Southern African Muckraking

Southern African Muckraking

300 years of investigative journalism that has shaped the region

Edited by
Anton Harber

This book was produced with the support of the
Konrad-Adenauer-Stiftung

First published by Jacana Media (Pty) Ltd in 2018

10 Orange Street
Sunnyside
Auckland Park 2092
South Africa
+2711 628 3200
www.jacana.co.za

© Individual contributers, 2018

All rights reserved.

ISBN 978-1-4314-2782-6

Cover design by Shawn Paikin
Editing by Lara Jacob
Proofreading by Megan Mance
Index by Josh Bryson
Set in MrsEaves 10.3/14pt
Printed by ABC Press
Job no. 003385

See a complete list of Jacana titles at www.jacana.co.za

Contents

Introduction – Anton Harber ix

A farmer, the governor and The Memorial
  – *Introduced by Kevin Davie* 1
A convert encounters a king – *Introduced by Hlonipha Mokoena* 8
'Discontent permeates the whole district'
  – *Introduced by Peter Limb* 14
Breaking the Peace – *Introduced by Irwin Manoim* 19
Impi yamakhanda: The war of the heads
  – *Introduced by Benedict Carton* 24
The conspiracy against black voters – *Introduced by Robert Edgar* 36
The Free State women's anti-pass protests
  – *Introduced by Peter Limb* 42
The heroic struggles of black women – *Introduced by Robert Edgar* 48
The mysterious disappearance of an anti-fascist campaigner
  – *Introduced by Raymond Joseph* 54
Ruth First: The obligation to dissent – *Introduced by Catherine Higgs* ... 61
Mr Drum goes to work in Bethal – *Introduced by Anton Harber* 69
The Sekhukhuneland Revolt – *Introduced by Peter Delius* 76
The living dead – *Introduced by Indra de Lanerole* 85
The hidden starvation – *Introduced by Benjamin Pogrund* 92
The secret organisation at the heart of apartheid
  – *Introduced by Raymond Joseph* 100
Abusive prison conditions in apartheid South Africa
  – *Introduced by Benjamin Pogrund* 109

'An endless chain' of political trials — *Introduced by Jo-Ann Bekker* 118
The investigative nun — *Introduced by Andrew Meldrum* 125
Muldergate: The scandal that ousted a prime minister and his
    successor — *Introduced by Raymond Joseph* 132
Exposed: Parliament is opening today!
    — *Introduced by Mbongeni Mbingo* 141
The Matola Raid: 'Why do grown men tell such lies?'
    — *Introduced by Paul Fauvet* 145
Robert Mugabe's 'moment of madness'
    — *Introduced by Andrew Meldrum* 153
The death of Samora Machel — *Introduced by Paul Fauvet* 163
Exposing military atrocities — *Introduced by Gwen Lister* 169
The Willowgate Scandal that caused the fall of the mighty
    — *Introduced by Geoffrey Nyarota* 172
The 'bloody trail' of the apartheid police
    — *Introduced by Tim du Plessis* 180
Exposing the 'Third Force' behind South Africa's pre-election
    violence — *Introduced by Philippa Garson* 188
Zimbabwe's land grab — *Introduced by Antony Sguazzin* 197
Angola's first muckraker — *Introduced by Claudia Gastrow* 203
Who wants to kill Albano Silva and why?
    — *Introduced by Erika Rodrigues* 209
When the lion wakes up — *Introduced by Tanya Pampalone* 215
Tackling a high-flying king — *Introduced by Mbongeni Mbingo* 223
The tenacious, pugnacious corporate vigilante
    — *Introduced by Reg Rumney* 228
A local story becomes a national scandal and ousts a
    prime minister — *Introduced by Finnigan wa Simbeye* 235
On the wrong side of development
    — *Introduced by John Aerni-Flessner* 240
Why Mount Frere's babies die — *Introduced by Harry Dugmore* 247
The dark, deadly art of witchcraft and the plight of albinos
    — *Introduced by Bob Wekesa* 254
The truth about President Jacob Zuma laid bare
    — *Introduced by Nic Dawes* 260
Killing rhinos for profit — *Introduced by Ron Nixon* 267

'Never set foot in this place ever again' — *Introduced by Joel Konopo* .. 273
Diamonds, soldiers, torture and corruption
  — *Introduced by Justin Pearce* 278
The massacre of Huambo — *Introduced by Justin Pearce* 284
Shattering the stereotype: Botswana's military millionaires
  — *Introduced by Evelyn Groenink* 289
All the generals' licences — *Introduced by Evelyn Groenink* 295
Joseph Kabila's family fortune — *Introduced by Franz Wild* 301
Fake degrees and documents
  — *Introduced by Letshwiti Batlhalefi Tutwane* 309
Reporting mystery murders, Gwanda became one
  — *Introduced by Bob Wekesa* 317
#GuptaLeaks: 'We have a game changer'
  — *Introduced by Anton Harber* 326
The Guptas come to Lesotho
  — *Introduced by Lekhetho Ntsukunyane* 335

Acknowledgements 341
Permissions 343
The Contributors 348
Index 357

To the cast of wonderful characters at the core of this book, the investigative journalists, whose courage and commitment put them among the finest people in the world, and without whom there would be less justice and accountability in southern Africa. And to the editors, owners, funders and readers who backed them.

Introduction

Anton Harber

Journalist Mandy Rossouw was driving through the Nkandla area of KwaZulu-Natal on a summer's day in 2009 looking for people to interview for a light feature on what it was like to have a head of state as a neighbour when she noticed some building activity at President Jacob Zuma's rural home. She spoke to some of the contractors on site, snuck a look at the plans and realised she had stumbled onto something.

'President Jacob Zuma is expanding his remote family homestead at Nkandla in rural KwaZulu-Natal for a whopping price of R65 million – and the taxpayer is footing the largest chunk of the bill,' was her opening line in the *Mail & Guardian* a few weeks later, after she had done some digging. The story drew a fierce reaction, especially when it emerged that she had underestimated the cost, and it turned out to be the kernel of a saga that was to grip South Africa in the next few years, carrying the seeds of the early end of Jacob Zuma's presidency nine years later (see page 260).

Tanzanian journalist Finnigan wa Simbeye in 2005 read in a local Kiswahili newspaper a minor report of a ministerial decision to reverse a pipeline contract to a local company. He checked it out, and learnt that this was a briefcase company with fake credentials. When the same company popped up in the privatisation of the country's energy utility, Simbeye was on to it. His reporting linked the company to high-level politicians, leading to a parliamentary inquiry, which ended with the resignation of Prime Minister Edward Lowassa. Along the way, Simbeye and his colleagues faced a combination of threats to his life and offers of massive bribes to back off the story (see page 235).

Sometimes, it is a photograph that encapsulates a situation so clearly that it provides the breakthrough for a journalist. Namibian editor Gwen Lister had been hearing for some time in 1987 that the South African occupying army was parading the bodies of South West African People's Organisation (Swapo) guerrillas they had killed in a most gruesome fashion, but faced consistent denials and threats of prosecution if she could not prove the case. A brave individual who stole a Polaroid photograph sealed the story. That edition of the paper was banned but only after it had sold out (see page 169).

South African reporter Jacques Pauw, on the other hand, sat on the information about the South African police death squad at Vlakplaas for about a decade, until circumstances allowed him to publish and blow open the dark heart of the apartheid state. The *Vrye Weekblad* newspaper that carried the story suffered legal and extra-legal pressure for some years until its closure (see page 180).

When Henry Nxumalo wanted to write about prison conditions in 1950s Johannesburg, he decided to get himself arrested to see conditions for himself. He wandered the streets of Johannesburg without the pass that black men were obliged to carry at all times, even acting drunk, but failed to get the attention of the police for a few days until he broke a shop window. His story became an exemplar of undercover, first-hand, enterprise reporting (see page 69).

It was Zimbabwean *Daily Gazette* editor Brian Latham who, hearing of talk that farms bought for resettlement were being leased to senior government officials, instinctively assigned his best-known reporter, Basildon Peta, and his new junior, Antony Squazzin, who had been on the job only three months, to investigate a story that would go on to shape that country and its politics for the next two decades (see page 197).

Peter Godwin dressed as a priest to get past the curfew in Matabeleland and reported on the Gukurahundi killings of the 1980s and Andrew Meldrum and his colleagues had to hide in a hospital cupboard to avoid soldiers searching for journalists working on the story. Their derring-do gave us early and important signs of the brutal authoritarianism that came to characterise Robert Mugabe's government in Zimbabwe (see page 153).

As instances of investigative journalism, these stories are highly varied. Some involved years of digging, others came from fortuitous discovery or the instinct of an alert editor. Some were based on documents, some started with rumours and others came from well-placed sources. Some involved lots of footwork, others were done on the desk, telephone and – more recently – the laptop and internet. Many were about government abuse of power, some were about the private sector and a few highlighted social conditions and their causes. Most were done by independent media, a few came from journalists whose sole form of distribution was the fax machine and at least one was done by a state-owned newspaper (Willowgate, page 172). Some were done by people who would not consider themselves primarily as journalists, but lawyers and activists, working for non-profit organisations – even a Catholic nun. But all of these also had much in common. All of them told us things that someone with power and authority did not want us to know. They involved determination and courage in taking on influential people and institutions. Most of the journalists involved shared a disdain and distrust for those with power and authority. All had an important impact on the society they wrote about, sometimes dislodging those who were abusing their power or authority. And each of them stands as a model of the journalism of exposé and accountability. It is this kind of journalism and the work of these brave individuals, and their supportive editors, that this book is intended to highlight and honour.

Why muckraking?

The paradox of investigative reporting is that in pursuit of the loftiest of objectives it often brings out the ugliest aspects of the societies we live in. It usually involves a great deal of digging in the darkest places and hanging out with scum, which is why we call these journalists muckrakers – those who dig around in the dirt. These journalists usually have disdain for those who peddle the 'sunshine journalism', which is based on the belief that society is best served by highlighting the good and the positive over the ugly and unjust, and contempt for journalists who like to be seen with celebrities. They are journalistic disrupters; those who strive not just to reflect on our societies but to question, probe and make uncomfortable those who wield power and authority. Their natural mode is distrust and they have an instinct for the muck. But they are usually doing it for the public good.

The muckraker label originates in America, from a speech by US President Teddy Roosevelt in 1906 on which he called on journalists to focus on more than just the dirt, to also look up and see the blue sky. It was a period in which a band of now-legendary American journalists – including Upton Sinclair, Frank Norris, Jacob Riis, Lincoln Steffens, Ida Tarbell and Ray Stannard Baker – exposed a great deal of government and business corruption. Roosevelt was a progressive and grateful for at least some of the exposés these journalists were responsible for, but he also warned that 'the man who did nothing else (but scrape the muck) was certain to become a force of evil' (Shiffrin, 2017).

Journalists have embraced the sobriquet with some pride, knowing that they may spend their time in the muck, they might be hard-nosed and cynical, but their work was a force for reform, improvement and the public good. The American muckrakers could take considerable credit for worker protections, food safety laws and other reforms that exist in the US today (Shiffrin, 2017), just as our African muckrakers have had a hand in the downfall of bad leaders, the jailing of crooks and a number of social and political reforms.

Why use the American term? I do so because it so usefully encapsulates the grinding, behind-the-scenes routine of much of the work of reporters, along with the reminder of their contribution to the public good. Little of the daily work of investigative reporting has the romance and excitement that we see in *All the President's Men*, the book and film of the infamous Watergate exposé which brought down US President Richard Nixon. Much of it is humdrum and mundane, and most muckraking journalists are a nerdy lot, without the glamour – and certainly not the panache – of actors like Robert Redford and Dustin Hoffman, who starred in the film *Watergate*. More often it is a case of chasing small-time, local corruption and the petty abusers of power, a crucial function but with little of the fame and acclamation that comes with the big national stories. It is usually built on the slow, grinding collection of information, the gradual building of contacts and sources, and the study of data to turn rumour and talk and suspicion into proof.

It was also a pragmatic decision to use muckraking in our title. It links us to two preceding and important volumes: *Global Muckraking* (2014) and *African Muckraking* (2017), both edited by Anya Shiffrin, the latter with George Lugalambi. The first book highlighted case studies from the global south, and included some African material. The latter homed in on this continent and had some southern African material. It was the important work of those volumes that drew our attention to how much material there was from this sub-continent and the value of bringing it to light.

Filling the gaps

Presently, we have few local texts for our students and young journalists to draw on, and it is our hope that this anthology provides role models and inspiration for a younger generation, as well as an appreciation of the work of their predecessors who built the best elements of our journalism tradition. Too little of our media and journalism history has been recorded in anything other than personal and often self-aggrandising memoirs, and my hope is to make available some of the material that can inform a fuller knowledge of this rich history.

I have taken an expansive view of investigative reporting, which might irritate the purists. We are familiar with the mainstream work, which involves the most famous stories such as the Information Scandal in South Africa in the 1970s, the Willowgate exposé in Zimbabwe in the 1980s and the anti-corruption work of Carlos Cardoso in Mozambique. This work follows a familiar format and fits more or less globally conventional notions of investigative reporting, and there is no denying its importance and its place at the core of this book. But if we were to confine ourselves to only this kind of work, we would be excluding a number of important exposés that break from these conventional patterns and arise out of the particular conditions and circumstances of this sub-continent. There has been work by non-profit organisations, activists and lawyers, or even commissioned by political organisations; some published in pamphlets, reports or official submissions – the kind of material that would be unlikely to be included in a northern hemisphere collection because they fall outside of the traditional Western journalism canon.

To understand why we have cast our net wide enough to include some of these, one has to understand the history of the media in this part of the world, how circumscribed it has been and how journalists and their allies have worked around this to get these stories into the public arena and confront those with power and authority.

The barriers to investigative reporting

Colonial governments did not afford their subjects the relative freedom of expression they allowed at home, keeping a much tighter grip on those they didn't recognise as citizens. Methods included preventing the importation of printing presses, allowing the publication of only state-controlled newspapers and jailing those who spoke out. These practices were carried forward into the independent post-1958 era, when mostly one-party states favoured a 'developmental' and 'patriotic' media, controlled top-down as part of a national and nationalist project.

Writing about six of these countries, Tawana Kupe described neatly how colonial inheritances shaped media structures in the post-colonial period:

> The history of colonialism, apartheid and post-independence political

developments has influenced media systems and structures in these six countries, and media policy and regulatory practices. Repressive political systems often leave an entrenched culture and practices of media control that are deeply ingrained and difficult to eradicate ...

Except for South Africa, which formally went the clear route of firmly entrenching media freedom and freedom of expression in its constitution, the other countries demonstrate degrees of continuity rather than radical departures from colonial media practices (in Berger, 2008: 37).

Under these circumstances, much of the muckraking work was done by activists and politicians, often with limited choices for publication and dissemination, and having to shape their work as formal research or petitioning to avoid censorship. There has been a revolving door between journalism, politics and activism, with individuals such as John Dube, J.T. Jabavu, Ruth First and Carlos Cardoso carrying their politics into their journalism and their journalism into their fight for rights. Interestingly, in South Africa, this was also true for the founding fathers of apartheid, with D.F. Malan and Hendrik Verwoerd both having started out as campaigning editors before becoming prime ministers. Richard Msimang and Sol Plaatje did their remarkable work on the impact of the 1913 Land Act – a cataclysmic moment that shaped this country and still defines its politics and economy – on behalf of the ANC, in the form of representations to present to the colonial authorities in London. And often the work had to be wrapped in metaphor and double-entendre to avoid the blunt knives of censors, such as when John Dube wrote circuitously about the violence in Natal in 1906 (see page 24).

Alongside the traditional inverted triangle of the hard news story, designed for maximum brevity and impact, stand reports that can be deliberately obtuse, circumambulatory and wrapped in officialise to confound authorities. In eSwatini (Swaziland), the last country with an executive monarchy and with a deeply traditional population, journalists have to carefully carve out the space to raise issues that the king might view as a challenge. It may be the only place where a report on the date for the opening of parliament required investigation, led to the jailing of the journalist and could be hailed as a triumph for representative democracy (see page 141).

If we were to apply a conventional view of investigative journalism and the methods, outlets, language and style associated with it, some of this important work would be neglected. Yet it forms a critical element in the tradition of investigative and campaigning work, and our history would be bereft without it. To take a wider view of investigative reporting is an act of inclusiveness and enrichment, providing, I hope, material that will get readers thinking about issues of independence and commitment, and the workings of campaigning journalism or accountability reporting, particularly in repressive states.

Most of the countries of southern Africa only moved to a more open society, allowing at least in principle for an independent media and journalism, with the shift to multiparty democracy in the early 1990s. But we have learnt that the habits and scars – and the tools – of repression are not wiped away overnight. In a number of these countries – such as Zimbabwe, eSwatini and Botswana – governments used a mixture of threat and cajoling, dressed up as false patriotism or trumped up security concerns, to limit the scope and impact of independent journalists, even when their constitutions offered protection for this work. Some governments used the power of their advertising – since government in many of these countries is the source of the bulk of media revenue – to keep media in line, and even resorted to undercover activity, surveillance, arrest, bombings and assassinations to prevent the scrutiny of reporters. Examples of arrests come from eSwatini and South Africa; examples of bombings come notably from Zimbabwe, where the *Daily News* offices were devastated by two bombs in 2000 and 2001; and five of the cases in this book ended in the death or disappearance of the journalist: Carlos Cardoso in Mozambique, Ricardo de Mello in Angola, George Heard and Ruth First in South Africa and Azory Gwanda in Tanzania. Ruth First died as the result of a bomb while she was a researcher in Mozambique many years after leaving South Africa, though the bomb could be said to have been aimed at what she represented in all aspects of her life, including her earlier journalism. Both Heard and Gwanda's disappearances – more than 50 years apart – remain tragically unresolved.

Journalists have had to fight every inch of the way for the realisation of the constitutional and verbal commitments to free speech, using the courts, collective organisation, international lobbying and – above all – their pens, cameras and laptops to establish their rights, and defend them.

A hostile environment

Another key impediment to independent journalism in this region has been financial: the capacity of independent media to invest in complicated and risky reporting, as well as the cost of defending their journalists and their work. Financial constraints, particularly in recent years, which have seen the decline of print advertising and readership in many countries, have been a – if not *the* – major contributor to what is often a hostile newsroom environment for reporting that challenges those with authority and wealth. It does not help that in many of these countries, such as Botswana, Zimbabwe and South Africa, private media has to compete with subsidised public media, which often operates in the same commercial space.

The Media Institute of Southern Africa (MISA) put it succinctly in its annual review *So This is Democracy 2017*:

> A closer look reveals an environment for media and citizenry that is highly volatile, hotly contested and often under pressure, a landscape where the insidious and subtle erosion of free speech rights is compounded both by the media's struggle for economic survival and its relevance to citizens who all too easily disown their media and the critical role it plays in keeping power to account (MISA, 2018: 10).

Tough political conditions are often compounded by media owners unable or unwilling to invest in the kind of reporting that costs money and carries a high risk of inviting the attention of authorities and their lawyers, and alienating advertisers. That is why some of the most important work is done by smaller, 'alternative' publications, best exemplified by those who published important stories by fax in Angola and Mozambique during the 1990s (see pages 203 and 209). One of the advantages of not having a strong commercial base is that it sometimes gives these publications the space to be bolder and braver because they are less concerned about the reactions of advertisers. It is my personal experience that smaller, less-resourced publications have to work harder to get attention and this provides an incentive for the unique content that comes with venturing into the territory that presents greater commercial risk.

Of course, we are talking about a diverse group of countries with different experiences. In some countries – notably South Africa and Namibia – elements of the media and investigative journalists played an important role in exposing colonial and apartheid injustices and in mobilising and organising resistance. This was done sometimes by parts of the mainstream media but most often by 'alternative' voices, which sprang up in periods of heightened political activity.

Botswana provides an interesting case study because it is a country that has been hailed as an African model of stability, democracy and economic growth.

It does not have media freedoms explicitly protected in its constitution, and media freedom has been severely constrained by a combination of financial and political pressures. Most newspapers only started in the 1980s and have struggled to survive. In the words of media law and journalism lecturer, Dr Lethwiti Tutwana, 'At best the government expected journalism of timidity, a streak of journalism that bowed to power and was essentially public relations aimed at promoting government and its figureheads. At worst it expected "development journalism", a euphemism for an element of public education fused with governmental praise. It got both.'

But there are also severe financial constraints in the media industry. 'With a small economy informed by a population of only two million people, Botswana's media houses do not have the resources to marshal serious investigative journalism. The owners are also by and large not keen to engage in such and are not dedicated to journalism as a platform to hold power accountable. They see the media as a business like any other. So sometimes the resource deficit is exaggerated. What lacks in the main is commitment to the media as a watchdog of society,' Tutwana writes. In addition, there are 'tough, antiquated laws that are inimical to watchdog journalism ... (These laws) have a chilling effect on press freedom. Some of these laws, despite Botswana's much vaunted democratic credentials, threaten custodial sentences' (Personal correspondence, 2018).

As you can tell from the Botswana stories in this collection, this has allowed for the questionable accumulation of wealth and power in political families, protected from scrutiny. But in recent years, the formation of a local investigative unit, INK, has challenged the status quo and started to build an investigative tradition. And this has been accompanied by work from an international consortium of investigative reporters, the African Investigative Publishing Collective (AIPC), built around the online magazine, ZAM.

In Tanzania for over two decades after independence, the state and ruling party dominated the media: the official *Daily News* and *Sunday News* were the English newspapers while *Uhuru*, published by the ruling party, was the only Kiswahili paper. According to journalist Finnigan wa Simbeye: 'In 1990 when economic liberalisation took off in earnest, private newspapers, radio and television stations came aboard which also allowed investigative reporting to emerge. The earlier investigative report which sent shock waves in the early 1990s was Stan Katabaro's investigations into an Omanese royal family that was given a game-controlled area in Loliondo, Northern Tanzania, for sport hunting which led to displacement of thousands of Maasai pastoralists.'

But it was not all smooth sailing. 'Katabalo, who investigated the story for many months and published in a Kiswahili tabloid called *Heko*, died of a mysterious disease in the mid-1990s. *Heko* also closed shop shortly afterwards.'

Another ground-breaking investigation – and an example of work done by an NGO – was by Transparency International's representative in Tanzania, Brian Cocksey, in the mid-1990s involving a corrupt power generation contract signed between state power firm, Tanesco, and Malaysian-based Melchmar International. 'The deal which involved top-notch politicians, businessmen and the Malaysians brought to the fore the first ever grand corruption power deal,' Simbeye says.

'So, investigative journalism started in the 1990s because there was now more press freedom and economic liberalisation brought about grand corruption among elite politicians and bureaucrats by business people seeking state favours … Today investigative reporting in Tanzania is very vibrant, in fact many newspapers doing fine in the market are writing investigative stories' (Interview, 2018).

So muckraking may be happening more than ever before, but the conditions are tough, the risks high. MISA's annual report says of Tanzania:

> President John Magufuli's crackdown on all criticism and dissent is both subtle and overt, and weighted against popular political and economic reforms. This makes it difficult for advocates to navigate the terrain of harnessing support to fight for fundamental rights when Magufuli's fiscal policy decisions reflect the strengthening of an economic sector. Citizens and stakeholders overlook infringements on freedom of expression and media freedoms. His shrewd skill in crafting law under the guise of regulation is in fact constricting the space for opinions and in essence is creating a police state. Opposition politicians and journalists including the exiled Ansbert Ngurumo and the still-missing Azory Gwanda are on a growing list of the dead, disappeared and detained (MISA, 2018: 10).

MISA also had strong words to say about Zambia:

> The Zambian political and social landscape was peppered with incidents ranging from the death of a student from Copperbelt University who was injured by police during a protest, to the bombing of a privately owned media house in Lusaka and the declaration

of a state of emergency following a spate of arson attacks on public installations (MISA, 2018: 10).

The establishment in recent years of a loose network of dedicated investigative units – such as INK in Gaborone, NMM Centre in Lesotho, and amaBhungane in Johannesburg/Cape Town – with the support of philanthropists and international foundations, has made a significant impact. As a result, stories from these countries are concentrated in the latter section of this chronological book, reflecting a recent regional boom in this work. While this development is heartening, it is notable that much of the work has to be done and funded from outside conventional newsrooms, though often published or broadcast in partnership with traditional outlets. This philanthropic support has been invaluable, but it is questionable whether it is sustainable.

In Lesotho, the four journalists who came together to form the MNN Centre for Investigative Journalism (MNNCIJ) had together had over 35 years of experience in conventional newsrooms, and faced every frustration. 'We had all faced serious challenges pursuing investigative in the conventional newsrooms we had worked in,' founding editor Lekhetho Ntsukunyane told me. 'There was no time and resources but even where journalists worked overtime to compile an investigative piece, the story might not be published because of political and advertising pressure on the publications. Tens of such stories pitched and written by us did not see the light of the day while we were in conventional newsrooms' (Personal correspondence, 2018).

Increased newspaper competition, however, pushed some to take risks in recent years – but the consequences were severe. In 2016, when *Lesotho Times* and *Sunday Express* editor, Lloyd Mutungamiri, and reporter Keiso Mohloboli published a story exposing an exit deal between the government and the Lesotho army commander, there was an assassination attempt on Mutungamiri and he was shot multiple times. Mohloboli fled to South Africa. In another instance, Ntsukunyane was arrested and forced to reveal his sources for an article he had written in the *Lesotho Times* in 2014. These are just a few examples of how reporters and editors were treated.

Ntsukunya Mohloboli, Billy Ntaote and Sechaba Mokhethi teamed up with Ntsukunyane to form their independent investigative journalism centre in July 2017 after receiving seed funding from George Soros's Open Society Institute of Southern Africa (OSISA). As you will see from the material in this book, that quickly paid off, as did cooperation between such centres in different countries.

Activists as journalists

Some of the reporting was done by activists or non-government civil society organisations, who moved to fill the space in the absence of newsrooms that can do it. An example of this is the report on the Lesotho Highlands Water Project in this collection, where an NGO has stepped in to do the kind of investigation and publishing that you might normally expect from a newsroom. I include this because it fits into the broad definition of muckraking, and it is important to consider the role played by work of this kind to supplement more conventional newsroom journalism. South African journalists will recall the role played by human rights organisations such as the Black Sash and the Detainees Parents Support Committee in doing research and publishing formal reports under apartheid censorship, often then picked up and disseminated by the news media. In Rhodesia, we have the example of the Catholic nun, Sister Janice McLaughlin, who used the church's networks and protection to gather and publish the truth of the war of independence, which was then picked up by other media. Those who draw a neat line between such work and that of the newsrooms are not taking account of the symbiotic relationship that often exists between them, and the value of these organisations doing muckraking work when newsrooms are constrained from doing it.

The conflation of campaigning and journalism does raise issues. If not subjected to the rigours and principles of journalism, this work can be partisan, partial and untrustworthy. But the best of it applies the same principles of honesty, truth and accuracy as would a professional journalist, though neither would deny their point of view or subjectivity. And the contributions of such organisations and individuals have been invaluable.

Hidden gems

The most interesting part of compiling this collection has been the discovery of a number of hidden gems, work that has been forgotten and needs to be brought back into the public debate. I have been teaching the history of investigative reporting at the University of the Witwatersrand for over a decade and always started in this country in the 1950s, with the work of Henry Nxumalo at *Drum* magazine and Ruth First at *The Guardian*. This book starts 250 years earlier and highlights some remarkable work in the intervening period, hopefully enriching our knowledge and understanding of the depth and range of this tradition and its evolution, and providing plenty of material for further discussion, debate and study (not to mention improving our teaching).

This collection highlights a long and rich tradition of investigative and campaigning journalism in some of these countries, with the first entry coming from more than three centuries ago, and a recent surge in most of the remaining countries of southern Africa. What shines through is the role these journalists have played not just in exposing instances of wrongdoing and injustice, but in the long-term promotion of a culture of accountability and openness in the public and private sectors, the fundamental traits of effective democracy.

There have been instances where those purporting to be investigative reporters have allowed themselves to be used by political factions and special interests, and have done damage to the public interest, but the spread and range of stories in this anthology should highlight how these occasional aberrations are overwhelmed by the amount of good work done over three centuries.

While the earlier years are peopled by individualistic, remarkable and, often colourful, stand-out characters, the more recent trend is towards cooperative work by large, sometimes cross-border, teams. This is a global trend, as demonstrated by the Panama Papers and Paradise Papers, two large-scale data dumps that brought together journalists across the world to break stories of a scale and significance that went beyond national borders. The best example from this region is the 19-member team from three different media operations that led the #GuptaLeaks exposé. The team was pulled together from the *Daily Maverick* website that first got the leak, the amaBhungane team, which brought its research and investigative skills, and *News24*, the country's biggest news outlet, which brought audience and clout. It stands as something of a model of mutually beneficial cooperation across different media groups and types. Interestingly, it was spurred on by competition with the rival Tiso Blackstar media group, which brought a team of their own reporters together from the *Sunday Times*, the *Business Day* and the *Sowetan* newspapers, and their online partners in *TimesLive*, to find the stories in the same data dump. In this case, we can celebrate the value of journalistic competition and cooperation in parallel (see page 326).

A number of recent stories have come from large-scale data dumps, enabled by digital records, email and large-scale computer memory. One even came from satellite digital imagery. Journalists who used to hope for a few sheets of official paperwork now make extensive use of masses of data delivered on hard drives and measured in terabytes, too lengthy to read and requiring advanced technical skills to access and analyse. The ease of copying and communicating digital data has proved a nightmare for those who want to keep secrets, and a boon for those journalists with the computer and technical skills now as essential to their work as the slow tasks of human contact with sources and whistleblowers.

But the development of electronic tools has also enhanced the power of authorities to keep tabs on and interfere with journalists in their work. This can include the monitoring of cell phones to track journalists and their sources, invasions of their computers and emails, and straightforward manipulation of electronic material in an attempt to divert and deceive. The security measures that the #GuptaLeaks team felt it necessary to take give a taste of how this affects reporters: they stopped using cellphones and relied on face-to-face conversations in the outdoors for sensitive issues, and every member of the team was given a new laptop that was kept off-line (see page 326).

The gaps in the range of work tell their own story. Most of the examples here are about government corruption and malfeasance. There are fewer examinations of the private sector and its share of crooks and thieves, and only the occasional story in areas such as religion and sport, health and the environment. Social conditions get important but sporadic mention.

The work has the most impact when legal and political structures play their role in bringing crooks and scoundrels to book. Journalists are, after all, just one cog in the machinery of accountability. They can expose the scandals, but it depends on prosecutors, police, the courts and the public to play their part. In many of these countries, these institutions do not always have the strength and independence to do so, the public too disempowered or governments – such as in Zimbabwe and Angola – too entrenched to care. But the growing number of exposés must give hope and fodder for those who want to see a blossoming of democracy, justice and good governance in this part of the world.

Inclusions and omissions

This anthology is a selection of some of the best and most interesting investigative journalism from southern Africa, but makes no claim to be comprehensive or exhaustive. Selection has been based on an attempt to ensure a diverse and representative spread of different kinds of work covering a long period and many countries, so I apologise in advance for good work that has been omitted. Some inclusions were fortuitous, such as when I found copies of Ricardo de Mello's *Impartial Fax* in the hands of one of his friends after a long and frustrating search; some omissions were unintended, as I failed to find or get permission to use material in time. And in the end, the selection has to be subjective and practical.

I have used only a few pieces of the work of foreign correspondents because the focus has deliberately been on the work of locally based journalists. This is not to downplay the role of foreign correspondents, some of whom have done important investigative reporting from this part of the world and have often worked in partnership with local journalists and outlets. I know from my own experience that joint publication with an international voice often provided cover for our work under apartheid and made authorities think twice about acting against us. Sometimes we even fed stories to foreign correspondents so that we could report them back here with less risk than if we broke them ourselves. But it is local work, much of it neglected and forgotten, that needs to be highlighted.

A significant exclusion has been broadcasting journalism and this is done solely for practical reasons. While most of the important investigative work in this region has come from print, because of government domination of the broadcasting industry, there have been some notable pockets of important work in television and radio in recent years. We could not do justice to that work in this book, and hope to do so in more multimedia follow-ups.

Each case study in this book consists of an introduction by an expert on the topic and extracts from the original investigations as published. For these extracts, we have stuck with original – and sometimes archaic or eccentric – spellings of names and places. We did so for the sake of authenticity, though this has led to some style inconsistencies.

References

Berger, Guy and Barret, Elizabeth. 2008. *50 Years of Journalism*. Johannesburg: Africa Editors' Forum, Highway Africa, Media Foundation for West Africa.
Schiffrin, A. 2014. *Global Muckraking*. New York: The New Press.
Schiffrin, A. 2017. *African Muckraking*. Johannesburg: Jacana Media.
MISA. 2018. *So this is Democracy?* Windhoek, Namibia: Media Institute of Southern Africa.
ZAM magazine. Available at: www.zammagazine.com/engage/about-zam, accessed on 15 August 2018.

1705, SOUTH AFRICA

A farmer, the governor and The Memorial

INTRODUCED BY KEVIN DAVIE

If we were to scour available records for when a piece of text was first used as an exposé in what would become South Africa, 1705 would be a good year to check. The text is *The Memorial*, 38 charges brought by lead author Adam Tas against Governor Willem Adriaan van der Stel. A private company, the Dutch East India Company (VoC), was then a little more than 100 years old and had been in the Cape for more than 50 years.

Built on the core foundational value of monopoly, what limited trade the company allowed locally was on its terms. The company's first commander, Jan van Riebeeck, had allocated parcels of land to a small number of its people to become free burghers.

By the time Simon van der Stel was commander and later governor, 1679 to 1699, the free farmers had spread across what is now the winelands. The governor was all powerful, lording over this domain and answering only to the Heeren XVII, the VoC directors in distant Amsterdam.

Leo Fouché, in his *Diary of Adam Tas* (1914), a 400-page treatise written in both Dutch and English, examined what happened next. Van der Stel's son, Willem Adriaan van der Stel, governor from 1699, set about using his position to feather his personal nest, laying out and developing a gilded estate at Vergelegen, three-days' wagon journey from Cape Town. The governor and his friends, on Fouché's telling, became so big they could supply the entire market themselves. Willem Adriaan duly fixed the key markets for his circle, thus controlling the meat, wine, timber and fish trade. The free farmers felt the lifeblood draining away.

Enter Adam Tas. Born in 1668 in Amsterdam, Tas had arrived in the Cape in 1697 as a free burgher. His uncle was Henning Husing, the richest farmer in the Cape and the main supplier of beef to the VoC. Tas began in low-level clerical positions in the VoC, but elevated himself dramatically through his marriage in 1703 to a wealthy widow, Elizabeth van Brakel, and he was now lording over a handsome spread of land in Stellenbosch.

By the spring of 1705, the free farmers, facing ruin, petitioned the Heeren XVII. With Tas, the 'elegant writer' as author, they composed *The Memorial*. The 63 signatories consisted of both French and Dutch farmer colonists in near equal numbers, and *The Memorial* was smuggled to Amsterdam to the XVII.

Fouché says of the complaint: 'It appears the governor had in his service over 60 white servants of the company, 20 of them upon his 18 cattle stations across the mountains. Upon those outside stations he had 18,000 sheep and 1,000 head of cattle, besides the stock carried at Vergelegen and elsewhere in Hottentots Holland, as well as Robben Island, Visser's Hok, Zoutvliet, etc.'

Fouché writes that when Willem Adriaan heard of the complaint in February 1706, he arrested Tas and confiscated his papers, including a draft copy of *The Memorial*.

Tas and other ringleaders were imprisoned at the Castle. 'There, two soldiers, with drawn swords, kept guard over him day and night; the chimney of his cell was walled up, his meat and drink were examined, as well as any comforts sent to him,' writes Fouché. In all Tas was incarcerated for 13 months and 17 days. So dire were the conditions in the Castle gaol that the company's doctor warned the arrested men could die.

Willem Adriaan mounted a spirited defence, refuting all the charges in the *Kortie Deductie* (counter defence), a 1,098-point refutation of *The Memorial*. He also went on a charm offensive. According to Fouché: 'Van der Stel summoned the citizens of Cape Town to the Castle where to their amazement they were met with the most courteous of receptions. He regaled them all, blacks, and liberated slaves and convicts included, with wine, beer, coffee and tobacco.' He collected 240 signatories to a testimonial of good conduct, which declared him to be a person of honour and virtue.

Fouché's version – that Willem Adriaan was a basic scoundrel – was supported by others, including Abraham Bogaert, a visitor to the Cape who described these events in his *Historical Journey* of 1711 and historian/curator George McCall Theal.

But an archivist at the Cape Archives, H.C.T. Liebbrandt, in 1888 published accounts using material from the archive, principally the *Kortie*

Deductie and confessions by Tas (made under duress, according to Fouché) and others retracting their earlier claims. In this version Willem Adriaan was cast as a wise ruler brought down by a wicked conspiracy by the colonist farmers (Liebbrandt, 1897).

Unfortunately for Willem Adriaan though, the XVII, in their own inquiry, found against him. In April 1707, the decision of the XVII reached the Cape: he was dismissed as governor.

Fouché devoted his *Diary of Adam Tas* to interrogating whether Willem Adriaan was a saint or sinner, checking, for instance, claims and counter-claims regarding his assets: 'The governor asserts that he owned 400 morgen; the Land Registers prove that he owned 613. He asserts that he had planted 200,000 vine-stocks; the official measurements prove that he must have had 500,000 at least. He admits having had over 250 work people in his employ; the burghers prove he had 350. He admits having had eight cattle stations, with some 20,000 sheep and 1000 cattle … When we consider the restricted character of the market at the Cape, the vast scale of his farming operation is sufficient itself to condemn Van der Stel.'

For Fouché, *The Memorial* was more than just a list of complaints against the governor, but a kind of Magna Carta for the boers. Tas and company 'clearly formulated and so stoutly maintained the rights and privileges of the colonists, it may therefore be said with justice that they laid the foundations of our political consciousness'. Willem Adriaan, Fouché wrote, scorned his adversaries by calling them 'boeren' or Boers. This 'denotes no caste or class; it designates a nation. The new-born people has received its name.'

In what may come as a surprise to anyone force-fed this history in heroic, white terms by apartheid education, the Van der Stels were actually of mixed race, Simon's mother being, in Fouché's words, a coloured woman, Monica da Costa. 'Her son, Simon was a man of remarkable qualities,' Fouché writes, but, echoing the racism of the time, continues: 'As is frequently the case with persons of mixed blood, the throwback occurred in the third generation. The impression that Willem Adriaan leaves us is of the half Oriental. His character was not without its more admirable features, but he lacked balance and self-control, and the moral sense seems to have been found to be entirely wanting.'

Patric Tariq Mellet, who describes himself as a heritage activist, sees race to have been a key factor in the dispute, where Willem Adriaan, perhaps because of his mixed-race ancestry, was sympathetic to the cause of a group of emerging free farmers, both black and mixed-race. And they supported him, as indicated by the 240 signatures he received for his petition.

Tas, says Mellet, accused Willem Adriaan of advancing the interests of the free blacks who would 'attack all Christians, good or bad without distinction, and swamp them.' This quote continues: 'Not much can be expected from our slaves; we can also not expect much better and even less from the Kaffirs, Mulattos, Mestocis, Casticos and all that black brood living among us, who have been bred from marriages and other forms of intermingling with European and African Christians. For there is not trusting the blood of Ham, especially as the black people are constantly being favoured and pushed forward.'

The white farmers, on this account, rose up to protect their narrow interests against those of the wider community. The XVII, says Mellet, noted that the number of signatories to Willem Adriaan's petition, 240, far exceeded the 63 who signed with Tas. He says the VoC found for the farmer colonists because so many of the signatories were French, the VoC being worried about exacerbating French-Dutch tensions.

One thing should be clear: Tas was no working-class hero. The story is that he returned to his estate, which he re-named Libertas. No great reforms flowed from this rebellion. The VoC remained in charge for another 100 years, slavery was only done away with after 140 years and democracy was a full 280 years distant.

References

Fouche, Leo. 1914. *The Diary of Adam Tas (1705–1706)*. London: Longmans, *Green and Co.*

Leibbrandt, H.C.V. 1897. *Precis of the Archives of the Cape of Good Hope: The Defence of Willem Adriaan van der Stel*. Cape Town: WA Richards and Sons, Government Printers.

Mellet, Patric Tariq. 2016. *The Story of The First Two 'Coloured' Governors at The Cape – Simon & Willem Van der Stel*. Available at: www.bruinou.com, accessed on 17 August 2018.

The Memorial

Adam Tas, 1705

HON GENTLEMEN, Pressed by high necessity, we humbly take the liberty to lay our just complaints before you, especially because we are not only very much oppressed here by an unjust and haughty domination of the present governor, Willem

A FARMER, THE GOVERNOR AND THE MEMORIAL

Adriaan van der Stel, but treated worse than slaves. Bearing in mind we are free burghers and subjects of the States-General, it can easily be conceived that this unheard of oppression must redouble our sorrows. What they are, we have decided in all truth to communicate as briefly as possible to your Honours as the unshakeable maintainers of right and fairness.

1. You are informed that the Governor has built, about twelve hours distant from the Cape, a country seat, large beyond measure, and of such broad dimensions, as if it were a whole town. Besides that, he possesses very many lands on whose area at least 50 farmers would be able to earn their living. He sows on that place annually an immense quantity of corn and has also planted a vineyard there of more than 400,000 vines. He possesses fully 800 head of cattle and 10,000 sheep. On that farm there are more than 60 Company's servants, subalterns, sailors and soldiers. All these people draw their pay, salary and rations from the Company, but the Governor uses them for his own private purposes. He has besides, on the same place and in his private service, some of the best slaves of the Company — as much as 100. He also uses for his own service daily the Company's smiths and wagon makers, and has for his wagons, ploughs, and what further belongs to agriculture, made from the Company's iron, whilst the wood is cut for him in the Company's forests.

2. Besides the country seat, the governor has, beyond the mountains of the Hottentots Holland, 15 cattle stations, where he pastures his flocks, which stations are taken care of by Company's servants and slaves, who likewise mind the cattle.

3. They sent out a large number of men with powder and bullet; from some Hottentots they bartered cattle, from others they took cattle violently and in a detestable manner, extorting the animals from the natives. All these unmannerly ways of bartering are matters of very evil consequence, by which the Hottentots are not only made desperate, but may be tempted to wreak their vengeance for injustice done to them, on the innocent. Of this there are already examples.

4. Minister [Petrus Kaken, an ally of Willem Adriaan van

der Stel, who participated in the cattle raids] is one of the largest agriculturists here, and notwithstanding his other emoluments [he receives a monthly pay of f120[1] from the Company], it is nevertheless true he makes no work whatever of religion, as he occupies himself much more with his lands than with his pulpit.
5. The Governor makes his daily work of his farm and its surroundings. We point to the continual riding and driving to that spot where he sometimes resides two, three, four, five, six and more weeks without once looking after the affairs of the Company or the Castle.
6. The Governor forbids the burghers free pasture for their cattle, and if anyone in his opinion comes too near him with his cattle, he threatens him that he will have his arms and legs beaten to pieces, and with such threats they are turned away.
7. In the same manner the ex-Governor [Simon van der Stel] treats his neighbours, for he also teases them as much as he can.
8. Of the same doings is the Governor's brother, the so-called Squire Frans van der Stel, as full of them as an egg is full of milk. He treats his neighbours in the most unjust manner in the world, and depending on his brother the Governor, he does as much evil as his bile can suggest.
9. A short time ago, it pleased this pretended Squire Frans to make a beastly, coarse and shameless request to a certain burgher, viz that he would greatly oblige the Squire and his brother the Governor, and show great friendship if he would give a good thrashing to two ex-burgher councillors [who] are both men of honour, so that they felt it.
10. From all the doings of the three gentlemen mentioned one must conclude that they not only imagine that everything is free for them [that they can do what they like], but that this whole land belongs to them in freehold, as they lord it over all.
11. The following takes place with European timber sent hither by the Company. The Governor has a selection made of the best beams, joints, spars, etc and then sends them to his farm. The worst that is left is given to the freemen.'

---

1 F or fl was the symbol for the Dutch guilder, which was derived from the florin.

12. Moreover, all access to the forests has been cut off to the burghers, so that they cannot obtain the least bit of timber.
13. A poor widow had some paltry pieces of wood cut in one of the public forests, which are situated far enough from the Governor. The Governor ordered the Landdrost to demand Rds 50 from her as a fine.
14. The Governor has not only forbidden free trade in wine for the burghers, but they are even prevented from bringing their wines from their farms to the Cape.
15. The freemen are also forbidden to supply any refreshments, whether meat, wines or vegetables, to foreign ships, whether of the English or Danish nation.
16. When it happens the freemen bring any corn to the Cape, and have travelled over very heavy and difficult roads, they are obliged, with the same wagons and oxen, to convey from the Cape to his farm Vergelegen, heavy loads of beams, planks, etc.
17. There are many poor people, some of whom hardly possess a wagon and a span of oxen with which they are able to earn a penny by riding for one or other person. However, they receive nothing in the world for carriage from the Governor.
18. The Governor ordinarily delivers his corn to the bakers for 10, 12 or 15 guilders per muid. He pays no tithes, and the bakers are compelled to accept wheat at that price. Should they be inclined to refuse, he withdraws his favours from them, forbids them to bake, and threatens to ruin them.
19. For your Honours' information we state that last year was a very bad corn year for most of the freemen, so that no one among us could deliver any corn worth mentioning to the Company. But the Governor, his brother Frans, the minister, and others had a very good harvest, because they have a large quantity of land; but sold most of their corn to the bakers at a high rate, so the Company was much embarrassed for want of corn…

Your Honours' very submissive, and most obedient Servants.

1878, South Africa

A convert encounters a king

Introduced by Hlonipha Mokoena

'Such exaggerated accounts' – these words open John W. Colenso's preface to Magema Magwaza Fuze's 1878 essay on his visit to the Zulu king, Cetshwayo (written as Ketshwayo). Colenso had reason to begin by pointing to the hyperbole and sensationalism that were then pervading the reports about the reigning Zulu king. Importantly, he was also commenting on the reports that Cetshwayo was killing Christian converts and therefore causing missionaries and converts to flee the Zulu country (Zululand).

Colenso was therefore writing to quell the hysteria as well as introduce to the English-reading public an unknown voice, that of his convert, printer and amanuensis, Fuze. The essay is also about re-encounters, since Fuze, Colenso and other Bishopstowe converts had travelled to the Zulu country in 1859 to meet with the then reigning king, Mpande. In the latter account, the young converts met Cetshwayo, who was then an aspiring and ambitious prince evidently impatient with his father's rule and itching to become king. By 1877 when Fuze visits again as an adult, Cetshwayo was an exasperated monarch who not only had to deal with his subjects fleeing Zululand, crossing the Tugela (uThukela) and residing among the 'white people' (the colony of Natal), he also had to deal with pressure from his subjects to execute Christian converts who were seen as exercising a certain amount of 'occult' power by worshipping a foreign god. More importantly, his every action was being reported to the Natal colonial government and by implication also to Queen Victoria in England. These then are the anxieties that Fuze finds animating Zululand, since every step he took towards the Zulu king was also a step towards his possible execution. Colenso's preface was however not concerned with these intrigues, rather he wrote to reassure the English audience of Fuze's credentials – he is the manager of Colenso's printing office (and therefore a responsible and hardworking man); he is a 'Natal native' (and therefore thoroughly Anglicised and loyal to British ideals) and he is literate (and therefore able to transcribe verbatim the Zulu king's words). In other words, Colenso was at pains to inform the readers that 'such exaggerated accounts' can and should be discarded in favour of the account of a Zulu-speaking witness who had travelled to the Zulu king to make enquiries about the supposed killing of converts.

The road leading to Mayizekanye (written as Maïzekanye) – Cetshwayo's military residence – was not a straight line. Fuze made many detours and observed much protocol about visiting chiefs, commoners and relatives on his way to the king. This then makes his report an account of Zulu etiquette – home-cooked meals being prepared for travellers, cool beer offered to 'wet the lips', and gifts of goats, calves and heifers being offered to an esteemed guest of the king. In fact, there is so much detail of the manners and habits of the Zulu country that it is even tempting to call Fuze's essay an ethnography. The problem is, he was an outsider – a Christian convert from Natal, who played the harmonium and carried a watch. He was also busily scribbling on pieces of paper to the amusement of Zulu girls who were watching him talk to the king. He was therefore the object of people's curiosity and suspicion (plus he was riding a horse). Thus, when he met with Cetshwayo it was an encounter between two incommensurable worlds. Yet, the two found common ground – first, in the personality of Colenso who had by that time proved himself a necessary and useful ally of *uSuthu* (the Zulu royal house) and the exiled *amaHlubi* chief Langalibalele, who was by then a prisoner of the British in exile in Cape Town. These two personalities framed the conversation between Cetshwayo and Fuze, since the matter of the converts was expeditiously dealt with by Cetshwayo's denials that he had ordered the execution of converts.

The conversation between the two exceeded the crisis that had precipitated Fuze's visit: in the essay Fuze recounted how he told the king that conversion didn't mean *ukuhlubuka* (deserting one's ruler); that he told him that the Zulu people should allow 'Natal natives' to return to Zululand and educate and enlighten the Zulus; that the king should follow the footsteps of his uncle, Shaka, and execute *izanusi* (diviners) since it was these practitioners who were continually accusing converts of diabolic deeds; that he discussed with the king the attempts being made by Colenso and others to appeal the arbitrary judgement made against Langalibalele. All these dialogues were neatly compacted into a few minutes of conversation since the Zulu king didn't have time to waste.

Thus, what we hear in Fuze's 'A visit to King Ketshwayo' is a multivocal conversation about culture, politics, imperialism and what Fuze aptly summed up as 'how matters stand with black people, and how the black chiefs are attacked with accusations'. The article is therefore littered with prognostications of what eventually occurred in 1879 when the Zulu kingdom was destroyed, and Cetshwayo exiled and sent to Cape Town, there to begin his own unique relationship with the English monarch, Queen Victoria, and with British imperialism.

References

Garb, Tamar (ed). 2013. *African Photography from the Walther Collection: Distance and Desire: Encounters with the African Archive*. Göttingen: Steidl.
Guy, Jeff. 1994. *The Destruction of the Zulu Kingdom: The Civil War in Zululand, 1879–1884*. Pietermaritzburg: University of Natal Press. Original edition, 1979.
Mahoney, Michael R. 2012. *The Other Zulus: The Spread of Zulu Ethnicity in Colonial South Africa*. Durham & London: Duke University Press.
Mokoena, Hlonipha. 2011. *Magema Fuze: The Making of a Kholwa Intellectual*. Scottsville: University of KwaZulu-Natal Press.
Parsons, Neil. 2003. 'No longer rare birds in London': Zulu, Ndebele, Gaza and Swazi envoys to England, 1882–1894' in Gretchen Holbrook Gertzina (ed), *Black Victorians/Black Victoriana*. New Brunswick: Rutgers University Press.
Webb, Colin de B. & John. B. Wright. 1987. *A Zulu King Speaks: Statements Made by Cetshwayo kaMpande on the History and Customs of his People*. Pietermaritzburg & Durban: University of Natal Press & Killie Campbell Africana Library.

A Visit to King Ketshwayo

Magema Magwaza Fuze, *Macmillan's Magazine* (UK), 1878

Well! On the day when we left my father's kraal, we went and crossed the Buffalo into Zululand, and went on to Njuba's, which was reached at midday, and we got to Esigedhleni, a kraal of Matshana's, in the evening. I sent a man to report me to Matshana, and was given a hut for myself and party; and shortly there arrived a leg of beef uncooked, which we grilled and ate, and slept. In the morning, Matshana sent for me, and I went to him, into a hut of his *isigodhlo*. I asked him about the killing

A CONVERT ENCOUNTERS A KING

of people, saying, 'I am very much surprised to hear the stories about killing in Zululand. But I should very much wish to hear clearly from you, sir, if it is really true that I too shall be likely to be killed ...' Said Matshana, 'I know nothing about any such matter here in Zululand. No one is killed, if he has not done wrong' ...

... When we had gone outside the hut I saw two converts, young men.

Well! We sat down with those two converts under the shade of a tree under a kraal, and I began to ask about the evil things I had heard as to the killing of converts. They told me that two converts had been killed and this is the account which they gave me:

There was a man of Gaozi's who had been a convert for two years. When Gaozi first heard that this man wished to become a convert he tried to prevent it, and collected his council to inquire closely about the conversion of that man. But as the man would not abandon his conversion, the Induna Gaozi let him alone ... but he ordered that the king should not be told about the matter. So things remained until a whole year had passed. But afterwards, when the second year was nearly at an end, the missionary Mondi (Mr Oftebro) went and told the king about that man's conversion ... The king was astonished to hear that it had been hidden from him by Gaozi, and sent a man to hear the truth about it from Gaozi. When Gaozi heard that, he was alarmed thinking that the missionary had gone to inform against him to the king ... and he sent an *impi* to kill the man at once, before Ketshwayo had sent a word of reply to him ...

... July 23: Since I have reached this (king's) kraal, I have not seen the king till this day. This morning at 8am, we went into the Chief Induna Mnyamana, I and Mfunzi, and Nkisimane, and Mboza, and he gave us some beer. As we came out from the Chief Induna, we saw the king standing at the top of the kraal speaking with his people, who were seated in great numbers; he was standing at the entrance to the cattle kraal. On seeing him we went up to pay our respects. Ketshwayo is a black *ikehla* (head-ringed man), resembling his father (the late Mpande), and firm in flesh. He is large, but his body is firm, not flabby, like bodies of other large men among the Zulus. His face does not look so well as it did formerly. He had on today a spotted blanket. After paying our respects, we went down to the bottom of the kraal. When the people went away from before him, the king sent to call us, he still standing at the same place. We came to him and sat down, I spoke with him as follows:

Magema: Ndabezita, I have come here with the desire to see you ... I wish to know about that which is said by people, viz. that you are killing people continually, without having tried their cause, and although the man may not be worthy of death. For you see, sir, those reports last year very much grieved Sobantu, till at last he sent to you, and wrote letters to go to the chiefs over the sea on the words which were spoken in your name by Mfunzi and Nkisimane. Those words plainly showed that these reports were false, and so they were silenced who spread those evil reports about you. And now it will be a joyful thing for me to hear from my lord, the King Gumede, that truly such is the case...

Ketshwayo: Well! I am glad to hear what you say. You see Sobantu there is a father to me, he is not like other white men; his words are different from theirs, they are pleasant. And yet I do not know why he cares for me; he has not seen me from the time when he saw me quite a boy ... I hope that Sobantu will always have a care for me, for those white men are talking – talking – talking, and they want to come down with might upon me. But for my part, as I have done no wrong, I will not run away ... As for me, look you, I don't approve of killing a man. But the Zulu people are bad; it is they who wish to kill one another, whereas I do not allow it. Here, you see, are Mfunzi and Nkisimane still alive, whom people have been after continually, seeking that they should be killed. Well! How is it that they are still alive? And in the time to come you will find them still here.

Magema: Ndabezita, I should wish to hear also about those stories of converts whom it is said you are killing. For, when I was there at home, it was reported that three converts had come to inform Mr John (Shepstone) about them. And moreover, this very day, I find the missionaries and converts already gone, running away from you. I wish to know the meaning of this.

Ketshwayo: Au! They are liars! Do you hear what he says? I too don't understand the meaning of that. I only see that all the missionaries have gone away, without my knowing why they are gone away, without their having said a word to me, whereas I had treated them very kindly ...

1887, South Africa

'Discontent permeates the whole district'

Introduced by Peter Limb

John Tengo Jabavu (1859–1921), the doyen of the early black press in South Africa and a leading pioneer of African journalism, in 1884 launched his own paper, *Imvo Zabantsundu* (Black Opinion), in isiXhosa and English, after working since 1876 on the Lovedale mission paper *Isigidimi samaXhosa* (Xhosa Messenger). Xhosa journalism had emerged gradually within the mission presses but it was difficult to present investigative journalism, or even an independent voice, within their pages.

Jabavu, an active Wesleyan, travelled widely to church, and later political, conferences and often used these visits to report first hand at a time when financial resources for the black press were limited, and communications slow. This story was the editorial lead in the English columns of the issue. He combines on-the-spot reporting and interviewing of local people with in-depth analysis sensitive to background factors. He first sketches the terrain, underlining the isolation yet high population density of the essentially rural district, which was becoming an important source of migrant labour for the Rand mines and Free State farms and mines. There were some small urban settlements and mission stations nearby, notably Bensonvale Institution, about which he enthuses from his own sincere Christian perspective, and Wittebergen, but much of the population lay in scattered villages.

The story emphasises the need for a press attuned to local needs: in this region, remote from big cities, 'there is no Press to bring to light the thousand and one little worries'. Mindful both of how white readers might dismiss black people's complaints as 'trivial', and of his black interlocutors' urgings that he expose the injustices they face on a daily basis, Jabavu nicely connects 'little' and 'big' concerns of the people of Herschel district, in the Eastern Cape (Beinart, 1987). These are in fact 'big' worries: the severely administered pass laws resemble the tyranny of tsarist Russia. Local workers are caught in a vicious circle: needing to migrate to find work to pay taxes, they are denied the travel passes necessary to do so; if they succeed, when they return home they could be denied entry on spurious grounds that there is no space. Jabavu's focus on everyday life captures how the investigative journalist's domain is not just 'high politics'. Liberty needs a free press, without which the Africans of Herschel are dependent on the 'caprice' of officials. And yet, he is not despondent: the people are in an 'enquiring frame of mind, indicative of a hopeful future'. Across all this reporting, there is ample evidence that Jabavu has listened closely and with empathy to local voices, who urged him to publicise their plight.

Jabavu's journalistic style is persuasive, a well-weighted balance of matter-of-fact reporting and eloquent appeal for official action to address inequities. The ridiculous and callous bureaucratic run-around of the pass laws is likened to 'shutting up a man in a dark chamber and kicking him for not seeing'. Sufficient evidence of hardship is adduced to make the reader want to act, but there is also careful attention to moderate language so as not to call down the wrath of censors, who would in fact shut down *Imvo* during the South African War.

In this decade, Jabavu also helped build new modern black political organisations in the Eastern Cape. Electorally he supported the South African Party against the party of Cecil Rhodes. Later developments would leave him far behind progressive African opinion; his enmeshment with such patronage politics would see him oppose the formation and policies of the South African Native National Congress (later the African National Congress) in 1912 and fail to condemn the 1913 Natives' Land Act. Yet despite electoral pacts with white parties, his investigative eye discerned that Africans themselves had discovered the source of their predicaments, such that 'discontent permeates the whole district'.

In the 1920s, it would be the black women of Herschel who vigorously asserted for black rights. However, although *Imvo* here in 1887 does 'call for instant inquiry and redress', all it can offer is a rather forlorn hope that officials sensitive to black needs might be appointed; with an eye to official readers, Jabavu declares that the people's complaints are narrated with 'an assurance that they have simply to be mentioned to be corrected'. The report in this regard thus shows both Jabavu's forthright criticism of racial discrimination in the best traditions of 19th-century investigative journalism, but also the naïve or wishful thinking that was a hallmark of his studied moderation. This was typical of black political strategy of the day and would remain so over the next several decades.

References

Beinart, William. 1987. 'Amafelandawonye (the Die-hards)': Popular protest and women's movements in Herschel district in the 1920s', in William Beinart & Colin Bundy (eds), *Hidden Struggles in Rural South Africa: Politics and Popular Movements in the Transkei and Eastern Cape, 1890–1930*. Johannesburg: Ravan Press, pp. 222–69.

A peep at Herschel

John Tengu Jabavu, *Imvo Zabantsundu*, 23 November 1887

Herschel is essentially a Native district on the extreme north-east confines of the Cape Colony. It abuts on the southern border of Basutoland and the south-eastern limits of the Free State. Although it teems with thousands of the Queen's subjects, and is probably more thickly peopled than any division in the Colony, we hear very little of it. The Magistrate with his attenuated staff, three European missionaries and a few Native assistants, with the inevitable Trader are the only emblems of civilisation to be met with, here and there, in that expansive territory. The Wesleyan Society has, by sheer resolution, in spite of obstacles of no small moment, at last succeeded in planting an institution in the very centre of the reserve, the light from which is beginning to chase the surrounding darkness. With the revulsion of opinion in the country against Native education it would, however, be hazardous to predict how long it would take the Bensonvale Institution with its satellites in the form of those effective agencies for spreading light and sweetness – the station schools, to lighten up today's ignorance. Still we are not despondent. Any one approaching the district can hear the rattling among the dry bones; and already the people are in the enquiring frame of mind, indicative of a hopeful future.

In the meantime, from what we ascertained and observed on

'Discontent permeates the whole district'

the spot, it is quite clear that the liberties of the people under our benignant Queen might be in safer keeping. The Natives appear to have found this out for themselves with the result that discontent permeates the whole district, and the prestige of the government is at a low ebb. It has been said that the liberties we have under our gracious Queen rest on the basis of a free Press. We need hardly observe that they have no Press at Herschel. Consequently, their liberties rest upon the caprice of the Government officials for the time being in charge of the Magistracy. This being the case, it is obvious that for the good, effective and profitable government of a Native community in this stage, a solemn responsibility rests upon the Secretary for Native Affairs and the Government of which he is a member to see to it that officers thoroughly conversant with Native feelings and possessing the confidence of the people over whom they are placed are appointed to such points. This is supremely necessary both for the benefit of the governed and for the good name of those who govern. We confess we looked in vain for anything to show that these leading facts had been kept in view by the Government in meeting the circumstances of Herschel.

We propose to enumerate a few cases of dealings that appear to us to call for instant inquiry and redress. They rest upon the universal testimony of the Natives of Herschel, who desired us as representatives of the Press to give them publicity. We narrate the incidents with an assurance that they have simply to be mentioned to be corrected. It is represented that Natives are not allowed to address public meetings summoned at the Magistracy to consider questions affecting themselves unless they are headmen. Small as this grievance may appear to be to the uninitiated, it is very serious in the eyes of the Kafir whose natural propensity is 'to gas'. Perhaps we are restricting the area of the existence of this failing, for is it not from the European race that we have the standing sentence that 'confession is good for the soul?' We should have thought that the Secretary for Native Affairs would have enjoined it upon all his subordinates to allow the people to speak their mind, in order if possible to base Native government on the goodwill of the people.

The people of Herschel complain that they have been deprived of a good and desirable slice of their commonage on the pretext that it is reserved for the grazing of the horses of headmen when they attend meetings. This act is rendered more galling by the impounding of stock on this piece of unenclosed land, and the fact that they are deprived of the water that is in it.

Then the Pass regulations of Herschel cannot exist anywhere else out of Russia. It seems to be the fashion not to give people passes to leave the district in quest of work, unless they have paid their taxes. We found that the rigour with which Native taxes have been collected, and for dropping which we were complimenting the Government only the other day, has not been abandoned in Herschel. Of course it appears as a very singular thing to the Natives to be refused passes to go out to earn money for taxes, and then to be severely handled for not paying up. It is on a par with shutting up a man in a dark chamber and kicking him for not seeing. How long is this to last! Then it is urged that those who do succeed in obtaining passes to go out to work, when they return home after two or three years they are not allowed to enter the district, on the plea that there is no place for them.

There are other matters to which attention might be drawn, but the space at our disposal does not permit us to refer to them in this issue. But we have said enough to show that the Government has a duty to perform towards the weak and helpless subjects of Her Majesty in outlandish districts where there is no Press to bring to light the thousand and one little worries which render life a grievous burden. We shall doubtless be told that the cases we have mentioned are trivial, but it is the trivial things that make up the sum total of human happiness. Now, the effect of these things is contagious, and there is thus all the more reason to have them as far as possible removed so as to secure the smooth and satisfactory government of the people.

1902, South Africa

Breaking the Peace

Introduced by Irwin Manoim

The 'scoop' that earned Edgar Wallace a place in journalism history consisted of 75 words, none of them written by Wallace. 'PEACE' said the first of seven headlines piled above the tiny story, 'THE IRRECONCILABLES SUBMIT', said another, 'GENERAL SURRENDER' said a third. It was the biggest story of the twentieth century, or so it seemed then, when the century was just two years old. The authorities were apoplectic. Here was a newspaper, the *Daily Mail* of London, read by mere clerks and labourers, which had somehow learnt a closely guarded secret – that the Boer War had ended – before the British cabinet had been informed. Rival papers jeered that the story was a lie. But it wasn't and the mystery was: how did Wallace do it?

Edgar Wallace was the living embodiment of the journalist's romantic idea of what journalists should be: reckless, audacious, contemptuous of authority, cunning, courageous, a braggart and a conman. He wrote swiftly and atrociously, which did not stop him from forging a second career as one of the most prolific and successful writers of pulp fiction in the British Empire. The best-known photograph shows him with head thrown arrogantly back, hat at a jaunty angle, a cigarette dangling from an absurdly long cigarette holder, and a wicked glint in his eye.

Wallace was the illegitimate son of a penniless actress who parcelled him off to foster parents when he was a week old. The foster parents were equally poor, and had 10 other mouths to feed, but brought him up until the age of 12, when he left school for a series of tedious and short-lived jobs, interspersed by run-ins with the police. At 18, he joined the army in search of excitement. In six years he failed to encounter excitement, but his life changed when he was shipped off to South Africa, to serve as a medical orderly at The Castle. He never rose above the rank of private – to reach corporal required studying for an exam, which was too much effort.

For amusement, he wrote satirical ditties. One of them, mimicking the style of the poet of Empire, Rudyard Kipling, was written as a welcome to the great man who was about to visit the Cape. Wallace posted his poem to the *Cape Times*, whose editor, showing a fine nose for popular entertainment, published it on the day Kipling's ship docked, under a note pointing out that it had been written by an army private. Wallace was invited to meet Kipling, who advised him to stay away from writing, 'a splendid mistress, but a bad wife'.

Ignoring this, Wallace quit the army and began freelance writing, first for the *Cape Times* and then *Reuters*, his timing perfect because a war had broken out. He was now 24 years old. He graduated to full-time war correspondent of the *Daily Mail*, for whom he penned jingoistic articles about the courage of the Tommies and the perfidies of the Boers, which earned him the honour, rare in those days, of having his byline on his articles. But the real story began only near the end of the war.

That the Boers had lost the war was apparent to all but the Boers, who entered into and then exited peace talks at Middelburg and then Pretoria. In the opinion of Lord Herbert Kitchener, commander of the British forces, the press were to blame, because they published leaked information that spiked the deals. When it came to the third round of talks, Kitchener decreed that they be held at a distant camp in Vereeniging, surrounded by high barbed wire fences and patrolled round the clock by guards. Military censors had to approve all cables sent out of the country, and reporters were forbidden from even mentioning that talks were being held.

Wallace, who had never been fond of British army officers, was determined to beat the censors. The great benefit of his six years in the army was that he had an old crony who happened to be one of the guards at the camp, and who shared Wallace's contempt for military authority. Each day, Wallace would travel in the train that ran from the Vaal River, border of Kruger's republic, to Pretoria. He would sit, nonchalantly smoking a pipe and reading the newspaper. But there was a point at which the train briefly came in sight of the Vereeniging camp. As the train came by, his friend (Wallace kept the man's name a secret) would stroll to the fence and wipe his brow with a coloured handkerchief. A red handkerchief meant 'a hitch in the talks'. A blue one meant 'progress is being made'. A white one meant 'the deal has been struck'. It seems likely that there were some more nuanced in-between signals, perhaps using hand gestures as well as handkerchiefs – or wiping the nose instead of the brow – but Wallace was coy about those details. His anonymous friend, after all, was in serious breach of military regulations.

The next problem was getting the news to London without alerting the censors. Wallace met up with a minor-league Randlord named Harry Freeman Cohen, who played the stock market in partnership with his London-based brother. Wallace later described Freeman Cohen as 'the whitest man I ever met', presumably referring to the man's fine sense of sportsmanship rather than his complexion. Cohen would send buy and sell notes to his brother, who went by the curious name of Caesar Cohen. Wallace persuaded him to also send coded messages on his behalf, for Caesar to pass on to the *Daily Mail*.

There were a number of different codes and messages, but the ones that mattered worked like this. Cohen would send a message: 'Have bought you Rand Collieries at 40s 6d'. If the number of shares was 100, the situation was unchanged. As the number crept up, the situation became increasingly favourable. By 700 shares, there was high confidence of a deal. When the number reached 1000, peace was absolutely assured. There was also a negative code. If he cabled 'Have sold Rand Collieries shares at 40s 6d', it meant the situation was deteriorating. At 100 shares, it was unsatisfactory. If it reached 1000 shares, then a deal was absolutely off.

Given the sudden surge in telegram activity from Freeman Cohen, the military censors, who were not quite as dim-witted as journalists like to think, demanded that he show proof that he actually owned the shares. This was not difficult – Freeman Cohen was a major shareholder in Rand Collieries. His great interest in the fortunes of Rand Collieries thus made some sense. The censors did not ask again.

The Vereeniging talks went on for days. Only the *Daily Mail* in London was confident enough to publish reports on the progress of the negotiations. Other correspondents were hanging about the gates of the camp, waiting for snippets and getting nothing. It was a mystery who the *Daily Mail* correspondent might be, since the articles carried no byline. Wallace was the obvious culprit, and both the military authorities and jealous rival journalists confronted him. But no one had seen him at the camp, he was not filing any cables, and he explained that he was tired of the endless waiting when nothing was happening and was busying himself with his own affairs.

By 16 May 1902, the *Daily Mail* was already announcing there was high confidence that a deal was likely. But the big story broke on Friday, 30 May:

> The Boers, meeting at Vereeniging, have practically agreed to accept peace: only certain more or less minor details remain to be settled and

they are not expected to affect the broad decision arrived at.

The Boer delegates returned to Vereeniging on Wednesday, and it is understood that they will exercise their full weight in favour of peace.

The government is expected to make its formal statement on, probably, next Monday, in both Houses of Parliament.

That was it. Three sentences. An unknown desk editor in London must have written the article, adding just a hint of caution in case it turned out wrong, and spicing it up with a few plausible bits of speculation. The government had nothing to say. On the Saturday, rival papers jeered that the *Daily Mail* had it all wrong. But, in fact the peace accord was signed that night and somehow Wallace was a day ahead. Kitchener was unable to get details of the settlement through to London until Sunday – there had been a break in the cable. It was only late on Monday morning that Arthur Balfour, the Prime Minister, confirmed to Parliament that peace had indeed been signed.

Wallace became both a hero and a villain. Alfred Harmsworth, owner of the *Daily Mail*, congratulated him and invited him to a grand dinner of celebration at the Savoy Hotel in London. The military censors announced that for breach of the censorship rules his permit as a war correspondent be permanently withdrawn and a medal he was owed would not be awarded. 'One scarcely knows whether to be amused or saddened by the puerility of the War Office,' replied Wallace.

There is just a little more to add to the story. A few weeks later, Harry Freeman Cohen was drinking at Heath's Bar on Pritchard Street, Johannesburg, with the morose and broke proprietor of the *Standard and Diggers News*, once the leading morning paper in Johannesburg, but shuttered by the British for being too friendly to the Boers. Cohen, having had a little taste of the excitements of journalism, proposed on the spot to buy it. He knew only one journalist, Edgar Wallace, whom he offered the job of editor, at a salary that far exceeded what the *Daily Mail* were paying him. Untroubled by his own lack of newsroom or editing experience, Wallace accepted immediately. He also suggested a new name for the newspaper, in honour of his previous employer: *The Rand Daily Mail*.

References

Daily Mail, May to June 1902, London.
Kaplan, Mendel & Robertson, Marian (eds). 1991. *Founders and Followers, Johannesburg Jewry 1187–1915*. Cape Town: Vlaeberg.
Lane, Margaret. 1939. *Edgar Wallace: Biography of a Phenomenon*. London: The Book Club.
Mervis, Joel. 1989. *The Fourth Estate: A Newspaper Story*. Johannesburg: Jonathan Ball.

Peace

Edgar Wallace, *Daily Mail*, 30 March 1902

PEACE
BOER LEADERS REPLY
THE IRRECONCILABLES TO SUBMIT
ABANDONMENT OF INDEPENDENCE
GENERAL SURRENDER
PROBABLY ANNOUNCEMENT ON MONDAY
REASON FOR DELAY

The Boers, meeting at Vereeniging, have practically agreed to accept peace: only certain more or less minor details remain to be settled, and they are not expected to affect the broad decision arrived at.

The Boer delegates return to Vereeniging from Pretoria on Wednesday, and it is understood they will exercise their full weight in favour of peace.

The Government is expected to make its formal statement on, probably, next Monday in both Houses of Parliament.

1906, SOUTH AFRICA

Impi yamakhanda
The war of the heads

INTRODUCED BY BENEDICT CARTON

John Langalibalele Dube (1871–1946) remains one of South Africa's most versatile luminaries. He pioneered modern Zulu nationalism and became the founding president of the South African Native National Congress, the predecessor of Nelson Mandela's liberation movement. An impressive body of scholarship examines Dube's politics, particularly the ways that Christianity and ethnicity shaped his activism (Marks, 1986; La Hausse, 2000; Hughes, 2011; Odendaal, 2013). Yet, to date only a few published works are devoted to the study of his life as a newspaper man in British-ruled Natal (Davis Jnr, 1997; Mokoena, 2016). He wrote 'The man's head' and 'Colour', reproduced below. Appearing in *Ilanga laseNatal* (*The Natal Sun*), a Zulu-language weekly that he edited, these articles bookended a tumultuous period in 1906. That year Dube covered the biggest story of his career: *Impi yamakhanda*, the 'war of the heads', an insurrection fuelled by Zulu youths opposing a £1 poll tax (Hadebe, 2001; 2003). In tracing the causes and consequences of this conflict, Dube established himself as an investigative reporter. Yet while it is tempting to focus on *Impi yamakhanda* as the moment he realised the power of journalism to expose wrongdoing, it was Dube's formative faith that truly sparked his interest in muckraking.

Early on, Dube learnt about searching inquiry in a mission setting that encouraged Christians to believe that Africans deserved the same God-given opportunities and protections as settlers. He grew up in Inanda, a hamlet of converts, *amakholwa*, outside Durban. His father James (Ukakonina) was a Congregationalist pastor of the American Board of Commissioners for Foreign Missions, known by the acronym ABCFM (Marks, 1986: 43–4;

Houle 2011). Dedication to the gospel never severed James's bond with his mother Mayembe's traditional amaQadi lineage. He regaled his children with tales of her patriarch, the *inkosi* (chief) whose fame 'excited the jealousy ... of the (Zulu) king'. John Dube carried his ancestral pride into American Zulu Mission (AZM) schools, particularly Amanzimtoti Theological (Adams College) where he read New Testament primers, morality tales (*Izinganekwane*), and *Pilgrim's Progress*, the latter being a remarkably accessible text in Africa (Hofmeyr, 2003: 27–8; Hughes, 2011: 1–3, 27). During Dube's adolescence, mother-tongue literacy took precedence over English proficiency, which may explain his mastery of evocative isiZulu writing (Dube, 1892: 16–8). In the pages of *Ilanga* he seemed to delight in enlivening articles with double-edged phrases, at once stinging white rulers and baffling censorious translators (*Ilanga*, 25 March 1906).

Dube encountered newspapers through American Board proselytisers whose beat was the drama of evangelism. His mission teachers had among their goals to expand the scope of religious reporting. Some served as foreign correspondents for the *Missionary Herald*, ABCFM's periodical which claimed to chronicle what ailed Christian civilisation, namely primitive sin (Wilcox, 1884; 1886). For its part, *Ilanga* professed to record what afflicted African civilisation, if for a different purpose: to uncover colonial transgression. Young Dube admired ABCFM representatives who advanced freedom, equality and knowledge. His mentor, Reverend William Wilcox, not only cherished the First Amendment right to expression; he affirmed that a 'white man born ... in a Zulu kraal will have the thoughts and feelings of a Zulu'. When Cecil Rhodes apparently asked Wilcox for the assistance of one 'good nigger', Wilcox rebuked the 'empire builder': '*good* but I call him a *man*' (Wilcox, 1925: 19, 202; Hughes, 2001; 2011: 86–91). Wilcox shepherded John into adulthood after the protégé lost his father James and mother Elizabeth (Namazi Shangase) to fatal illnesses. Together, the acolyte and reverend would introduce South Africa to the 'industrial' aim of Booker T. Washington's Tuskegee Institute in Alabama, which sought to train artisans and teachers to serve their black communities. Dube eventually implemented this 'self-help' curriculum in his own institute, Ohlange (Wilcox, 1927; Keita, 2009).

Wilcox helped create Ohlange by forging an educational pipeline that facilitated the enrolment of AZM pupils in American schools promoting the Tuskegee vision (Washington, 1897). In 1887 Dube went overseas to enter the undergraduate bridging programme, or 'preparatory department', of Oberlin College, Wilcox's alma mater in Ohio (*Summit County Beacon*, 5

October 1887). Oberlin instructors taught the composition of fact (rhetoric) and printing, journalism skills that Dube brought back with him to Natal at the end of 1891.

Five years later he returned to the US, accompanied by his wife Nokutela. John Dube attended Union Missionary Training Institute in Brooklyn, completing a theology course that culminated in his ordination as a Congregational minister (Wilcox, 1963: 42–4; Marable, 1979: 23–38). The couple stayed three years in a nation overrun by white vigilantes who lynched black men accused of violating white womanhood. Prominent African Americans such as Henry McNeal Turner, Bishop of the African Methodist Episcopal (AME) church, assailed this mind set: 'Southern (white) fanatics' declare '(t)hat if you free the negro he will want to marry our daughters and sisters.' He questioned the presumption: 'What do we want with their daughters and sisters? We have as much beauty as they' (quoted in Feimster, 2009: 53).

Lynching was an ordinary occurrence when John and Nokutela toured East Coast states to 'solicit aid' for their proposed Tuskegee in Natal. In November 1896, their 'refined' presentations won praise from the New York *Tribune* (Hughes, 2011: 65). Months later this paper sensationalised the killing of Samuel Holt, an African American suspected of assault and homicide. A white mob in Georgia burned him at the stake and cut away 'his ears, fingers, and other portions of his body' (Patterson, 1998: 194–5). A few years before Dube departed for Oberlin settlers in his colony, frenzied by 'rape scares', also instigated vigilante aggression, although they stopped short of extra-judicial executions of Zulu-speaking Africans (Martens, 2002: 379–400).

In May 1897 John Dube likely passed through Georgia on his way to Alabama to meet Washington and give a commencement address at Tuskegee (*Birmingham News, Montgomery Advertiser*; both 28 May 1897); this event inspired his 'Zulu's message,' a future plea to 'Afro-Americans' to uplift Natal natives (Vinson & Edgar, 2008: 243–4). In May 1897 Dube also told graduating 'sons and daughters' of Hampton Institute in Virginia: 'your forefathers came from Africa … (while) I have come … to learn something of industrial education. … (and) I think a few of you might go out and teach as you are taught … (to) revolutionize … the Zulus.' In terms celebrating Ethiopianism – a prophetic creed rejecting white-controlled Christianity in fulfilment of Psalm 68:31, 'Ethiopia shall soon stretch her hands unto God' – Dube offered a refuge: '(I)f the Negro is ever really to have a country it will be Africa' (*Southern Workman*, 1 July 1897).

In due course Natal authorities would blame 'exported' Ethiopianism for stoking 'primitive' Zulu violence in 1906, an accusation Dube denied, if obliquely: 'if the people of this country were to be taught the Gospel, then it could not be taught ... by Europeans' (*Evidence, Natal Native Commission, 1906–7*: 962). He alluded to this sentiment in a letter to the Tuskegee founder (Harlan, 1989: 338–9). Still, Dube was careful about airing radical thoughts, giving himself cover by criticising Ethiopian-type adherents who wanted to overthrow white rule (*Ilanga*, 2 March 1906; 16 March 1906). Most important, his 1897 American speeches signalled his coming of age as a nascent Pan-Africanist echoing Henry Turner. The next year this AME Bishop visited South Africa to enfold 'native' Christians, Xhosas and Zulus among them, in a movement settling his black brethren on 'the continent' to spur development from Liberia to the Cape Colony (Campbell, 1995: 136–8). This ideal of traversing borders and boosting Africans appealed to Dube (La Hausse, 2000: 13). He valued connections fostered by crossing the Atlantic, especially journeys that enabled him and his brother Charles to study in the US (Charles attended Wilberforce, an Ohio AME-supported university).

AME revivalism coincided with American expansionism. The latter, in turn, animated the US press headlining 'Yankee' imperialism in Cuba and comparing the 'war spirit', vented on the home front through 'sundry lynchings', to 'Great Britain's aggression in South Africa' (*Washington Post*, 31 August 1900). With the Dubes residing in Brooklyn, a notorious incident of 'lynch-law' deposed the multi-racial elected government in Wilmington, North Carolina. The Red Shirts, a group venerating the Ku Klux Klan, executed this coup d'etat in 1898, reinforced by white veterans shooting a Gatling gun from the Cuban theatre. The paramilitary murdered black bystanders and drove their families into nearby swamps. An associate of Turner, Baptist Reverend Charles Morris, was so traumatised by the massacre that he left America to preach '(a)mong the Zulus' (*Cleveland Gazette*, 31 March 1900; Carton & Vinson, 2017: 59–70); his 'Negro' evangelism was featured in *Ilanga* (*Ilanga*, 16 March 1906). As 'Colour' went to press, Dube was cataloguing evidence of lethal attacks by vengeful Natal soldiers on non-combatant Zulus. Indeed, by August 1906 – the month the article was conceived – he was not only well aware of the shared legacy of racial retribution in South Africa and the United States, but Dube likely anticipated the echo over international telegraph lines carrying news that Booker Washington's 'Negro improvement' activism had incited white marauders to kill African Americans in Atlanta (Painter, 1987: 216–9).

When John Dube returned to Natal from his second American sojourn, he well recognised how the 'lynch-law' mentality – particularly its calculated terror and transnational reach – posed an existential threat to black people enduring white supremacy. Thus, he accelerated his plan to create two institutions that would ensure 'the last shall be first'. The police surveilling Dube's 'seditious' activity recorded this biblical phrase, along with 'and the first shall be last' (quoted in Vinson & Edgar, 2008: 244).

In 1901 John and Nokutela Dube finished the construction of Ohlange. This vocational oasis gave Zulus a chance, he proclaimed, to 'keep pace with (white) civilization', unlike 'the Red Indians of America' (*Evidence, Natal Native Commission, 1906–7*: 961). Two years later, in February, the Dubes launched *Ilanga laseNatal*. It followed the trail originally blazed by *Ipepa loHlanga* (*National Newspaper*), if not this periodical's final trajectory. In 1903 *Ipepa loHlanga*, edited by Mark Hadebe, headed for closure (Mokoena, 2016: 369–70). Committed to publishing isiZulu articles along with a few columns in English, isiXhosa and Sesotho, *Ilanga* adopted a didactic tone, commending piety and admonishing sycophancy. Dube reserved special ire for peers collaborating with 'foreigners' to restrict oral and printed Zulu 'literature'. One editorial scolded the AZM teacher Ngazana Lutuli for aiding a government effort to codify isiZulu orthography (La Hausse, 2000: 12).

During the paper's first decade one subject seemed to overshadow all others, spreading protests against a £1 poll tax imposed on unmarried men over the age of eighteen (Hadebe, 2001; 2003). The revenue-raising measure targeted single African migrant labourers earning cash (Marks, 1970: 138–42). Dube set out to discover whether this unrest portended something more ominous. Were the combative youths, he wondered, enflaming generational struggles between junior commoners and traditional leaders? No other newspaper so clarified the combustible interplay between politics and culture provoking war in 1906. Dube referenced generational struggles in Natal as African patriarchs were surrendering more resources to settlers (soon after a succession of environmental disasters – rinderpest, drought and locusts – had devastated crops and livestock). Seeing their material birthright diminished, some Zulu youths perceived the apparent elder acquiescence to colonial exactions as an act of betrayal, and increasingly defied senior authority by flouting filial obligations (Carton, 2000). *Ilanga* illuminated these dynamics to warn government that it had disturbed a hornet's nest, and to alert readers that reactive opposition to the poll tax, incited by intense social discord, made all Africans vulnerable to the firepower of vindictive colonists. The sources informing Dube were probably associated with his Ngcobo Qadi lineage as well as AZM counterparts who lived along the coast, north from Durban to the Tugela River, like the Maphumulo division. At another remove, he likely received tips from Zulus in Pietermaritzburg and southern reserves around Ixopo, an area dotted by ABCFM stations. Finally, his most prized informants may have been 'native interpreters' – and *Ilanga* supporters – serving the magistrate.

When 'The man's head' first appeared, Dube's public insistence on payment of the new £1 obligation was well known (*Ilanga*, 26 February 1906). Seeming to play a different tune, his March 1906 article portrayed anti-poll tax as a reasonable outcry expressed with slogans and mock war-dancing, *ukugiya*, that physically harmed no one. Displeased with this characterisation, Natal authorities indignantly summoned Dube. Their showdown gave *Ilanga* a chance to present the editor's starring role in a scene titled, 'I Governor noMafukuzela', where Dube, the 'tireless man' (uMafukuzela), addressed the overlord's rebukes (*Ilanga*, 28 May 1906). Soon protestors abandoned their voluble approach and, instead, wielded spears in regiments that confronted law enforcers; several white policemen were slain. In Ixopo and Dumisa, militants rallied to the promises of 'Ethiopianism' (Report Magistrate, Lower Umzimkulu, January 1906; Report Inspector Philips, Dumisa, April 1906). By April, some of them had joined armed rebels streaming towards the Tugela Valley. Deploying hit-and-run tactics, they skirmished the Natal army, coiled to strike with Gatling guns and field batteries. The guerrillas called their campaign *impi yamakhanda*. Colonists, however, coined it Bhambatha's uprising, so designated for the ringleader, amaZondi *inkosi* Bhambatha kaMancinza who was either accused by whites of plotting treason or honoured by Zulus for galvanising resistance. In June, Bhambatha's forces concentrated in the Nkandla forest. It was a fatal error; government troops trapped the rebels and annihilated them with cannon fire. 'Mop up' units then scoured the countryside, targeting real and imagined insurgents, torching homesteads and selling seized livestock to fund these operations (Marks, 1970: 239–40; Carton, 2000: 122). Over the next two months another phase of *impi yamakhanda* turned Maphumulo into a war zone (Guy, 2005). That settlers embraced their self-appointed prerogative in these martial zones – of 'licking the niggers into shape' and 'knocking the hell out of them' (Marks, 1970: 177) – did not surprise *Ilanga*. In 'Colour' Dube urged Zulu readers to see their predicament, as hunted people, in the way that African Americans understood the peril of lynching. Vengeful colonists pervaded South Africa, he asserted, so one could not separate them from ordinary 'natives', and vice versa. Thus, it was incumbent on *abantu* (Africans) and *abelungu* (Europeans) to stem the hatred spawned by white supremacy. In the wake of 'Umbala', Dube contacted his Tuskegee hero, explaining that 'the prejudice of our white people' grimly mirrored 'the Southern States in America' (Harlan, 1989: 339).

'The man's head' depicts this hatred and the predatory men like Colonel Leuchars who embodied it. The article describes a series of events, beginning one morning in February 1906, when George Leuchars, a former minister of Native Affairs, and his 'vultures' hovered on the horizon while *inkosi* Gobizembe paraded his young men before Magistrate Ernst Dunn. Directed to hand over their £1, they refused and stormed off, according to Dunn's memos. The magistrate moved to another location in Maphumulo to meet *inkosi* Swayimani [sic] and his 'boys' (Statement Nkomonopondo, March 1906; Minute Magistrate Dunn, February 1906). These young men thrusted sticks in the air, Dunn noted, and shouted '(t)hey had no money' (Statement Swayimana, March 1906; Statement Sergeant Mhlazana, March 1906). Swayimani [sic] cracked his *sjambok*, a whip, striking some 'boys' but these lashes 'had not the desired effect'. After the assembly dispersed, Dunn quipped, 'the whole were ... ungovernable by either myself or their Chief'. Hours later he summoned poll tax payers of *inkosi* Meseni to Galliard's Store. A crowd formed and jeered, 'they were being eaten up by Government'. Dunn blustered: '(i)f they were here to pay, well and good, if not they had to go' (Minute Magistrate Dunn, February 1906). They left.

Galliard's was Dunn's last afternoon stop. Back at the magistracy he penned a document sounding the alarm: 'the brutes here ... shout at me *"Iya asikutela gade satsho enza ngokutanda"* (Get away. We are not going to pay ... Do as you please), and *gwiya* [e.g., simulate combat in dance steps]' (Minute Magistrate Dunn to Under Secretary for Native Affairs, February 1906). Dunn witnessed the sparks of a gathering blaze. The narratives of 'The man's head' coincided with the magistrate's reports. With no apparent access to Dunn's records, Dube probably reconstructed what happened from details supplied by eyewitnesses who remembered the day the poll tax collection failed. Convinced force would defuse strife in Maphumulo, Leuchars told Gobizembe to surrender 300 poll tax evaders. Unsatisfied with the turnout, Leuchars ordered the *inkosi* to clear out his homestead and blew it up. Within days, Gobizembe was banished. Leuchars wanted similarly to punish Meseni and Swayimani [sic] (Interview, Colonel Leuchars & Swayimana, March 1906; Stuart 1913: 149–50).

References

Birmingham News (Alabama), 28 May 1897.
Campbell, J. 1995. *Songs of Zion: The African Methodist Episcopal Church in the United States and South Africa*. New York: Oxford University Press.
Carton, B. 2000. *Blood from Your Children: The Colonial Origins of African Generational Conflict*. Charlottesville: University of Virginia Press.
Carton, B. & Vinson, R. 2017. 'Ethiopia shall stretch from America to Africa: The pan-African crusade of Charles Morris', in D. Hodgson & J. Byfield (eds), *Global Africa: Into the Twenty-first Century*. Berkeley: University of California Press, pp. 59–70.
Cleveland Gazette, 31 March 1900.
Davis Jr., R. 1997. '"Qude Maniki!" John L. Dube, Pioneer editor of *Ilanga Lase Natal*', in L. Switzer (ed), *South Africa's Alternative Press: Voices of Protest and Resistance 1880s–1960s*. Cambridge: Cambridge University Press, pp. 83–99.
Dube, J. 1892. *A Familiar Talk Upon My Native Land and Some Things Found There*. Rochester, NY: R.M. Swinburne and Co.
Evidence Natal Native Affairs Commission 1906–7. 1907. Testimony of J.L. Dube, 5 April 1907: 961–962. 8/3/76, 1/NCP, Pietermaritzburg Archives Repository (PAR), South Africa.
Feimster, C. 2009. *Southern Horrors: Women and the Politics of Rape and Lynching*. Cambridge, MA: Harvard University Press.
Gasa, E. 1999. '*John L. Dube, his Ilanga laseNatali* and the *natal administration, 1903–1910*'. PhD thesis, *University* of Zululand.
Guy, J. 2005. *The Maphumulo Uprising: War, Law and Ritual in the Zulu Rebellion*. Scottsville: University of KwaZulu-Natal Press.
Hadebe, M. 2001. 'Isidumo sokulwa eRichmond'. Unpublished paper, University of Natal, Durban.
Hadebe, M. 2003. 'A contextualization and examination of the *Impi Yamakhanda* (1906 uprising) as reported by J.L. Dube in *Ilanga laseNatali*, with special focus on Dube's attitude to Dinuzulu as indicated in his reportage on the treason trial of Dinuzulu'. MA thesis, University of Natal, Durban.
Harlan, L. (ed). 1989. *The Booker T. Washington Papers*, vol. 9. Urbana, IL: University of Illinois Press.
Hofmeyr, I. 2003. *The Portable Bunyan: A Transnational History of the Pilgrim's Progress*. Princeton: Princeton University Press.
Houle, R. 2011. *Making African Christianity: Africans Reimagining Their Faith in Colonial South Africa*. Bethlehem, PA: Lehigh University Press.
Hughes, H. 2001. 'Doubly elite: Exploring the life of John Langalibalele Dube'. *Journal of Southern African Studies* 27(3): 445–58.
Hughes, H. 2011. *First President: A Life of John L. Dube, Founding President of the ANC*. Johannesburg: Jacana Media.
Interview between Colonel Leuchars and Chief Swayimana, 11 March 1906, Maphumulo Martial Law Misc. Report 1906, 1/MPO 5/4, PAR.
Keita, C. 2009. *Cemetery Stories: A Rebel Missionary in South Africa*. Mogoya Productions.
Ilanga laseNatal (*Ilanga*), 26 February, 2 March, 16 March, 25 March, 28 May; 1906.
La Hausse de Lalouviere, P. 2000. *Restless Identities: Signatures of Nationalism, Zulu Ethnicity and History in the Lives of Petros Lamula (c.1881–1948) and Lymon Maling (1889–1936)*. Pietermaritzburg: University of KwaZulu-Natal Press.
Marable, M. 1979. 'South African nationalism in Brooklyn: John L. Dube's activities

in New York State, 1887–1899'. *Afro-Americans in New York Life and History*, 3(1): 23–38.

Marks, S. 1970. *Reluctant Rebellion: The 1906–8 Disturbances in Natal*. Oxford: Oxford University Press.

Marks, S. 1986. *The Ambiguities of Dependence in South Africa: Class, Nationalism, and the State in Twentieth-Century Natal*. Johannesburg: Ravan Press.

Martens, J. 2002. 'Settler homes, manhood and "Houseboys": An analysis of Natal's rape scare of 1886'. *Journal of Southern African Studies*, 28(2): 379–400.

Minute Magistrate Dunn, Maphumulo, 5 February 1906, 400/06, 1/SNA 1/1/335, PAR.

Minute Magistrate Dunn, Maphumulo, to Under Secretary for Native Affairs, Pietermaritzburg, 2 February 1906, 1/SNA 1/1/335, PAR.

Mokoena, H. 2016. 'The afterlife of words: Magema Fuze, bilingual print journalism and the making of a self-archive', in D. Peterson, E. Hunter & S. Newell (eds), *African Print Cultures: Newspapers and Their Public in the Twentieth Century*. Ann Arbor: University of Michigan Press, pp. 361–88.

Montgomery Advertiser (Alabama), 28 May 1897.

Odendaal, A. 2013. *The Founders: The Origins of the ANC and the Struggle for Democracy in South Africa*. Lexington, KY: University of Kentucky Press.

Painter, N. 1987. *Standing at Armageddon: The United States, 1877–1919*. New York: W.W. Norton.

Patterson, O. 1998. *Rituals of Blood: Consequences of Slavery in Two American Centuries*. Washington, DC: Civitas Counterpoint.

Report Inspector Phillips, Dumisa, 22 April 1906, 1051/1906, 1/SNA 1/1/339, PAR.

Report Magistrate Lower Umzimkulu, 29 January 1906, 33/1906, 1/SNA 1/4/15, PAR.

Southern Workman, 1 July 1897.

Statement of Nkomonopondo, 5 March 1906, Maphumulo Martial Law Misc. Report 1906 (Zulu Rebellion), 1/MPO 5/4, PAR.

Statement of Sergeant Mhlazana, 19 March 1906, *Rex vs. Umgodi et al.*, 1426/1906, 1/SNA 1/1/341, PAR.

Statement of Swayimana, 8 March 1906, Maphumulo Martial Law Misc. Report 1906, 1/MPO 5/4, PAR.

Stuart, J. 1913. *A History of the Zulu Rebellion 1906 and of Dinuzulu's Arrest, Trial and Expatriation*. London: MacMillan.

Summit County Beacon (Ohio), 5 October 1887.

Washington, B. 1897. 'Fourth U.L.A. lecture: The negro problem in the black belt of the South'. *Oberlin Review*, February (np). Wilcox Papers, Oberlin College Archives, OH. *Washington Post*, 31 August 1900.

Wilcox, M. 1963. *Proud Endeavorer: The Story of a Yankee on a Mission to South Africa*. New York: Graphic Press.

Wilcox, (Rev.) W. 1884. 'Umzila Mission'. *Missionary Herald* 80: 186.

Wilcox, (Rev.) W. 1886. 'Umzila Mission'. *Missionary Herald* 83: 20.

Wilcox, W. 1925. *The Man from An African Jungle*. New York: Macmillan.

Wilcox, W. 1927. 'The Booker Washington of South Africa'. *Oberlin Alumni Magazine*, March (np). Wilcox Papers, Oberlin College Archives, OH.

The Man's Head

John Dube, *Ilanga laseNatal*, 26 February 1906
Translated by Benedict Carton, with assistance from Dingani Mthethwa and J. Sabelo Ntshangase

Our attention has been with Maphumulo and Ixopo, now we turn our focus to the place of Dumisa where *inkosi* Jack together with his headmen, or councillors, went to the magistrate to report that their young men refused to pay the poll tax. Today I learned something new about black people. *Amakhosi* find a way to settle the problem with white authority by blaming angry boys for refusing to pay for the tax, and thereby maintain good standing with government. On the other hand, when the boys are caught they blame *amakhosi* for having instructed them to refuse paying taxes. Therefore, Gobizembe was arrested because those young men of his father who performed a dance simulating combat (*ukugiya*) in the face of the magistrate, chanting 'we will never pay,' now smear Gobizembe 'with poop on his face,' blaming him for instructing the boys not to obey (government) agreeably. Jack is now imprisoned, he is saying that his people refuse to pay, but who knows, when they are brought to book perhaps they will say that Jack is lying. I don't understand people anymore. When you look at all these things you wonder if armed resistance can be launched by these people! *Ilanga* said this amounts to nothing. Members of the taxing authority do not accept the spears brought by Gobizembe's people, they believed those spears are not the weapons typically carried in war. The spears brought forward were dug-up throw-aways from the trash heap. Shoo! Do you think they will bring their real fighting spears right away? Lushazi (Colonel Leuchars) is ready to confiscate Gobizembe's cattle and sell them.

Mshofeni has already paid one hundred cows for refusing to identify his people who show contempt to the high political power.

The question is whether Gobizembe's people will be divided up under other *amakhosi* or a new *inkosi* will be appointed over them, you will never know the intentions of the authorities.

On Monday there was a trial against the people who killed policemen at Mafuze district. The trial was handled in the government court. Manjongwe and others did not attend the trial because they were sick. Twenty people were convicted that day.

The vultures are hovering and it seems the days are numbered for *amakhosi* Meseni and Swayimani [sic] (they are the next target). It is said that Meseni, *inkosi* of the Qwabe has been commanded to give up one hundred men who defied the Magistrate at Gillands [Galliard's] on February 1st. Swayimani [sic] was also made to produce fifty young men who defied the Magistrate on the same day. Leuchars (called umfo ka) knows the power of a conquering warrior, he will eat up (seize) their cattle too. We pity Gobizembe, while death awaits many others.

Just before going to press we hear that Gobizembe and his brother Paul are in Stanger, the site of the magistrate. Leuchars appears not satisfied with the severe punishment inflicted on them. There is a lesson delivered to the man who disobeys government. The whites want to prove to us that we are really under their heel. There is turmoil at Swayimani [sic] and Meseni because they have been directed to hand over the boys who defied the Magistrate. If they fail to surrender those men, Leuchars is out there ready to bring the heavy hand and nobody can stop him from enforcing compliance.

Colour

John Dube, *Ilanga laseNatal*, 28 September 1928
Translated by Benedict Carton, with assistance from Dingani Mthethwa and J. Sabelo Ntshangase

The question of colour has become the pressing topic! [In this opening sentence, the idiom, *indaba egudwini*, means 'everyone is talking about an electrifying topic'. The locative, *egudwini*, refers to the *igudu*, a communal pipe passed between smokers.] Bad news came by telegraph that thirty black people were killed in America following a dispute over women [the killing refers to the

August 1906 Atlanta 'race riots']. The whites have said that the blacks violated [*ukupoqa*, 'to force in a violating way', alluding to sexual assault] white women and black people have said the same with regard to their own women. Bishop Turner of the African Methodist Church speaking in New York said it would be a good thing if the black people of America were taken across to West Africa. He is now speaking to rich Americans to help transport black people [from the United States] to West Africa. There is a conflict between white and black colour when they come together. Although Bishop Turner makes this argument, the question is will he prevent white people from going to West Africa? As soon as the white people arrive in West Africa, the conflict will kindle there. Before the arrival of white people in our country, there was no problem between the whites and blacks. Now it has started. The black people in America have been well educated yet the hatred in the [former Confederate] South is serious. We are begging our white authorities [listen closely], arrange better ways of treating black people so that the time will not arise that hatred between white people and black people will become as serious as it is in the Southern States of America where the black person is falsely accused of committing a violent act against a white woman and taken from the prison cell and shot without a trial. You who are the Natal authorities protect the future generations and avoid everything causing the hatred that can pass to our children. What you have seen in America and other places are sufficient to make you wise and to encourage you to establish the best treatment for black people.

1909, SOUTH AFRICA

The conspiracy against black voters

INTRODUCED BY ROBERT EDGAR

Alan Kirkland Soga (1861–1938) was a journalist who took up the cause of African voters in the early 20th century. One of four sons of Reverend Tiyo Soga and Janet Burnside, he was sent to Scotland at the age of seven with two of his brothers for his schooling and eventually studied law in Glasgow (Allen, 1904; Switzer, 1997; Odendaal, 2013). On his return to the Cape Colony, he was employed as a civil servant in the native affairs department and applied his legal training as an acting resident magistrate at St Mark's in southern Transkei. After Cape Prime Minister Cecil Rhodes replaced him with a white and demoted him to a lesser position in the labour department, he angrily resigned and turned to journalism. When the East London leader, Walter Rubusana, established *Izwi la Bantu* (*Voice of the People*) in November 1897, Soga was soon appointed its editor. Printed bi-weekly by the Eagle Printing Press Company in East London, it billed itself as the 'leading Native paper of the Border' and usually consisted of four pages, three primarily written in isiXhosa and one in English aimed at a European readership.

Izwi was South Africa's second independent black newspaper, established thirteen years after John Tengo Jabavu's *Imvo Zabantsundu*, printed in nearby King Williams Town. Unlike *Imvo*, which allied itself with a white political party, *Izwi* stressed the need for a broad African nationalism and was tied to the South African Native Congress (SANC), which established branches in the Eastern Cape. Soga's *Izwi* took strong positions criticising the suppression of the Bhambatha rebellion in Natal and other white policies. He also kept abreast of events in England and the United States, and he exchanged copies of *Izwi* for newspapers from those countries. An admirer of Booker T. Washington, he was well informed about African American opinion and expressed his desire to convene in America 'a conference of black men from different parts of the world to discuss the black man's future and the potential for unity' (Allen, 1904).

In 1907, British colonial officials announced their intention to merge four of their southern African colonies into a Union of South Africa. White delegates from Natal, Cape, Transvaal and Orange River provinces met in Durban in November 1908 to discuss the formation of a Union. The following February, they announced a draft South Africa Act that ensured whites would dominate the new Union. It stipulated that only men of European descent could serve in Parliament and that African and coloured men would not be allowed to vote in the Transvaal, Natal and Orange River. A small number of male Africans and coloureds in the Cape who met education and property qualifications – about 20,000 voters comprising about 15 per cent of the whole Cape electorate – would retain their franchise.

Before the draft Act was announced, Soga penned an opinion piece in which he argued for maintaining the Cape's qualified franchise and extending it to the other colonies. He tried to assuage white fears that an expanded black vote would lead to inter-racial marriages and sexual relations and that black voters would ever outnumber white voters. And he did not argue for extending the vote to all blacks. Those Africans like him who qualified for the vote, he observed, were proud of their 'civilised' status in contrast with the 'mass of people to whom they belong (who) are still living in barbarism ...' (*Izwi la Bantu*, 2 February 1909).

The announcement of the draft Act provoked a harsh reaction from black leaders such as Rubusana, Soga and John Dube. Black delegates representing the four colonies met in Bloemfontein in late March to establish the South African Native Convention (SANC). It was the first time African leaders from all over the country had met together. Soga was selected as the SANC's general secretary. The SANC accepted the idea of Union, but only if black people were granted equal rights and the qualified franchise for blacks was extended to the whole country.

That was the backdrop for Soga's editorial, 'The South African Conspiracy Act and the Natives', in which he assessed the forces blocking the extension of the black vote. One was the British government, which had missed an opportunity at the signing of the Vereeniging Peace Treaty ending the Anglo-Boer War in 1902 to extend political rights to blacks. Instead, they deferred a decision on this issue until self-government was implemented in the colonies. That ensured that whites would control decisions about any future political dispensation. By the time the draft Act was being considered, political power had shifted to white South African interests, and Soga identified two groups as the 'storm centre' of the plot to block the extension of black political rights. The first was white Transvaal politicians who were not prepared to yield on granting any political rights to blacks. The second was the white press (including his hometown newspaper, *The Daily Dispatch*), which he labelled as 'representatives of the big lions of plutocracy'. He maintained the white press was owned by and served white capitalist interests, especially the Randlords who were concerned with maintaining segregation and insuring supplies of cheap black labour.

Soga's fiery rhetoric did not translate into militant action. Like most members of the black educated elite, he was very conscious of his status and preferred to bring about change through public debates in newspapers and following constitutional processes. Soga's views certainly made little impact on white leaders. The white National Convention approved the draft Act in May 1909 with no changes in its language and sent a delegation to London to lobby the British Parliament to adopt their Act. In response, the SANC sent its own nine-person delegation to represent black views, but their effort came to naught when Parliament ratified the Act with few changes and the Union of South Africa came into being in May 1910 (Plaut, 2016).

References

Allen, S.A. 1904. 'Mr Alan Kirkland Soga', *Coloured American Magazine*, February 1904.
Odendaal, André. 2013. *The Founders*. Johannesburg: Jacana Media.
Plaut, Martin. 2016. *Promise and Despair: The First Struggle for a Non-Racial South Africa*. Johannesburg: Jacana Media.
Switzer, Les. 1997. *South Africa's Alternative Press Voices of Protest and Resistance 1880s–1960s*. New York: Cambridge University Press.

The South African Conspiracy Act and the Natives

Alan Kirkland Soga, *Izwi la Bantu*, 23 November 1909

The local daily is highly incorrect at us for describing the compromise on the native franchise right under the Union as a great betrayal. We might better have described it as the South African Conspiracy Act. But when the *Daily Dispatch* accuses us of 'adopting an inflammatory tone and language calculated to appeal to the worst passions of its readers', we can but reply that we expected no better from a special leader of a shameless complot ... The *Dispatch* need not be afraid of dividing the whites against the blacks or vice versa. This could not be more surely done than will be done by the present Draft Act if it is permitted to pass in its present form. The ingenuity of that paper's attempts to appease criticism is only equalled by its aptitude for misrepresenting the true significance of the native position. But we are neither going to be beguiled by the plausibilities of the allied press nor their threats of the possible evils of agitating the native mind, and we are glad to see that it recognises with some misgivings that 'it is becoming daily more and more clear that a very considerable agitation is about to be undertaken with regard to the Native and Coloured franchise.' Good! We hope that the natives will throw fear to the winds, and will proceed, as they are accustomed to do in a free country to give free expression to their opinions, and to exercise the constitutional rights of public meeting, in as public a manner and as constitutional a way as the laws of this country permit.

Applied to their accomplices at the Cape, the word 'betrayal' is most suitable, but the captains of this complot reside in the Transvaal. That is the storm centre, and the centre of political discord in South Africa.

The reasons for this conspiracy against the Natives are too deeply rooted in our economic and race question to be satisfactorily dealt with in a brief article. The *Daily Dispatch* observes that this feeling, 'call it prejudice' as Dr Jameson remarked at Grahamstown 'or call it what you like', requires time for its removal and argues from that, that the Natives would be wrong in agitating against the Draft Act. It says further: The Cape delegates did all they could short of breaking up the Conference to secure greater privileges for the Coloured people, and indeed a very strenuous attempt was made in the Convention to secure a general franchise which would have fulfilled Mr Rhode's words — 'Equal rights for all civilised men.' But the other Colonies would have either accepted a Union in which the coloured franchise was maintained in the Cape Colony, or of leaving the conference.

It also threatens dire consequences – 'disaster in the breaking up of the Union' and warns the natives to be careful – 'in case there will arise in the country an agitation against the Native vote which will sweep it away forever' ... At one stroke they sweep away the work of half a century and the dearest possession of 20,000 voters who represent the more ignorant millions. The educated and cultured few are forced back on the mass to be ruled under guardianship over again ... Prejudice in this case however (plausible word) is used as a red herring, for there is no doubt of its existence. It is equally true (and this is the point the *Dispatch* carefully forgets) it is a prejudice fomented, promoted and kept constantly before the public by a cultured press, the jackals of the big lions of plutocracy which stand to gain by that dirty work, as the idle rich have always stood to gain in every country by degradation of the proletariat. True enough the root of race hatred in this country on the political plane (as witness the Asiatic treatment in the Transvaal) lies in economic reasons, aggravated in the case of the natives by their colour and ignorance, but on the moral plane, it is cunning and capital that keeps alive through a perverted press system those passions and prejudices which would die out quickly were the axe and the guillotine or the hangman's rope threatened the writers or were they controlled by those Christian principles of which they love to boast. Those who are blind to the attitude of the allied press, and the degrading way which it panders to the basest passions of the ignorant mob, and the lynching theme have overlooked the leading features of the allied press of Cape Town, Johannesburg, Pretoria, Bloemfontein, Kimberley and need we add East London. These prejudices are kept alive by a crusade of the most offensive description, and so far as they ordinarily refer to the black or coloured section it is as a rule in terms of contempt for their 'inferiority', their 'brutality', their 'ruffianism', their 'hereditary and irredeemable savagery', their 'drunken obscenity and insolence to white men' and their 'indecency to white women'. This latter which has now been developed by constant nursing and exaggeration into a hideous Black Peril is a trump card and is placed at the price of the lives of many innocent victims whose lives are forfeit at the nod of any white harridan or kitchen tyrant ... Now to trace the conspiracy. It is easily traced by those who have followed contemporary history. The political faction in the principal states have been co-operating in freezing out the educated natives and coloured people while the late war was yet in its infancy ... We know at any rate that some of the chief conspirators who arranged the Vereeniging compact were present in the Convention. Today as yesterday they are agreed in 'sitting on' the black man. The first notable act in the drama was that dark blot on the Empire — the failure to protect the Native and Coloured rights in the Peace Treaty. That sin rests with the Imperial Government, chiefly through the advisers of the British Cabinet at the end some of whom are sitting on this Convention. It will be remembered (we write from memory) that Clause VIII left the door open for the prospective enfranchisement of the natives when Responsible Government was granted. The Coloured people urged with a reasonableness which has never been refuted that they were excluded from the effect of the Clause. Deputations and petitions were sent to the Home authorities claiming the exercise of solemn treaties, and assurances of protecting the constitutional rights of the native and coloured subjects of the King and also the loyalty and good conduct of both sections, and their fidelity to the British Crown during the war, but the superior strategy of the so-called cultured capitalist class who were now playing their game for cheap labour, intervening with their press, their cables, and confidential men worked for the failure of the legitimate efforts of those people in a good cause ...

1913, SOUTH AFRICA

The Free State women's anti-pass protests

INTRODUCED BY PETER LIMB

The three newspapers featured here, *Abantu-Batho* (*People*), founded by Pixley ka Isaka Seme, *Indian Opinion* of Mahatma Gandhi and *Tsala ea Batho* (*People's Friend*) of Sol Plaatje, were among the most courageous investigative papers of the day.

South African journalism in 1913 was marked by domination of the white-owned press. Black newspapers lacked adequate revenue and relied on a readership with greatly restricted incomes. However, enterprising editors such as J.T. Jabavu, John Dube and Solomon Plaatje managed to keep going the first generation of the independent black press, including these three papers. By 1913, this golden age of the black-owned press was limping along, but would soon go into steep decline.

The two articles are closely connected in political and gender context. The eyewitness reports tell stories of campaigning by African women against the pass laws. The first, from *Abantu-Batho*, gives voice to vigorous protests by Winburg women in June 1913. *Indian Opinion* reprinted it, assuring it wider readership. The writer records the dialogue with the location superintendent, highlights the women's own views (unusual in press reports then, and more so in *Abantu-Batho*), and describes in detail the women's festive, yet deadly serious and disciplined, demonstration, vividly capturing their grim determination to continue until victory and their disdain of these 'dirty papers' (passes).

The contemporary press rarely carried reporter names and authorship of the first article is unclear. Plaatje was in the region at the time, but aspects of style suggest it may not have been him (Willan, 2018a). Direct connection with *Abantu-Batho* is also less evident, though editors Cleopas Kunene and

Daniel Letanka attended Congress gatherings in the area and prominent local Congress activists such as Edward Sauer Mochochoko are possible authors, as are black women of Winburg who wrote letters to the press on passes. It may even have been a white sympathiser, as in Winburg lawyer Antonie Baumann and his wife Marie, who defended the women. Irrespective of authorship, the article is a fine piece of investigative reporting that captures the features and colour of the protests, people involved and their causes.

The author of the second piece is likely Plaatje. A celebrated South African journalist (Limb, 2016; Willan, 2018b), he travelled across the Free State at the time campaigning against the Land Act and pass laws. White Free State politicians had strongly promoted the Act and pass laws and Plaatje's journalism, like that of Gandhi, had long targeted their prejudice. Here we see Plaatje's direct investigative reporting as, together with local female activists, he visits the women in prison and takes up their cause using characteristic striking metaphor and clear logical argument, deftly combining measured fact with principled commitment. His investigations continued for months after. This is Plaatje at his best as an eloquent and probing investigative journalist campaigning against the Land Act and the imposition of passes on black women.

The impact of both pieces was considerable. Circulation of the black press then was limited, but copies were passed from hand to hand and such reports fed into a growing stream of protest. The women had courageously taken the lead, and press accounts of their defiance such as these stung men into action, as seen in huge anti-pass protests in 1919. The 1913 women's protests were not forgotten and were invoked as a symbol of liberation movement struggle in the grim apartheid years. The stories aroused great indignation and helped swell the numbers of the nascent Congress and give direction to its new policies that if in retrospect might appear tame, nevertheless were bold for their time and enabled Congress to mark out a national, critical approach much removed from the *hamba kahle* ('Go in peace') approach of Jabavu. They also show black newspaper networks sharing investigative reports, which in turn helped strengthen wider black unity, for example between the ANC and the African Political Organisation and its organ, APO.

The gender ramifications of the reports are particularly interesting. Plaatje in this and earlier reports championed recognition of women's political role. Moreover, whereas elsewhere direct female participation in Congress was very limited, women delegates were active in the Free State Congress. And, white papers of the day commented that 'the spirit of revolt' among protestors was in part induced by their reports of suffragette protests in England (*Bloemfontein Post*, 29 May 1913). Importantly, Plaatje went on the road and joined women in gaol to listen closely to their stories.

REFERENCES

Bloemfontein Post, 29 May 1913; also cited in Julia Wells, 'The history of black women's struggle against pass laws in South Africa 1900–1960', PhD Columbia University, 1982, p. 122.
Limb, Peter. 2016. 'The print world of the press and *Native Life in South Africa*', in Janet Remington, Brian Willan & Bheki Peterson (eds), *Sol Plaatje's* Native Life in South Africa, *Past and Present*. Johannesburg: Wits University Press.
Willan, Brian. 2018a. Email to Peter Limb, 1 April.
Willan, Brian. 2018b. *Sol Plaatje: A Life of Solomon Tshekisho Plaatje, 1876–1932*. Johannesburg: Jacana Media.

NATIVE WOMEN'S BRAVE STAND

Indian Opinion, 2 August 1913, reprinted from *Abantu-Batho*, July 1913

In Winburg – the oldest town in the Free State – as soon as the women heard what the Bloemfontein women had done and were doing (observes the native newspaper, *Abantu*), they also decided to take action. A meeting was immediately called, in which it was agreed that all the passes be collected and delivered to the proper authorities with the intimation that the papers will not be wanted any longer. On Monday, June 2, all the women of the location assembled at the square and formed themselves into a procession and proceeded towards the town. On reaching the gate dividing the town and the location they stopped, and all the passes were collected from each individual, young and old, and were wrapped up in a rag and the bundle was carried onwards. Being led by three big tall women, they marched 10 by 10 through the town. The three leaders had flags of the Union Jack as an emblem of freedom and liberty. Young women and girls had sticks, whips and sjamboks. The old ladies had long broom-sticks in their hands. There was no outward demonstration; no noise, no shouting or singing — in fact, one woman in the crowd tried to sing and demonstrate, but she was quickly stopped by the others; sticks and sjamboks being instantly applied to silence the woman who dared to make noise of any sort! The procession was quiet and very impressive; so much so that for want of a biercoach and two black horses, it might have resembled a funeral procession. Nevertheless, the women went on bravely and resolutely, pledged never to carry the obnoxious passes again. The same paper thus amplifies the account:

The Town Hall was reached. A clerk appeared, and the women demanded to see the Superintendent of the Location. He was soon found, and when he appeared he said: 'Oh! You people almost frightened me. What's wrong?'

'We've brought your passes: we don't want them any more', spoke one of the leaders, showing the little bundle. The Superintendent said: 'I don't want the dirty things!'

'Where shall I put them?' asked the same woman, and then threw the bundle down at the door, whereas the Superintendent had pointed to some other direction where to put the 'dirty' papers. But eventually he called a clerk or official to pick the bundle up and commanded him to burn it at the yard yonder. The women were also standing in the yard, and so the bundle was picked up, and at a further corner a match was lit and put into the bundle. Thus, in the presence of the Superintendent and before all the women, the 'dirty' passes were burnt into ashes!

To an outsider it was an amusing little ceremony, but to the women it meant much and more than the Superintendent himself realised.

The Superintendent then said the married women need not carry passes, but that all young ones must. The leaders protested against their daughters being compelled to carry passes as if they were loose girls. The Superintendent, however, took down the names of the three leaders, and then made the rest file in fives so as to count them. They numbered 162. He told them to go away quietly, and promised to bring their grievances before the Town Council and would report the result to the Location Vigilance Committee. The crowd, satisfied for the time, dispersed quietly without noise or singing or other demonstration.

The scene was a great contrast to that which I described to your readers a little while ago about the Bloemfontein women of the Waaihoek Location. At Winburg everything was done quite simply and orderly — the forming of the procession; the solemn delivery of passes by each individual; the impressiveness of the march towards the Town Hall; the gentle manner in which the 'dirty' bundle was thrown down in front of the Superintendent; the short, interesting ceremony of the burning of passes; the quiet and orderly way in which the crowd dispersed — each act, one by one, showed in remarkable degree what combination can do, what great victory boldness and determination can win. One wondered how these women kept their tempers and remained orderly throughout, more especially when one remembered those wild and violent scenes of big political demonstrations by the women of England — the disorderly and unwoman-like scenes one so often witnessed in Hyde Park, or Trafalgar-square, or on the Bristol Downs. There was no doubt at Winburg as to which demonstration was more ladylike in conduct and manner.

The day after I asked one of the women who had taken part as to what they would do next. She said, 'We won't carry passes, and we are determined to go to Edenburg (meaning to gaol) and to reduce the Pass Law into ashes, as we did the "dirty papers".' This was without doubt a solemn declaration representing the united opinion of all other women, not only in Winburg, but throughout the Free State.

THE WAR OF DEGRADATION! THE IMPRISONED WOMEN: HAPPINESS IN ADVERSITY

Sol Plaatje, *Tsala ea Batho*, 16 August 1913

Denied the right to wear their own boots, but determined to return to gaol till the stubborn Bloemfontein Municipality gathers some sense.

Last Sunday morning, in company with Mrs Pitso and Mr and Mrs Michael Petrus, our editor visited the 34 native and coloured women of Bloemfontein, who were sentenced to two months' hard (labour) under the exceptional 'Free' State conditions, which forces native women to carry passes. They are incarcerated at the Kroonstad gaol, to which they were transferred from Edenburg. They are keenly determined to fight the pass business to its bitterest end. They are subsisting on the coarsest diet, but recognise they have not gone to Kroonstad to enjoy themselves but to fight bitterly for their liberty. Their only complaint is that if the Union government or whoever feels benefited by their imprisonment, had no boots to offer them doing their imprisonment, he could at least have allowed them to wear their own shoes. This is denied them, they are told, by the Doctor's orders. Perhaps it will be good for his profession if 34 coloured women can contract disease and became invalids for the rest of their lives; who knows? Any way, they are determined that until the Bloemfontein Municipality shakes off its imbecility, they are prepared to return to prison; and, if necessary, die there, but they are determined that the struggle will only end when the Bloemfontein Municipality ceases to send male policemen to accost respectable coloured women in the streets and order them to turn out their skirt pockets for the Badge of Degradation. Some of the most refined ... women of Bloemfontein are negotiating the pebbles and the cement floor with the bare skins of their feet. There is no doubt that the pain ... is having a serious effect upon them. ... For they present the appearance of ... sheep suffering from foot and mouth disease. We admire their determination, and their incarceration has, if anything, only served to harden their hearts. And we were glad to find the preparations at Bloemfontein showing that a rousing welcome is awaiting them on their glorious homecoming on the 24th.

1936, South Africa

The heroic struggles of black women

Introduced by Robert Edgar

Jameson Gilbert Coka (1910–1960s) was a journalist whose columns in the mid-1930s introduced an African American audience to the plight of black South Africans. Born on a white farm near Vryheid in KwaZulu-Natal, his father was a sharecropper who moved his family into Vryheid when the white farmer demanded the labour of one of his sons. An avid reader of books and newspapers, Jameson was so inspired by the message of uplift of the African American educator Booker T. Washington that he decided to 'be instrumental in uplifting Africans to a position they formerly occupied during the heyday of Egypt, Ethiopia, Timbuctoo and Prester John' (Coka, 1936a). Showing exceptional promise as a student, he was awarded a bursary to attend one of the premier African schools, Amanzimtoti Institute (Adams College), where he received a junior certificate.

After returning as a teacher to Vryheid, he was drawn into the Industrial and Commercial Workers' Union (ICU) in 1927, which, with a membership of around 100,000, was then the largest black organisation in South Africa and was mobilising black workers all over the country. He attended local and national meetings and eventually became its assistant district secretary for the East Rand. However, within a few years, the ICU went into a steep decline because of leadership rivalries and the administrative misuse of funds, and Coka found different work as an interpreter-clerk at Grey's Hospital in Durban.

Coka's ICU experience seasoned him politically for his initial ventures into journalism in the late 1920s. He contributed columns to the ICU newspaper *The Workers' Herald* and to *Abantu-Batho*'s successor, *Ikwezi le Afrika*, run by Pixley Seme, a lawyer and African National Congress (ANC) leader. Coka began selling issues of *Ikwezi* on the streets of Johannesburg, but after reporting on a conference of the Natal ANC, he was promoted to overseeing other newsagents for the paper and reporting on Transvaal news. He found it 'adventuresome to go from town to town in the Reef canvassing for the support of a newspaper. I learnt that, all things equal, the contents of a journal are its decisive factor' (Coka, 1936a).

Once *Ikwezi* folded after a few years, Coka struggled to find outlets for his pieces. He 'bombarded several newspapers' with articles and endured a stream of rejection slips. But then the *Sunday Times* began printing his submissions. That brought in some income, but not, as Coka noted, at the same rate as a white journalist earned. 'No African receives the usual journalistic rates. He is paid "as a native". The white press was almost inaccessible to an African writer unless he happened to share anti-Africanism. It would rather publish third-rate stuff from white contributors than from Africans' (Coka, 1936a). Coka was candid about the barriers he faced as a black journalist. 'To be a freelance journalist in South Africa is no joke, especially when one has woolly hair. He gets no access to newspaper files, public archives, museums and public libraries' (Coka, 1936a).

After joining the Communist Party, he wrote for its newspaper, the *South African Worker*, for a while, but he was expelled from the Party as a 'reformist' during its fierce internal ideological battles in the mid-1930s. Living in Western Native Township, he then established his own newspaper, the *African Liberator*, which featured a Pan-African tone and ran regular features on the Italian invasion of Ethiopia that had a special appeal to an African readership. Although he admitted that his newspaper was 'leading a dog and cat existence', he expressed hope 'that in time it will stand on its legs' (Coka, 1936a). However, his newspaper lasted but one year.

Since his exposure to Marcus Garvey's Pan-African ideas as a youngster, Coka had expressed an interested in establishing international ties 'among Negroes all the world over'. He found an avenue for accomplishing this through Claude Barnett's Associated Negro Press (ANP), a Chicago-based news service begun in 1919 that serviced African American newspapers several times a week with news features and columns (Coka, 1936b). Barnett wrote Coka: 'We will be glad to have you ... discussing those situations regarding our brethren in South Africa which you think should be known by the Negroes of America' (Barnett, 1936). In 1934 and 1936 Coka contributed 16 columns on such varied topics as black South African urban life, the African press, white missionaries and black churches, an African dramatic society and the disenfranchisement of African politically. Given their own struggles with Jim Crow America, African American readers readily identified with the oppression black South Africans were experiencing with white supremacy.

Coka's 'How African women make a living' was one of several of his columns that focused on the challenges African women faced living in the Witwatersrand. Since the First World War, African women had been streaming from black reserves into the urban areas despite government policy that did not accept Africans as permanent urban residents (Wells, 1993). They often came alone because their husbands had abandoned them when they migrated to the urban areas and started second families. Coka captured the vulnerability of these women whose employment opportunities were severely constricted. They became mainstays in white homes as domestic servants replacing African men who were moving into industry. Living in rooms in the back yards of white homes or spending long hours going back and forth to their own homes in the townships, domestic servants were exploited and were very vulnerable to the sexual advances of men – both their white male employers and young and old African men.

African women also earned extra money by washing and ironing clothes for whites, hawking food, and illegally home brewing beer. For many African women beer brewing was an independent but risky source of income since white municipal officials, aiming to gain a monopoly over beer to generate revenue to pay for white administration in the locations, unleashed the police with their pick-up vans to arrest women brewers.

REFERENCES

Coka, Gilbert. 1936a. 'The story of Gilbert Coka, of the Zulu tribe of South Africa', in Margery Perham (ed), *Ten Africans: A Collection of Life Stories*. London: Faber.
Coka, Gilbert. 1936b. 'Letter to Claude Barnett, 1 February 1936.' Claude Barnett Papers, Chicago Historical Society, Chicago.
Horne, Gerald. 2017. *Rise and Fall of the Associated Negro Press: Claude Barnett's Pan African News and the Jim Crow Paradox*. Urbana: University of Illinois Press.
Well, Julia. 1993. *We Now Demand! The History of Women's Resistance to Pass Laws in South Africa*. Johannesburg: Wits University Press.

How African Women Make Their Living

Jameson Coka, *Capitol Plaindealer* (Topeka, Kansas), 22 November 1936

It is easy for African women to get into employment. It is hard for them to get a living wage. The difficulties of making a living wage are so great that maternal love overcomes repugnance to work inadequately paid so that the mother may at least have a few cents for her off-spring. And the field of Negro women is restricted.

Women usually get into domestic service for Europeans where they are employed in various capacities — house-wives, child-nurses, and cooking. This is fairly easy because every European, no matter how poor, requires a black servant. There is so much poverty among Negroes, that they take any crumbs which fall from the masters' table.

Women are compelled to increase the family income by going out to work. Husbands do not earn sufficiently to keep families. Fathers neglect the education of their children through poverty and sometimes owing to a hope that when they go to work at an early age and bring home some money they are better assets than when after college training they are thrown into the streets.

Women employed in domestic service sometimes live in their employer's premises. These are often at the back yard in close proximity to lavatories. They are not encouraged to have visitors. Sometimes even husbands are prohibited from seeing their wives. Morally this is bad, for it leads them into all sorts of temptations.

Single girls living in that way are constantly exposed to the ravishes of unprincipled young and old men who are slaves to their beastly lusts. Brought up with no principles, pursuing no high ideals, they become moral wrecks. They get into the habit of illicit cohabitation with men. In many instances degraded and lascivious Europeans molest them and at times mislead the gullible. Living in employers' premises exposes our women to sundry evils.

It is martyrdom for those who live in segregated ghettoes to arrive and leave their working places in time. First they travel long distances by bus, tram or train if fares are available. If not, they have to walk. In any case stations and tram and bus termini are often far from their working places. They dissipate energy in walking to their destinations. They have to start work at 4am. Engaged in all the multifarious household drudgeries they have half an hour for breakfast and one hour for rest. They are obliged to work until 8pm. And after that they have to return to their homes. Thus they have little time to attend to their families. Their young children are often left to the care of others hardly older.

Girls often dislike to return to their homes. Fatigued and weary — hard worked and with little opportunity of recreation they become narrow in outlook, cramped in development, sensual in self-expression and thus become easy victims. They have neither regular working hours nor a standard wage. They accept what employers are prepared to give. They have no conception of organisation and are victimised and exploited to their master's satisfaction without let or hindrance. The average wage of a domestic servant is $6 per month.

Washing and ironing for Europeans provide many Negroes with livelihoods. Every hour of the day they are seen with huge bundles of dirty linen from town and as often with big bundles of clean and ironed clothes. Women of all ages, young girls hardly in their teens and old matrons all carry the eternal washing. Europeans find it cheaper to have it thus done than to send it to laundries.

Poor African women provide their own soap, water, coal, wood and fares. For that and their hard work they receive $2 per month. Lucky indeed are the few who receive $6. And those heavy bundles of washing stunt the growth of young girls and stunt the growth of unborn children because many pregnant mothers have to carry those staggering weights. Apart from that, constant washing and ironing develop kidney troubles and thus seriously impair the health not only of mothers but of the unborn.

Illicit liquor traffic with its constant round of arrests, degradations, vice-spreading, demoralisation of men and women, breaking up of homes, direct incentiveness to prostitution and debauchery is too sordid to need further comment. Yet many

African mothers and daughters fall into that in order to eke their living ...

With the greatness of the depression the activities of women to earn livings have grown. They have largely taken to hawking foodstuffs and crochet goods. They sell sweet potatoes, boned meat, fat-cakes, fruits and tea. This is not only true of women in urban areas but even in the rural areas.

The nursing profession as giving a genteel occupation has suddenly come to the forefront as a career for fairly educated African girls. They are to be found in every hospital which gives facilities for their training. While probationers their pay is low, $5 per month in the first year to $15 in the final year. When employed they usually earn from $25 to $60. Missionary hospitals, mine hospitals and municipal hospitals usually give them an opening. They get uniform and quarters and are the most highly paid Africans in general.

Teaching has lost its popularity owing to the low pay which teachers receive. A female teacher holding the same qualifications as men and doing the same work receives less pay. And then the unscrupulousness of some missionaries exceeds belief because they take unqualified teachers so as to pay them lower wages. Teachers usually earn $9–$25. Out of this they are expected to be dressed and keep their families. So far then have our women gone in the industrial area. They do no factory work because that is a 'white' preserve. They do no clerical work for there are no African businesses to engage them and they have not yet climbed into the higher professions.

Competition is rife and keen in every field, but Negro women are gallantly trying to keep body and soul together. They make a braver show than men. Many keep homes either as wives or daughters and their heroic struggles for bare existence would draw tears from an angel. However, they plod along as best they can and bravely shoulder their burdens.

1937–45, SOUTH AFRICA

The mysterious disappearance of an anti-fascist campaigner

INTRODUCED BY RAYMOND JOSEPH

The disappearance without a trace in 1945 of celebrated political reporter, columnist and ace investigative journalist George Heard is one of the most enduring unsolved mysteries of South African journalism.

Heard, 39 at the time of his disappearance, had reported extensively on the rise of the Ossewabrandwag (OB) – the Ox Wagon Sentinel, a secretive anti-British and pro-Nazi Afrikaner paramilitary organisation that opposed South Africa entering the Second World War. His relentless exposés of the OB, as well as the activities of a pro-Nazi 'fifth column' in South Africa played a key role in a crackdown of the OB and its militant wing, the Stormjaers. Thousands were placed in internment camps for the duration of the war.

Among them were B.J. 'John' Vorster, who later became prime minister of South Africa, and Hendrik van den Bergh, who went on to head up the feared Bureau for State Security (BOSS). Heard also exposed a cabal of pro-Hitler supporters in the South African Broadcasting Corporation (SABC) who were so powerful that they were able to limit Prime Minister Jan Smuts's access to the national broadcaster. Some senior members of the SABC were dismissed, and several were sent to internment camps as a direct result of Heard's reporting.

A gifted public speaker, Heard earned the ire of the *Rand Daily Mail*'s board of directors – who were nervous of his 'leftist' reputation – when he began addressing public rallies supporting the war effort against Nazi Germany. Although he abhorred the repression of Stalin's communism, he nevertheless made speeches vigorously backing the campaign to aid Soviet Russia, by then an ally, to strengthen the second front it had opened against

Adolf Hitler's armies. But, while the communists in South Africa claimed him as one of their own, he was in reality a left-liberal democrat.

His speeches exposing the appallingly low wages paid to black mine workers would also have angered and embarrassed the Chamber of Mines and stuffy Rand Club-influenced board. Given an ultimatum to stop his public speaking, he chose to resign and enlisted in the navy as an ordinary seaman rather than accept the offer of a commission by friends in government.

At the time of his disappearance on 8 August 1945, Heard was a lieutenant and second-in-command on the frigate *Good Hope*, which was docked in Cape Town. The war in Europe had ended a few months earlier and the end of the war in the Far East was only weeks away. Heard, who was due to be demobbed and looking forward to re-entering the world of journalism, was last seen leaving his ship for shore leave. Then, despite being seen around Cape Town over the next few hours, he vanished into thin air.

Heard had a shrewd grasp of politics and an intense dislike of fascism and Nazis. Heard shot to national prominence in 1937 after he pulled off a major scoop for the *Rand Daily Mail* when he reported a remarkably accurate forecast of Finance Minister N.C. 'Klaasie' Havenga's upcoming budget. He was charged under the Official Secrets Act and when he appeared in court he refused to be sworn, telling the court: '... I must decline because I cannot give evidence.' His sentence of eight days in prison for contempt was suspended so he could appeal, but before his appeal could be heard the government, perhaps fearing embarrassment if Heard's clearly high-level source was revealed, withdrew the charges.

After that people flocked to him with confidential information, his son Tony, a former editor of the *Cape Times*, wrote in his autobiography, *Cape of Storms*.

But it was George Heard's commitment to the Allied cause and his unequivocal stand against Hitler's Nazi Germany for which he became best known as a journalist. Under *Sunday Times* editor Langley Levy, Heard reported widely on the growing threat of a 'fifth column' of pro-German subversives active in South Africa. Their activities included dynamiting power and telephone lines, and railway tracks.

An example of his hard-hitting reporting is the story headlined 'Storm troops mean new racialism', published on 14 April 1940. It began thus: 'Modelled on the example of Hitler's Germany, and deriving something from the experience of the strike commandos in the Rand Revolt of 1922, the new "armies" of South Africa have become actively militant in their aims, semi-military in their organisation. The Ossewa Brandwag and the resuscitated Handhawersbond (League of Defenders) are familiar specimens of the new kind of unofficial "army", but they are not by any means the only ones.' A month later, on 26 May 1940, in what former *Sunday Times* editor Joel Mervis called a 'masterpiece of investigative journalism', an explosive exposé by Heard revealed how the OB was secretly organising to overthrow the government. Headlined 'Brandwag is a menace to South Africa', with the strap head: 'Private uniformed army is being raised', it laid bare the OB's plans to 'create a rival organisation to the Union Defence Force'.

Still the mystery of Heard's death lingers on: Tony Heard and his older brother Raymond, also a journalist, have spent years trying to get to the bottom of their father's death. Tony says that at one stage his father was warned by a contact that his name was on a 'death list', but it did not deter him. He says that they have uncovered circumstantial evidence strongly suggesting that their father was assassinated by 'a known OB killer' named Felix van Breda, who was later hanged for another murder. They have 'strong suspicions' of who ordered the hit, but have never been able to confirm it. 'I have been told of an intelligence report that says George was taken to Joburg and his body was put down the Apex Mine in Tembisa on the East Rand,' says Tony Heard (Interview, April 2018).

Joel Mervis wrote: 'So ended the life of a talented courageous journalist. He was already assistant editor of the *Rand Daily Mail* when he enlisted and inevitably would have become editor of the *Rand Daily Mail* or the *Sunday Times*. Who can doubt that his skill and forceful personality would have made a very special impact on newspapers?'

REFERENCES

Bennett, Benjamin. 1973. *Some Don't Hang*. Cape Town: H. Timmins.
Heard, Tony. 1990. *The Cape of Storms*. Johannesburg: Ravan Press.
Mervis, Joel. 1989. *The Fourth Estate*. Johannesburg: Jonathan Ball.

Expected Budget Concessions: Big Increase in Provision for Old-Age Pensions

George Heard, *Sunday Times*, 13 March 1937

A substantial increase in the provision for old-age pensions will be one of the outstanding popular features of the Budget which the Minister of Finance, Mr N.C. Havenga, will present to Parliament on Monday.

I have reason to anticipate that an amount of about £750,000 will be earmarked for this purpose and that the maximum pension payable to aged persons will be raised from £30 to £42 a year.

At the same time the means test will be greatly relaxed, and it is probable that the pensionable age in the case of women will be reduced from 65 to 60.

Handsome provision will also be made for the payment of pensions in cases of invalidity. When he makes his statement on Monday Mr Havenga will be in a position to dispose of a total sum of nearly £10,000,000. His surplus for the year now ending is likely to be in the neighbourhood of £5,250,000. While on the present basis of taxation, even allowing for substantially increased expenditure, he will have an excess on next year's accounts of at least £400,000.

Tried to Stop War Message by Gen Smuts

George Heard, *Sunday Times*, 10 December 1939

Ever since the outbreak of war, strenuous efforts have been made within the South African Broadcasting Corporation to frustrate the decision of Parliament and the policy of the Union Government.

When General Smuts became Prime Minister of the Union he prepared a message to be broadcast to the South African nation. In this message he set out clearly the reason that he induced Parliament to declare war on Germany.

The statement was, from every point of view, an objective one; yet strenuous efforts were made to prevent it from being broadcast. The authorities raised all sorts of objections and difficulties, and it was only after counsel's opinion had been taken that the message was allowed to go on air.

Counsel's opinion was that the South African Broadcasting Corporation could not refuse to broadcast the Prime Minister's statement. The authorities were compelled to accept the inevitable and General Smuts's statement was broadcast to the nation.

The question that arises, however, is why the Broadcasting Corporation objected to General Smuts's statement ...

Brandwag is a Menace to S.A.

George Heard, *Sunday Times*, 26 May 1940

Behind the plain words addressed to members of the Ossewa-Brandwag by a Bloemfontein Defence Force Commander the other day lies a grave warning for all South Africa.

We shall ignore it at our peril.

In every corner of the Union to-day the Ossewa-Brandwag is engaged in a campaign whose only object can be to subvert the constitutional authority of this country.

Its 'recruiting' officers are everywhere – in the Railways, in the Post Office, in every Department of State. Already they have done incalculable mischief.

On the Railways they have persuaded dozens of young men not to join up with the new Railways and Harbours Brigade. In other departments they have dissuaded Defence Force recruits from taking the new oath to serve anywhere in Africa.

There was a time, perhaps, when these surface manifestations of the activities ... could be lightly disregarded, but that time has passed ...

THE MYSTERIOUS DISAPPEARANCE OF AN ANTI-FASCIST CAMPAIGNER

Menace of the 'Fifth Column' in South Africa

George Heard, *Sunday Times*, 21 April 1940

The time has come for South Africa to start war against Germany. For more than seven months Hitler's 'fifth column' has been operating almost unhindered in every part of the Union. Already it has gained great strategic objectives. It now threatens to encompass in South Africa what its counterparts have already accomplished in Austria, Czechoslovakia, Poland and Norway.

Throughout the country today, in so-called 'cultural' organisations, in factories, in great State undertakings, in school rooms, in private houses along the Reef and elsewhere, the agents of the 'fifth column' are conducting their subversive activities, aided and abetted by their new-found South African allies.

The 'fifth column' is the inspiration for all the anti-British propaganda which is now sweeping the country: it is the instrument for perpetuating Nazi trade with the Union. It is the author of countless attempts — many of them all too successful — to undermine the loyalty of thousands of simple-minded South Africans ...

Storm Troops Mean New Racialism

George Heard, *Sunday Times*, 14 April 1940

The 'private army' with its storm troopers and its fighting commandos is rearing its ugly head among the people of South Africa.

Modelled on the example of Hitler's Germany, and deriving something from the experience of strike commandos in the Rand revolt of 1922, the new 'armies' of South Africa have become actively militant in their aims, semi-military in their organisation.

The Ossewa-Brandwag and the resuscitated Handhawersbond are familiar specimens of the new kind of unofficial 'army', but they are not by any means the only ones.

Throughout the country to-day, aspiring politicians and 'culture' leaders are gathering around them the nucleus of a 'fighting' commando, pledged to defend the interests of Afrikanerdom and to confound its enemies.

The unifying connection between these mushroom 'armies' is not easy to trace, but the underlying purpose is essentially the same. The military outlook is identical ...

1947–83, SOUTH AFRICA

Ruth First: The obligation to dissent

INTRODUCED BY CATHERINE HIGGS

Ruth First was a South African socialist, a political journalist and a fierce critic of both the segregated South African state in which she grew up and the apartheid state which emerged after 1948. As a journalist, she wrote for a variety of leftist newspapers, including the *Guardian* and *Fighting Talk*. In 1963, she was arrested and then re-arrested under the 90-day detention law, a wide-ranging law that allowed anyone suspected of communist activity or considered a threat to the state to be held without trial. First spent 117 days in jail, most of it in solitary confinement, and published a memoir of her experience in 1965. By then, she had joined her husband Joe Slovo in exile in London. He had escaped South Africa after joining Nelson Mandela and his colleagues in founding Umkhonto weSizwe, the military wing of the African National Congress (ANC), which opposed the apartheid state (First, 2009: vii–ix). First remained active in the anti-apartheid movement abroad and refashioned herself as an academic. She wrote eight books, among them *South-West Africa* (1963), *The Barrel of a Gun* (1970), *The South African Connection: Western Investment in Apartheid* (1972) and, with Ann Scott, a well-received biography of the South African writer, Olive Schreiner (1980) (First & Scott, 1980; Williams, 1982: 55; Harlow, 2002: 232). First was murdered on 17 August 1982 when a bomb exploded as she opened a box of books in her office at Eduardo Mondlane University in Maputo, Mozambique, where she had taught since 1977. The bomb, sent by the South African Security Branch, blew a hole through the exterior wall of the building (Saul, 2014: 122). First's last book, *Black Gold: The Mozambican Miner, Proletarian and Peasant*, was published posthumously in 1983.

First was born in Johannesburg, South Africa in 1925 to parents who had escaped Russia's pogroms and immigrated as children from Latvia and Lithuania in the early 1900s. Julius Fürst and Tilly Levitan met at a Jewish government school in then-segregated South Africa and married in 1924. Both were committed socialists and members of the Communist Party of South Africa. Fürst ran a mattress factory with his brother; Levitan was the demanding intellectual who both berated her daughter and helped shape her political views (Pinnock, 1997: 308–9; First, 2009: i). First's intense interactions with her own mother were arguably recaptured in the fictionalised depiction of First's relationship with her eldest daughter, Shawn Slovo, who wrote and produced the 1988 film, *A World Apart*, about her mother's 1963 arrest (Slovo, 1988; Pinnock, 1997: 309; Saul, 2014: 122).

In 1942, First entered the University of the Witwatersrand, where she studied social science and was active in the Young Communist League and edited their newspaper. In 1946, the strike by 100,000 African mineworkers seeking a minimum wage prompted her to quit a 'boring' and 'sycophantic' job with the city of Johannesburg. She volunteered for the mineworkers, cranking out strike leaflets on a mimeograph machine. 'When the mine strike was over,' she recalled, 'I became a journalist.' Journalism would become the vehicle through which she protested the racially framed inequity that defined South Africa. By 1947, at 22, she had been appointed the Johannesburg editor of the *Guardian* (Webb, 2015: 9; Pinnock, 1997: 310, 312).

Her first major story for the *Guardian* was an exposé of the conditions of farm labour in Bethal, about 160 kilometres east of Johannesburg. A short newspaper article by the activist Anglican priest, the Reverend Michael Scott, brought the story to First's attention. Together, First and Scott visited Bethal in July 1947. Bethal was rural and Afrikaans speaking. Local farmers were suspicious of two English speakers from Johannesburg; this reflected an antipathy that stretched back to before the brutal South African War fought between the British and the Afrikaners from 1899 to 1902. Bethal farmers depended on seasonal labour to sow and harvest potatoes. They were unhappy with the series of reports First and Scott published in the *Guardian*, depicting the abuse of 40,000 farm workers, contracted mostly from Nyasaland (modern-day Malawi) and Rhodesia (modern-day Zimbabwe). Most black South Africans refused to work on Bethal's farms – so strongly were they associated with 'callous brutality, ill-treatment and violent death' (Webb, 2015: 14, quoting Murray, 1997: 75).

First's Bethal articles in the *Guardian* did lead to a government inquiry but not to any tangible improvements in workers' lives (*Guardian*, 3 July 1947; Pinnock, 1997: 312–4). In December 1947, members of the ANC in Bethal reported that 'workers were still locked up in compounds after the work was done, and then driven out the following day with whips and dogs' (Webb, 2015: 15). First continued to follow the story. As editor of *Fighting Talk* she published an article on Bethal in 1956 (Webb, 2015: 15). By then, a great deal had changed. The National Party government was elected on an apartheid platform in 1948, and quickly introduced the heightened form of segregation that characterised apartheid. The South African Communist Party was banned in 1950.

In 1960, First was banned from practising journalism. She and Slovo, who remained prominent anti-apartheid activists, were closely watched by the police. In 1963, a search of their home turned up a copy of *Fighting Talk* – by then a prohibited publication – and First was arrested under the 90-day detention law (First, 2009: 1, 44). Released after ninety days and then immediately rearrested, she broke under the psychological harassment of her interrogators. She was never physically tortured. Fearful that she may have exposed fellow activists, she attempted suicide in an effort to protect them from her weakness. It was a courageous and political act.

As shaken as First had been by her imprisonment, she quickly rebounded to the fierce and critical thinker that both intimidated friends and colleagues and endeared her to them. As her fellow activist John S. Saul recalled: 'I doubt there is anyone who knew Ruth First well who didn't have difficult moments with her. She was tough, demanding, even occasionally domineering. She was forged in a hard school, a revolutionary socialist and a woman fighting consistently and unflaggingly against racism, chauvinism and capitalist exploitation in the teeth of one of the most brutal regimes the world has ever seen' (Pinnock, 2014: 98–9; Saul, 2014: 122). She also did not hesitate to criticise the left for its shortcomings or blind spots; this was clear in *The Barrel of a Gun: Political Power in Africa and the Coup d'État*, her critique of the first decade of postcolonial independence in Africa. As the historian Shula Marks observed, 'Criticism of Africa's ruling elite was still muted on the left' when the book was published in 1970. For First, 'who cared passionately about the liberation of Africa,' writing *The Barrel of a Gun* embodied, in Marks's view, 'the courage, intellectual integrity and independence of mind which characterised Ruth's approach to politics both within southern Africa and more widely' (Marks, 1983: 126–7).

Black Gold, First's last book, written while she was teaching and researching at Eduardo Mondlane University in Mozambique, was published in 1983. Its style reflected an observation by her husband, Joe Slovo, who 'suggested that she always had too much on her plate, too many deadlines before her, and that her "facility for the flow of words was sometimes an impediment to a more finished structure"' (Webb, 2015: 10). *Black Gold*, however, involved an extensive set of interviews with Mozambican miners working in South Africa and traced the impact of their wages on their families and communities in Mozambique. The book included excerpts of the interviews and photographs of the miners. Her assessment of the long-term health of South Africa's mining industry would prove prescient.

In 2014, Ruth First's legacy was celebrated in an issue of the *Review of African Political Economy*, twenty years after South Africa's first democratic election, which elected Nelson Mandela of the ANC to the presidency. The contributors included John Saul, who had worked with First in Mozambique. Saul wondered what First might think of the modern state, which in his opinion had been '"recolonized" by a still dominant Empire of Capital' (Saul, 2014: 123). We cannot know though: *The Barrel of a Gun*, with its unflinching criticism of corruption and coup d'états in newly independent African states in 1970, might give us a hint (First, 1970). As Saul notes, 'the extent that such a question haunts us – or, at least, haunts me – is a measure of how courageous, independent-minded and strong a writer-activist she was, and of how much we all still miss her clear and principled voice' (Saul, 2014: 124).

References

First, Ruth. 1970. *The Barrel of a Gun: Political Power in Africa and the Coup d'État*. London: Allen Lane.
First, Ruth. 1983. *Black Gold: The Mozambican Miner, Proletarian and Peasant*. Sussex, UK: Harvester Press/New York: St. Martin's Press.
First, Ruth. 2009. *117 Days: An Account of Confinement and Interrogation under the South Africa 90-Day Detention Law*. New York: Penguin Books.
First, Ruth & Scott, Ann. 1980. *Olive Schreiner: A Biography*. London: Andre Deutsch.
Harlow, Barbara. 2002. 'Looked class, talked red: Sketches of Ruth First and redlined South Africa', *Meridians*, 3(1).
Marks, Shula. 1983. 'Ruth First: A tribute', *Journal of Southern African Studies*, 10(1).
Murray, M.J. 1997. 'Factories in the fields: Capitalist farming in the Bethal district', in Alan H. Jeeves & Jonathan Crush (eds), *White Farms, Black Labour: The State and Agrarian Change in South Africa, 1910–1950*. Oxford: James Currey.
Pinnock, Don. 1997. 'Writing Left: The journalism of Ruth First and the *Guardian* in the 1950s', in Les Switzer (ed.), *South Africa's Alternative Press: Voices of Protest and Resistance*. Cambridge: Cambridge University Press.

Pinnock, D. 2014. 'Building an alternative consensus for political action: Ruth First as journalist and activist.' *Review of African Political Economy*, 41: 139.
Saul, John S. 2014. 'More comfortably without her?: Ruth First as writer and activist,' *Review of African Political Economy*, 41: 139.
Slovo, S. 1988. *A World Apart*. Atlantic Entertainment Group, DVD.
Webb, Christopher. 2015. '*Fighting Talk*: Ruth First's early journalism, 1947–1950', *Review of African Political Economy*, 42: 143.
Williams, Gavin. 1982. 'Ruth First: A preliminary bibliography', *Review of African Political Economy*, 25.

Ruth First, *The Guardian*, 3 July 1947

It is not every day that the Johannesburg reporter of the *Guardian* meets an African farm labourer who, when asked to describe the conditions on the farm on which he works, silently takes off his shirt to show large weals ... and scars whipped on his back ... He cannot really explain why. He knows that after the whipping he came in to the town to lay a charge with the magistrate; was then handed 11s. 4d. by his employer (pay for several weeks' work) and told he was discharged. This is the story of 'Work Nyeilande', 15-year-old (note his age) contracted labourer from Nyasaland.

We met him in Bethal about a mile from the centre of the town as we went to inspect two corrugated iron structures to which contracted labourers are brought in batches of 50 or 60 every Friday by the local farmers' recruiting organisation. These labourers are recruited in the Northern Transvaal after crossing the border illegally from Rhodesia or Nyasaland in search of work. They are locked in the central compound for three or four days until they have been allocated to the local farmers.

What are the conditions of these contracted farm labourers? They were eager to tell us.

They sign on for a six-month contract under which the most handsome remuneration is £2 for 30 working days. ... They are housed in barn-like buildings with concrete floors, often no windows, and no chimney or hole in the roof for smoke from the braziers or open flames in tins suspended from the roof with wire, which serve as lights. We saw not a single blanket in any of these compounds. The labourers sleep on sacks.

117 Days

Ruth First, 1965

I was appalled by the events of the last three days. They had beaten me. I had allowed myself to be beaten. I had pulled back from the brink just in time, but had it been in time? I was wide open to emotional blackmail, and the blackmailer was myself. They had tried for three months to find cracks in my armour and had found some. The search was still on. Some, many perhaps, of my weaknesses had been revealed to the Security Branch; if they had any inkling of others, I would have no reserves left. I could no longer hold to an intransigent stand because I had already moved from it. It was too late to say stoically that I would say nothing, not one word, to them.

Sleep had been a refuge in the cell; now it had fled. On top of sleeplessness I had nausea and diarrhoea. It all spelled anxiety I suppose, but an anxiety that had got out of hand and that I could no longer control with my own resources. I asked for a visit from my own doctor.

The days were grey and melancholy. I barely noticed the exercise periods. I had reeled back from a precipice of collapse but I felt worse than ever. I was persecuted by the dishonour of having made a statement, even the start of a statement. Give nothing, I had always believed; the more you give the more they think you know, and the more demanding they become. I had never planned to give anything, but how could I be the judge? It would be impossible to explain such an act, to live it down … My air of confidence had always been useful in keeping others from knowing how easily assailed and self-consciously vulnerable I was; it had worked many a time, but it could do nothing for me now. I had presided over my collapse with a combination of knowingness and utter miscalculation. My conceit and self-centredness had at last undone me. I had thought to pit myself against the Security Branch in their own lair. What had I hoped to learn?

Black Gold

Ruth First, 1983

This study of the worker-peasants of the south of Mozambique, who have been locked into both mine work and peasant household production, captures the end of an era whose demise is being ushered in by a two-fold series of events. The first has been the accession to power of Frelimo, and its commitment to restructuring the Mozambican economy and the eventual ending of migrant labour. Second, there have been two forms of labour displacement by the mining industry. These have been influenced partly by Frelimo's victory and its implications for the balance of political power in Southern Africa, but they have principally derived from changes in the pattern of capital accumulation and employment in the South African mining industry.

There have been two forms of labour displacement in mining. The first has been the substitution of capital for labour in an extended programme of mechanisation, especially in recently developed mines. The scope for substituting machinery for labour in the South African gold mines is limited, given the cost conditions and technical requirements of deep-level South African gold mining; and technical changes will not end the industry's dependence on large numbers of African workers, but they will bring about changes in the size and the structure of the African labour force. According to projections for employment levels in mining for the rest of this century, employment in gold mining in South Africa will fall by about 65 per cent, from 424,992 to some 148,000 in the year 2000. The expansion of coal and base metal mining, which is increasingly exploited by open-cast and highly capital-intensive techniques, will keep total employment in mining up to its 1977 total.

The second form of labour displacement is the substitution of South Africans for other mine labour. The alarming projections for African unemployment in South Africa, as both industry and agriculture reduce their labour requirements, suggest that the present trend towards the internalisation of mine labour supply will be at the continuing expense of labour recruited from outside. After 1974 ... the ratio between 'foreign' and South African labour was dramatically reversed. By 1976 the proportion of 'foreign' workers on the mines had dropped to 57 per cent; by 1977, it was 48 per cent; by 1979 it had fallen lower still, to 46 per cent. As the trend continues, the African labour force of the mines will be drawn increasingly from the South African 'Bantustans', especially the Transkei and the Ciskei. This does not mean that the Chamber of Mines will cease all importations of labour from the outside supply areas, but that it will perfect its strategy of spreading its supply of controlled labour inputs.

1952, SOUTH AFRICA

Mr Drum goes to work in Bethal

INTRODUCED BY ANTON HARBER

Founded in 1951, *Drum* magazine captured the emerging sprit of defiance in post-war South Africa, giving a voice to a new urban culture that was radicalising black opposition politics and expressing itself in a burst of creativity in writing, music and dance. As the apartheid government, which had come to power in 1948, tightened its grip, the African National Congress (ANC) turned to protest and defiance under the youthful influence of Nelson Mandela and Walter Sisulu. The few racially mixed areas around the big cities were cauldrons of political and cultural activity through the 1950s, and Sophiatown, on the outskirts of Johannesburg, was one such area.

Under the patronage of Jim Bailey, heir to a mining fortune, and the editorship of Anthony Sampson, later to become Mandela's biographer, *Drum* captured this Sophiatown spirit. It was a commercial venture, which came out monthly, but was driven by the maverick Bailey's passion for black journalists, Sampson's knack for finding talent, and a brilliant team of writers and photographers, such as Can Themba, Nat Nakasa, Casey Motsitsi, Lewis Nkosi and Bob Gosani.

The magazine's pages carried a heady mix of American-style gangsters, radical politicians, illegal taverns, jazz singers, sex across the colour line, and tough exposés in print and picture. It was a pioneer expression of an exuberant and confident African perspective, celebrating African leadership, achievement and creativity. East and West African editions turned it into an early Pan-African venture, distributed in eight countries, with considerable success.

One man in particular, Henry Nxumalo, who often wrote under the name

Mr Drum, pioneered first-hand investigative reporting, immersing himself in stories to give vivid descriptions of his life under white minority rule. He tackled the toughest stories, such as prison and labour conditions, and church segregation, with extraordinary courage.

In 1954, to experience and write about harsh conditions in a Johannesburg prison, Nxumalo set out to have himself arrested for not carrying the notorious pass book which all black men were obliged to have with them at all times. After a few days of frustration, he broke a shop window to get the attention of the police.

Since authorities had denied previous reports of the conditions in the jail, 'we believed that only by sending a member of our own staff to jail could we be certain of an accurate report,' the editor wrote.

Nxumalo told his story of racism, violence and degradation in deadpan language: 'I was kicked and thrashed every day. I saw many other prisoners being thrashed daily. I was never told what was expected of me. Sometimes I guessed wrong and got into trouble ... all prisoners were called Kaffirs at all times.'

He described the 'tausa', a strange dance that naked prisoners returning from work had to go through to show that they were not hiding anything on their bodies. *Drum* photographer Bob Gosani, who was himself to become a legend at the magazine, pretended to be doing a fashion shoot with an office secretary on top of a nearby building of the prison to get a picture that remains one of the most unforgettable images of the indignities of apartheid. There was an outcry, and shortly afterwards a new law was passed with severe penalties for publishing 'false information' about prisons.

Nxumalo's most politically significant work, however, was in exposing brutal labour conditions on farms. In 1952 he focused on Bethal, a major farming area east of Johannesburg known for its use of prison labour and for a series of convictions of farmers for assault and brutality. He interviewed workers who told of being tricked into signing contracts to work in slave-like conditions, and to confirm the details he signed up himself. Pictures showed prisoners being transported in wire cages on the back of trucks to work on the farm.

Others wrote about farm conditions, but Nxumalo was the only one to go in and experience it himself. In 1955, he wrote a piece headlined 'I worked on Snyman's farm'. Snyman was a notorious farmer in Rustenburg, west of Johannesburg, who had been repeatedly convicted for assaulting his workers. Nxumalo wrote of back-breaking corn picking with bare hands, numerous assaults by the farmer, and how workers were kept against their will. When he felt he could work no longer, he was told: 'On this farm, you don't just quit when you want to.' He was asked for his pass. 'He tore it up into little pieces and threw them away on the lawn. 'Now you can't leave without my permission: I can have you arrested and imprisoned.' Mr Drum fled in the dead of night.

Again, his piece was accompanied by an extraordinary set of photographers, taken covertly, including a silhouette of a guard on a horse wielding a whip.

Nxumalo was stabbed to death in 1957 while on his way to meet a source while investigating an illegal abortion racket by a well-known doctor. His murderer was never identified, but it was widely presumed to be related to the story.

Repeated coverage of these labour conditions by Nxumalo and others led to an organised potato boycott in 1959, a critical moment in the mobilisation of the ANC. But the severe security clampdown after the Sharpeville massacre of 1960 and the arrest of most political leaders drove many of the *Drum* writers into exile, and the magazine never recovered. The residents of Sophiatown were forcibly removed in the 1980s. It is still published, though the current version bears little resemblance to the magazine of the 1950s.

In 2005, Nxumalo was given the Order of Ikhamanaga in Silver by the ANC government and a Johannesburg street was named after him. *Drum* is remembered as a high moment in the history of black journalism, and a symbol of what it might have been if apartheid had not crushed its spirit.

REFERENCES

Sampson, Anthony. 1983. *Drum: The Making of a Magazine*. Cape Town: Jonathan Ball.
Nicol, Mike. 1991. *A Good-Looking Corpse: The World of Drum – Jazz and Gangsters, Hope and Defiance*. London: Secker & Warburg.
Choonoo, Neville. 1997. 'The Sophiatown generation', in Les Switzer (ed), *South Africa's Alternative Press*. Cambridge, UK: Cambridge University Press.
Gready, Paul. 2015. 'The Sophiatown writers of the fifties', *Journal of Southern African Studies*, 16(1): 139–65.
Copies of the magazine can be found at Bailey's African History Archives: www.baha.co.za.

The Story of Bethal

Henry Nxumalo, *Drum*, 1952

For many years Bethal has been notorious for the ill-treatment of the African labourers on the farms. As far back as April 12, 1929, there was a case (Rex v. Nafte, at the Circuit Court at Bethal) of a farmer who was found guilty of tying a labourer by his feet from a tree and flogging him to death, pouring scalding water into his mouth when he cried for water ... On June 3, 1947 (see De Echo Bethal of 6.6.47) there was a case of a farmer assaulting two labourers, setting his dog on them, flogging them and chaining them together for the night; and only a week later, on June 11 (De Echo, 13.6.47), a farm foreman was found guilty of striking a labourer with a sjambok and setting his dog on him ... These cases all came up in court and were strongly condemned by the magistrates; Mr B.H. Wooler described the incident as being sordid, despicable and reminiscent of slavery, and the local European, De Echo, described the conditions disclosed as being 'tantamount to slave-driving'. And it seems clear that for every case that came before a magistrate there were many more that were never found out ...

Conditions still bad

Since 1947 there have been many statements made to the effect that conditions at Bethal have improved, and in 1949 an act was passed to safeguard the interests of labourers under contract. More inspectors were appointed by the Director of Native Labour, were supposed to supervise and witness the signing of contracts, and to satisfy themselves that they were fully understood by the recruits.

But, in spite of everything said to the contrary, there is still plenty of evidence that conditions at Bethal and the system which causes them are a disgrace to the country ...

Mr Drum finds out

In order to discover the truth about the way contracts are signed, Mr DRUM himself decided to become a farm recruit. He was soon picked up outside the Pass Office by one of the touts or 'runners' who look out for unemployed Africans, and are paid for each man they collect for the agencies ... He said he had no pass, and, with many others, was told that he would be given a pass if he signed a contract to go and work out of Johannesburg: this is the normal way of dealing with people without passes. He chose to work on a farm in Springs, and was sent to _____'s compound, where he waited nearly a day before he could sign the contract.

Running past the contract

When the contract came to be signed the interpreter read out a small part of the contract to a number of recruits together, while the attesting officer held a pencil over the contract ...

N. A. D. African Clerk (calling roll of everyone on the contract sheet): you're going to work on a farm in the Middleburg district; you are on a six months' contract. You will be paid £3 a month, plus food and quarters. When you leave here you will be given an advance of 5s. for pocket money, 10s. 4d. for food, and 14s. 5d. for train fare. The total amount will be deducted from your first months' wages. Have you got that?

Mr DRUM and other recruits: Yes.

Clerk: You will now proceed to touch the pencil.

Mr DRUM: But I was told before that I was going to be sent to a farm in Springs. Why am I now going to Middleburg?

Clerk: I'm telling you where you are going, according to your contract sheet, and nothing else.

So Mr DRUM refused to touch the pencil when he reached the attesting officer, and was told to wait outside for his pass.

The other recruits then ran past the attesting officer, each (holding) the pencil for a moment, which was not even touching the paper ... As a result of holding a pencil for a second (50 recruits were attested in a few minutes), the recruits were considered to be bound to a contract. But in fact the contract had not been fully understood. So it seems that none of the contracts 'signed' in this way are valid at all (Native Labour Regulation Act of 1911, as amended 1949).

Touts' trick

A man from Nyasaland described how the touts employed by a certain labour agency in his country worked. There was a certain boundary which many people crossed in order to get to the Union. The touts wait there to intercept, and when they saw one trying to cross the area they immediately pounced on him and threatened him with arrest for trespass if he did not accept the offer of a contract for work for South Africa as a waiter. The victim only realised on arriving in the Union that he had been tricked and contracted to work on a farm ...

Compulsion, not persuasion

We wish to emphasise that while the Industrial Revolution is causing as much chaos in South Africa as it caused in 19-century Europe, no lessons have been learnt from the industrial past (whatsoever). The same abuse of labour is repeated in the same style.

Farm prisons and contracted labour bypass the normal need to attract men by improved working conditions and higher wages. They depend upon compulsion, not persuasion.

Most men who touch a pencil for a farm contract are hungry, ignorant and urgently in need of work. Once they have touched a pencil they have handed themselves to an unknown employer in an unknown area under largely unknown conditions.

It is obvious that care has been taken by the authorities to protect these people.

We asked, when farm life is so often satisfactory, what are the conditions which have given Bethal so fearful and exceptional (a) history — and we reply, it is the system; the farm contract system that has had so vile a result ...

1958, SOUTH AFRICA

The Sekhukhuneland Revolt

INTRODUCED BY PETER DELIUS

On 16 May 1958 violence broke out in Sekhukhuneland. Within a few days, nine people had been killed, many more had been wounded and numerous buildings and vehicles had been torched. A police column was despatched to the area, which set about trying to restore order with a heavy hand and limited results. Journalists scrambled to describe and account for this turn of events. The area had been the heartland of the Pedi kingdom in the 19th century but by the 1950s it was a remote reserve area far removed from the usual haunts and interests of the press. Any white people who wanted to travel there had to request special permission to do so. Few applied and even fewer were granted permits. Once violence erupted the area was completely sealed off and the African National Congress was banned.

Newspapers made some attempt to cover the story but without access and contacts, they served up poor fare. Journalists reached for the tried and tested tropes of primordial tribal violence and an atavistic desire to return to a lost past to explain these far-off events. The *Rand Daily Mail*, which at least gave the story space, nonetheless provided a pastiche of colonial assumptions by way of analysis:

> The Bapedi, tribesmen who were once all powerful rulers of Sekukuniland took up arms again last week for the first time in sixty years. They have reverted to guerrilla-like tactics in an attempt to regain their lost power and past glory ... Now behind the brown clouds of dust in caves the dreaded 'babolai' (killers) wait.

This rendition evoked images of the Mau Mau uprising in Kenya from 1952. It had sent shudders of fear through settler worlds and inspired the circulation of lurid and blood-soaked tales of barbarous Africans within colonial society in Africa and beyond. It has, however, since been revealed that the British treated the Kikiyu with considerably more systematic violence and cruelty than Mau Mau rebels inflicted on their enemies.

The Sekhukhuneland Revolt was a profoundly significant episode in 20th-century South African history. The eventual defeat of the rebels was a turning point in the imposition of apartheid's rural designs. But the linkages that formed between the Communist Party, the ANC and the rebels in the course of the resistance left a vital legacy for later struggles. The willingness of the rebels to take up arms in defence of their freedom also gave pause for thought for some leaders of the ANC and the Communist Party and contributed to the decision to launch the armed struggle a few years later. In addition, the networks generated in the revolt provided some of the first recruits for the ANC's military win, Umkhonto weSizwe. But at the time, these events were met by the mainstream media with a combination of incomprehension and racist fantasy.

In stark contrast to this trickle of tendentious reporting, a little known, independent, left-wing journal, *Africa South*, published an account of the rising penned by James Fairbairn which provided profound insights into what was taking place. He located the revolt in the context of the apartheid state's attempts to corral black farming and to co-opt chiefs through the introduction of the Bantu authorities system. He also highlighted the role of migrant workers in organising the resistance and he provided a reasonably full narrative of key events. His article has been amplified and modified by more recent research but its main points have not been overturned. It remains a valuable historical source.

I first encountered Fairbairn's article in the 1970s when I started research on Pedi history for my PhD. Both the author and the journal, *Africa South*, were previously unknown to me. (For the history of *Africa South*, see page 86.) I assumed that the author was writing under a pseudonym. But it took an embarrassing amount of time before it dawned on me that the name harked back to John Fairbairn, one of the editors of *South African Commercial Advertiser* in the 1820s. It was South Africa's first independent newspaper and its resonance with realities of the 1950s was underscored by its repeated banning by the governor.

James Fairbairn was the *nom de plume* of Jack Halpern. Born in 1927 in Berlin, his parents fled Nazi Germany and settled in Johannesburg. He became a journalist and correspondent for the left-leaning *Reynolds News* and the *New Statesman*. He also edited the publications of the South African Institute of

Race Relations (IRR). His archived papers suggest that he had a wide range of contacts in liberal left circles. But this mainly white network would have had limited information on events in Sekhukhuneland. Members of both the ANC and the Communist Party played a part in organising the resistance but my research suggests at that time that white communists and the higher echelons of the ANC had a very limited understanding of their members' activities in the reserves.

So how did Halpern get his information? One part of the answer is that his position at IRR allowed him access to its developed network of contacts that penetrated far deeper into rural areas than most. Elements of his report echo material that the Institute gathered at the time, but did not publish. A key source for his report, as well as for the IRR information, is likely to have been members of the Anglican Church. An Anglican secondary school in the area had recently been closed as a result of Bantu Education but Jane Furse Hospital remained open. One of the leaders of the resistance, Godfrey Mogaramedi Sekhukhune, was a male nurse at the hospital and probably a key informant for Halpern and others.

In 1960 Halpern moved to Southern Rhodesia and worked there as a journalist until he was expelled in 1963. After arriving in Britain, Halpern served as Secretary-General of Amnesty International from 1964–5. He also published *South Africa's Hostages: Basutoland, Bechuanaland & Swaziland* in 1965. He died on 11 May 1973. In his later years when he looked back over a long and distinguished career he probably would not have guessed that his pioneering account of the Sekhukhuneland Revolt would have such lasting significance.

References

Delius, Peter. 1996 *A Lion Amongst the Cattle*. Johannesburg: Heinemann and Ravan Press.
Halpern, Jack. 1965. *South Africa's Hostages: Basutoland, Bechuanaland & Swaziland*. London: Penguin Books.
Material on Halpern is located in the Institute of Race Relations Collection held in the Wits Library; Institute of Commonwealth Studies Library, London University; Jack Halpern Papers were donated to the Institute of Race Relations by Jack Halpern's widow.

The Sekhukhuneland Terror

James Fairbairn (Jack Halpern), *Africa South,* October 1958, South Africa

Behind the mass murder trial of Bapedi tribesmen from the 'sealed off' Reserve of Sekhukhuneland, lies the story of their people's resistance to the Nationalist Government's Bantu Authorities – and of the intrigue, intimidation and armed force which the Native Affairs Department (NAD) has employed to make them accept this final tightening of the screws of White control over African tribal life.

The Bantu Authorities Act, which was passed in 1951 without any consultation with the African people, changed the traditional forms of African tribal and rural local government without providing for any form of African political expression ...

To understand recent events in this loosely defined area, which lies in the Lulu Mountains of the Eastern Transvaal, one must remember that its native Bapedi 'group' were amongst the very last of the Bantu tribes to be conquered by the White man in South Africa ... Disputes about the succession of Sekhukhune I, who was finally defeated and deposed by the British, were settled in 1883; the Bapedi were disarmed; and for the past 70 years the inter-linked Bapedi, Bakoni and Batau peoples have lived in as much peace as the impact of successive White laws, taxes and agricultural betterment schemes permitted them ...

No sooner had the Bantu Education Act been passed in 1954, however, than the NAD took over the Jane Furse Mission school run by 'Father Huddleston's friends', and abolished its three high school classes. The principal, a Pedi, resigned in protest against the Act, and considerable resentment was aroused, fanned by the dictatorial manner in which the local NAD agricultural officer is said to have imposed stock restrictions, new local taxes and even residential bars to the Bapedi's traditional polygamy.

When, therefore, Dr Verwoerd himself held an *indaba* a few months later with Eastern Transvaal chiefs and counsellors to explain the blessings of his Bantu Authorities and Bantu Education Acts, the Bapedi representatives were unimpressed.

Their Regent, Moroamoche, returned home and called a 'report-back' meeting, the assembled tribe rejected the Bantu Authorities system – and the four-year war of attrition with the NAD, which has turned Sekhukhuneland into today's Government-occupied armed camp, began.

A network of spies and informers was established throughout the Reserve, but even by May 1956, only four headmen had been persuaded to back Bantu Authorities. When attempts were made to trick Moroamoche into signing Bantu Authorities papers, his counsellors pulled him away physically, and in June 1956, a tribal gathering once more decisively rejected Bantu Authorities, though a few more headmen had been 'won round'. In November, the local officials having failed, no less a person than Mr C.W. Prinsloo, Chief Information Officer of the NAD, came to promise the Bapedi a railway bus service, a new secondary school, a clinic, a post office and a telephone if they accepted Bantu Authorities. The Bapedi, however, resolutely refused the bribe. Rumour spread that Maroamoche was to be deposed, and the tribal council dismissed its secretary and head councillor, whom it suspected of intriguing with Prinsloo to foist Bantu Authorities on them. Phetedi Thulare, a senior member of the royal house who had been working in Johannesburg as a messenger, became secretary in March, 1957 – and was deported without warning exactly one month later.

Mr Prinsloo's repeated unofficial offers, in the pseudo-Bantu idiom beloved by his chief Verwoerd, to bring the two deportees 'out of his stomach' if the tribe accepted Bantu Authorities, were rejected; but by July 5 of last year, he had apparently bullied Moroamoche into submission. The setting up of a Bapedi Bantu Authority was gazetted. Some 8,000 members of the tribe then donned ceremonial dress and gathered from as far as 20 miles away, at Mohaletse, where they presented a petition bearing 30,000 signatures to NAD officials, demanding the return of their exiled 'sons'.

Their petition was completely ignored and, although two new secondary schools were set up, matters came to a head at the end of last November. On the 29th, the Bapedi Authority was disestablished 'for lack of support', and on the 30th the regional

Chief Native Commissioner, backed by an armed police convoy, informed Moroamoche at Mohaletse that he was suspended as Regent for a month. Simultaneously, seven men were arrested, and two of them, including the new tribal secretary, immediately deported. The five others were gaoled on charges of obstructing the authorities. It is perhaps significant that one of these five subsequently made application to the Supreme Court, on December 4, when his counsel alleged that the police at Schoonoord, the Sekhukhuneland administrative centre, had refused him access to his client. The matter was settled out of Court after ready access to the accused was promised, and the State agreed to bear the costs of the application. In February of this year, three of the five men were acquitted and minor fines imposed on the other two.

Before this, however, the Government decided to reverse the history of over a century, and to facilitate the setting up of Bantu Authorities by separating the 'Bapedi' from the 'Bakoni'. The removal of the latter to the Nebo part of Sekhukhuneland under their 'own' Native Commissioner was begun, but they have reportedly been trickling back to their old homes recently.

At the end of last year Moroamoche's suspension was extended for another three months, and after this the Government, which was simultaneously encountering stiff resistance from the Bafurutse around Zeerust, quickened the pace of its persuasion.

Acting under a law of 1927, Dr Verwoerd took powers on February 28 of this year to 'seal off' any Native area at will ...

On March 7 this proclamation was applied to the Bapedi part of Sekhukhuneland (as well as to Zeerust and a third Reserve), and since then, reliable first-hand reports have been understandably hard to come by. However, the Government's publicly taken measures speak for themselves.

On March 11 Moroamoche won a Supreme Court appeal against his continued suspension, on the grounds that the Government had not given him the chance to defend himself, demanded by the law it had invoked. With impressive promptness, the Government re-suspended him on the very next day – this time under a different law which contained no such 'democratic' safeguards.

Five days later the African National Congress was declared an illegal organisation in Sekhukhuneland — once more through a mere proclamation in a Government Gazette — and anyone even giving its 'thumbs up' sign or 'Afrika!' greeting became liable to a fine of £300 and three years' imprisonment.

On March 21 Moroamoche was deported, without any warning, to Cala in the Transkei, together with his wife and one child; and shortly afterwards, on April 1, the Bantu Trust, which is in effect the NAD, took over all functions of the disestablished Bapedi Authority.

One would think that there was nothing except remaining alive which the Bapedi could now do, but apparently they were not yet crushed. At Easter the primary school at Mohaletse was permanently closed down as a result of a boycott, and its 300 children reportedly barred from all other schools.

Heavy police reinforcements were brought into the area and, after several 'nominees' had refused the position, an attempt was made to set up a retired Pedi police sergeant as acting Regent of the tribe, which promptly rejected him. As the boycott of schools became general, heavy police reinforcements took over the Reserve, headed by a special mobile column under Detective Sergeant Jan Hendrick van Rooyen, already notorious for his unbridled terrorism whilst commanding a similar force in Zeerust.

Tension rose as police raids increased, and the by-now inevitable flow of blood began on May 16. An armed police detachment arrested Phasoane Nkadimeng, a minor chief who had been threatened with deposition because of his opposition to Bantu Authorities, as well as his brother and a senior counsellor. Phasoane's villagers apparently rushed up, surrounded the police van into which their chief had been thrust, and held it to prevent his being driven off. What followed is a sadly familiar story. The police claim that stones began to fly, and that they were reluctantly forced to open fire in self-defence. Four men were shot dead, and six men and a woman wounded. The police van roared off, and the enraged crowd took its revenge on the nearest Government 'collaborationists'. The wave of retributory violence spread, and for several days assaults and arson swept the

Reserve. Seven more tribesmen died, and many were seriously wounded.

Convoys of fresh police reinforcements were rushed to Sekhukhuneland under the personal command of top brass, including Col C. de Wet van Wyk, Deputy Commissioner of the South African Police, and the arrests of the tribesmen now facing murder charges began – many of them reportedly 'smelt out' by 'loyal' headmen.

On May 26 yet another Government Gazette proclamation made the carrying of 'dangerous weapons', which include the heavy 'kierrie' sticks and indispensable knives habitually carried by tribesmen, punishable by a year's imprisonment and/or a £100 fine or whipping.

I will not attempt to recount the many harsh sentences which have been imposed by local courts there under the various and incredibly restrictive decrees now in force. In some cases, the timely intervention of White lawyers has led to the noting of appeals, but the authorities alone know how many other convictions there have been. Meetings of more than ten Africans have, of course, been banned together with all other possibilities of even verbal protest, and those reporters who have been allowed into the area entered it under the strictest official supervision. Their 'sight-seeing tour', though otherwise barren, did provide one final touch to fill in the public's picture of enlightened White guardianship.

Standing in front of a smoking, sealed-off Reserve occupied by sten-gun carrying police, Mr C.W. Prinsloo and his fellow Native Affairs Department 'information' officers explained what the 'real' cause of the trouble in Sekhukhuneland was. The 20,000 strong Bapedi, said Mr Prinsloo, were (after 75 disarmed years of White rule) trying to maintain an 'assegai empire' over their 280,000-strong Bakoni neighbours, and were therefore against the 'progress' brought about by new chiefs appointed by the Government. But the terrorised Bakoni need not worry, Mr Prinsloo assured the world, for the Government would protect them and deliver them from oppression.

I know of at least one Bakoni headman who will be glad of Mr Prinsloo's assurances – one Frank Maserumule, who, after being rewarded for his espousal of Bantu Authorities by being made chief of a brand new village which the NAD had set up at Nebo for the Bakoni it had forced to move from northern Sekhukhuneland, was forced to flee for his life from the wrath of his enforced subjects.

1961, South Africa

The living dead

Introduced by Indra de Lanerole

'The living dead' is an investigation of banishment, which was one of the cruellest tools used by the apartheid government in the 1950s and 1960s to silence their opponents. It describes the fates of 116 black South Africans who were removed from their homes without charge or trial and sent into internal exile, 'imprisoned in utter isolation', far away from work, family and friends. Many of the banished were traditional leaders in rural areas who resisted government actions. Some were over 70 years old. One was a 16-year-old girl. To be banished it was not necessary for someone to have committed any offence, but – as the Department of Bantu Affairs put in 1965 – only that 'their presence in an area gave rise to dissension and dissatisfaction and was consequently detrimental to good government' (Badat, 2013: 320).

Helen Joseph was not a professional journalist but a union organiser and political activist aligned with the African National Congress (ANC) which was banned the year before this article was published. She was one of the accused in the Treason Trial of 1956–61, along with Mandela and many other leaders of the Congress movement. In 1959, Joseph and Lillian Ngoyi, both leaders in the Federation of South African Women, were asked by the ANC to identify how many people had been banished, who they were and to find ways of helping them. Can Temba, *Drum* magazine's 'ace reporter', had written an excellent exposé of the banishment camp at Frenchdale farm near Mafeking in 1956 (Badat, 2013) and other press stories had covered some individual cases. The two women set up a new organisation, the Human Rights Welfare Committee, and began assembling information and making contact with some of the banished and their families. They also raised money to start sending food and other support to some of them.

Joseph wrote the article based on this research. Though she was campaigning on behalf of the banished, the article is not polemical. It is packed with stories, facts and analysis. It reflects exactly the work we understand to be that of the investigative journalist – carefully assembling and interrogating legal and other public documents, speaking to those affected, gathering stories, compiling data and drawing attention to the actions of the state.

It wasn't until the year after she wrote this article, when the Treason Trial had ended and her travel restrictions were lifted, that she was able to investigate the issue further. With her friends, Joe Morolong and Amina Cachalia, she went on a road trip to visit the banished and the families they left behind. Following this trip, she became the first person in South Africa to be placed under house arrest. She smuggled out her account of the banished and this journey was published later outside the country as a book, titled *Tomorrow's Sun*. After this, the apartheid government reduced their use of banishment, something which her ground-breaking work may have been partly responsible for, although new laws gave the government extensive new powers to restrict movement. Winnie Mandela was later to become the most famous banished person when she was removed from Soweto and sent to Brandfort. Joseph's house arrest continued, with one break, into the 1980s. She died just before South Africa's first democratic elections in 1994.

This article was published in *Africa South*, a journal that between 1956 and 1961 brought together the writings of journalists, activists, intellectuals and political leaders. It published an extraordinary group of people, including Nelson Mandela, Walter Sisulu, Ruth First and Julius Nyerere. Ronald Segal, the publisher and editor, described it as a magazine that would connect the political struggle in South Africa, the anti-colonial movements on the continent and the civil rights movements in the US (Daymond & Sandwith, 2011: 20). From 1960 onwards with the ANC's banning, it was published as *Africa South in Exile* from London.

Articles like Joseph's point to an important strand in the history of investigative journalism in South Africa – its close and complex relationships to social and political movements and social justice organisations, including the church. Can Temba is easy to place in the traditional picture of the lone, independent, hard-drinking, male investigative journalist, meeting contacts in bars. His story on the banished appeared in *Drum*, a magazine which combined investigations with celebrations of the musicians and boxers of the era. Helen Joseph's committed journalism belongs in another tradition along with that of John Dube and Ruth First, published in political journals from *Ilanga* to *The Weekly Guardian* and *Africa South*. These diverse strands continue today with investigative teams like aMabunghane transforming themselves into non-profit organisations and others working closely with social justice organisations and movements.

At the 2017 Global Investigative Journalism Conference in Johannesburg, the economist Joseph Stiglitz said he didn't think the market now could sustain such journalism. 'The living dead' reminds us that there may be spaces to look for the continuation of this work outside of traditional newsrooms.

REFERENCES

Badat, Saleem. 2013. *The Forgotten People: Political Banishment Under Apartheid.* Leiden, Netherlands: Brill.
Daymond, M.J. & Corrine Sandwith (eds). 2011. *Africa South: Viewpoints, 1956–1961.* Scottsville: University of KwaZulu-Natal Press.
Joseph, Helen. 1966. *Tomorrow's Sun: A Smuggled Journal from South Africa.* London: Hutchinson.
Joseph, Helen. 1986. *Side by Side.* London: Morrow.
Steiglitz, Joseph. Interview at Global Investigative Journalism Conference, 18 November 2017. Available at: https://gijc2017.org/2017/11/19/stiglitz-on-truth-trump-inequality-and-investigative-journalism/, accessed on 7 June 2018.
The full collection of articles from Africa South is available online in the digital archive at the University of KwaZulu-Natal: www.disa.ukzn.ac.za/as. The full article is available here: www.disa.ukzn.ac.za/sites/default/files/pdf_files/asjul61.5.pdf

The Living Dead

Helen Joseph, *Africa South*, July 1961

'It is not Mhlupeki that died but me, because what they have done to him they will do to me!' So wrote a lonely, desperate man after years of hopeless banishment when he heard of the death of another exile. 'You are like a person who has been buried alive,' wrote another.

In South Africa's shameful history, one of the ugliest chapters is that of the stealthy, relentless persecution of the individual who opposed government policies. Only recently has the scandal of banishment been brought to light, the power that can and does pluck an African from the midst of his family and cast him into the most remote and abandoned parts of the country – there to live, perhaps to die, to suffer and starve or to stretch out his survival by poorly paid labour, if and when he can get it.

It is all quite legal, this banishment without trial, all neatly enshrined in an Act of Parliament passed many years ago ...

Over 30 years ago, General Hertzog, as Minister of Native Affairs, in introducing the Native Administration Bill, said that the power to move a 'Native' from one place to another was an 'excellent provision'. The Bill provided that the Governor-General had power to remove a whole tribe from one place to another – presumably to enable whites to occupy the tribe's land, the Mamatola tribe was removed under this section. General Hertzog said that the powers to remove a 'Native' could be used against stock thieves, but there is reason to believe that he had in mind political leaders rather than stock thieves ...

It remained for the Nationalist Government, however, to realise and exploit the full powers of this Act of Parliament. The opponents of Bantu Authorities – the puppet regimes established by the Government – have been the real victims, perhaps because the limelight of publicity is not so easily focused on the Reserves, and indeed for nearly six years these banishments went on almost unnoticed ...

The true background to this savage system of banishment emerges from the stories of the banished people themselves. The appalling history of the Matlala deportation speaks less blandly than the Minister.

In 1953 and 1954, following opposition to the imposition of Bantu Authorities, altogether 20 men and three women were deported from the Matlala Reserve in the Northern Transvaal. They were and still are scattered all over the country. Of these 23 men and women, five men have already died in exile and 16 are still living in their place of banishment. Only two have ever been released, and both died soon after they returned home. At least two of the men who died in exile were receiving no government allowance and had no employment. They were old and sickly, and it seems clear they died of starvation. Only a few of these banished people are known to be in employment, and up to now, not one has received any government assistance.

The conditions of the families they left behind them in the Matlala Reserve is pitiable. Children grow up in rags, unable to go to school; some drift away to the local town or to the farms in order to earn £1 or £1 10s a month. The wives are not allowed by the Chief to plough; for mere existence they depend on the food they can beg from neighbours. In some cases, the huts of the deportees were burnt down and demolished by the Bantu Authorities' Chief immediately after the deportation, and all livestock was confiscated.

Wives were called to the Chief's office and told they could be taken to join their husbands, but that they would not be brought back again; if they refused, they were threatened with deportation. In two cases where the husbands have died, the wives were merely informed by the Chief; they have not received any of their husbands' clothes or belongings as proof of death. Only in one instance was the husband's body returned for burial, but no belongings were returned with the body.

This is the story told by the widow of Frans Ramare, who died – according to the report of other deportees in the area – alone and starving, in Zululand.

'One morning he was called to the Chief's place. This was the last time we saw him. He never came back to say goodbye to his two wives and children. We later learned from the people that our husband was banished. Since then we never hear anything, until one day we got a message from the Chief saying that Mr Frans Ramare passed away in exile. That was all. We never received anything from the Government about our husband's death and we did not see anything like his clothes, which could be used to prove to us that our husband is really dead. Since the banishment of our husband, we never received any letter from him. We never knew of his sickness until his death was reported, and we don't even know the date he passed away.'

Wherever there is opposition to Government plans, to Bantu Authorities, particularly in the tribal areas, the Government pounces on one or two individuals, summarily arrests and then removes them as far as possible ... Chief Mopedi served a prison sentence for refusing to cull cattle and repair fences; and *after* serving his sentence for this defiance of authority and non-co-operation, he was deported in 1954 from Witzieshoek to Groblersdaal; his wife was deported too. After two years, he was taken from Groblersdaal to Frenchdale; he is still there ...

The Government record is an ugly one. One hundred and sixteen Africans have been arbitrarily removed from their homes since 1948. One hundred and sixteen human beings have been arrested, thrown into police cells, handcuffed and taken under police custody to desolate areas, flung into an empty shed or hut, with nothing but the clothes on their bodies and, of course, the generous allowance – sometimes – of £2 a month to spend. Only there isn't anywhere to spend the money ...

What has happened to the 116 deportees during the years? Forty-eight are still in exile; 10 are known to have escaped from South Africa; 41 have been released, some for only specific periods of probation; 11 have died in the camps, probably without medical attention of any sort, possibly for lack of it. Six are missing and cannot be traced, unless the Minister will provide the information which until now he has refused to give ...

The two main camps for the banished people are at Frenchdale and Driefontein. They are not large; provision is only made for 8 deportees in Frenchdale and 12 in Driefontein. But they are stark and bare, in semi-desert areas, many hot and isolated miles from the nearest towns. Hyenas prowl around Frenchdale at night; the nearest store is 12 miles away and the nearest bus stop for Mafeking is 14 miles from the camp. True, the deportees may leave the camp freely and travel into Mafeking – if they walk the distance to the bus; but they must live in the camp ...

In both these camps there exist no opporutnities for employment and the deportees in Driefontein depend upon government allowances of £2 a month. In Frenchdale the deportees from Witzieshoek refused to accept anything from the Government; they maintained that they would rather starve. There is no work, no occupation. The deportes say: 'We are waiting to go home.' It is a long wait ...

The camps are not the end of the story. Other deportees are scattered over the Northern Transvaal, over Natal and Zululand – one here, one there, many miles from each other. Right up to the Rhodesian border, to the edge of Swaziland, in the heart of Zululand, in the Transkei, in the Cape, they can be found – if you know where to look for them.

The living dead

With cruel ingenuity, the man from the Transkei is banished to the Northern Transval, so that he may be isolated from those around him, until he learns to speak the new language; the Sesotho-speaking men from Zeerust and Sekhukhuneland are sent to the borders of Swaziland, to the heart of Zululand, so that they too must struggle with an unknown tongue. Employment? They may work as labourers for a few pounds a month — these men who were leaders among their own people, who were trade unionists, chiefs, university students — or they may be put to herding cattle …

Ben Baartman wrote: 'My experience of banishment is that you are just taken to an empty town and nobody seems to care for you. You are given neither food nor any sort of job through which you can support yourself. In other words you are like a person who has been buried alive' …

1962, South Africa

The hidden starvation

Introduced by Benjamin Pogrund

Starvation among blacks was rife in South Africa in the early 1960s. But it was hidden. Apartheid's victims had no power. They suffered and died, out of sight in city hospital wards and in rural areas.

Two years of devastating drought in the north-east of the country helped to bring the issue into the open. Attention was first focused on the plight of (white) farmers. Then came a new private organisation, Kupugani, the Nutrition Corporation, created to provide high-protein soup powder on a mass scale to the poor. It wanted publicity and the *Rand Daily Mail* was willing to help. Stirred by Kupugani's information about the extent of starvation, editor Laurence Gandar agreed to embark on a major exposé.

Gandar was already famed for his probing, relentless analyses of the evils of apartheid. He also had a newsroom which had become skilled in aggressive chasing after news, and sub-editors with a flair for eye-catching design and headlines. The *Mail* now entered a new phase, the first South African newspaper to put together a dedicated investigative team.

'Starvation: A national scandal', the front page announced on Monday, 1 October 1962.

The campaign began with reports from the drought areas by Keith Abendroth of the *Mail's* Pretoria Bureau: 'Pellagra and kwashiorkor – the dreaded, deadly malnutrition and starvation diseases – are the constant companions of thousands of African children in Shilwane, in the remote north-eastern Transvaal.

'In kraals in the sun-scorched Drakensberg mountains and in the normally lush Thabina, Letsitele and Letaba valleys the infant mortality rate among Africans is climbing and the incidence of pellagra particularly is 10 times higher than it was three years ago ...'

By then I had spent weeks investigating and researching. I learnt that the Infant Mortality Rate – the number of deaths before the age of one – revealed the grim story: for whites, it was 27 per 1000; for blacks, anything up to 400. A prime source was Kupugani's national organiser, Neil Alcock, a farmer with immense understanding of agriculture and driven to ensure food security for all. My secret source was Dr Sam Wayburne, chief paediatrician at Baragwanath Hospital: he risked his job by taking me through his wards to see starvation victims – shrunken babies, two to a cot. It was horrific.

I also tapped into a resource which no one ever bothered to look at: the annual reports of city medical officers of health. Dry as dust, difficult to get hold of, they yielded damning statistics and comments about baby deaths.

So by Day 3, when my reports began, we were well prepared: in a succession of reports we presented emotional words about dying babies and starving people, and published difficult-to-look-at photographs of kwashiorkor babies. Underlying everything, we reported fact after fact.

The results were immediate. The Nationalist government condemned us: our picture of the drought areas was 'unfavourable and distorted'. As our reporting continued the attacks rose. I was called a liar in Parliament. The then *Transvaler* newspaper, the National Party's organ, sneered at us as 'die hongersnood koerant' (the malnutrition newspaper) and said our pictures of starving babies were fakes. Dr Wayburne told me that a *Transvaler* reporter had arrived and said he had the job of checking everything I was writing. He demanded a tour of the kwashiorkor wards: 'After walking through the first ward he was green in the face,' said Wayburne. 'He declined my offer to look at the next ward.' The *Transvaler* went on abusing us.

Meanwhile, however, our Pretoria Bureau was conveying a different message to me from senior officials: Keep going, we need to pressure the politicians. The public response was staggering. Outrage and anger erupted about the extent of starvation; money poured in for Kupugani.

After 10 days of non-stop exposés, Gandar wrote a front-page editorial, 'END THIS SCANDAL!' with the message: 'Prevention, prevention, prevention'. I followed up with a week-long swing deep into rural KwaZulu with Alcock, from one church mission hospital to another, checking levels of starvation and what food was needed. That led to renewed campaigning late in November, with another article titled, 'The price of hunger'.

> 'Detailed statistics of the extent of kwashiorkor and malnutrition in the rural areas do not exist,' I reported. 'When babies die they are buried without ceremony. African parents see no point in walking miles to the

nearest Government office to notify the death.

'But every authoritative statement by doctors and nutritionists makes clear the gravity of the situation.'

We went into a new dimension, to give readers broader perspective about the causes of malnutrition. 'The death toll and misery caused by kwashiorkor can be ended by emergency measures to ensure that every baby has one pint of milk a day,' I reported. But malnutrition needed prolonged effort to deal with complex factors: poverty, which prevented people from buying enough of the right foods; ignorance, which resulted in mothers giving babies the wrong foods and failing to observe elementary rules of hygiene; migratory labour, which broke up family life, causing instability and illegitimacy; detribalisation had good and bad results, including the lowering of moral standards; rural reserves were overcrowded and eroded. 'The land cannot support the people who live on it. Disease is inevitable,' I wrote.

'None of these causes can be viewed in isolation. They hang together, and must be fought as one.'

Grim hunt in the bush for their food

Benjamin Pogrund, *Rand Daily Mail*, 3 October 1962

Mass starvation has driven Africans in part of the Eastern Transvaal back to Stone Age conditions. They are living on wild fruit picked from bushes.

In other parts of the Eastern and Northern Transvaal:
- Children sometimes go without food for two or three days.
- Many adults eat mealie meal – and nothing else – only every second day.
- Hospitals are overcrowded with malnutrition cases.
- In one area Africans believe that an epidemic has broken out. They have no name for it. The 'epidemic' is pellagra, due to malnutrition ...

These are the findings of two nutrition experts, both members of the Nutrition Corporation (Kupugani) – Mr Neil Alcock, the national organiser, and Mr Carl Keyter – after a tour of the drought-stricken areas.

Mr Alcock and Mr Keyter say that in Potgietersrus, the one district where famine conditions have received wide publicity — money is being used by a relief committee and the government to feed about 6000 Africans, mainly children, out of a total population of 108,000.

'Only an insignificant proportion are being fed. The surface has only been scratched.'

Most government officials are aware of the serious situation in their areas and would like to help. But they want official approval from a higher authority ...

Although drought conditions have aggravated the situation 'we were very much aware that malnutrition was a permanent condition of the people and existed long before the drought'.

They found that an estimated 20 percent of the people of Sekukuniland suffer from advanced malnutrition diseases such as pellagra, kwashiorkor and scurvy.

In the Maandagshoek-Steelpoort area 'we found a rural community who had reverted to Stone Age conditions.

'They had no mealie meal, and lived solely on the wild mapoeshan, a yellow date-like fruit which they picked from bushes and soaked overnight in water to make them more palatable.'

The basic diet of Africans in the reserves is mealie meal every day — or every two days; meat once a week — or once a fortnight. Yet in some areas farmers periodically destroy their surplus crops.

The Africans do not have milk, vegetables, merogo or other supplementary foods.

Near Nelspruit, Trichardtsdal, Bushbuckridge, Tzaneen and Warmbaths areas, periodic surpluses arise and are destroyed by farmers. The surpluses cover all types of food: dairy, oranges, vegetables, pineapples and bananas.

In Sekukuniland, 12 miles from large citrus-growing lands, there is widespread scurvy — caused by lack of vitamin C found in oranges. The symptoms of scurvy are bleeding gums and fissured lips.

In Trichardtsdal, farmers leave chopped bananas to rot on

the ground to fertilise the soil.

Hunger: The facts are in sick beds

Benjamin Pogrund, *Rand Daily Mail*, 4 October 1962

Ulcers on the eye-balls and on the mouth, swollen bellies, deep open cracks behind the elbows and knees, wasted bodies, sparse and feathery hair, blisters, a scaly rash, listlessness and misery — these are the visible, obvious signs of starvation and malnutrition.

They are found in kwashiorkor and pellagra cases.

Left unchecked, they lead to death. Cured, permanent liver damage remains.

There is no shortage of calories or protein in South Africa as a whole.

Yet the facts are that thousands die each year from either direct malnutrition — kwashiorkor and pellagra — or from allied diseases.

The death toll statistics have reached proportions where they no longer have meaning in human terms!

- 10,000 non-White deaths a year from gastro-enteritis in the urban areas alone.
- 10,000 African deaths a year from tuberculosis.
- Up to 800 children a year admitted to Johannesburg's Baragwanath Hospital with kwashiorkor. One in five of them die.
- Another 3000 a year treated as out-patients for the same disease.
- And no one has any idea of the exact situation in the rural areas. Putting it at its best, nutrition experts say it is as bad as in the cities.

The only clues come from reports that the majority of cases admitted to a hospital in a Northern Transvaal African reserve suffer from malnutrition, that children with kwashiorkor pour into Durban hospitals from the surrounding rural areas; and that many of Baragwanath's cases are also from the rural areas.

However staggering the available statistics, they are still only part of the total picture ... the greater mass – of chronic malnutrition – is hidden.

The implications for South Africa and for the affected individuals are far-reaching and devastating:
- Growth is stunted. The adult in his mid-twenties is physically weak, easily susceptible to a host of diseases.
- Workers, one step away from starvation, cannot do their jobs properly. Their employers call them 'lazy' and 'stupid' – and the loss of productivity and the effects of absenteeism are incalculable.
- Women start off malnourished and become worse with each pregnancy. They cannot give their babies a fair start in life.

Left to itself, malnutrition can only continue to grow with each succeeding generation. Not only ethical principles, but also sound economic facts call for South Africa to end a scourge that need not exist in our land of riches.

The children suffer more than any

Benjamin Pogrund, *Rand Daily Mail*, 5 October 1962

'Because of the serious drought in parts of the country and in view of the potato surplus, the Potato Board has decided to make potatoes available to farmers for cattle feed at a nominal price.' – Announced in Pretoria yesterday.

The children suffer most. Underfed, wrongly fed, their bodies offer no resistance when illness comes.

The result is a rate of death among African infants which is as high as, if not higher than, the world's most backward areas.

Two years ago, Durban reported that of every 1000 African babies, 246 died within their first year. This has dropped by 30 per cent, since the start of a feeding scheme.

In 1960, Johannesburg's African infant mortality rate was 122 per 1000; last year it was 92. Cape Town's figure is 144 and Kimberley's is 89. The Director of the National Nutrition Research Institute, Dr F.W. Quass, has said that estimates of African infant deaths throughout South Africa range from 100 to 400.

In contrast: India 185 per 1000; Egypt: 141; Ghana: 90; Nigeria: 76.

South Africa's national average for Whites is 27 per 1000. This compares favourably with Britain, the United States and Australia.

A major cause of the big killers among African and Coloured children – gastro-enteritis and bronchopneumonia – is malnutrition.

Gastro-enteritis accounts for one-third of African children's deaths – 10,000 a year in the urban areas.

A survey among doctors by the National Nutrition Research Institute indicated that, of 200,000 child patients, 22 per cent suffered from deficiencies linked to malnutrition.

A senior doctor at Johannesburg's Baragwanath Hospital states that, apart from the 3800 direct cases of kwashiorkor each year, 'tens of thousands of other children who came for treatment have a background of malnutrition'.

Cape Town's medical officer has reported that the percentage of non-White deaths is seven times greater than that for Whites. Among Whites, nearly five per cent of all deaths are under five years of age. Among Africans, 57 per cent.

A survey at the Red Cross Children's Hospital in Cape Town showed that half the children who came as out-patients were underweight; of all the children at the hospital, 16 per cent suffered the 'grossest degree' from diseases caused by malnutrition.

Malnutrition is also believed to affect mental development. That is what the available evidence indicates.

One study carried out in the Valley of a Thousand Hills, Natal, was on a group of African children a year after they had recovered from kwashiorkor.

The children were found to be apathetic, lacking in intelligence and initiative, acting only when given orders.

'They were like zombies in horror films, automatons,' said the report.

South Africa's other great scourge, tuberculosis, is linked with malnutrition on the simple basis that an underfed body falls easy prey to infection. The country has an estimated 150,000–

200,000 tuberculosis victims. At least half of them are walking around undetected, in many cases spreading the disease still further. In 1948, the state spent R500,000 to combat tuberculosis. Now the figure has grown to R13m.

Yet the number of new cases reported by SANTA – 160 a day, nearly all non-Whites – has shown little sign of decreasing. For those who still do not believe the gravity and extent of malnutrition in South Africa, here are the views of some of the men who know the situation:

'It is evident that malnutrition and its associated deficiency diseases exist to a far greater extent than even the most pessimistic nutritionist expected.' – Dr F.W. Quass, director of the National Nutrition Research Institute, September 20, 1961.

'There is little doubt that serious malnutrition occurs among the lower sections of our population, and until this is seriously and whole-heartedly tackled by all authorities, no improvement in the incidence of gastro-enteritis, kwashiorkor, broncho-pneumonia and tuberculosis can be expected.' – Dr E.D. Cooper, Cape Town's Medical Officer of Health, 1960 Annual Report.

1963–78, South Africa

The secret organisation at the heart of apartheid

Introduced by Raymond Joseph

The investigation into the Afrikaner Broederbond, the elite secret organisation that infiltrated the South African government and society at the highest levels, was one of the longest running in the history of South African journalism. It spanned three decades – and three journalism generations – with a majority of the reporting done by four reporters working at different times for the *Sunday Times*.

Between them they exposed a shocking story of state capture that was deeply rooted in South African politics and the ruling National Party. The organisation's all-male members included the elite of Afrikanerdom, who profited through their membership with position, power and, in some cases, access to government contracts and tenders.

'The South African Government today is the Broederbond and the Broederbond is the Government,' wrote journalists Hans Strydom and Ivor Wilkins in their 1978 book *The Super Afrikaners*. 'No Afrikaner government can rule South Africa without the support of the Broederbond. No Nationalist Afrikaner can become Prime Minister unless he comes from the organisation's select ranks.

'From this pinnacle of executive control over South Africa's affairs, the organisation's 12,393 members permeate every aspect of the Republic's life. Through its network of more than 800 cells in the villages and cities of South Africa, the organisation has infiltrated members into town and city councils, school boards, agricultural unions, the State-controlled radio and television networks, industry and commerce,' they wrote.

The organisation invited very few working-class members into its ranks.

Explaining the reason for this, Strydom and Wilkins wrote: 'The reason is simple: The Broederbond has become the home of the rich and powerful Super-Afrikaners. They have been so successful in advancing their own careers and finances by being Broeders that the gap between them and the Afrikaner worker will simply not be comfortable in that company.'

The reporters involved in exposing the organisation were a disparate group of characters: Charles Bloomberg, the son of a Jewish dental mechanic and a close friend of Nelson Mandela, fled South Africa after receiving death threats because of his relentless exposés; Hennie Serfontein, who had worked closely with Bloomberg, then took over the Broederbond beat at the *Sunday Times*. Serfontein, from a conservative Afrikaner background, worked briefly for the liberal Progressive Party, before becoming a full-time journalist and later a documentary filmmaker; Strydom began his journalism career in the Afrikaans press before ending it as news editor of the *Sunday Times*. Wilkins, the only one of them still alive, worked as a news photographer, journalist and political writer in South Africa, before emigrating in 1987. He now edits a yachting magazine in New Zealand.

All of them produced books about the Broederbond: Serfontein's *Brotherhood of Power* and Strydom and Wilkins' *The Super Afrikaners*, were both published in 1978. Bloomberg's *Christian Nationalism and the Rise of the Afrikaner Broederbond in South Africa, 1918–48*, was published in 1990.

Two editors also played a key role in the ground-breaking reporting on the Broederbond: Joel Mervis, an astute journalist who transformed the *Sunday Times* into South Africa's biggest, most influential newspaper, and his successor, Tertius Myburgh.

Bloomberg began breaking stories about the inner workings of the Broederbond in the early 1960s, after a trove of Broederbond documents were leaked to him by Professor Albert Geyser, a clergyman and the son of a prominent Broederbond member. Geyser experienced a Damascus Road conversion after he was appointed to a Dutch Reformed Church commission set up to find theological backing for apartheid. What he found changed him forever and he was charged with heresy after he began to criticise apartheid and the Bond.

Geyser received the documents from the Reverend Beyers Naude – whose father was one of the founders of the organisation – who had sought his theological advice on their content. Naude later angered the National Party after he spoke out against apartheid and both he and his anti-apartheid Christian Institute were banned in 1977. For seven years, he was confined to his home and not allowed to speak to more than one person at a time.

Week after week, beginning in April 1963, Bloomberg broke news stories that exposed the hidden hand of the Bond in South African politics, religion and the formulation of the apartheid laws that governed life in the country. Bloomberg, and later Serfontein, wrote their stories under a *Sunday Times* reporter byline as they feared for their safety. After several months, police raided the *Sunday Times* in October 1963. Stand-in editor Louis Welch, who had suspected a raid and moved some of the unused documents to a safer place, handed over a file of already-published documents. 'For good measure he reproduced more of them on the Sunday after the raid,' Mervis wrote in his book *The Fourth Estate*.

The next big break in the story came in January 1978 after an unnamed Broederbond member handed Wilkins and Strydom what was the most comprehensive trove yet of secret documents. For the next six weeks, the *Sunday Times* ran a series, revealing some of the deepest secrets of the Bond and how it controlled South Africa.

Journalist John Matisonn, who alleged in his book *God, Spies and Lies* that Myburgh had been a high-level spy, claims Myburgh prematurely shut down the reporting on the Broederbond before it had run its course.

An indication of just how far the tentacles of the Broederbond reached came when lists of the names and details of more than 10,000 Broederbond members, which had been captured in the *Sunday Times*' new publishing system, were mysteriously deleted. There were also attempts to stop the publication of *The Super Afrikaners*. First the bookbinders pulled out of the project at the last minute, according to Wilkins. Then Penguin, which through a subsidiary company had lucrative government contracts for school textbooks, was not prepared to risk that lucrative business, and pulled out as publishers. By then Jonathan Ball, who was eager to launch his new publishing company with a book that would attract attention, took on the book.

'He had some difficulty securing a printer for the same reasons. By the time he got to contract a bookbinder he was being quite cagey about telling anybody what the project was about,' says Wilkins. 'When the bookbinder discovered it was about the Broederbond, he refused to touch it. This was right at the last minute and it was a big blow.'

And just as both Bloomberg and Serfontein had feared for their safety, so too did Wilkins and Strydom. 'We weren't quite sure what the reaction would be. We were certainly aware of the hit squads,' says Wilkins. 'It wasn't that long since the Durban academic Rick Turner was gunned down in his own home. Tertius arranged for armed bodyguards for Hans and me. There were other harassments though. My phone was very clearly tapped and I would frequently get heavy-breathing calls in the middle of the night. This continued on and off for years and I developed paranoia about going into dark car parks ... after being followed several times late at night with footsteps that stopped when I stopped and then carried on when I carried on – just like the movies. Hans had a harder time of it. He had a scary phone call where the caller named Hans's kids, the schools they attended and the buses they took to get there. The family cat was killed and left on their doorstep. He also had a problem with his bank withdrawing his mortgage and giving him a hard time.'

The publication of the secret membership lists and the exposing of the inner secrets of the Broederbond had far-reaching consequences, remembers Wilkins. 'It caused huge divisions within Afrikanerdom and split families. Within Afrikaner ranks, the reactions were quite complex. Some were outraged by a sense of envy – they could see how they had missed out by not being included in the ranks, with all the privileges and contracts and appointments that went with it. Some young Afrikaners were appalled that their fathers were part of it.'

With the unbanning of the African National Congress and other liberation organisations and the freeing of political prisoners in 1990, an already weakened Broederbond began losing its grip on government and its role in defining policy. In 1993, 78 years after it was founded and just before the dawn of democracy in South Africa, the Broederbond became an open organisation that still functions today to serve and promote Afrikaner interests.

But looking back, it is clear that the beginning of the end for the Broederbond had begun many years earlier, thanks to the bravery and dogged reporting of four exceptional investigative journalists.

REFERENCES

Matisonn, John. 2015. *God, Spies and Lies*. Cape Town: Missing Ink.
Mervis, Joel. 1989. *The Fourth Estate*. Johannesburg: Jonathan Ball Publishers.
Wilkins, Ivor & Strydom, Hans. 2012. *The Super Afrikaners*. Johannesburg: Jonathan Ball Publishers.
Interview Ivor Wilkins: April 2018, email.
Interview Peter Wilhelm: April 2018, Cape Town.

Broeder plan to oust DRC new dealers

Sunday Times, April 1964

A secret Broederbond plan to oust 'new deal' leaders of the 1,800,000-member Nederduits Gereformeerde Kerk, outlaw theological criticism of apartheid, and tighten the Broederbond stranglehold on church affairs is causing growing friction in the DRC.

Details of the plan – disclosed today for the first time – show a direct link between Broederbond decisions and DRC policy.

The Broederbond inspired moves in the NGK Transvaal Synods this month to:

- Ban public criticism of DRC policies, especially on race matters
- Boycott and smear the independent inter-church journal, *Pro Veritate*
- Clip the wings of the 'new deal' Southern Transvaal moderator, Dr C.F. Beyers Naude, who edits *Pro Veritate*

Each of these decisions – as the accompanying photostats reveal – was secretly hatched behind closed doors several months ago by the Bond's 11-member Uitvoerende Raad ...

News disclosures stun Broederbond

Sunday Times, April 1964

Stunned by the *Sunday Times*'s exposure of its undercover activities, the Broederbond through its chairman, Dr P.J. Meyer, this week started an extensive witch-hunt to discover the source of the leak and ordered an all-round tightening-up of security measures and secrecy ...

Police raid proves photostats are authentic

Sunday Times, October 1964

This week's police raid proved beyond doubt the authenticity of photostats of Broederbond documents published by the *Sunday Times* — and has ended any doubts among Afrikaans-speaking people about their genuineness.

The sensational disclosures of Broederbond influence in many spheres, published during the past few months, shocked and startled readers. On Tuesday, for the first time months after *Sunday Times* disclosures, the police acted in response to an official Broederbond complaint that a copy of their constitution had been stolen from their offices ...

Top Natal education jobs go to Afrikaners

Ivor Wilkins, *Sunday Times*, 23 January 1977

English speakers have been manoeuvered out of top jobs in Natal's Education Department. In a recent reshuffle two leading educationists were passed over for the job of deputy director.

It went to a less senior Afrikaner. There are now fears that succession to the director of education's job has been arranged to be kept in Afrikaner hands. If this happens, English-speaking South Africans will lose their voice on the powerful Committee of Education Heads, which coordinates education throughout South Africa.

It is also feared that the Broederbond's ambition to control education in South Africa will have been achieved ...

Broeder master plan exposed

Ivor Wilkins, *Sunday Times*, 15 January 1978

Secret Broederbond papers in the possession of the *Sunday Times* disclose that the powerful underground organisation has drawn up an enormous 'master plan' to secure the survival of whites in South Africa.

The plan, drawn up in the wake of the Soweto riots in 1976, is set out in a series of detailed papers circulated to the Broederbond's 11,000 members through its network of cells.

The third paper in the series, *'Die Strategie'* (The Strategy), outlines a massive scheme to harness the entire economy – private and public sectors – to resettle Africans in the Bantustans on an enormous scale ... worked out a plan to indoctrinate the entire population ... to accept the 'Christian national' viewpoint.

Broederbond plans for more white babies

Ivor Wilkins, *Sunday Times*, 5 February 1978

The Afrikaner Broederbond has formulated a secret plan to boost the white – and particularly the Afrikaner – population of South Africa.

The plan is disclosed in secret Broederbond papers now in the possession of the *Sunday Times*.

It says the white birthrate must double, the black birthrate must be reduced and white immigration must be stepped up.

The Broederbond plans to 'stimulate' South Africa's population dynamics to ensure that whites at least maintain their prominent position ...

THE SECRET ORGANISATION AT THE HEART OF APARTHEID

New leaks show up the Broeder turmoil

Hans Strydom, *Sunday Times*, 19 November 1978

A new set of Broederbond documents handed to the *Sunday Times* has disclosed that the underground organisation was shaken to the core by publication of its secrets in the *Sunday Times* early this year.

A picture of shock and anger emerges from the latest newsletters circulated to the organisation's 12,000 members since that massive 'leak' of documents ... More than 70 Broederbond cells were at one stage suspended because they were suspected of leaking information to the *Sunday Times* ...

Who's who in the Broederbond?

Ivor Wilkins and Hans Strydom, *Sunday Times*, 26 November 1978

The South African Government today is the Broederbond and the Broederbond is the Government. No Afrikaner government can rule South Africa without the support of the Broederbond. No Nationalist Afrikaner can become Prime Minister unless he comes from the organisation's select ranks.

The Prime Minister, Mr P.W. Botha, is a Broeder. Mr John Vorster, the former Prime Minister, is a prominent member — as were his three predecessors, Dr D.F. Malan, Advocate J.G. Strijdom and Dr H.F. Verwoerd. Every member except two of the Vorster Cabinet was a Broederbonder.

From this pinnacle of executive control over South Africa's affairs, the organisation's 12,393 member permeate every aspect of the Republic's life. Through its network of more than 800 cells in the villages and cities of South Africa, the organisation has infiltrated members into town and city councils, school boards, agricultural unions, the State-controlled radio and television networks, industry and commerce, banks and building societies.

Its membership spirals insidiously upwards through the strata of South African society, into the provincial administrations, the Departments of Education, Planning, Roads and Works, the hospital services, universities, the quasi-State corporations, the public service, the National Party caucuses, working through the administrators until it finally reaches its apex in the offices of the Prime Minister and the State President ...

How the Broederbond captures those top jobs ... and how it chooses the Super-Afrikaners to fill them

Ivor Wilkins and Hans Strydom, *Sunday Times*, 17 December 1978

Broederbond vigorously disputes claims that it pushes members into top positions.

It cites its rule stating that members must not abuse their positions.

This sounds right and proper, but the position in reality is totally different: Broeders do hold top positions in almost every sphere of South African life.

The key lies in this: To serve Afrikanerdom as they see it, they must do everything in their power to ensure that genuine Afrikaners have control of key positions. To them, obviously, 'genuine Afrikaners' mean Broeders. Why else were they handpicked by extremely strict criteria to join this exclusive organisation of Super-Afrikaners? ...

1965, South Africa

Abusive Prison Conditions in Apartheid South Africa

Introduced by Benjamin Pogrund

The Prisons Act of 1959 modernised the regulations for South African jails. But section 44(f) also created a new crime: publishing 'false information' about prisons or prisoners, 'knowing the same to be false or without taking reasonable steps to verify such information'. Publishing pictures of prisons and prisoners were prohibited.

Everyone understood that the government's aim was to suppress news about prisoners, that nothing could now be published about prisons. So nothing was. The next year this became critical: the Sharpeville massacre was followed by the banning of the African National Congress and Pan-Africanist Congress and a six-month State of Emergency was declared. Several thousand anti-apartheid activists were detained without trial and more than 18,000 black men were packed into prisons as alleged 'vagrants'.

During the Emergency, as the *Rand Daily Mail's* African affairs reporter, I worked with Obed Musi (an exceptionally brave reporter) of *Golden City Post* to expose the deaths of scores of the 'vagrants' at Modderbee prison, Benoni, from pneumonia caused by lack of food, clothing and blankets in the winter cold. I asked the prisons department for comment, making publication possible; later, I found the comments were lies. Questions I asked at other times were ignored or evaded.

In 1961, I gained first-hand knowledge of our prisons: I was jailed for a few days in the Old Fort in Hillbrow, Johannesburg, for refusing to identify an informant. I was isolated in the 'white' section but managed contact with several prisoners. Soon enough, information began reaching me about widespread abuse and cruelty inflicted on the masses of black criminal prisoners, the more than a thousand black political prisoners on Robben Island, and the dozen or so white political prisoners in Pretoria Local Prison.

In 1965, editor Laurence Gandar assigned me to start an investigative unit, the country's first, to be a very modest model of the ground-breaking investigative journalism of the London *Sunday Times'* Insight. Prisons were our first target. I consulted the *Mail's* chief legal adviser, Kelsey Stuart, about section 44(f): what were 'reasonable steps'? Stuart's skilled advice was crucial to making the *Mail* what it was, going against the 'when in doubt, leave out' maxim which newspapers invariably applied, and instead pushing to publish the maximum.

I drew up a 112-point questionnaire about prison conditions, contacted lawyers and spread the message in Johannesburg's underworld that I wanted to speak to ex-convicts.

Luck intervened. Holidaying in Durban I met Harold Strachan, an artist newly released after three years' imprisonment for teaching Umkhonto weSizwe, the ANC's armed wing, to make bombs. In hours of interviewing and recording him, I was impressed by his detailed descriptions of what he had suffered and witnessed in prison. I became convinced of his accuracy and truthfulness.

Strachan had already been visited by the Security Police and been asked questions known as a prelude to 'banning', which once imposed would make it illegal to publish anything he said. I intended using him only as background for the wider prison investigation. That's when I had the idea: he spoke so vividly and credibly, why not a first-person report? Gandar and Stuart agreed. I threw myself into writing his recorded 35,000 words down to 11,700. We brought Strachan to Johannesburg, Stuart questioned him minutely about my text, put him under oath, and declared himself satisfied that I had taken 'reasonable steps'.

Starting on Wednesday, 30 June 1965 we published Strachan's recordings over three days with the headline: 'Three years "inside": The staggering story of life in some of our prisons'. Some of the details might seem tame in light of terrible things now reported in prisons. But at the time they were electrifying, revealing the unknown, especially because we were in such outright defiance of the authoritarian government.

The first police raid on the *Mail* was on a Thursday, and they seized my text to prevent publication of the third report. But we outwitted them and the *Mail* carried it in full the next day. Anticipating police action, I had taken the precaution of getting Strachan to go on holiday with his family before publication began; he returned home on Friday morning to find a car full of dishevelled and angry security policemen who had been waiting since the day before to serve a banning order on him. So we foiled them that way too.

I was also following leads at Cinderella Prison, Boksburg. The Johannesburg *Sunday Times* published ahead of us, but on 30 July the *Mail* waded in with another massive report: 'Detailed evidence of the electric shock torture and beating of prisoners at Cinderella Prison have been given by two jail warders and two African ex-convicts.' I wrote after interviewing Head Warder Johannes Theron, Warder Gysbert van Schalkwyk, and Isaac Setshedi and Filisberto Taimo. Stuart questioned each of them and they signed my reports under oath. It was a horror story.

We were subject to a series of police raids to seize documents. From the prime minister down, we were assailed for our 'abominable lies'. Afrikaner nationalist newspapers, abetted by some English-language newspapers, abused us as traitors with heavy threats of what was going to be done to us. The SABC, the government-controlled broadcaster, ran a sustained smear campaign against us. Official rage was all the greater because our initial reports, and then the government's crude responses, went worldwide.

The government went for our informants, arresting and charging them with perjury and giving 'false information' about prison conditions. We had an early taste of how far the government would go: Van Schalkwyk, aged 22, broke in court under an unscrupulous prosecutor, Percy Yutar (who later, in an Appellate Court ruling, had to pay me damages for libel). Overnight, public opinion – among whites, that is, because blacks knew the truth from bitter experience – turned against us. At the *Mail*, many colleagues were hostile towards Gandar and me.

The might of the state was thrown at us for the next four years. Unending court actions, seizing our passports (I got mine back more than five years later), police surveillance, death threats and shots fired at the *Mail* building in Main Street, Johannesburg; many of my ex-convict contacts were frightened away.

The *Mail* paid for the legal defence of all our informants. But we had no hope: Stuart had advised that any criminal charges would have to be based on each report taken as a whole. However, prosecutors plucked out a sentence here and there, or a few words, and put together a string of charges, each with its own penalty. Serving prisoners were subject to irresistible pressure to testify against us: the prospect of early release or merely better treatment. The government could draw from an almost limitless pool of prisoners, plus warders, to testify about a specific event in a specific prison at a specific time on a specific day. It was impossible for us, except only occasionally, to refute the avalanche of lies.

Strachan was convicted. Sentenced to 18 months, he was, surprisingly, released after a year – into banning and house arrest. The Cinderella informants were all jailed – except we got Isaac Setshedi acquitted on appeal. He showed astonishing courage: the police arrested him and tried to intimidate him by inventing murder and robbery charges; when he stood firm they tried blandishment, giving him fried eggs for breakfast. Setshedi stuck with the truth.

Finally Gandar and I were put on trial. Virtually all the prosecution's 100 witnesses were organised perjurers. Even the brilliant Sydney Kentridge, our lead counsel, could not break most of them as they told their rehearsed stories. From the start, it was a foregone conclusion that Judge-President Piet Cillie would find us guilty, and we expected to be jailed. He did convict us but our defence was so strong that even he could not impose prison sentences. Gandar was fined and I was given a suspended sentence. That was hailed as a victory. I felt I had been through a replay of Frans Kafka's *The Trial*. It ended in July 1969 and I resumed full-time journalism.

Cillie's judgment gave the government what it wanted: nothing could be published about prisoners or prisons unless the department of prisons approved it. Silence again descended.

But it was different behind the high walls. The government could not admit it while in the midst of its public denunciations of our reports, but change swept through prisons. On Robben Island, much of the cruelty ended and living conditions improved. Black criminal prisoners throughout the country were now issued as a matter of course with socks and shoes and jerseys; the three-quarter 'tsotsi' shorts were replaced by long trousers. Life became more bearable.

There was another plus. The board of the *Mail's* owner, South African Associated Newspapers (SAAN), consisted of white, conservative members of the English business establishment. Most were deeply upset about the *Mail's* brutal conflict with the government, especially because of hints that they might also be charged. At least a year's profits went into paying for the four years' prison saga. But not the slightest pressure was applied to Gandar and me to recant. Our greatest and unlikely defender was the chairman, a mild-mannered accountant, Cecil Payne. It was a triumph for press freedom.

The board did try to get rid of Gandar because of his political views. An editorial revolt made them think again: Gandar was made editor-in-chief in charge of opinion, and Raymond Louw was appointed editor. He took the *Rand Daily Mail* to new fighting heights during the next decade.

Three years 'inside': The staggering story of life in some of our prisons

By Harold Strachan as told to Benjamin Pogrund, *Rand Daily Mail*, 30 June 1965

I was sent first to the Port Elizabeth North End Prison and was there for about five weeks. The European section of this prison was generally known among prisoners as a 'hobo' gaol, occupied mainly by short-term prisoners ...

We had a flush toilet in the cell which is quite unusual for prisons I have been in. But an interesting thing about this toilet was that you didn't only defecate in it, but you also washed in it; you brushed your teeth in it.

They had sufficient bathroom facilities. They had a very spick-and-span shower room with hot water and everything laid on, but we weren't allowed to use this because it had been beautifully polished – floor, taps and so forth – and mats were laid on the floor to keep it nice and tidy, and prisoners were seldom allowed to go in there.

It was kept clean for inspection.

We were obliged to shower twice a week in cold water in another shower house in the back of the corridor where we were. The section warder would not allow us to go even to this little bathroom in the morning, and hard as it is to believe, one would stand up with one's toothbrush while a man was actually sitting on the pan, wait for him to finish and say: 'Come on, get up, I want to brush my teeth.'

And he would get up amidst all this bloody stink, and he would flush the thing. Then a man would flush it again and then dip his toothbrush in the water and brush his teeth. Or wash his hands and face in it ...

In other ways too, the place was appallingly dirty. The

blankets were covered with semen. They smelled of sweat; were exceedingly thin and worn out, and the place was terribly cold. Many of the windows were broken.

The food came from the kitchen in aluminium dixies, always grubby, never free from grease.

Some of the hoboes in the jail were quite comical. There was a bloke, for example, with socks tattooed on his feet and a collar and tie tattooed on his neck, and he came in wearing just a jacket, shirt and shoes.

ORDEAL IN A PRISON YARD ... THEY LAUGHED AS A MAN CROUCHED NAKED — WAITING

By Harold Strachan as told to Benjamin Pogrund, *Rand Daily Mail*, 2 July 1965

I want to talk about assaults. I did not see any serious assaults at Pretoria Central. The worst assaults I have seen were on non-European prisoners at Pretoria Local Prison.

For example, I remember walking back to our section from the exercise yard, conducted by a head warder. There were two doors on either side of the passage through which we were walking and through these two doors across the passage, Africans were carrying heavy bags of food on their shoulders, bent forward.

We had to walk past and as a political I was never allowed to see or come into contact with any non-European prisoners.

Instead of asking the men to keep away the head warder kicked one of them in the belly. The man sort of staggered back, holding onto the bag on his back.

This is typical — this happened often. I saw it from my cell window. Orders were often accompanied by a blow. We saw Africans being driven into their section — we peeked through our windows — they were driven in like animals by *poyisas* [black warders] with sticks and with leather straps.

They used the long double strap of their truncheons or keys as a whip. Each man as he came past running would get a blow with the whip. Our window at one time overlooked the yard and the non-European reception office at the Pretoria Local and we could see these men being driven across the yard for showering or other purposes by these *poyisas* with these straps.

We could see these men also being hit with fists and open hands. We could see them coming in a column two-abreast, that is, 'two two' as they put it, and being thrashed as they rushed into the prison.

We could hear the same men rushing up the stairs and then into the section above us with the same cries as we had heard in the yard, and we could hear the blows following.

This was general. But the worst I saw anywhere in gaol were those on Africans at the hospital, and sometimes non-European patients in the hospital at Pretoria Local. For most of my time there the hospital yard was straight under my window.

All prisoners when they came into prison went to the hospital to get examined and so forth. Non-European prisoners who had to see the doctors were brought out at about 6.15 in the morning, and it could be freezing cold in Pretoria.

They stood naked, 60, 70, 80, of them at a time. Huddled up like birds trying to keep warm, like poultry, stark naked.

They had to stand with frost thick on the ground, barefoot, clutching each other to try to keep warm. Shivering.

And they would stand there until the doctor came at 9 o'clock. Sometimes later. Now and then one of these *poyisas* would allow them to pick up a garment to drape over their shoulders. Otherwise they just stood naked until the doctor came.

I have seen prisoners get a blow, as they were inoculated, or from one of the prisoners who worked in the hospital. Sometimes this happened in the presence of a doctor.

I also saw occasional assaults on the patients themselves. I saw one man who was apparently suspected of smuggling dagga, dragged out of the hospital by a warder — Kruger — whom we called 'Florence Nightingale'.

This warder was a burly man with a deformed face. He dragged out this prisoner who was wearing the hospital grey robe, and forced him to kneel down on all fours, stripped naked in front of all the other patients who were allowed to sit around in the sun during the day.

They were laughing at this man and other African prisoners

standing around were also laughing at him.

Forced him to kneel while the African prisoner who acted as hospital orderly stood with an enema can of soap and water. The enema was administered. The prisoner was stood up; blood was dripping down his legs; he was not allowed to get rid of this soapy water. It was blue soap. I saw them making it. He had to stand with his buttocks clenched together with his hands.

He was then forced to jump around from leg to leg, doing a sort of quick march, a sort of knees up to a horizontal position but still clutching his buttocks so the stuff couldn't come out.

The burly warder kicked him as he jumped in this way, kicked him on his arms, his back, his hips and his belly. Until finally a pot was brought out by one of the African prisoners ...

On another occasion I saw a prisoner carried into the prison yard on a blanket, the corners held by other African prisoners. He might have been shamming because many prisoners, like soldiers, swing the lead, and they like to get into hospital where the food is slightly better.

Anyway this man was put on the ground and he was lying there immobile. After a while he stirred.

Two of the warders had a consultation and apparently decided the man was shamming.

One of the warders took his wooden truncheon and, sitting down, let it fall on the forehead of this man on the ground – I suppose about 20 or 30 times. Bong, bong, bong – as you might do with a pencil on a table, letting it fall with its own weight. But this was a truncheon falling from six inches. As it turned out, the man was unconscious – fortunately, for he didn't feel this lot going on.

Behind prison bars there's torture

By Harold Strachan as told to Benjamin Pogrund, *Rand Daily Mail*, 30 July 1965

Detailed evidence of the electric shock torture and beating of prisoners at Boksburg's Cinderella Prison have been given by two jail white warders and two African ex-convicts. Warder Gysbert van Schalkwyk, 22, said a black prisoner, Aaron, was questioned about money found in a cell:

Chief Warder Louis van der Merwe instructed the prison hospital's warder, Erasmus, 'om hom te brand' (to burn him).

Aaron, naked, climbed on to a bed with a red rubber top, on which a convict hospital orderly had sprinkled water.

Six convicts held Aaron down – four holding his legs and two his arms. Then Aaron had water sprinkled over his body by a convict.

Erasmus had two wires with shiny points at the ends. The wires were connected to a beige-painted machine, which was normally used in the hospital for heat treatment. This machine was plugged into an electric power-point in the wall.

Erasmus held the one shiny point on Aaron's shoulder and arms. The other point he just played anywhere on Aaron's body – on his stomach, his legs, private parts, chest, neck – and when Aaron screamed, also on his mouth and tongue ...

I have seen this shock treatment being done many times. I have seen at least 15 to 25 convicts getting this treatment.

All the warders at Cinderella Prison know that it happens. But they are too scared to talk about it.

1965, South Africa

'An endless chain' of political trials

Introduced by Jo-Ann Bekker

In his memoir, *The Sword and the Pen: Six Decades on the Political Frontier*, the late journalist, editor and author Allister Sparks described his Eastern Cape court reports in the mid-1960s as his 'most creditworthy achievement'.

Senior journalists seldom cover lower courts, and Sparks was a *Rand Daily Mail* political correspondent when given this assignment. But those were extraordinary times. Hendrik Verwoerd, the architect of apartheid, was prime minister. The African National Congress (ANC) and Pan-Africanist Congress were banned, their leaders in jail or exile. In the Eastern Cape, the main stronghold of these organisations, more than 900 rank-and-file members and supporters had been arrested by the Port Elizabeth security police, and 817 of these men and women were prosecuted.

Sparks was tipped off about the trial by activist and writer Mary Benson. The court cases were held in isolated small towns beyond the range and resources of Port Elizabeth attorneys and newspapers. It was largely due to Johannesburg-based advocates, appointed by the Defence and Aid Fund, that the trialists were defended. And it was largely due to Sparks's two-part feature 'The trial of 800' on July 22/23 1965 that – to quote the *Mail's* front-page editorial – 'the full extent and intensity of the political trials' was first exposed.

Part 1 (reprinted here) explained that magistrates were restricted to hearing cases that carried maximum sentences of three years. But in these trials, charges relating to ANC membership were split into several counts, each carrying penalties of three years' imprisonment. Trialists who had been acquitted, or had served their time, were charged with another aspect of the same offence, denied bail, and tried and jailed again.

'AN ENDLESS CHAIN' OF POLITICAL TRIALS

Part 2, 'Operation Defence', examined the efforts of the Defence and Aid Fund to secure advocates for the trialists and assist their families. After wage earners were jailed, many dependents subsisted on donations. Thirty-five families had been forced to leave Port Elizabeth, Sparks reported.

When reporting on individual trials, Sparks's task was to expose legal irregularities without contravening contempt of court legislation.

'All I needed to do was state the statutory limitations applying to magistrates' court hearings early in my reports, then report straightforwardly what was actually happening in these cases, being careful not to relate the one to the other. That would leave readers able to relate the two aspects of the report for themselves without exposing me to a contempt charge for directly implying that the magistrates were cheating. It worked' (Sparks, 2016: 235).

His memoir mentioned the case of 47-year-old Port Elizabeth nursing sister Zebia Mpendu, sole provider of three children, who was detained for 15 months before being brought to trial (*Rand Daily Mail*, 1 July 1965; 27 August 1965; 22 July 1965). 'I still remember the look of bewilderment on Zibia Mpendu's face as she was led away to the waiting prison van. Nine years in jail for going to a meeting. Unbelievable. Outrageous. But inescapable' (Sparks, 2016: 237).

The power of this recollection is diluted by inaccuracies: the spelling of Mpendu's name, the charges she faced and her sentence – four years. But these errors say more about memory and fact checking than the impression Mpendu's trial made on Sparks. In 1968 his newspaper reported a further blow to the nursing sister: she was struck off the nurses roll for 'disgraceful conduct' as a result of her conviction.

Assessing the impact of his coverage, Sparks wrote:

> My reports on this protracted violation of legal procedure attracted international attention. Both *The Guardian* in London and *The New York Times* ran lengthy articles on the trials, which in turn helped prompt the legal authorities to take a closer look at what had happened. The cases all went on review to the Supreme Court, which declared the splitting of charges to be illegal and lopped 2000 years off the collective sentences.
>
> Looking back over 66 years of journalism, I guess that should rank as my most creditworthy achievement' (2016: 238).

There are exaggerations in these paragraphs. The overseas reports appeared seven months after Sparks' features and appear to have used the Defence and Aid Fund as their primary source (Leyleveld 1966; Uys 1966). Sparks provided no reference for his figure of 2000 years. Another source states the Fund 'got the sentences of 158 men reduced, keeping them out of prison for a total of 258 years' (SAHO: para 13).

Nevertheless, Sparks' contribution was significant. Other newspapers had covered individual trials, but his 'Trial of 800' was the first analysis of the government's efforts to keep ordinary ANC supporters imprisoned. His reports were quoted in the Institute of Race Relations' annual surveys (Horrell, 1966: 87–90; Horrell, 1967: 54–6) and were followed by questions in parliament (Horrell, 1966: 87).

State repression continued. In March 1966, the Fund was declared an unlawful organisation. Police swooped on its branches and froze all accounts, including R3,000 in its Port Elizabeth coffers (*Rand Daily Mail*, 19 March 1966). In April – two months after his front-page story 'South Africa set to reconvict foes' (Lelyveld, 1966) – *The New York Times* correspondent was given a week to leave the country (Lelyveld, 1986; *Rand Daily Mail*, 23 April 1966).

But by 1967, the endless chain of political trials had been broken (Horrell, 1968).

REFERENCES

Lelyveld, Joseph. 1966. 'South Africa set to reconvict foes; 162 ending terms face new trials in same cases'. *The New York Times*, 16 February.
Lelyveld, Joseph. 1986. *Move Your Shadow: South Africa Black and White*. Johannesburg & London: Jonathan Ball Publishers in association with Michael Joseph.
Horrell, Muriel (compiler). 1966. *A Survey of Race Relations in South Africa*. Johannesburg: South African Institute of Race Relations.
Horrell, Muriel (compiler). 1967. *A Survey of Race Relations in South Africa*. Johannesburg: South African Institute of Race Relations.
Horrell, Muriel (compiler). 1968. *A Survey of Race Relations in South Africa*. Johannesburg: South African Institute of Race Relations.
Rand Daily Mail. 1965. 'Sympathy for A.N.C. unchanged – witness', 1 July.
Rand Daily Mail. 1965. 'Trial of 800' (editorial), 24 July.
Rand Daily Mail. 1965. 'Police methods not in best tradition', 27 August.
Rand Daily Mail. 1966. 'Defence and Aid', 19 March.
Rand Daily Mail. 1966. 'Police swoop on Aid Fund', 19 March.
Rand Daily Mail. 1966. 'Lelyveld moved to London: "I tried to do an honest job"', 23 April.
Rand Daily Mail. 1967. 'Members of ANC get jail terms', 29 September.

Rand Daily Mail. 1968. 'Nurse is struck off roll', 22 July.
South African History Online, 'The International Defence and Aid Fund', para 13. Available at: www.sahistory.org.za/topic/international-defence-and-aid-fund-idaf-3, accessed on 27 April 2018.
Sparks, Allister. 1965. 'The Trial of 800', *Rand Daily Mail*, 22 July.
Sparks, Allister. 1965. 'The Trial of 800: Operation Defence', *Rand Daily Mail*, 23 July.
Sparks, Allister. 2016. *The Sword and the Pen: Six Decades on the Political Frontier.* Johannesburg & Cape Town: Jonathan Ball.
Uys, Stanley. 1966. 'South Africa: New trials for 162 in jail', *The Observer*, 20 February.

The trial of 800

Allister Sparks, *Rand Daily Mail*, Thursday, July 22, 1965

The Security Branch man spoke with quiet emphasis. 'We mean,' he said, 'to have peace and quiet in this area for the next ten years.'

His meaning was plain enough. For years the Eastern Cape area, and especially Port Elizabeth, has been the main stronghold of the African National Congress.

Now, with the national leaders of the A.N.C. already on Robben Island, the political police are moving in against the rank-and-file numbers in the Eastern Cape stronghold.

In the last year and a half 918 people have been arrested in the two Port Elizabeth townships. Except for 101 who have had the charges against them withdrawn (mostly members who have turned against their comrades and given evidence for the State), few of these can have much hope of knowing freedom again within the next 10 years.

It does not always mean much for them to be acquitted by the courts. Of the 26 who have so far been found not guilty, at least 10 have been rearrested and recharged and are once more in jail either awaiting trial or serving sentences. There are three recorded cases of men rearrested a fourth time after being thrice freed either by the courts or by having the charges against them withdrawn.

The only prisoner so far to complete his sentence (on appeal his 2½-year jail term was reduced to nine months) was brought to court the day before he was due for release, recharged, refused bail and taken back to jail as an awaiting-trial prisoner.

So far 452 people have been sentenced to a total of 2,339 years. Not for sabotage or other forms of violence (there have been only 17 such cases, dealt with separately in the Grahamstown Supreme Court), but for what are in effect technical offences: mostly membership of the banned A.N.C., collecting funds for it, distributing pamphlets, attending meetings and allowing premises to be used for meetings.

There are a further 298 awaiting trial — all in custody.

And it can be a long business awaiting trial. The record is held by Tommy Charlieman, a Uitenhage man, who was held for 19 months in four different areas before being released (according to his attorney no formal charge was ever put) — only to be rearrested and returned to custody. Now he has at last been tried and is serving an eight-year sentence.

Zebia Mpendu, a middle-aged nursing sister who is the sole support of three children, is now appearing in court after waiting in jail 15 months for the trial to begin. Many others have waited more than a year.

And over them all, those in jail awaiting trial and those in jail after trial, hangs the widely used power of the Minister of Justice to place them under house arrest or other restrictions when their judicial punishment is over.

Thus Operation Peace and Quiet. It is all strictly within the law — South African law.

A striking feature of the trials themselves has been the severity of the sentences.

Whereas three alleged members of the Central Committee of the Communist Party were sentenced in Johannesburg to five years, scores of rank-and-file members of the A.N.C. have been sentenced in the Eastern Cape to seven or eight years and some to as much as 12 years.

Whereas alleged lay members of the Communist Party — found by the court to have collected subscriptions, distributed leaflets, painted slogans and attended more than 20 cell meetings — were sentenced to two years, an African schoolmaster, Barnett Chezi, was sentenced to three years for allowing his choir to perform at an A.N.C. fund-raising concert. On appeal Chezi's sentence was reduced to one year.

One reason why the Eastern Cape sentences have been heavier is because the charges have been split into more counts. Allegations such as collecting subscriptions, distributing leaflets and attending meetings are set out as separate counts each carrying a possible three-year sentence (the maximum jurisdiction of a regional court).

Thus, for example, an African charged with subscribing to the funds of the A.N.C., with allowing his house to be used for meetings and with distributing pamphlets on three separate occasions (he was not even charged with being a member) was sentenced recently to 10 years — 2½ for the subscriptions, 1½ and two for each distribution of pamphlets.

Another possible reason is that, though the charges do not allege violence, many State witnesses have tended to emphasise the theme of violence in their evidence — testifying, for example, that an accused person advocated violence while attending an A.N.C. meeting, or that the subscriptions he collected were to buy guns and bombs.

The justification for this was challenged by defence counsel in a recent case; he described it as a 'heinous' attempt by State witnesses to embroider the evidence so as to 'aggravate sentences'.

The point at issue in this case, as in many others, was the New Plan adopted by the A.N.C. in 1961. Accomplices giving evidence for the State said the New Plan 'involved violence'; the defence claimed it was only an organizational device for working underground and that violence was limited to an elite corps in the Umkonto we Size sabotage movement.

The defence also produced court records from other cases, including the Rivonia Trial, to support its claim that the same State witnesses had previously described the New Plan without mentioning violence.

It was significant, said counsel, that in an earlier case in which no evidence had been led to associate the New Plan with violence, regional executive members of the A.N.C. had been sentenced to only 18 months.

A number of accomplices have given evidence several times. One, described by a defending advocate as 'a professional witness,' has testified against more than 60 associates. The courts invariably order that their names may not be revealed in Press reports, and one of the prosecution's most frequent grounds for opposing bail has been that to free a prisoner from custody would be to endanger the witnesses' lives.

If the prosecution is right about this, then the witnesses may well have a special interest in long sentences for the accused.

Another striking feature of this operation is that it has so far gone almost unnoticed by the public. Even in Port Elizabeth itself there are few Whites who realise that a massive political crackdown is taking place around them.

This is not due entirely to a comfortable White obtuseness. The trials themselves, though not secret, are the next best thing: almost invariably they are held *in camera* and in remote country courts — in Humansdorp, Cradock, Somerset East, Graaff-Reinet, Addo and Port Alfred.

The official explanation is that this is to prevent demonstrations and avoid clogging the Port Elizabeth courts. But it has other results as well.

Though the Press is entitled to attend, it often cannot. The Port Elizabeth newspapers are not large enough to be able to detach three or four experienced reporters to cover out-of-town courts continuously for two years or more. So many of the cases are left to inexperienced country correspondents, or are not reported at all.

1977, RHODESIA

The investigative nun

INTRODUCED BY ANDREW MELDRUM

Rhodesia's war to maintain white minority rule was raging in 1977 and so was the government's effort to control the press.

Following the collapse of Portuguese colonial rule in 1975, the Mozambican government allowed Robert Mugabe's nationalist guerrillas to be based in the country and the fighters infiltrated the long, mountainous and porous border with Rhodesia. Attacks in Rhodesia increased dramatically and casualties mounted, both of white soldiers and civilians but especially of the country's black rural farmers.

Prime Minister Ian Smith's Rhodesian Front regime maintained strict censorship of the domestic press and considerable controls over the foreign press to prevent coverage that suggested the African nationalists were gaining momentum or that they had a justified cause. Rhodesia's newspapers were directly censored by government officials. The *Rhodesia Herald*, for instance, had numerous blank spaces where stories had been taken out. The empty columns became so glaring that the Rhodesian government ordered that the spaces should be filled by uncontroversial articles.

Rhodesian censorship even extended to controlling what was written about Great Zimbabwe, the stone walled city in the country's southeast that thrived between the 12th and 15th centuries. Archaeologists determined that the structures, the oldest and largest masonry constructions in pre-colonial Africa, were built and inhabited by the local Shona people. But the Rhodesians did not want it known that blacks had created the impressive structures and promoted the myth that the walls had been built by followers of the Queen of Sheba or the Phoenicians. Peter Garlake, the senior inspector of monuments for Rhodesia, who did well-respected work which showed that Great Zimbabwe was built by the local Shona people, was censored and forced to leave the country in 1970.

The domestic publication most critical of the Rhodesian government and which described the aims of the African nationalist parties was *Moto*, which means fire in Shona, a weekly published by the Catholic Church. It was a thorn in the side of Rhodesian Front government, which in 1970 deported its editor, the Swiss priest Father Michael Traber. *Moto* continued with a local staff until it was banned by the Smith regime in 1974.

Foreign correspondents were also restricted. Journalists who went on rare trips with Rhodesian forces were required to submit their work to censors. Many reporters working for the foreign press found themselves staying in the capital Salisbury (now Harare) and speaking to a limited group of sources and writing carefully about the war, in order to avoid being thrown out of the country. Several journalists were forced to leave.

The ground-breaking book, *None but Ourselves*, by Julie Frederikse highlights with wide-ranging interviews the Rhodesian regime's efforts to control the flow of information about the war. Into that repressive environment came a modest, soft-spoken Catholic nun from the United States. Sister Janice McLaughlin, of the Maryknoll order, came to Rhodesia in 1977 to do work for the Catholic Commission for Justice and Peace. As part of her work she wrote dispatches for a newsletter published by the London-based Catholic Institute for International Relations.

Taking advantage of the Catholic Church's network of sources across Rhodesia, McLaughlin gathered information about brutal aspects of the war that the Rhodesian government had tried to gloss over. One of those was the creation of 'protected villages', created by the Rhodesian regime to prevent black rural farmers from interacting with, and giving assistance to, the nationalist guerrillas. The villages were ostensibly to protect the civilians from the violence of the guerrillas, but they were large rural camps behind barbed wire. McLaughlin described how rural families saw their homes destroyed by Rhodesian forces and were forced to build new homes, at their own expense, in the camps. With inadequate water and sanitation, and far from their fields, the camps were very unpopular.

Gathering figures of the numbers of protected villages across the country and how many people were in them, McLaughlin showed that there were more than 580,000 people in the 'protected villages', more than twice the official number given by the Rhodesian government.

McLaughlin also documented the difficult conditions in the camps. And she provided information for a map that showed the cluster of protected villages along Rhodesia's border with Mozambique.

McLaughlin also wrote that the Rhodesian army was perpetrating systematic torture of people suspected of supporting the nationalist cause and that the Rhodesian forces could do so with the knowledge that they would be granted immunity from prosecution. After interviewing people who had survived abuse, McLaughlin wrote harrowing accounts of how rural black Zimbabweans were severely beaten and burned by Rhodesian troops.

Even though she was writing for small Catholic publications, McLaughlin's work caught the attention of the Rhodesian authorities. She was arrested in August 1977 and accused of being a 'communist and self-confessed supporter of terrorism' and was refused bail. She was held in solitary confinement in Chikurubi Prison on the edge of the capital for three weeks, when she was released and deported.

'The Rhodesian regime was trying to silence my work. But the international attention surrounding my arrest created a lot of interest in my work,' said McLaughlin. 'My articles were in small, relatively unknown publications. But after I was thrown in jail, all kinds of publications reprinted my work. Many more people saw my exposés as a result.'

Following her deportation, McLaughlin worked for the Washington Office on Africa, a church-based lobby group to educate the American public and Congress about African affairs. In 1979, McLaughlin started work for the Zimbabwe Project, an initiative set up by a consortium of Catholic donors to assist refugees from the war in Rhodesia. She was based in Mozambique for two years, visiting refugee camps for which she raised funds and purchased supplies.

After Zimbabwe's independence in 1980, McLaughlin worked with the government to build nine schools for former refugees and war veterans and to develop a system of education that linked academic subjects with technical training. 'On the frontline: Rural Catholic missions and Zimbabwe's liberation war', her thesis for a doctorate in religious studies from the University of Zimbabwe, was published by Baobab Books in Harare in 1995.

In 2008 McLaughlin was elected president of the Maryknoll Sisters in the US. After retiring from that position in 2015, she returned to Zimbabwe where she continues community development work, including efforts to stop human trafficking from Zimbabwe.

Protected villages on the increase

Janice McLaughlin, Catholic Institute for International Affairs newsletter (London), August 1977

At the last count (30 May), there were approximately 203 protected villages [PVs] in Rhodesia, housing more than half a million people. These figures from informed sources on the spot are double the official government estimates of 250,000, or 'a twelfth of the local tribal population'.

The figures continue to climb as the government steps up its programme to establish protected villages in almost all operation areas. During the past rainy season (March) more than 100 new villages were established which would involve about 20,000 people, according to the government's estimates of 2,000 people per village.

Nineteen tribal trust lands in Mashonaland and Manicaland are already affected, and two in Victoria Province. The people in the Wankie area of Matabeleland have also been told they are to move into PVs. Chweshe TTL, just 45 miles north of Salisbury, where the first village was established in 1974, continues to have the highest village population with 120,000 people living in 21 villages.

It is difficult to get accurate figures of the villages, not only because they are going up fast, but because they also come down as quickly. They are popular targets for the guerrillas who cut the fences, liberate the people inside and burn down the huts. At the end of May, the Provincial Commissioner for Internal Affairs, Mr Geoffrey Henson, admitted that since the beginning of the year there had been 70 guerrilla attacks on the villages. This is probably an underestimate.

The guerrillas have also played havoc on the village administration by attacking personnel of the Minister of Internal Affairs who are responsible for running the villages. On July 1, the Minister, Mr Jack Mussett, stated in Parliament that his department had suffered high casualties with 114 killed, 25 missing or abducted and 243 wounded. He interpreted this to mean that the villages were successfully disturbing the guerrillas and said, 'protected villages are proving to be a thorn in the side of the enemy'.

... (He said:) 'I will not try and pretend that the exercise has been without hardship or difficulties for the African men, women and children involved. It is a tremendous upheaval for any person to have to leave his or her home and to change from a traditional easy-going rural way of life to an urban type of existence with the constraints imposed by the needs of security. However, these temporary disadvantages must be balanced against the over-riding advantages of being able to live in comparative safety ...'

The people affected to not think much of this advantage. Few have anything to fear from the guerrillas and feel no need to be 'protected' from them. They are still in danger from the security forces and can be submitted to interrogation which includes torture and beating. There have been many cases of rape in the 'keeps', as the villages are called locally, and District Assistants are now to confiscate the passes (*situpas*) of the women which allow them to move in and out of the village, and to force the women to sleep with them in order to retrieve the passes.

The 'urban type of existence' mentioned consists of a small amount of space (often 15 square metres per family), lack of sanitary facilities, clean water and sufficient food. People must build new houses from whatever they can salvage from these former dwellings and receive no compensation for the property they lose. Families are moved up to five kilometres from their fields and are often unable to produce enough to feed themselves. Their cattle are kept outside the village and are frequently stolen. The education of children is interrupted and sometimes terminated for good (47 schools have been closed because the population was moved into protected villages). The people are kept behind fences almost like prisoners and must call out their numbers and be registered when entering and leaving the village ...

'The protected villages are completely unacceptable to us,' said one man from Chiweshe TTL. 'A person can't like living in 15 square metres.' Another man explained: 'The people really hate this government for making them leave their homes and move to a crowded place with no shelter. They would rather starve than accept help from the government.'

'If we are asking to be put into the villages, then why does the government have to come and burn our houses to force us to move?' asked another man who described what had happened recently in the Tanda Tribal Trust Land. The people there had been given notice to move. They refused, saying they were quite safe, and there was no reason to leave their villages. On 4 July 1977, the security forces came and burned down six villages containing approximately 60 families each – Dzikit, Shuwa, Ngurune, Nufunde, Chatambudza and Huta. As a result of this incident, an estimated 2,880 people are now living in the bush. They maintain that they are prepared to stay in the bush rather than live in a protected village.

The chairman of the Chiweshe Residents Association ... described some of the problems in the PVs, including lack of clean water, lowering of education standards, increases of venereal disease and the depletion of natural vegetation ...

While the government has rejected claims of starvation within the 'keeps' ... it is a fact that voluntary agencies and organisations have often had to come to the rescue. Last year, the Emergency Relief Committee of Christian Care spent more than $60,000 providing food, clothing, blankets, accommodation, education and health services to residents of the protected villages ...

Another report from Dande TTL in the north says, 'Aid of any kind is most urgently needed for Mabomo and Chapoto. Mabomo was resettled in the bush without clinic, school, stores, post offices, etc. No cattle Chapoto is cut off from the outside world through war activities ... Malaria is rampant ...' From Chiweshe a report states, 'Most desperate need of the people is safe sanitary facilities. Insufficient and polluted water poses a related problem to health and Chishewe has been noted for the incidence of typhoid in the past.'

More than half a million people have been forced to live in such difficult conditions and to create new lives from nothing. The real irony is that in many areas the guerrillas move in and out of the villages freely ... If the villages fail to cut off the guerrillas from the local population, what purpose do they serve except to make life miserable for their inhabitants?

Rhodesian army pursues policy of systematic torture

Janice McLaughlin, Catholic Institute for International Affairs newsletter (London), August 1977

Reports of torture at the hands of government security forces continue to be the rule rather than the exception. Furthermore, under the provisions of the Indemnity and Compensation Act, a soldier or other government official can torture or kill a prisoner and the matter cannot be brought to court if the Minister certifies that the action was committed in good faith to suppress terrorism or to maintain public order ...

There is a realisation by the commanders of the security forces that they cannot win the war. This realisation appears now to be shared by some ordinary soldiers ...

The practice of torture has become a common event in the lives of people in the rural areas. Schools are frequent targets of interrogation campaigns. One common method of torturing students which leaves no tell-tale marks is the towel and hose method. The students are stripped naked, a towel is put over their faces and running water is sprayed in their mouths and noses through a hose ...

1978, SOUTH AFRICA

Muldergate: The scandal that ousted a prime minister and his successor

INTRODUCED BY RAYMOND JOSEPH

'It was nearly midnight at Miami International Airport. The lean figure in the St Moritz sweater stood up from a table near the Braniff Airline counter. Mervyn Rees stretched out his hand and said: "Dr Rhoodie, I presume?"'

So begins *Muldergate* (also known as the Info Scandal) by *Rand Daily Mail* investigative reporters Mervyn Rees and Chris Day. Published in 1980, the book details the clandestine web of department of information secret projects run by Eschel Rhoodie, and paid for out of a multi-million rand, secret slush fund.

Rhoodie, the former secretary of the department of information, was on the run as his elaborate propaganda war to polish the tarnished image of apartheid South Africa was unravelling back home. Millions had been spent on dozens of secret projects that included buying influence and politicians, attempts to buy foreign newspapers, and launching the *Citizen* newspaper and several magazines in South Africa. The launch of the pro-government *Citizen* came after a failed attempt to buy the anti-apartheid *Rand Daily Mail*.

Journalist Gordon Winter, an infamous government spy working inside the South African media, referred to some of these projects in his 1981 book *Inside BOSS*. 'Some of the secret projects mounted by the South African Information Department and BOSS were mindboggling,' he wrote. 'Hand-picked men had been used to run sporting groups and cultural organisations which pretended to be unbiased but were totally controlled by Pretoria. Publishers had secretly been given large sums to bring out a wide variety of pro-government books glamorizing the "South African way of life".'

In the weeks after the airport meeting, Rees and Day spent many days grilling Rhoodie as he revealed details of secret projects he had set up. In many cases he confirmed what they already knew, or filled in missing parts of the jigsaw of information they had collected. They also learned of projects they knew nothing about.

'It was a series of disclosures that were to reverberate in the corridors of power in the United States, various African States, Britain, France, Holland, Germany, Norway, Japan, Israel and Latin America where Rhoodie had bought and sold opinion formers and decision makers from a massive slush fund,' Rees and Day wrote in their book.

The late-night airport meeting was the culmination of a two-year investigation that spanned four continents, and had transformed Day and Rees into 'international lounge lizards' as they travelled the world following leads. Their investigation helped change the course of South African history. It played a major role in toppling Prime Minister John Vorster and split the National Party government. It also helped prematurely end the political career of Minister of Information Connie Mulder, who had been a frontrunner to succeed Vorster. And it brought down Hendrik van den Bergh, the all-powerful head of the sinister and secretive BOSS, the Bureau for State Security, who was a key player in the scandal.

The very real dangers faced by reporters digging into the scandal became clear when Van den Bergh chillingly told the Erasmus Commission of Inquiry into the Info Scandal that he had men under his command who would kill on his orders. 'I have enough men to commit murder if I tell them: Kill ... I don't care who the prey is. These are the type of men I have ...'

Muldergate was a high point in South African journalism, comparable to Watergate, which had brought down US President Richard Nixon a few years earlier. And as with Watergate's Bob Woodward and Carl Bernstein's 'Deep Throat', Rees and Day also had a source deep inside the establishment. Their source, a man they dubbed 'Myrtle', has never been identified. More than anything, it is a story about tenacious, old-fashioned, shoe leather journalism, with the reporters spending long hours poring over thousands of property and company registration documents trying to unravel the web of secret projects and companies that Rhoodie had set up.

While many journalists on different publications worked on the story, the real credit must go to Rees and Day, and Kitt Katzin of the *Sunday Express*, an investigative reporter on a small newspaper that punched far above its weight.

From the very beginning it was clear that it was going to be a game of high stakes poker with the future of the *Rand Daily Mail* on the line. Early on, *Mail* editor Allister Sparks, aware that a misstep could give the government the opportunity to close the *Mail* down, insisted that they not publish until they could do it in a comprehensive series of reports, preferably with simultaneous publication in overseas newspapers.

The *Mail* was finally pushed into publishing when Rees, frustrated at Sparks holding back publication, fed Katzin with information that he already had, but was unable to corroborate until then, according to former *The Star* editor Harvey Tyson, in his memoir *Editors Under Fire*. Tyson wrote that Rees had confirmed this for the first time in an interview with journalist Jo-Anne Richards (Tyson, 1993: 239).

Richards said: 'Mervyn told me that he was frustrated as he had been working on the story for so long and wanted to run with it, but Allister was nervous. He said the only way he could force Sparks's hand was to feed some of his info to Kitt Katzin. Once the *Express* ran the *Citizen* story the floodgates were opened and the *Mail* began running the stories that Mervyn had been working on for so long (Interview, August 2018).

And with the *Mail* being a known target for BOSS and Special Branch spies, Sparks demanded absolute secrecy, with even senior colleagues not being briefed on the investigation. An exception was the editors of the *Mail's* sister papers – the *Cape Times* in Cape Town, the *Natal Mercury* in Durban, the *EP Herald* in Port Elizabeth and the *Daily Dispatch* in East London – who helped fund the investigation and who would meet from time to time to be briefed by Sparks.

Like most investigations, the story began with a tip-off, in the form of a phone call to Rees from a trusted source in August 1977. His source introduced him to a highly placed civil servant who told him about corruption in high places, much of it centred on the department of information. With little more to go on, Rees began working the Pretoria cocktail circuit and also looking for contacts in the many government departments in South Africa's administrative capital, starting with minions lower down the food chain.

His search led him to a woman who had worked for the department of information, but left after her affair with a senior government official turned sour. She in turn told him the names of three other women, who had been 'hurt'. Rees (1980) later wrote:

> Women, in fact, played a prominent role in Muldergate, adding enormous colour to an already lurid tale. For many months newspapers

delved into the private lives of South Africa's most prominent politicians and key personalities in the Info Scandal. What emerged was a picture of moral hypocrisy in which absolute power acted as an aphrodisiac to men who used their influence to seduce women both in South Africa and abroad.

Meanwhile Katzin was beavering away at the *Express*, a sister paper to the *Mail*. He was a meticulous reporter whose good looks and boyish charm hid a dogged and hard-edged side to his character. His flow of Info-related exposés quickly earned him a national reputation as a reporter – and some high praise from the Afrikaans media.

The Citizen bubble finally burst on 29 October 1978, when the *Express* published a page-one lead under Katzin's byline headlined: 'The *Citizen* secrets revealed'. The *Mail* followed the next day with a comprehensive story they'd been sitting on.

A bombshell followed a few days later when Judge Anton Mostert, who had been investigating the department of information, called a press conference where he announced that the *Citizen*, despite denials by Mulder and others, had been financed out of state funds. 'It's all true', crowed the *Mail* the next day.

The story opened the floodgates that led to the toppling of Vorster and the fall from grace of Mulder – and thrust P.W. Botha into power.

In his book *Gods, Spies and Lies*, John Matisonn, the *Express*'s political editor at the time, speculates that the information, based on a secret report by Auditor General Gerald Barrie, was leaked to tip the balance of power that helped Botha become prime minister. It was the ultimate irony that it was the 'hated' English Press – particularly the *Rand Daily Mail* – that many staunch Nationalist Party members had trusted to share information that exposed one of the biggest scandals in both their party's and South Africa's political history.

References

Matisonn, John. 2015. *God, Spies and Lies*. Cape Town: Missing Ink.
Mervis, Joel. 1989. *The Fourth Estate*. Johannesburg: Jonathan Ball.
Rees, Mervyn & Day, Chris. 1980. *Muldergate*. Johannesburg: Macmillan.
Tyson, Harvey. 1993. *Editors Under Fire*. Johannesburg: Random House.
Winter, Gordon. 1981. *Inside BOSS*. London: A. Lane.

Secret Revealed: Nat English newspaper bankrolled by Info secret funds

Kitt Katzin, *Sunday Express*, 29 October 1978

The *Sunday Express* can dislose today that the Nationalist English daily newspaper, *The Citizen*, has been financed heavily by public money channeled through massive — and secret — public funds.

This means that taxpayers, without their knowledge, have been paying millions of rands — the total could top R12 million — towards the maintenance of an English-language Government-supporting newspaper.

Not even Parliament knows officially that it has been happening. In fact, it was specifically denied in Parliament only four months ago ...

Missing Millions

Mervyn Rees, *Rand Daily Mail*, 30 October 1978

The *Rand Daily Mail* can today reveal that not only were millions of rands in State funds secretly allocated by the Government to finance the Nationalist English daily newspaper, *The Citizen*, but that an amount of R13 million 'disappeared' en route to *The Citizen*.

Attempts by the Government to recover the R13 million over a period of more than a year failed — as the money had been put into private enterprise in a bid to help an ailing company, despite the fact that *The Citizen* was desperately short of funds ...

The *Mail* can also disclose today that the Department of Information was forced, because of the misappropriation, to raise a loan believed to consist of millions of rands in Switzerland to continue to finance *The Citizen* operation.

This means that not only have the taxpayers financed without their knowledge the losses incurred by *The Citizen* — estimated by the Nationalist Sunday newspaper *Rapport* to be R4 million a year — but they have also financed the secret amount of R13 million that disappeared into the private sector.

The *Mail* has been told that the loan raised in Switzerland was repaid earlier this year — with funds that had been allocated for another, equally vast and controversial secret project overseas in 1975.

According to the *Mail's* informants, the funding of *The Citizen* was so secretive that not even some prominent people associated with the newspaper were aware of the true source of the funds.

At least one of the Department of Information's 'front men', however, is known to have been paid an amount of R20,000 annually and tax-free for his covert services.

The *Mail*, however, also has information about the launching of the secret *Citizen* project and knows the identities of the central characters involved, as well as the code names that were used ... When one of the Cabinet Ministers made the discovery he was horrified that funds from his department were being used by the Department of Information for this purpose.

Info's U.S. Paper Bid

Mervyn Rees, *Rand Daily Mail*, 1 November 1978

Dr Eschel Rhoodie sent R10 million of the Department of Information's secret fund to the United States to buy the influential *Washington Star* newspaper.

The money was sent by Dr Rhoodie, then Secretary for Information, to Mr John McGoff, the right-wing American publisher who is a close friend of both Dr Rhoodie and Dr Connie Mulder, former Minister of Information.

Flop you paid for

Mervy Rees, *Rand Daily Mail*, 2 November 1978

More than R800,000 of Department of Information money was used by South African film magnate Mr Andre Pieterse to help finance *Golden Rendezvous*, an Alistair MacLean adventure film, starring Richard Harris, which was an international flop.

The *Rand Daily Mail* on Tuesday disclosed that the money was set aside out of secret funds for commercial film projects.

Mr Pieterse is a director of Film Trust (Pty) Ltd which had investments in *Golden Rendezvous*. Together with Pretoria advocate, Mr Retief van Rooyen, he was a director of Thor Communicators – a Department of Information 'front organisation'.

Mr Van Rooyen was the man who told the *Mail* he had given a special briefing on Department of Information projects to three Cabinet Ministers shortly before Mr P.W. Botha was elected Prime Minister ... The sources say he ploughed more than R800,000 of this money into *Golden Rendezvous*. The *Mail* can find no evidence that the money has been paid back to the Government.

It's all true!

Mervyn Rees, *Rand Daily Mail*, 3 November 1978

South Africa's biggest political bombshell burst yesterday when Mr Justice Anton Mostert made public startling evidence which has confirmed reports in the *Rand Daily Mail* and *Sunday Express* of massive misuse of public money through Department of Information secret funds.

Judge Mostert released evidence which shows beyond doubt that *The Citizen* newspaper was financed out of State funds.

And in evidence under oath, Mr Louis Luyt named the former Prime Minister, Mr Vorster, the Minister of Plural Relations, Dr Connie Mulder, and General Hendrick van den Bergh, former head of the Bureau of State Security, as key figures in the secret project to finance the newspaper.

A NATION SWINDLED

Rand Daily Mail, 6 December 1978

In a series of sensational findings and disclosures, the Erasmus Commission last night blasted former Department of Information and those involved with it.

The Commission, whose report will be debated by Parliament tomorrow, revealed 'irrefutable indications of large-scale irregularities and exploitation' of the Department's massive R64,000,000 secret fund, including possible theft and fraud 'through which the State suffered great losses'.

DEPT SPENT R32M TO FUND *THE CITIZEN*

Rand Daily Mail, 6 December 1978

Project Annemarie – the secret code name for the Department of Information's *The Citizen* newspaper project – absorbed almost half of the Department's R64,000,000 secret fund, the Erasmus Commission's report discloses.

The total amount spent on *The Citizen* up to the time of the appointment of the Commission in November was R31,907,732,73 – almost R5,000,000 more than the R27,000,000 the *Rand Daily Mail* estimated had been spent on the project. The amount has still not been recovered.

This amount included R220,000 from the secret fund to enable *The Citizen* to sponsor the 1976 Grand Prix.

One of the most sensational findings involving *The Citizen* was the Commission's conclusion that the newspaper was intended and had acted as a vehicle of National Party policy.

Rhoodie's mansion in Miami's millionaire row

Mervyn Rees, *Rand Daily Mail,* 9 December 1978

This is the lavish mansion at Miami Beach, Florida, which Dr Eschel Rhoodie bought out of his huge secret fund – made up mostly of money from the Defence Special Fund.

The *Rand Daily Mail* traced the R278,000 mansion after an exhaustive search which took it to Millionaire's Row on the island of La Gorce in Biscayne Bay.

This is the luxurious front view.

Behind are sweeping lawns, a large swimming pool and mooring for a sea-going yacht.

Beside the mansion is the famous La Gorce Golf Course.

The *Mail* can disclose today that Dr Rhoodie, the former Secretary for Information, bought the mansion out of the R10 million in secret fund money originally allocated to buy the *Washington Star*.

The house was purchased in 1975 in the name of Pinetree Drive Company, a company run by Mr Daniel J. McGoff, brother of Mr John McGoff, the Michigan publisher and president of the Panax Corporation, who tried to buy the *Washington Star*.

1983, SWAZILAND

Exposed: Parliament is opening today!

INTRODUCED BY MBONGENI MBINGO

It's September 1982 and King Sobhuza II is dead. He has ruled Swaziland from his birth in July 1899 and after 83 years he has outlived friends and foes alike and carved an economic, political and social legacy that is widely acknowledged and revered. Now departed, how would Swazis, who had known no other government, proceed? They could retain the executive monarchy, choose constitutional monarchy as in Lesotho, or go the way of Botswana to become a republic.

Shortly after independence in 1972, parliament had approved a motion calling on the king to dissolve the house and assume executive power. This ended a brief honeymoon with an accountable parliamentary system and set the stage for King Sobhuza to issue his infamous 1973 Decree, dissolving parliament, banning political parties, suspending human rights and sending his political rivals to prison. As executive monarch, he ruled with a prime minister and a council of ministers.

In 1978, the king introduced a new experiment in political representation that forbade political parties, so that candidates were elected on individual merit. This set the tone for a future parliament that would be a tame appendage of the government. However, King Sobhuza died in the last year of this experiment, leaving his royal Dlamini house to sort out myriad constitutional dilemmas. A mourning period ensued during which all key national activities, including parliament, were suspended.

Top of the sensitive urgent issues was finding a successor. King Sobhuza was reputed to have over 70 wives and hundreds of eligible sons. No less important was to manage the transition process that included formulating surrogate mechanisms for managing a modern government and at the same time re-enacting ancient succession rituals that had not been performed for almost a century. Under the circumstances, parliament was a problem that could not be solved by simply ignoring it. What to do with parliament was debated within the traditional royal circles, although it was considered an irritant at a time when the nation was dealing with pressing issues.

The stakes were high. Some careers, like that of Prime Minister Prince Mabandla, depended on parliament. Mabandla was a reformist who believed in strong parliamentary governance. He had made powerful enemies among the royalty by appointing South African judge Ismail Mahomed to chair a commission of inquiry to investigate corruption. The investigation had implicated several powerful royal courtiers, who were saved from arrest only by King Sobhuza's intervention. Now their knives were out for Mabandla. The prime minister also calculated that his political survival depended on a standing parliament to clarify the separation of powers. For that he needed a royal pronouncement through the Queen Regent's speech from the throne. But even he could not take the risk of suggesting an opening of parliament.

Similarly, among the members of parliament were politicians who saw the opportunity to revive their political ambitions. They needed parliament's suspension lifted. Civil society was quite pleased with the prime minister for his stance on corruption. They also supported a modernist outlook of governance that would not tightly be controlled within the reed barriers of the Lobamba Royal Kraal.

The fate of parliament was a smouldering coal within the confines of the royal family. No one could dare publicly speak about the issue. In the days after King Sobhuza's death, James Dhlamini, a maverick journalist of the *Times of Swaziland*, elected to spend his days digging around Lobamba where he had struck a rich seam of gold that he mined for stories. He interviewed several unnamed sources, among them senior leaders of the House of Parliament, suspected to include the Speaker himself.

On 24 February 1983, he broke the story of the date of the opening of parliament in a four-paragraph front page story, which gave only the facts and little indication of the significance of this leak.

Preparations for the opening of parliament normally take months. Yet here was an article suggesting an opening of parliament in the next few hours that no one had mentioned. The royal authorities exploded in fury. The reporter received a surprise summons for an urgent royal audience with the Queen Regent. After a brief interview, he was taken straight to the nearby Lobamba

Police Station and locked up under the infamous 1973 Decree that allowed the minister of justice to order anyone arrested and jailed for renewable terms of 60 days without trial.

Nonetheless, he had forced the elders to act. They scrambled. The prime minister quickly penned a speech for the throne to be read at the opening of parliament. It reaffirmed the separation of powers and the sanctity of the institution of parliament as a key accountability framework and outlined the responsibility of the prime minister and cabinet to parliament and the head of state. He took the precaution of pre-recording the speech so that it was read over radio at the same time as it was being delivered in parliament. Except that it was never read.

His detractors among the royal counsellors did not sit back. Unbeknown to the prime minister, they too penned their own speech for the throne, and were waiting at the steps of parliament. The Queen Regent, being a woman in mourning, was not allowed to address the public and sent an emissary. After the ceremonial welcome by a guard of honour, the emissary was taking his seat when powerful princes accosted him. They switched his speech and ordered him to read a different version, which subordinated the prime minister to the royal advisors.

Incensed, the prime minister ordered the culprits arrested and thrown in jail for sedition. They were there a few days before their comrades pressured the Queen Regent to release them and to focus her rage at the prime minister. The tide had turned. The prime minister learnt they were considering charging him with treason, and hopped over the border to become a refugee in neighbouring South Africa.

Dlamini's story had an enormous impact. The power play between royal factions and the government spilled into the public space. Students took to the streets, a groundswell that fermented the formation of the People's United Democratic Movement (PUDEMO), a political party that the government has since proscribed as a terrorist organisation.

The Queen Regent also did not last long. A few weeks later, she was replaced by the mother of the teenager, Prince Makhosetive, who had been selected to be king. Parliament resumed work and has not been disturbed to date. Civil society continued to pressure government and finally won the restoration of constitutional rule.

Parliament set to resume tomorrow

James Dhlamini, *Swaziland Times*, 24 February 1983

The Queen Regent will officially open the first session of parliament tomorrow.

She will address a joint sitting of both Houses and then declare the session open. After her departure, both houses will adjourn until Monday.

On Monday, the Prime Minister, Prince Mabandla, is scheduled to present a Bill with a certificate of urgency to be debated, but its title was not immediately available.

On Tuesday, the Minister of Finance, Mr James Simelane, will present his budget speech.

1983, MOZAMBIQUE

The Matola Raid: 'Why do grown men tell such lies?'

INTRODUCED BY PAUL FAUVET

Within a year of achieving independence in 1975, Mozambique found itself at war with the white supremacist regime headed by Ian Smith in what was then Rhodesia.

The Mozambican government, headed by President Samora Machel, implemented United Nations sanctions against Rhodesia from March 1976. This cut off the Smith regime's main routes to the sea, the Mozambican ports of Beira and Maputo. The Rhodesians hit back by sponsoring a rebel group which took the name Mozambique National Resistance (Renamo), whose leadership initially came from former agents of the Portuguese secret police, the PIDE, and deserters from Frelimo, the Mozambican liberation movement. A Renamo radio station was set up, 'Voz da Africa Livre' (Voice of Free Africa), which openly gave its address as a post box in a city still known as Salisbury.

Initially, Renamo was little more than an irregular unit in the Rhodesian armed forces. But after the Lancaster House agreement on Zimbabwean independence in 1979, the entire Renamo operation, including its radio station, was transferred to South Africa, where it came under the command of South African Military Intelligence.

Relations between Maputo and Pretoria were already strained, as the apartheid regime worked to undermine the Frelimo government economically. It cut South African traffic through the Maputo rail and port system, reduced the recruitment of Mozambicans to work on the South African gold mines, whose remittances were an important source of foreign exchange, and crucially ended the agreement that South Africa had with Portugal whereby the miners' deferred pay was received in gold at a preferential price. This was effectively a subsidy to the Portuguese colonial government, and South Africa terminated it shortly after Mozambican independence.

But after the fall of the Smith regime, Pretoria adopted military measures aimed at undermining or overthrowing Frelimo. Renamo was given training facilities in eastern Transvaal, and under South African direction it greatly expanded its operations within Mozambique, striking at the transport and electricity networks.

South Africa also occasionally used its own forces. On 30 January 1981, South African commandos slipped over the border and hit houses in the city of Matola, adjacent to Maputo, where 14 members of the ANC, and a passing Portuguese electrician who got in the way, were murdered. A 15th ANC member was kidnapped and later executed when he refused to collaborate.

As became habitual in its attacks on the Frontline States, Pretoria claimed that its targets were 'ANC terrorist bases'. Although those murdered were certainly members of the ANC's armed wing, Umkhonto weSizwe, the houses raided were simply where they were sleeping.

Pretoria also resorted to assassinations. The most notorious of these on Mozambican soil came on 17 August 1982, when a parcel bomb killed ANC and SACP militant Ruth First.

Matola was the target for a further South African raid, this time from the air, in 1983. This raid was at the centre of a major apartheid propaganda offensive, including saying that journalists were prevented from visiting the scene. I was one of those who quickly drove the 12 kilometres from Maputo to see the damage, arriving about 90 minutes after the raid. Nobody stopped us from wandering around Matola at will and seeing the places attacked – such as the Somopal factory and Francisco Morgadinho's house. Mozambique New Agency (AIM) photographer Anders Nilsson could take pictures of the dead Somopal workers before the bodies had been moved. The following is the piece I wrote for AIM, dissecting the raid.

Tell me lies about Matola

Paul Fauvet, Mozambique News Agency (AIM), June 1983

South African aircraft strafed and rocketed the city of Matola, which adjoins Maputo, on the morning of 23 May 1983, killing six people and wounding a further 39. The targets were all Mozambican and civilian, although the Pretoria regime claimed it had attacked 'ANC military bases'.

AIM journalists were among the first on the scene shortly after the air raid, and could see with their own eyes that the South African claims bore no relation to reality.

The men who run South Africa's propaganda services are noted neither for their truthfulness nor for their subtlety. Their justifications for South Africa's aggressive stance towards its neighbours are couched in the language of the school bully and the inveterate liar.

The propaganda operation mounted by the regime around the 23-May air raid against Matola was based on a tissue of falsehood. It is hard to find a single sentence on the subject spoken or written by any South African official that does not contain at least one crude lie.

Take the case of the 'warning' radioed to the Maputo airport control tower. On 24 May, the day after the raid, the Johannesburg *Rand Daily Mail* blasted this headline all over its front page: 'Mike Zero One calls Maputo and tells startled Air Control: KEEP OUT OF IT OR OUR PLANES WILL HIT BACK'.

The opening paragraph read: 'Minutes before SAAF Impalas launched a blitz attack on ANC bases in Maputo yesterday morning, an Air Force officer warned the Mozambique government not to interfere, or else action would be taken against it.'

The paper was quoting a press conference given in Pretoria by a South African Air Force spokesman, Brigadier Kobus Bosman. The *Mail* went on to quote the 'warning' in full: 'This is Mike Zero One. I have an important message for you. Tell your military HQ that aircraft are conducting operations in your area against the ANC. We have no quarrel with the Frelimo government and any interference with these aircraft will result in immediate retaliation.' Not surprisingly, the Maputo Tower was taken aback at this, and the message was repeated, adding the words, 'Do you understand?'

Many South African papers, both English and Afrikaans, gave prominence to this aspect of the raid, for it rang a pleasant bell in the memories of many South African whites. It recalled the Rhodesian Operation Green Leader against Zambia in 1979: during this operation a Rhodesian air force pilot had contacted the Lusaka airport control tower to tell the Zambians that ZAPU camps were being attacked and the Zambian air force should not interfere.

Operation Green Leader became the shared property of racist pride in Rhodesia and South Africa, in those months before the Smith regime finally bowed before guerrilla and international pressure at Lancaster House. It 'proved' the military superiority of the whites (the awkward fact that white Rhodesia still went down to defeat could always be blamed on 'Lord carry-on-selling-the-white-man-down-the-river-Carrington', as the then British Foreign Secretary was referred to in the correspondence columns of the South African government mouthpiece *The Citizen*).

But the South African echo of Green Leader at Matola was flawed in one crucial aspect. The Rhodesian warning had been serious — it was made before the raid started. But the South Africans worked on the novel principle of bomb first, warn later. For the Impalas and Mirages that raided Matola were already outside Mozambican airspace and returning to the Hoedspruit base in the Transvaal when the Maputo tower received the message from 'Mike Zero One'.

The raid was a quick hit-and-run affair, lasting from 07.22am until 07.25am. It was at 07.34am that Mozambican flight captain Antonio Ferreira da Silva asked for clearance from the control tower and took his LAM (Mozambique Airlines) Boeing 737 into the air on a routine flight to Beira. One minute later the message from 'Mike Zero One' broke into Captain da Silva's communications with the tower. The synchronised clock attached to the recorder which tapes all conversations between the tower and incoming and outgoing aircraft read 07.35am. The raid had finished a full 10 minutes previously.

The South African military also told journalists that they had originally planned the raid for 21 May, but had been forced to delay it 'because of bad weather'. In fact, the weather had been fine on 21 May. Displaying internationally verifiable weather charts, Dr Jaïme Peres of Mozambique's meteorological services told

The Matola Raid: 'Why do grown men tell such lies?'

local and foreign reporters a few days later that there had been 'good visibility' all the way from Pretoria to Maputo, and also along the coast from Durban to Xai-Xai, some 200 kilometres north of Maputo. Maybe the South Africans had delayed the raid — but if so, it certainly wasn't because of the weather.

Another lie to tumble from the lips of verbose South African officers was that a South African Airways (SAA) flight to Maputo, scheduled to arrive in the Mozambican capital at 08.20am, had not taken off from Johannesburg's Jan Smuts airport because the Mozambican government had ordered the closure of Mozambican airspace. The truth was that the order to close the country's airspace was not issued by the Council of Ministers until 08.20. Five minutes earlier, Hussene A. Hussene, Maputo's chief air traffic controller, received a phone call from Johannesburg saying that the SAA plane had not taken off because of a 'technical fault'. At 09.00 a telex was received from Johannesburg repeating the same story. The telex read: 'Delay due technical.' Obviously the South African military had told SAA not to fly to Maputo that day, and a few hours later tried to present the disruption to flight timetables as being due to Mozambican actions.

The biggest lie of all, of course, was the supposed justification for the raid. It was against 'ANC bases'. According to the South African spokesmen, six of these had been hit, and in the process a Mozambican missile base had been 'neutralised'.

Uncritically, the South African press splashed these claims across their front pages. A *Rand Daily Mail* picture showed the grinning Brigadier Bosman standing before a model of Matola showing one of the alleged bases. Mozambicans who saw that picture instantly recognised the target as the house of Francisco Morgadinho. Morgadinho has nothing to do with the ANC — he is the director of Intermark, Mozambique's state advertising company. He and his wife have lived in their Matola home since 1969. That didn't stop the South Africans from pumping rockets into it.

In reality, the targets hit were a jam factory and its crèche, about 14 private houses (three of which had been occupied by South African refugees in the past), one reed hut by the banks of the Matola River and two electricity pylons. As the week passed, dozens of journalists visited the sites attacked.

The South Africans were not budging from their story, however. They claimed what had been hit were 'two logistical headquarters responsible for supplying weapons and explosives to terrorists', an ANC 'command headquarters', a transit facility referred to as 'Main Camp', and houses where 'terrorism' in urban and rural Transvaal was planned.

A convincing number of bodies was needed to go with such an impressive list of targets – and clearly the number of victims had to be greater than the number of deaths caused by the ANC's car bomb at the South African Air Force HQ in Pretoria the previous Friday. So the figure of 64 was dreamed off the top of some South African official's head. It was neatly broken down into 41 'ANC terrorists', 17 'Frelimo soldiers' and six civilians. Faithfully, the South African press reported all of this, not stopping to ask how the pilots of fast flying aircraft who were over Matola for no more than three minutes could have given such an exact body count.

In fact, there were six fatalities, three workers at the Somopal jam factory, one six-year-old child, one Mozambican soldier, and one South African refugee (killed almost by accident as he was washing a car in a Matola street).

The South Africans did try to explain the discrepancy between their version of the raid and what reporters in Matola saw. Quoted in the *Rand Daily Mail* of 25 May, a South African military statement claimed it was 'an obvious fact' that the area of the raid had been cordoned off by the Mozambicans.

The South African ambassador in London, Marais Steyn, gave an interview to the BBC in which he claimed: 'We've attacked terrorist bases outside South Africa before, and after these attacks the host countries' actions have followed a definite pattern. That pattern is to wait some hours before they take reporters into the area; often only near the area, after they have manipulated the evidence, removed certain bodies and done other things.'

Sergio Vieira, then Mozambique's Agriculture Minister, replied to Steyn. Two days after the raid, he told a rally at the damaged factory what Steyn had said. Gasps of disbelief arose

The Matola Raid: 'Why do grown men tell such lies?'

from the crowd as he translated Steyn's claim that their factory was a military base. 'Why do grown men tell such lies?' he asked.

And what other raids was Steyn referring to? The attacks into Angola, Lesotho and Mozambique have all been different in nature, sharing only a common murderous quality. In Maputo on 23 May nobody escorted journalists to Matola. They simply got into their cars and drove there, unaccompanied. The first journalists (from Mozambican and western media) were on the spot within an hour of the raid.

So what Steyn wishes us to believe is that within that hour Mozambican forces managed to disguise a military installation as a jam factory, replacing guns with piles of grapefruit, bombs with packing cases, artillery with lines of industrial machinery, while at the same time hiding not only 58 corpses but all traces of blood.

In the days following the raid, dozens of foreign reporters, based in South Africa, Zimbabwe and Kenya, visited Matola. They did not see any 'ANC bases', any 'neutralised' missile sites, nor any sign of the extra 58 corpses claimed by the South Africans, and nor did the diplomats who toured Matola the afternoon following the attack.

The South Africans also claimed, repeatedly, that there had been no resistance to the Matola raid, that no Mozambican forces had opened fire. This claim serves several purposes. It implies that the 'warning' was successful, that Mozambican soldiers are cowardly or incompetent or both, and that the South African Air Force is more or less invincible, able to strike at neighbouring states with impunity.

In fact, Mozambique's defence forces did respond. In the streets of Matola militiamen unslung their rifles and took potshots at the enemy planes. This may not have been militarily effective, but it did show a fairly high degree of morale and a willingness to fight back. More importantly, anti-aircraft batteries opened fire at three places. According to both the Ministry of Defence and civilian eye-witnesses, two of the Impalas tried to attack the Matola oil refinery, but were driven away by anti-aircraft fire. Planes that overflew the Radio Mozambique transmitters in Matola were also fired on. The two Mirages that swooped on the bridge over the Matola River also came under fire, and it is likely that this prompt response saved the bridge (although it cost one of the defending soldiers his life).

It is true that none of the attacking planes was brought down (although eye witnesses said they saw smoke trailing from two of the planes, and anti-aircraft captain Ilidio Ombe told Mozambican television viewers that optical instruments indicated that at least some of the planes had been hit). The story might have been different had Mozambique used all its defences. But there was a problem: the attack coincided with the arrival of a Mozambique Airlines DC10 from Paris. This was no coincidence: the South Africans had timed the raid carefully. Mozambique may have been inhibited from using its most effective defence, for fear that the missiles might home in on the largest object in the sky — the DC10 coming in to land.

The Matola raid was widely billed as 'retaliation' for an ANC car bomb in Pretoria. Yet the bomb was in no way the responsibility of Mozambique. ANC members are quite capable of undertaking military action without assistance from Mozambique.

Apartheid mythology is that South Africa is a healthy 'evolving' society, by and large quite a peaceful place, disrupted by a handful of 'terrorists' from outside the country. This is the mythology of every regime threatened by its own people. The headline in the *Johannesburg Star* on the Pretoria bomb unintentionally gave the game away. 'Oh God! It was like war' was the *Star*'s headline. Precisely. It is war — and the war was declared by the apartheid regime over 20 years ago, with the Sharpeville massacre and the subsequent outlawing of the ANC.

1983–87, ZIMBABWE

Robert Mugabe's 'moment of madness'

INTRODUCED BY ANDREW MELDRUM

Of all the stains on Robert Mugabe's tumultuous 37-year rule of Zimbabwe, the bloodiest, most indelible was the Gukurahundi, or what many call the Matabeleland Massacres. The Gukurahundi, derived from a Shona word for 'the early rains that blow away the chaff', happened from 1983 through 1987 when the Zimbabwe National Army's Fifth Brigade rampaged through the south-western provinces of Matabeleland North and South and parts of Midlands province and attacked rural Ndebele communities, killing an estimated 10,000 to 20,000 civilians.

The residents of rural villages were rounded up and forced to attend all-night rallies for Mugabe's ruling party, Zimbabwe African National Union – Patriotic Front (ZANU-PF). Community leaders were beaten and sometimes killed in front of the gatherings. Men, young and old, were forced to dig graves, then shot and buried in them. Surviving community members were made to dance on top of the fresh graves. Some families were pushed into huts that were set on fire and they either burned to death or were shot dead when they tried to escape. The troops spread terror, destruction and death across the home area of Zimbabwe's Ndebele ethnic minority, which makes up about 20 per cent of the country's population.

The Fifth Brigade consisted of 3,000 troops, virtually all Shona speakers. The brigade had received special counter-insurgency training by North Korean advisors and were known as Mugabe's elite praetorian guard, directly answerable to his office. Their arms, equipment and uniforms were different from the rest of the army, including distinctive red berets. With the prolonged, deadly brutality of the Matabeleland campaigns, the Fifth Brigade was trying to stamp out rural support for anti-government rebels who had carried out a series of violent protests and killings.

Peace and stability flourished throughout the rest of Zimbabwe and in the capital, Harare, in the 1980s, so it was hard to comprehend that Matabeleland was in the grip of the horrors of the Gukurahundi.

Journalists, both Zimbabwean and foreign, played a significant role in exposing the killings and bringing the atrocities to the attention of the world. Despite the widespread violence and large number of people affected, it was not an easy story to uncover. The government denied the army's abuses and placed a curfew over the area, curbing travel by civilians and making it difficult and dangerous for journalists to investigate. The state-controlled media, comprising all Zimbabwe's television and radio broadcasters, the daily newspapers and the national news agency, dismissed the reports of massacres as fabrications. Those who spoke out about the killings were excoriated by government officials. Some foreign journalists who reported on the killings were expelled.

Within days of the Fifth Brigade being deployed into Matabeleland in January 1983, reports of murders began to surface. Early accounts of the mass killings came from the Bulawayo *Chronicle* and local magazines also reported some incidents. Opposition leader Joshua Nkomo and members of his Zimbabwe African People's Union (ZAPU) party, who represented Matabeleland, spoke out in parliament. 'People are daily being killed like chickens,' said William Kona, a ZAPU MP, on 26 January 1983.

Nick Worrall, the correspondent for *The Guardian*, was one of the first of the international media to report on Gukurahundi, publishing stories in early February 1983. By the end of March, Worrall had been thrown out of Zimbabwe.

I was a young, idealistic American journalist, who had come to report about the transformation of the country from white minority-ruled Rhodesia to majority-ruled Zimbabwe. I was committed to illustrating how Zimbabwe was a beacon of multi-racial democracy showing South Africa the way out of apartheid. I had not anticipated reporting on atrocities perpetrated by Mugabe's army against the minority Ndebele people, but the insistent accounts of the killings convinced me to investigate.

The stories from individuals were horrific, but difficult to verify. It was also hard to confirm the bigger picture, that the incidents reported were part of a larger campaign. The Catholic church was an important resource because of its network of churches, mission schools and medical clinics across Matabeleland and its commitment to human rights in the country.

In mid-February 1983, I went to Bulawayo with three other journalists.

A Zimbabwean Catholic priest took us to a church and told us that hundreds of people had fled Matabeleland North for Bulawayo, hoping that they would find safety in the city, the provincial capital. He led us to the basement and as we went down the stairs we saw the space was filled with scores of people. We asked who would speak to us on the record about the killings and virtually all raised their hands. They wanted their stories to be told.

We four journalists divided up and each interviewed between 10 and 20 people, taking down names, ages, places, dates and the names of those killed. Each interview was harrowing as people told of family members and neighbours being murdered by the Fifth Brigade. The people's faces showed the shock of fresh trauma, with some speaking of killings just days earlier. After nearly two hours, we had notebooks full of accounts and together we had the names of nearly 100 people who had been killed, according to the eyewitnesses.

The next morning we drove into the cordoned off area of Matabeleland North on the main road to Victoria Falls. We stopped at a Catholic hospital where the wards were full of people with severe burns, broken bones, bullet wounds and stabbings. The staff showed us people sleeping outside, behind the hospital, who were also receiving treatment. As we were interviewing them, a doctor rushed in, saying that army troops had arrived and were searching for us. The four of us hid in a closet and held our breaths as we heard the heavy boot steps through the wards. They left and we departed quickly afterwards.

We were convinced that the killings were being carried out on a massive scale across the Matabeleland North province. Soon our dispatches were being published in the *Washington Post*, the *Philadelphia Inquirer*, Agence France-Presse and other media outlets.

The Catholic bishop of Bulawayo, Henry Karlen, compiled a series of accounts of atrocities in Matabeleland and travelled to Harare to deliver the report to Mugabe, who agreed to investigate. In April 1983 the army lifted the curfew it had imposed over a large part of Matabeleland North and the reports of killings ebbed. It seemed that the bishop's meeting and the press reports persuaded Mugabe to pull back the Fifth Brigade.

But in January 1984 there was a second wave. This time the army troops concentrated on Matabeleland South where a curfew was imposed. Hundreds of residents were rounded up and held in mass detention centres. In addition to the violence that occurred behind the curtain of the curfew, the army banned food deliveries to the province, on the grounds that food was going to anti-government rebels. Zimbabwe was in the grip of a three-year drought and the peasant farmers of semi-arid Matabeleland were some of the worst affected.

The troops manned roadblocks and seized bags of the staple maize meal. The ban on food meant that families, villages and entire districts became desperately hungry. Journalists were barred from going in.

Despite the ban, I managed to drive into the area and saw soldiers stopping vehicles and confiscating food. I spoke to mission priests who told of the hunger and the arrests.

Zimbabwean journalist Peter Godwin wrote dramatic stories for Britain's *Sunday Times*, describing how he snuck into Matabeleland South disguised as a priest and discovered a mine shaft where bodies had been dumped. Godwin's stories caused a sensation and captured international attention on the violence.

The brigade's campaigns in 1983 and 1984 were the most severe and deadly but the military continued to impose a harsh repression over the Matabeleland region through 1987.

The Gukurahundi came after 150 years of rivalry between the Shona and Ndebele peoples. The antagonism between the two ethnic groups was evident in the nationalist struggle against white-minority Rhodesian rule. Ndebele leader Nkomo and his ZAPU movement received support from the Soviet Union and its military wing was based in Zambia to the north. Mugabe's ZANU-PF got Chinese support and was based in Mozambique to the east. In the 1980 elections that brought Zimbabwe to independence, Mugabe and ZANU-PF won the support of the country's Shona majority while Nkomo and ZAPU were confined to about 20 per cent of the vote. Mugabe brought Nkomo and ZAPU into an uneasy alliance in 1980, but Nkomo balked at Mugabe's moves to create a one-party state. This set off a chain of events that led to the Gukurahundi.

In February 1982 Mugabe's then security minister Emmerson Mnangagwa announced the discovery of large arms caches that had been hidden by Nkomo's military wing to be used against Mugabe's government. Nkomo and two other members of his party were sacked from their Cabinet positions. Top leaders of Nkomo's military wing were arrested and charged with treason.

Unhappy to see Nkomo fired from government and their military leaders jailed, several thousand members of Nkomo's military wing deserted from the army. Some violently protested against the Mugabe government. Six foreign tourists were kidnapped and killed, some 20 white farmers in the Matabeleland area were shot dead. In response to this sporadic anti-government violence, the Fifth Brigade was sent in to Matabeleland. The brutality against the civilian population was to eradicate local support for the rebels, called dissidents by the Mugabe government.

Historian Stuart Doran, in his book *Kingdom, Power, Glory: Mugabe, ZANU and the Quest For Supremacy 1960–1987*, makes a compelling argument that the Gukurahundi was an attempt by Mugabe to dismantle support for Nkomo and ZAPU in order to create a one-party state.

The bloody campaigns of 1983 and 1984 did little to change the political allegiance of Matabeleland's people who voted solidly for Nkomo and ZAPU in the 1985 elections. The troubles in Matabeleland did not end until December 1987 when Mugabe and Nkomo signed the Unity Accord merging the two parties and bringing Nkomo back into the government.

Mugabe commissioned an investigation into the Matabeleland killings, chaired by Simplisius Chihambakwe, but the report was never made public. To right that omission an independent investigation was commissioned by two Zimbabwean non-governmental organisations, the Legal Resources Foundation and the Catholic Commission for Justice and Peace. 'Breaking the silence: A report on the disturbances in Matabeleland and the Midlands' was published in 1997. The authoritative investigation drew on more than 1,000 interviews and many documents to piece together an account of the abuses.

The Gukurahundi has had a lasting impact in Zimbabwe. More than 35 years later it still has a bitter influence on Zimbabwe's political life and ethnic relations. Those at the head of the chain of command have not been held to account. When Emmerson Mnangagwa succeeded Mugabe as Zimbabwe's president in November 2017, he was questioned about his role in the Gukurahundi, as the country's security minister during the deadly campaigns. He refused to accept responsibility and avoided committing to a new investigation, saying that old wounds should not be re-opened. Perence Shiri, the head of the Fifth Brigade during the killings, rose in power to become the head of Zimbabwe's air force and Mnangagwa appointed him the minister of agriculture. Robert Mugabe has never accepted responsibility or apologised for the killings, calling them a 'moment of madness.'

Mugabe troops leave trail of death

Nick Worrall, *The Guardian* (London), 2 February 1983

I watched yesterday as the body of school teacher Austin Ngwenya was buried in Bulawayo. Relatives said that he was bayoneted and shot dead on Tuesday last week by soldiers of the Fifth Brigade.

Later, at the village of Fingo, in a poor peasant farming area 30 miles east of this city, I was shown the fresh graves of three other young men, all murdered, their relatives say, by fifth brigade troops.

These are among the perhaps dozens who have been killed by this special army unit, recruited from the northern trial area of Mashinaland and trained by North Korean instructors in isolation from the rest of the regular army, which went through training schemes managed by Commonwealth officers.

Ominous indications that the death toll may be higher still are provided by alleged 'death lists' which Zapu officials here say have come into their possession. One such list I was shown contained 38 names, including that of a local councillor.

Allegations made last week by the Zapu leader, Mr Joshua Nkomo, that the brigade was out of control were dismissed at the time by the Government as rubbish.

Yet yesterday a stream of people was reported to be fleeing the soldiers, flooding to Bulawayo from rural areas ... Well-informed sources here yesterday said that Mr Gumede, who wore dark glasses for his TV appearance, had been attacked by soldiers who burst into his house last week. He was severely beaten and is now preparing a report for Mr Mugabe. He refused to make any public comment.

... In each case, bereaved relatives named the killers as men of the Shona-speaking fifth army brigade, which was formed in 1981. The brigade has acquired a reputation for poor discipline and linked politically to the majority Zanu (PF) party.

Part of the brigade, possibly up to 2,000 men, was deployed in Matebeleland during last month to bolster a combined police-army anti-dissident force of about 5,000. The unit, sources said, was sent at a time when desertions of Ndebele soldiers from the army had reached worrying proportions and when dissident activity was on the increase.

People questioned in Bulawayo and Fino, however, said they had no idea why the unit operated in Mbembezi district for more than a week except to 'harass' the population for tribal and political reasons. No dissident activity has been reported there, nor does the open rocky terrain provide suitable cover for them.

... The ruthlessness of this new phase of the anti-dissident operations is shown by lists of people missing, people believed killed and people confirmed killed by the soldiers.

The list I was shown by a Zapu official had been compiled by a man who had fled from the town of Tsholotsho, north of Bulawayo, the headquarters of the security forces' operation. Another list names seven women killed in Nkai Forest ...

A young man I gave a lift to into Bulawayo said he was moving to Harare before everybody in his village was killed ...

In a statement last Friday, the Minister of State for Defence, who is in charge of the operation in Matebeleland, Mr Sydney Sekeramayi, said it would be 'regrettable' if innocent people were caught in crossfire between dissidents and security forces.

No one at Fingo yesterday was aware of any crossfire.

'Their targets are Zapu officials, teachers, nurses and young men suspected of fighting with Zipra (the former Zapu military wing) during the war,' said an old man ...

The fifth column that is shaking Zimbabwe

Nick Worrall, *The Guardian* (London), 3 February 1983

The killing of civilians by soldiers of Zimbabwe's fifth army brigade has revealed a considerable dilemma facing Prime Minister Robert Mugabe in tackling the problem of dissident violence which has terrorised Matebeleland for the past year.

On one hand Mr Mugabe and his security advisers believe that only military force can quell the actions of gunmen who have kidnapped, killed and violently robbed indiscriminately in the province.

On the other, the military force he employs must be loyal to the Zimbabwe government and Mr Mugabe's majority Zanu (PF) party.

At the same time they must be disciplined and trusted not to violate a sensitive tribal and political situation by alienating the Matebeleland people — almost one-fifth of the country's seven million — in the process of eliminating the dissidents, many of whose aims are no more than banditry.

Unfortunately, in less than two weeks after the fifth brigade was deployed in rural parts of the province, that trust appears to have been violated in a grim and brutal manner. Many in Matebeleland believe it is an outcome that might have been foreseen.

When a meeting of white farmers at Nyamandhlovu ... (was told) this brigade was being moved, the news was received with stunned silence ... The farmers' apprehension arose out of the reputation for indiscipline the brigade has earned — right or wrongly — since it was formed — under a 10-man North Korean military training team in late 1981 ...

The 5,000 men of the brigade were dubbed by a newspaper '*gukurahundi*' — a Shona expression which roughly means 'the winds that blow away the chaff' ...

Hundreds Reported Killed in Attacks by Zimbabwean Troops

Jay Ross, *Washington Post*, 26 February 1983

Zimbabwean soldiers have killed hundreds of civilians in the past month in an offensive against dissidents in the southwestern part of the country ... The North Korean-trained 5 Brigade, as it sweeps through rural districts, has created a climate of fear worse than what the people experienced during the country's bloody war for independence, veterans say.

At least five independent reports by church groups and relief workers have been sent to the government detailing killings, rapes and beatings by the 5,000-man brigade, composed mainly of troops from Prime Minister Robert Mugabe's former guerrilla army.

... the reports cite reliable estimates totaling more than 1,000 civilians killed in Matebeleland Province, the stronghold of opposition leader Joshua Nkomo's minority Ndebele tribe.

Mugabe told a rally last week that '5 Brigade would not leave Matebeleland until every dissident has been routed' ...

Nkomo denies any link with the rebels ... Military units and police have been excluded from the area during the 5 Brigade operations, more than 100 miles away from the area toured by the Zimbabwean press today.

The government has clamped a dusk-to-dawn curfew on most of the area between Bulawayo and Victoria Falls. Only government and military vehicles are allowed to enter ...

Zimbabwe curfew 'cuts off food to drought-hit areas'

Andrew Meldrum, *The Guardian* (London), 8 March 1984

The month-old army curfew in southern Matebeleland has cut off almost all food supplies to the drought-stricken area, bringing hunger to the estimated 450,000 people there, according to Church and international aid officials here.

The army is also carrying out a campaign of harassment of young people to dissuade them from helping the area's anti-government dissidents, villagers who have fled the curfew area claim.

Tensions and bitterness has grown as, on one side, accounts of army brutality come in from the curfew area and, on the other, atrocities by dissidents are reported. Last week, an opposition MP, Mr Sikwali Moyo, said he was badly beaten by soldiers for representing Mr Joshua Nkomo's Zapu party.

... 'Both the government troops and the dissidents have perpetrated atrocities.'

After the worst drought since the turn of the century, Matebeleland people rely on shops for food. The result of the curfew is that many have gone hungry.

One clergyman said people were eating grass.

An interdenominational group of Bulawayo churches sent a letter to the Prime Minister, Mr Robert Mugabe, warning of imminent widespread starvation and calling for an end to the hunger policy towards civilians. The Church leaders say they have received no response.

The new Minister of Home Affairs, Mr Simbi Mubako, said in

Parliament last month that 'food is flowing easily' into the curfew area. 'They (the Government) know that is not true,' said a pastor here. 'They know what's going on and they are not going to stop it.'

Zimbabwe massacre bodies found in mine

Peter Godwin, *Sunday Times* (London), 15 April 1984

A disused mine shaft, five miles from a Zimbabwean army camp in southern Matebeleland, has been used for the disposal of bodies in a three-month 'clean-up' operation against 'dissidents' who oppose the government of the prime minister, Robert Mugabe ... every night for 'many weeks' trucks arrived at the shaft from the direction of the army camp at Balaghwe. Corpses were unloaded and thrown in. Some bodies got snagged on cross-supports inside the interior. After each night's dumping, the locals say, explosives were used to cover the bodies with debris ...

Stench of death everywhere in Mugabe's siege of Matebeleland

Peter Godwin, *Sunday Times*, 15 April 1984, London

The heavily armed soldiers at the roadblock, five miles south of the city of Bulawayo, seemed unsure. They checked my identification thoroughly and after a brief discussion waved me through — the first journalist to enter southern Matebeleland after nine weeks of strict curfew ... The curfew was 'relaxed' last week on orders from the minister of state security in Harare ... Shops and stores have been allowed to open normally, and traffic has been permitted to flow in and out of the curfew zone. However, the minister then appeared to change his mind. In a second statement, he stressed that the dusk-to-dawn curfew remained in force and that no journalist would be allowed into southern Matebeleland for the time being. Between statements, I slipped into the area ...

1986, MOZAMBIQUE

The death of Samora Machel

INTRODUCED BY PAUL FAUVET

Mozambique's first president, Samora Machel, died on 19 October 1986 when his plane, a Soviet Tupolev 134, crashed into a hillside at Mbuzini, just inside South Africa. He was returning to Maputo from a summit held in Mbala, Zambia.

If there was a decisive date in the crisis leading to Machel's death it was 11 September 1986, when Machel flew to Malawi to confront the ageing dictator Hastings Banda of the possible consequences of his continuing support for the apartheid regime's surrogate army in Mozambique, the Mozambique National Resistance (Renamo).

When Banda proved uncooperative, Machel openly threatened his regime. On his return, he told reporters 'the South African military use Malawian territory to destabilise, to destroy the People's Republic of Mozambique'. In response, the Mozambican government 'will put missiles all along the Malawian border. Secondly, we will close Malawi's route through Mozambique to Zimbabwe and South Africa. Let them find some other route.'

Following these threats to the only African government allied to South Africa, the noises from Pretoria took on an increasingly harsh and belligerent tone. A landmine explosion in the Kangwane Bantustan on 6 October was the pretext for South African defence minister, Magnus Malan, to menace Machel personally.

Malan invoked the 1984 Nkomati non-aggression pact between South Africa and Mozambique, a pact which his government had repeatedly violated through its continued support for Renamo. 'The Nkomati Accord and landlines cannot exist side by side,' said Malan. 'If President Machel chooses landmines, South Africa will react accordingly ... If he chooses terrorism and revolution, he will clash head on with South Africa.'

South African military spokesmen fulminated that African National

Congress and South African Communist Party (SACP) leader Joe Slovo had been seen in Maputo with high-ranking government officials. (This was not a startling intelligence discovery – Machel and Slovo had, very publicly, stood shoulder to shoulder in March 1986 at the Maputo funeral of SACP General Secretary Moses Mabhida.)

The Frontline States held an emergency summit in Maputo on 12 October at which they declared that 'South Africa has already embarked on the road of fascism and of war against the peoples of southern Africa'. The summit backed Machel's tough stance against Malawi, denouncing Banda's regime for its 'complicity in the terrorist campaign against Mozambique'.

The last time he held an off-the-record briefing with Mozambican journalists, on 11 October, Machel did not hide his loathing of Banda and of Mobutu Sese Seko of Zaire. Carlos Cardoso, then the director of the Mozambique News Agency (AIM), was deeply worried by the deteriorating situation, and had a grim foreboding. He told Machel: 'They are going to try to kill you.' Machel replied that there had already been failed assassination plots. 'I am in their way,' he said. 'I have not sold out to anyone. My hands are clean.'

The strategy of the front line states was to try to separate Malawi and Zaire from Pretoria. On 19 October, Machel flew to Mbala in Zambia where he, and the Zambian and Angolan presidents, Kenneth Kaunda and Jose Eduardo dos Santos, planned to confront Mobutu over Zairean support for Unita, the rebel movement boosted by South African and US support.

Machel's plane never returned to Maputo. It was widely suspected that the plane crash was no accident, and that the South African military had planted a fake navigational beacon, luring the plane off course.

Samora Machel's death and South African radar

Paul Fauvet, AIM, December 1986

One major unanswered question concerning the crash of President Samora Machel's Tupolev 134 on 19 October 1986 is why South African air traffic control did not warn the pilot that he was off course and in danger of entering South African airspace.

The plane had been tracked on South African radar for hundreds of kilometres. According to the South African paper *Business Day* of 21 October, 'a top government source said "our guys had the plane on their radar, even when it was still over Zimbabwe"'.

Yet no warning was given to the doomed Tupolev, even as it headed for a militarily sensitive area. For the corner of the eastern Transvaal where the crash took place, near the junction of the Mozambican, Swazi and South African borders, is a total air exclusion zone.

It is also where at least two landmines had exploded in the previous fortnight, and military garrisons in the region had been strengthened in the days immediately preceding the crash.

Only a week after the disaster did the South African press address the problem of the radar. 'South African monitors paid little heed to Machel flight', announced a headline in the *Sunday Star* of 26 October. According to this story, when the plane disappeared from the radar screens, officials 'thought nothing of it', since it was not in South African airspace.

But, if they thought it was so unimportant, why had the radar been following it from Zimbabwe? The radars must also have detected, while it was still well inside Mozambique, that the plane's course was taking it into South Africa.

On 1 November, South African Foreign Minister Roelof Botha tried to explain away the behaviour of the South African radar operators in a television interview on the programme *Good Morning, South Africa*. According to Botha, the flight 'just disappeared from the screen. No-one monitoring that radar could or would have imagined that there was anything strange about it.'

'Every radar station has what we call a horizon beyond which it cannot see any object,' said Botha. 'You cannot see an aircraft once it has passed over a mountain, for instance, and is on the other side.'

'There are quite a number of flights in that vicinity of the Kruger Park and so on,' he continued. So the radar operators 'must be seeing virtually all the flights fading or disappearing at one stage or another'.

In this interview Botha tried to make out that there is heavy air traffic down the Mozambique/South Africa border at 21.00 on a Sunday night (in fact, as far as is known, the Tupolev was the only flight in the area that night), and that the radar lost the presidential plane when it disappeared behind a hill.

In other words, the Foreign Minister would like us to believe that South African radar is rather primitive and inefficient. In reality, South Africa possesses a highly sophisticated integrated military and civilian computer-assisted radar system, whose two main purposes are to assist in South African air strikes into neighbouring countries and to detect any plane entering South African airspace.

A good radar system needs to be placed high up, so that it can 'look' down to avoid the problem of planes hiding behind hills. Several radar stations located a good distance from one another will also make it difficult for any plane, whether accidentally or by design, to use the landscape to 'disappear' from radar vision.

This is, naturally, the kind of system we find in South Africa. Furthermore, it is not very secret. The South African papers themselves have written openly about it.

One of the main radar installations is at Mariepskop, 2,000 metres up, on the edge of the Drakensberg mountains. This is what the Johannesburg *Star* of 8 February 1975 had to say about this installation: 'Only metres away from where the Drakensberg escarpment falls to the Lowveld, the big scanner whirls silently around. It can pick up most aircraft movements from a large chunk of Botswana in the west, to Rhodesia in the north, to southern Mozambique and Natal in the east. Height finders are positioned nearby. They can calculate the height of any aircraft picked up by the scanner.'

Mariepskop is an early warning station, designed to give the alert against 'hostile aircraft approaching South Africa from over her borders'.

'All information gathered by the softly sweeping scanner — aircraft appear as tiny pinpricks of light on the screens — can be fed in computer form to the headquarters of South Africa's radar defence system at Devon. Virtually instant computer feedback from Devon can supply Mariepskop with the information needed to identify an aircraft.

'Besides Devon and Mariepskop, there are two other stations in the northern radar system, covering each other. The zones covered by the four stations overlap so each base can see the one next door.'

In other words, it should have been quite impossible for the presidential Tupolev to escape radar surveillance.

These radar defences are no joke: according to the *Star* of 29 November 1975, the Devon computer centre is 'buried under reinforced concrete capable of withstanding a ten kiloton nuclear explosion'.

The computers at Devon try to work out whether any intruding aircraft is 'friend or foe'. If they think it may be hostile, 'the controllers at Devon can call on a whole range of defences, including Mirages and other jet fighters, surface-to-air missiles and anti-aircraft cannon'.

This was what the South African radar system was like over a decade ago. Now it is even more sophisticated, particularly through South Africa's acquisition of the Plessey AR-3D computerised radar system, which was integrated into its air defences in 1982 ...

The 1979 Defence White Paper also made it clear that there were to be no 'holes' in the radar system. It said, 'The South African Air Force is constantly carrying out air reconnaissance. Various sensors are used in this process to obtain maximum information. Reconnaissance systems are constantly being modernised in order to keep abreast of operational requirements.'

Thus, from documents that are public knowledge, it is evident that South Africa can keep its entire border area under 24-hour radar surveillance, and the chance of any aircraft evading this is vanishingly small.

The conclusion to be drawn is that the Tupolev was on the radar screens up until the moment of its crash. The radar operators knew it was off course, knew it was entering South African airspace, knew the Libombos mountains posed a serious threat to the aircraft, and yet no warning was given no preventive action was taken.

The computer centre at Devon doubtless identified the plane

as Samora Machel's Tupolev. After all, there was nothing secret about the President's trip to Zambia, and the radars would have followed its journey from Maputo to Zambia earlier in the day. No other plane was expected along that route.

The South African authorities knew whose plane it was, they knew exactly when and where it crashed – and yet they did not inform the Mozambican authorities for another ten and a half hours. The first message was sent to Maputo at 06.50 the following morning.

1987, Namibia

Exposing military atrocities

Introduced by Gwen Lister

The years under apartheid were tough for journalists of *The Namibian* newspaper, which was founded in 1985. There were always consequences for much of our investigative reporting which then had to do mainly with exposing the dirty tricks and atrocities perpetrated by the South African colonial regime. These included bans, attacks on our offices, arrests of journalists and constant death threats and harassment.

It was difficult to report many of the acts of brutality by security forces, due to constant denials on the part of either the South African Defence Force (SADF) or police that they were responsible for gross human rights violations of civilians, especially those living in the war-torn north of the country bordering Angola, then known as Ovamboland to the locals or as the 'operational area' to the military occupiers.

For months we had claimed that on many occasions when the SADF killed insurgents of the Peoples' Liberation Army of Namibia (PLAN), fighting to free then South West Africa, they strapped the bodies to the sides of their Casspir armoured vehicles and paraded them through the towns and villages to inspire fear and to deter the local population from joining Swapo or giving support to their fighters who came across the border.

Again, the military denied they were responsible for any such actions. Finally, we were vindicated thanks to the bravery and foresight of a young activist from the north named Nico Kaiyamo. He sent us a Polaroid photograph he'd taken clandestinely of the macabre spectacle.

With the photograph already in our possession, and without telling them we had photographic evidence of the atrocity, we'd again approached police spokesperson Kierie du Rand for comment.

Another vehement denial was the response.

Our front page the next day was headlined 'Parade of death', and it featured the photograph prominently displayed, along with the police disclaimer. We did not at the time name the young man who'd taken the photograph at risk of his life because of the inevitable attrition that would ensue for him and his family.

The day after publication, that edition was banned by the Publications Control Board in Pretoria, but it had already sold out and proof had gone out into the world of the cruelties meted out to civilians under the jackboot of apartheid.

Parade of Death: Police and army deny public display of dead Swapo soldiers

The Namibian, 16 January 1987

Both the police and army have denied liability for an incident in northern Namibia on December 29 last year at midday, when the bodies of dead insurgents were paraded to locals at Ondobe near Oshikango, by members of the security forces.

In spite of numerous denials by police and army over the past year of the parading of corpses by security forces, the photographic evidence on this page is indisputable proof that this practice does take place.

Inspector Wally Bredenhann, Police Liaison Officer, denied knowledge of such an incident having taken place, when approached with a report of the Ondboe 'parade of corpses'.

The officer, after being given details concerning the incident, said that: 'The report about dead terrorists on Casspirs is not true.'

Residents reported that the Casspir had no marks of identification apart from the words 'Wolf Turbo 4'.

Deputy Attorney-General Mr Estienne Pretorius was unable to say offhand whether or not an incident of this nature constituted a criminal offence.

'No such documents have ever been submitted to this office, and we therefore have never had the opportunity to consider such a case.'

He said he was 'hesitant' about commenting without

researching the matter beforehand. He said his office would have to receive a formal complaint before deciding whether it was an offence.

A SWATF (South West African Territorial Force) spokesman refused to take note of the details concerning the incident, saying that the SA Defence Force (SADF) was a 'Christian organisation'.

'We have repeatedly confirmed that we do not indulge in such inhuman actions. If anyone did such a thing he would be prosecuted.'

Referring to the parade of dead bodies, he said the SADF did not need to brag about such incidents.

The Namibian approached both police and army concerning details of the incident, since the Casspir had no marks identifying it as a vehicle belonging to either branch of the security forces.

Approached for comment in the matter, Bishop James Kauluma, head of the Anglican Diocese of Namibia, said that he had frequently received reports of similar incidents in the past, citing the areas of Oshakati, Ondangu and Ongwediwa where they had apparently taken place.

Security forces invited members of the public to 'see their Swapo's'.

The security forces, he added, had 'gone past the point of self-respect and dignity'.

'One cannot do such inhuman things unless you are damaged psychologically or emotionally.

The photographs also vindicate this newspaper, which was last year chastised by security forces for carrying reports of similar incidents.

1988, ZIMBABWE

The Willowgate Scandal that caused the fall of the mighty

INTRODUCED BY GEOFFREY NYAROTA

The Willowgate Scandal, the most celebrated case of investigative journalism in the early days of Zimbabwe's independence, was exposed in 1988 in *The Chronicle*, a Bulawayo-based, state-owned daily newspaper.

This investigation became the first serious challenge posed by any newspaper to the fearsome régime of Robert Gabriel Mugabe, eight years after his ascendancy to power. Willowgate exploded during the first year of his first term as President of Zimbabwe. Up to 1987 he was Prime Minister.

The catalyst for the investigation into the corruption of several of Mugabe's ministers was the signing in December 1987 of the Unity Agreement between his ruling ZANU-PF party and PF-ZAPU, led by his long-standing political adversary, Dr Joshua Nkomo. This landmark agreement signalled the end of the notorious five-year *Gukurahundi* campaign waged by the Zimbabwe National Army's 5 Brigade in the Matabeleland and Midlands provinces, in which thousands of innocent citizens of Ndebele ethnic origin were massacred or brutally assaulted. To cover up the murderous campaign, Mugabe's government had enforced tight controls over the media, especially in Bulawayo.

The year 1988 ushered in a new era of relaxation of those controls. *The Chronicle* started to flex its muscles as reports of corruption within the ranks of government escalated. Alarmed, Mugabe warned the public not to make spurious allegations of corruption against his officials. Any allegations must be accompanied by evidence, he said.

The stage was set for the dramatic sequence of events that culminated in the investigation mounted by the newspaper into the corrupt acquisition of brand new motor vehicles from the Willowvale Mazda Motor Industries (WMMI), a motor vehicle-assembly plant in Harare, the capital city, more than 400 kilometres away.

Cabinet ministers bought almost the entire output as the vehicles came off the assembly line and disposed of them at breath-taking profit margins.

Due to the unavailability of foreign currency, Zimbabwe was faced with a serious shortage of new cars at the time. Buyers paying a deposit at the official car dealers waited for up to two years before taking delivery. Mugabe's cabinet devised a scheme whereby ministers were allocated one vehicle each directly from the Willowvale plant, which was partly owned by government. Some ministers exploited this loophole to purchase several cars each.

One minister acquired a total of 36 vehicles. One car was purchased for Z$29,000 in the morning and re-sold for a cool Z$105,000 that day. Business boomed as some of Mugabe's ministers became full-time car dealers.

The story began when Obert Mpofu, managing director of the Zimbabwe Grain Bag Company and a Member of Parliament, received a mysterious windfall by mail (*Chronicle*, 21 October 1988).

The cheque from WMMI was a refund for an overpayment on a vehicle. A cover letter explained that Mpofu had overpaid on a recently purchased truck. Mystified, Mpofu brought the cheque to me, as *Chronicle* editor. We immediately launched an investigation. The refund was in fact intended, not for Obert Mpofu, but for one Alford Mpofu, who had indeed overpaid on a vehicle. This simple clerical error triggered off a series of events that ultimately rocked the Mugabe government to its core.

Incensed assembly plant workers gave me the list of names of all officials who had fraudulently purchased vehicles, along with the engine and chassis numbers (*Chronicle*, 14 December 1988). We then traced the vehicles to the individuals or companies to whom they had been re-sold and found out the grossly inflated prices. We subjected the fraudulent ministers to rigorous interrogation.

The exposé was explosive when the story hit the streets. Readers queued to buy a copy of the hardly legible newspaper, as it came off a 57-year-old printing press.

One of the culprits, Enos Nkala, the temperamental Minister of Defence, who was then acting Minister of Home Affairs, took umbrage when we sought to interrogate him. He breathed fire on television, threatening to arrest my deputy, Davison Maruziva, and me (*Chronicle*, 14 December 1988). Senior police, army and intelligence officers visited my home. They revealed that they were under instruction to arrest me but were reluctant to do so. They suggested, instead, that I go into hiding. While hiding in my village, I was promoted to the specially created position of group public relations executive of Zimbabwe Newspapers, the government-owned publishing company.

Government could not ignore a scandal of such magnitude. Mugabe set up Zimbabwe's first official commission of inquiry, headed by Judge President Wilson Sandura (*Chronicle*, 29 December 1988).

When Mugabe's much-feared ministers were paraded before Sandura, the courtroom was packed with incredulous citizens unused to the unprecedented spectacle of usually haughty politicians being humbled as they lied under oath. The commission established that the allegations published by *The Chronicle* were authentic.

Five cabinet ministers and a provincial governor were forced to resign. In a tragic anti-climax, Maurice Nyagumbo, Mugabe's closest confidant and one of the ministers incriminated in multiple car deals, committed suicide. The rest were exonerated by the President.

There was a massive public outcry as details of the scandal unfolded. Outraged University of Zimbabwe students staged demonstrations and set on fire the official Mercedes-Benz of Vice-Chancellor Prof. Walter Kamba. Former ZANU-PF secretary general, Edgar Tekere, mounted a crusade against corruption, culminating in the formation of his own political party in 1989. He stood and lost as a presidential candidate against Mugabe in violence-ridden elections in 1990.

Reporting on the Willowgate Scandal, Michael Hiltzik of the *Los Angeles Times* said: 'What followed was a public inquiry into official corruption that has no parallel in sub-Saharan Africa and little enough anywhere else in the world.'

While the authorities took stern action against me as *Chronicle* editor and Maruziva, my deputy, the Willowgate Scandal signalled a turning point in the practice of journalism in Zimbabwe, away from the speech-reporting that had become a feature of journalism, especially in the vast government-controlled media empire. The scandal opened the flood gates of investigative reporting, especially in the privately owned newspapers.

While I lost my job at *The Chronicle*, I received more than fair compensation by way of international recognition: a Commonwealth Press Union Award for Excellence in Journalism in 1989, the Percy Qoboza Foreign Journalist Award a year later from the Association of Black Journalists in the USA; and seven further international awards over the years, including the World Association of Newspapers' Golden Pen Award and the prestigious UNESCO Guillermo Cano Press Freedom Award.

Big Racket in New Cars

Geoffrey Nyarota, *The Chronicle*, 21 October 1988

A cheque issued to a client by Willowvale Motor Industries, but sent to a different person in error, has led to the uncovering of what appears to be the tip of a massive iceberg, involving the illegal sale of new motor vehicles.

The practice whereby new vehicles are allocated to certain individuals in contravention of laid down regulations is, according to inside sources, widespread and allegedly involves top government officials who utilize their influence to direct officials at the car assembly plants to allocate new vehicles to certain people, some of whom are used only as fronts.

Toyota Cressidas, Nissan Sunnys and Mazda B2200 trucks have allegedly been allocated to dozens of people, mostly in Harare and Bulawayo.

It is alleged that in some cases the people receiving the cars have only had their names used, with money being provided to them by certain individuals who later collected the vehicles.

In other cases the new vehicles are delivered to registered car dealers in the normal way. The dealers are then instructed by 'people in the ministry' to sell the cars to specific individuals whose names are supplied.

Most of the vehicles have then been re-sold at highly inflated prices, with Toyota Cressidas sold in the box by Willowvale for around Z$29,000 being sold on the black market often within 48 hours of collection for up to Z$70,000.

Early this month Cde Obert Mpofu, the managing director of the Bulawayo firm, Zimbabwe Grain Bag Company and a non-Constituency Member of Parliament, could not believe his eyes when he received an unexpected cheque for Z$3,968.

His joy was short-lived, however, as closer inspection of the Willowvale Motors cheque revealed that it had in fact been made out to one A. Mpofu.

Mystified, Cde Mpofu contacted the assembly in Harare.

'They told me that Mr Mpofu, the managing director of Zimbabwe Grain Bag and MP had bought a truck from Willlowvale,' he said, 'and that he had telephoned the company the previous day asking for a refund as he had overpaid for the vehicle.'

Cde Mpofu said when he asked for further details he had been referred to a Mr Wilde at Willowvale. Mr Dudley Wilde, the factory manager at Willowvale, is said to have explained that he had acted on instructions from the Ministry of Industry and Technology to issue a car to Cde Mpofu. He is alleged to have said in confidence that the instructions had come from the Minister himself, Cde Callistus Ndlovu.

Mr Wilde said the Mpofu who had phoned the previous day asking for his refund had given his address as Kezi Shopping Centre, Box 1796, Bulawayo, and his contact telephone number as 74622, also in Bulawayo. While Kezi Shopping Centre is not listed in the phone directory, the BoldAds Commercial Directory of Bulawayo lists Box 1796 as being rented by the Wholesale Centre.

Wholesale Centre (Pvt) Ltd of 62 Main Street is listed in the telephone directory. The box number is given as 1796. The name and address of the manager are given. He is one Mr Manilarl Naran of 3382 Gorebridge Road, Killarney.

When *The Chronicle* rang the number 74622 the phone was answered at Spot-On, the large liquor wholesale outlet at the corner of Fort Street and 5th Avenue. Spot-On is also owned by Mr Manilarl Naran.

Mr Naran is a high-profile Bulawayo business tycoon with strong and equally prominent connections in top political circles. *The Chronicle* investigations revealed that the vehicle in question, a Mazda B1600 truck was collected on or about August 24 from the Willowvale plant on behalf of Cde Alford Mpofu, a manager at Spot-On, who has adamantly refused to answer any questions put to him. A cheque for Z$24,382.80 had been made out in favour of Willowvale in anticipation of the purchase of a diesel Mazda B2200 pick-up truck. Apparently none was available and the cheaper petrol model B1600 was allocated.

This accounted for the refund of the Z$3,968.40 which eventually landed on Cde Obert Mpofu's desk at Zimbabwe Grain Bag. But that is only part of the story. Another vehicle was collected at the same time, a Mazda B2200, purportedly purchased by a Cde Don Ndlovu, a part-time accountant at Spot-On. Cde Ndlovu says late in July or early in August he received a telephone call from the deputy secretary in the Ministry of Industry and Technology, Cde Elias Mabhena, who is also chairman of Willowvale, a company which is government-owned through the Industrial Development Corporation.

Cde Mabhena has since been promoted to the position of permanent secretary for the Ministry of Trade and Commerce.

Cde Ndlovu says that Cde Mabhena advised him that his name and that of Cde Alford Mpofu had been brought forward for new car allocations.

'When I asked him under what circumstances our names had been brought forward he said we were not to worry,' said Cde Ndlovu. 'All we were required to do was to supply certain details about ourselves.'

Cde Ndlovu said he and Cde Mpofu had then supplied the required details and Cde Mabhena had said that a Mr Gibson would contact them later. In due course, they contacted Mr Dave Gibson, managing director of Willowvale Motors.

'Mr Gibson said two trucks would be ready in about 10 days and Mr Wilde would contact us about that time,' said Cde Ndlovu.

'Later Mr (Manilarl) Naran asked us to go and see the manager of the Bank of Credit and Commerce in Bulawayo, Mr Aktar, who would issue us with cheques for the purchase of the vehicles.'

In August BCC issued two cheques in favour of Willowvale Motors, each for Z$24,382.80 and handed them to Cdes Don Ndlovu and Alford Mpofu. Cde Don Ndlovu apparently collected another cheque the following day, this time made out in favour of Leyland Motors and for Z$22,087.20 ...

Cde Ndlovu said an air ticket was later given to him and he flew up to Harare where a car had been hired for him.

He picked the car up at the airport and with a driver who

had also travelled from Bulawayo, he drove to Willowvale Motors where they saw Mr Wilde. After handing over the cheques they collected the two trucks, a B2200 and a B1600.

Cde Ndlovu then received a cheque for Z$3,968 to cover the difference on the B1600.

'I, however, lost the cheque when we went to Meikles for lunch,' he said. 'The cheque that Cde Obert Mpofu eventually received was a replacement cheque for the one that I had lost.'

He said when he arrived back in Bulawayo he contacted Cde Alford Mpofu who advised that 'CD has given instructions that the vehicles together with keys and the papers should be given to Mr Naran'.

Asked who 'CD' was, he said it was the Minister of Industry and Technology, Cde Callistus Dingiswayo Ndlovu.

'That was the last we ever saw of the cars,' said Cde Don Ndlovu. 'In fact, in the case of Cde Alford Mpofu I don't think he ever saw the truck' ...

Asked this week to explain in which circumstances instructions were issued to dealers to sell new vehicles only to certain individuals, Cde Lukas Mahoko, a senior administrative officer in the ministry said the practice whereby vehicles could be issued to certain individuals on advice from the ministry had been discontinued in 1986 after car dealers had complained.

'If individuals approach the ministry for new cars we tell that the ministry doesn't handle new cars,' he said. 'They must approach dealers direct.'

Asked to account for the letter which he signed in 1987 he said the letter had been written to the dealer on the instructions of the then deputy secretary in the ministry, Cde Elias Mabhena.

'Where this has happened we have always been instructed to do so from above. Most people who want cars go through him because he is the chairman of Willowvale.'

Back at Willowvale Mr Wilde said he received his instructions on the allocation of vehicles from above and he was not prepared to disclose any details.

'I have already received a threat on my life,' he said, 'and I am not prepared to give you anything that goes into the Press. All I'm doing is obeying instructions given to me. I don't want to get involved. I value my safety and that of my family.

Mr Dave Gibson ... said while he was aware something fishy was happening he did not know the extent of the racket.

'We are often asked to assist people who are alleged to have difficulties with transport in their businesses,' he says. 'The Ministry of Industry and Technology asks us to assist' ...

1989, SOUTH AFRICA

The 'bloody trail' of the apartheid police

INTRODUCED BY TIM DU PLESSIS

Investigative journalism was never the forté of the mainstream Afrikaans-language press in South Africa in the period covered by this book. The majority of Afrikaans newspapers founded in the 20th century were started for mainly political reasons, in most cases the advancement of Afrikaner nationalism. When the National Party came to power in South Africa in 1948, the Afrikaans papers considered their main mission to be the consolidation of Afrikaner political power. That was the closest they came to 'campaigning journalism'.

What passed for investigative journalism in Afrikaans newspapers consisted mainly of exposing so-called '*boereverneukers*' – small-town crooks, shysters and pyramid scheme operators in the Afrikaans community.

This mould was dramatically broken in the late 1980s when, at the height of the apartheid mayhem, courageous Afrikaans journalist Max du Preez founded *Vrye Weekblad* as an anti-apartheid weekly in Afrikaans. Du Preez cashed out his savings, asked for a few donations, took the giant leap of faith and bade farewell to the mainstream media.

Journalist Jacques Pauw was a reporter at Afrikaans Sunday paper *Rapport*, where he cut his teeth in investigative journalism when he helped expose the 'Kubus' Ponzi scheme run by serial fraudster Adriaan Nieuwoudt. When Du Preez announced the inception of *Vrye Weekblad*, the idealistic Pauw jumped at the opportunity.

The camaraderie between Du Preez and Pauw bore fruit less than a year later. *Vrye Weekblad* made the sensational revelation of the existence of apartheid South Africa's death squads, sanctioned and authorised by the government. Their story shook the Nationalist regime to its foundations and is widely recognised as one of the decisive moments in the final implosion of apartheid, destroying what little was left of the government's claims to moral cause.

In the early to mid-1980s, in the course of his reporting duties, Pauw had come into contact with one Dirk Coetzee, a former captain in the Gestapo-like security branch of the SA Police (SAP). Coetzee revealed to Pauw the existence of a nefarious outfit in the SAP by the name of Unit C1, based at Vlakplaas, an agricultural small-holding 30 kilometres west of Pretoria. Coetzee started the Vlakplaas operation in 1980 on instruction from the SAP high command and was its first commanding officer.

According to Coetzee, the overall mission of Vlakplaas (Unit C1) was the disruption and destruction of the activities of individuals and organisations involved in the political struggle against the apartheid regime. Their tactics were brutal and included the cold-blooded murders of activists, arson, merciless torture (often resulting in death), the bombing of buildings and carrying out assassinations using explosive devices and drive-by shootings.

But, as often happens when 'methods of barbarism' – to use the well-known historic phrase – are employed in the pursuit of political aims, Coetzee fell out with his superiors in the SAP. He was side-lined to a desk job and took medical retirement.

In graphic and comprehensive detail, Coetzee revealed to Pauw the full horrors of apartheid's death squads, including his own participation in a number of murders and other serious crimes.

When Pauw first heard these stories he was still employed by *Rapport* and knew full well the paper would never touch them. If truth be told, very few mainstream South African newspapers would.

Coetzee also told his tale of death to a mainstream Afrikaans newspaper editor, a prominent National Party member of Parliament and a Progressive Federal Party MP. None believed him or did anything, according to Pauw.

Once at *Vrye Weekblad*, he regularly discussed the Vlakplaas story with the editor, Du Preez. Both agreed the story needed to be told, but also knew what risks were involved. *Vrye Weekblad* was small and thinly resourced. By then a full-blown national state of emergency was in force in the country, including draconian media regulations, which made provision for the arbitrary closing of publications and prison sentences for 'transgressing' editors and reporters who dared to ignore these. Not to mention civil law suits that could result in life-long financial ruin for the journalists.

Assassinations that fitted the pattern in Coetzee's revelations continued to occur. On 1 May 1989, Wits academic and anti-apartheid activist David Webster was gunned down in front of his Johannesburg home and three months later, Swapo leader Anton Lubowski died a similar death in Windhoek, Namibia.

But as seasoned journalists, Pauw and Du Preez knew they needed more than Coetzee's word to publish his story. On his part, Coetzee was worried about his safety and raised the possibility of leaving the country.

A breakthrough came in October 1989 when anti-apartheid paper *The Weekly Mail* reported that a member of the SAP, one Butana Almond Nofemela, who had been convicted of murder, made sensational allegations about the existence of a hit squad in the SAP. He confessed to being a member and to his participation in several high-profile political murders.

Nofemela also revealed that Coetzee was his commander at Vlakplaas, in the process corroborating much of what Coetzee earlier told Pauw. Nofemela decided to speak up in an attempt to save his own life when he realised he was about to be executed.

At *Vrye Weekblad*, Pauw and Du Preez got going, now more determined than ever to get their story out. They argued that Afrikaans readers in particular needed to know what horrific deeds were being perpetrated in their name, ostensibly to retain Afrikaner political control.

Nofemela's revelations deeply rattled Coetzee. He feared assassination. He, more than anyone else, knew what these people were capable of. Since pouring his guts out to Pauw for the first time, Coetzee had also established a new life outside the SAP and was concerned over the safety of his young family.

At the same time, political change was accelerating in South Africa. The air was thick with rumour that the apartheid government, realising its iron grip on the country was slipping, was ready to enter into negotiations with the then outlawed liberation movements.

Du Preez came up with the idea that they seek the help of the African National Congress (ANC), asking them to assist in getting Coetzee out of the country. Banned in apartheid South Africa, the movement by the late 1980s attained the aura of a government-in-exile. It was the pre-eminent liberation movement with more diplomatic missions abroad than the Pretoria government.

When Du Preez and Pauw mentioned to Coetzee a possible escape plan involving the ANC, he was initially shocked, but after consulting his family he made the anguished decision to go along.

In November 1989, Coetzee and Pauw travelled to the resort island of Mauritius, where he was, once again, extensively interviewed by Pauw. After that Coetzee was placed in the care of the ANC in London.

The strategy to involve the then outlawed ANC was as risky as it was smart. If government agencies had found out about their plans, Du Preez and Pauw could face serious criminal charges, possibly including treason.

But the plan worked. On 17 November 1989 *Vrye Weekblad* hit the streets with a front-page banner headline reading 'Bloody trail of the SA Police'. In page after page the paper reported, in gruesome detail, how activists were tortured, maimed and murdered, many of them household names in the liberation struggle. By also revealing the internal structures and lines of command in Unit C2, *Vrye Weekblad* convincingly showed that Vlakplaas was no rogue operation, but an official project, authorised right up to the highest echelons of government.

The Vlakplaas story hit the country like a thunderbolt. It was also splashed across front pages and TV screens all over the world – an amazing achievement for a paper selling less than 20,000 copies per week and staffed by a small band of activist journalists.

The reaction of the apartheid government's propaganda machine was swift and predictable. Denial upon denial was issued. Vlakplaas was described as a mere training facility where 'rehabilitated' ANC cadres – called askaris – were housed.

'Every inch of dirt against Coetzee was paraded in public. He was branded a liar, perjurer, traitor, gangster and psychopath,' Pauw later wrote in the book *Tell Me No lies.*

The police used their 'contacts' in the mainstream media to discredit Coetzee and *Vrye Weekblad*. Coetzee had never left South Africa and was hiding in a delusional state somewhere on a farm, said *Rapport*. Another Afrikaans newspaper said one had to be mad to believe Coetzee while an English-language newspaper said that the ANC had paid the apartheid hitman R1 million to say what he said.

Vrye Weekblad also exposed Coetzee's successor at Vlakplaas, Colonel Eugene de Kock, who was dubbed 'Prime Evil' because of his prolific 'kill rate'. The newspaper later revealed that Vlakplaas was not disbanded after its exposure in the newspaper as officially declared by State President F.W. de Klerk, but continued after 1990 as a 'Third Force' that stoked violence between the ANC and the Inkatha political movement across the country.

But as the political drama of South Africa's transition to democracy unfolded, the bulk of the allegations over the murderous activities of the apartheid state's security apparatus was proven to be factual and correct.

Pauw said in an interview that *Vrye Weekblad* had made only one mistake in their exposure of Vlakplaas: it was much worse than what the newspaper originally thought. Because of its involvement in the so-called 'black-on-black' violence in the early 1990s, the death toll of Vlakplaas ran into the hundreds, maybe thousands of victims.

Testimony in courts and the proceedings of the Truth and Reconciliation Commission (TRC), established two years after the new South African government took over in 1994, confirmed the *Vrye Weekblad* reports. Pauw and Du Preez's decision to cooperate with the ANC in November 1989 was effectively vindicated when the TRC granted Coetzee full amnesty for the crimes he committed at Vlakplaas.

Vrye Weekblad closed its doors in January 1994, bankrupted by endless tax-funded litigation embarked upon by powerful apartheid figures and bureaucrats whose activities were exposed by the paper.

The Vlakplaas commander that succeeded Coetzee, Eugene de Kock, was arrested days after South Africa's first democratic election in April 1994 and two and a half years later, he was sentenced to several life sentences and 220 years' imprisonment.

The generals that made De Kock one of the most decorated policemen in history and gave him instructions to 'make a plan' to deal with targeted activists were never charged. The politicians that provided the secure environment in which the unit flourished, made available secret funds for clandestine operations and attended barbeques at Vlakplaas to thank De Kock for his sterling service denied any knowledge of the unit and its activities.

HIT SQUAD'S REGISTER OF TERROR

Jacques Pauw, *Vrye Weekblad*, 17 November 1989

Captain Dirk Coetzee admits that he had, until and including 1982, actively participated and helped plan various murders and terror attacks that were committed by the South African Police's special unit at Vlakplaas.

Then he still kept in touch with several members of the hit

squad and is aware of other acts of terror in the following years.

Here is his register of death:

The murder of the anti-apartheid activist and Durban lawyer Griffiths Mxenge: 'In November 1981 I was called from Vlakplaas to Durban by Brigadier Van der Hoven, the then head of Security in Natal, where I was instructed to kill Mxenge.

'The police knew that money for the ANC was channelled through him, but could not prove it. I was told to ensure that the murder looked like a robbery, because Van der Hoven said the police were not in the mood for another Biko case. The security police in Durban pointed out his home to us and informed us about his movements. Captain Koos Vermeulen, Warrant Officer (now Lieutenant) Paul van Dyk and I laced four pieces of meat with strychnine to poison his dogs with and gave it to my Askari's, Almond Nofomela, David Tshikalange, Brian Ngulungwa and one Joe.

'I instructed them clearly that he should be killed with knives and not be shot. I was then informed of all their movements: how they followed him, the poisoning of his three dogs and the trap they had set for him on the side of the road. They told me how they had stopped, kidnapped and taken him to the Umlazi Stadium where they stabbed him to death with knives. They also cut his throat and cut his ears off.

'After the incident I met them late at night at a pre-arranged meeting place where they had Mxenge's jacket, watch, wallet and car keys. They assured me that it looks like a robbery.

'I've since reported back to Van der Hoven, who instructed that the team must return to Pretoria.

'There I was called to Brigadier Marius Schoon, who very anxiously wanted to know if we had left any traces. He ordered that Mxenge's car should be burned immediately. It was done close to the Swaziland border.

'I later heard that General Johan Coetzee, then Head of the Security Police, after my report back, had been called out of a meeting to hear the news of the successful operation.

'The Askaris each received a R1,000 for their good work.'

The murder of two ANC members near Komatipoort: 'After the army's raid into Maputo in 1980, two suspected

ANC members, Vusi and Ghost, were kidnapped and brought into South Africa. Ghost was taken to Vlakplaas where he later willingly started to work with the police. Vusi was held in the police cells in Brits, where he had the attitude of "Charge me or shoot me".

'Schoon gave the instruction that Vusi and another captive ANC member that was held at Vlakplaas, Peter, had to be gotten rid of. I collected Vusi (his MK name) from the police cells and took him to an abandoned farm near the Kopfontein border post where Captain Koos Vermeulen and Peter were already waiting for us.

'I first let Vusi sign three different, predated invoices with three different pens so it would seem as if he was still alive and in our service three months later.

'Vermeulen and I poured poison, that had been prepared by the forensics laboratory, into their cold drink and beer. Everyone talked about Lothar's poison (General Lothar Neethling is head of the forensics laboratory). We were assured that 60 grams would be enough to let them die of a "heart attack". The poison would not work. We increased the dosage to 360 grams each, but nothing happened.

'We later took the two to Komatipoort where Paul van Dyk waited for us. From there we went to a farm nearby where Major Archie Flemington of Security at Komatipoort met us.

'We gave Vusi and Peter sleep medication that had also been prepared by the forensics laboratory. We had been asked beforehand to keep notes of the effects of the sleep medication. When the two 'terros/terries' were sufficiently confused, Vermeulen shot them through the head with Makarov pistol with a silencer.

'The two bodies were then burned along with wood and tyres that we found on a rubbish dump. It took seven hours before the bodies were burned out. The ash and the remains were dumped into the Komati River.

'During the burning of the two "terries" (terrorists) security men of Komatipoort told me how they had distributed strong alcohol, laced with poison, among ANC members in Maputo. The poison is injected through the lids of the bottles with a micro needle.'

(Other incidents listed:)

The burning of a 'second Biko' ...

The murder of activist Patrick Makau and a young child ...

The bomb attack on Chris Hani, military leader of Umkhonto We'Sizwe ...

The murder of (exiled journalist, researcher and activist) Ruth First ...

Hit on Marius Schoon ...

A diamond trader is killed by the hit squad ...

An ANC member is blown up in Swaziland ...

A kidnapping from Swaziland ...

The blowing-up of ANC offices in London ...

Coetzee speaks of several other days of terror that he personally was involved in or that he knew of. He speaks of other incidents, especially in Swaziland where ANC members were murdered and kidnapped.

1990–92, SOUTH AFRICA

Exposing the 'Third Force' behind South Africa's pre-election violence

INTRODUCED BY PHILIPPA GARSON

Political rivalry between the Zulu nationalist Inkatha movement and the United Democratic Front, aligned to the banned African National Congress (ANC), broke out in the mid-1980s in the South African province of Natal and the KwaZulu homeland. When Inkatha launched as a national political party, the Inkatha Freedom Party (IFP), in the township of Sebokeng, south of Johannesburg, in July 1990, violence erupted and spread rapidly to other townships in the country's economic hub.

Single-sex hostels, where many Zulu migrant workers resided, became bastions of Inkatha support. Horrific violence broke out between these hostel dwellers and ANC-supporting residents in many townships and adjacent shack settlements.

For the next few years, until the first democratic elections in 1994, conflict raged between the ANC and IFP in the Transvaal, KwaZulu, Natal and beyond, claiming as many as 16,000 lives. Many newspapers and observers attributed this so-called 'black-on-black' violence to political rivalry let loose after the unbanning of the ANC and other organisations in February 1990. This internecine violence, they argued, demonstrated that neither the ANC nor Inkatha was in control of its supporters in an era of intense jockeying for power during pre-democracy negotiations.

But the ANC, its allies and the alternative press – including *Weekly Mail*, *Vrye Weekblad* and *New Nation* – were of the view that a 'Third Force' was actively stoking the violence. Elements in the security forces – with the suspected sanction of top leaders in government – were engaged in covert attempts to foment the violence to weaken the ANC's support base and boost

Inkatha as a potential National Party ally. Whether these covert attempts were part of a renegade right-wing agenda inside the government to subvert negotiations or part of state-sanctioned policy was unclear.

The apartheid government had been engaged in a decade-long 'total onslaught' strategy to defeat liberation forces in Namibia, Zimbabwe, Angola and Mozambique, dispatching covert and special force units with brutal effect. This divide-and-rule strategy involved funding, arming and training counter-revolutionary armies. After the outbreak of Inkatha/ANC violence on the Reef, it became apparent to many observers that the security forces were doing the same at home, bolstering Inkatha to weaken the ANC.

Evidence of police partiality towards Inkatha during the conflict supported these claims, as did anecdotal evidence of the sporadic involvement of masked whites and non-South African blacks in the fighting. Random violence on trains, at funerals and vigils and in other contexts, seemed designed to wreak maximum havoc, claim as many lives as possible and perpetuate the cycle of violence. Nelson Mandela, church leaders and anti-apartheid activists repeatedly called on President F.W. de Klerk to purge his security forces of those colluding with Inkatha to stoke the violence.

But where was the proof? Government leaders continued to deny any collusion and the repeated refrain from Minister of Law and Order Adriaan Vlok was, 'bring us the evidence'.

Caprivi Trainees: On 21 September 1990, *Weekly Mail* journalist Eddie Koch reported that an elite unit of around 200 Inkatha fighters had been trained in guerrilla warfare at a secret Military Intelligence base in the Caprivi Strip, Namibia, in 1986. Under command of two SADF Special Force leaders, the fighters were reportedly trained for seven months to use heavy weaponry. The men returned to Ulundi where some then trained other Inkatha members. A former member of the Civil Co-operation Bureau, the SADF's covert death squad whose existence *Vrye Weekblad* had exposed in May that year, corroborated Koch's evidence. An SADF member stationed in Caprivi at the time and Inkatha members trained there, who had made statements to lawyers, also backed up the claims.

Koch further reported the existence of two training camps in KwaZulu for Renamo, the South African-supported Mozambican militia, and cited reports that former Renamo members were selling AK-47s to hostel-dwellers on the violence-wracked East Rand. Given the political climate at the time, Koch was not in a position to name his sources, some of whom may have been intelligence operatives in the ANC.

Inkathagate: In July 1991 *The Weekly Mail* and the *Guardian* newspapers simultaneously broke 'Inkathagate', which offered documentary proof of security police funding of Inkatha and its union, the United Workers Union of South Africa. Both De Klerk and Buthelezi were weakened by the exposé internationally and at home. Buthelezi managed to stay afloat while his subordinate, MZ Khumalo, took the rap. Shortly afterwards, Vlok and Defence Force chief Magnus Malan were removed as ministers of police and the military respectively and reassigned to less influential cabinet positions.

The Black Cats: Reporting on township violence in 1990 and 1991 for *The Weekly Mail*, I had developed strong contacts in the township of Wesselton, near Ermelo, where a civic association had organised rent boycotts to challenge corrupt local authorities. I reported on the activities of a group of vigilantes called the Black Cats that had been wreaking havoc there, singling out ANC-aligned activists to maim and kill. Gang members were often seen with local white policemen.

In early 1992, Mbongeni Khumalo, a senior Inkatha member, broke ranks and told *The Weekly Mail's* Koch about his own role in training the Caprivi paramilitary group and how members of the group had in turn trained other Inkatha members, including the Black Cats, to kill activists. Two Black Cats then gave detailed accounts to Garson and Koch about the weapons training gang members had received at a secret training camp and the crimes they'd committed back in Wesselton against ANC supporters. The Black Cat investigation showed how the MI-backed Caprivi trainees had participated in a cascading training model, recruiting vigilantes to join Inkatha and then training them to attack ANC-aligned activists.

The Black Cats alleged that local white policemen were complicit in arming them, initiating attacks and squashing investigations. They also charged that some Caprivi trainees had stoked violence in Wesselton itself. Among these was Daluxolo Luthuli, a former MK member turned Inkatha assassin, who led the training of the Black Cats.

The Weekly Mail arranged for the two Black Cats, whose lives had been threatened, to go into hiding. However, taking care of them proved challenging in the absence of a proper witness protection programme. In a devastating turn of events, the mother of one of the renegade Black Cats was killed in an apparent reprisal killing.

Soon afterwards, the Goldstone Commission of Inquiry, set up in July 1991 to investigate the causes of political violence, held a special hearing on the *The Weekly Mail's* exposés. The commission found that *The Weekly Mail* was justified in publishing Khumalo's allegations but concluded that there was insufficient proof that the Black Cats were part of a Military Intelligence-trained hit squad or that local white policemen were involved.

Later, the Truth and Reconciliation Commission concluded that the Black Cats had, together with Caprivi trainees, assassinated more than 20 ANC members. Furthermore, the TRC found that police had supplied the Black Cats with resources and covered up their involvement in ANC killings. The TRC also found that ANC-backed self-defence units were responsible for killing Black Cat members (TRC, 1998: 721).

Regarding the Third Force, the TRC found that while there was no evidence of a 'centrally directed, coherent and formally constituted third force', that 'a network of security and expert security force operatives' often acting with 'rightwing elements and or sectors of the IFP, fomented, initiated, faciliated and engaged in violence', which included 'random and targeted killings' (TRC, 1998: 692–710).

It was also revealed at the TRC that the training of the covert paramilitary unit at Caprivi was part of Operation Marion, a project of MI's Directorate of Special Tasks, similar to their Operation Katzen in the Eastern Cape. Luthuli and other Caprivi trainees also confirmed to the TRC that the Caprivi men were trained to be a hit squad and that he himself had led many attacks against UDF and later ANC leaders in KwaZulu and Natal (TRC Report, 1988).

Further corroboration of MI involvement in fostering the violence emerged with the eventual release in 2007 of the controversial Steyn Report, which alleged covert SADF involvement in the ANC/IFP violence on the Reef and in KwaZulu-Natal. Former SADF chief of staff Pierre Steyn had been tasked in November 1992 by De Klerk to look into third force activities by the SADF after the Goldstone Commission uncovered evidence of a network of SADF front companies connected to acts of violence and criminality.

Former security policeman and apartheid assassin Eugene de Kock would later confirm that he and his Vlakplaas colleagues had supplied heavy ammunition to Inkatha by the security police. However, after all these years, much of the truth about security force involvement in fomenting the violence has not come to light and few of those implicated have been brought to justice.

References and further reading

Ellis, Stephen. 1998. 'The historical significance of South Africa's third force', *Journal of Southern African Studies*, 24(2). Available at: https://openaccess.leidenuniv.nl/bitstream/handle/1887/9519/ASC-1241486-035.pdf, accessed on 18 August 2018.

Reports of the Goldstone Commission on the Prevention of Public Violence and Intimidation (1992–1994). 'Report by the committee appointed to inquire into allegations concerning front companies of the SADF and the training by the SADF of Inkatha supporters in the Caprivi in 1986', Vol. 2.

Taylor, Rupert & Shaw, Mark. 1998. 'The dying days of apartheid', in David R. Howarth & Aletta Norval (eds). *South Africa in Transition: New Theoretical Perspectives*. London: Palgrave Macmillan.

TRC Report. 1988. Available at: www.justice.gov.za/trc/report/, accessed on 15 August 2018.

Inkatha's Secret Training Base

Eddie Koch, *The Weekly Mail*, 21 September 1990

An elite unit of Inkatha fighters has been trained in guerrilla warfare by South African army officers at a secret base in the Caprivi Strip. This base, called Hippo and located on the banks of the Cuando River 80 kilometres west of Katimo Mulilo, fell under the control of the Chief of Staff Intelligence. This division of the South African Defence Force took over control of the Mozambique guerrilla group, Renamo, from the Rhodesian Central Intelligence Organisation in the 1970s and turned it into the clandestine force that it is today.

The Hippo base trained at least 200 Inkatha guerrillas in 1986. The SADF officer in charge of training was Major 'Jakes' Jacobs ... Some recruits remember being met by four white men who slapped them on the back and joked about how they were going to make soldiers of them.

At least two batches of Inkatha fighters, each about 100 strong, were trained to use AK-47s, RPG7 rocket launchers, G3 submachine guns, Browning machine guns and anti-personnel mines.

The course at Hippo lasted seven months and included lessons in urban and guerrilla warfare, use of explosives and demolition, and contra-mobilisation – a form of military intelligence work.

After training was completed the unit was divided into four divisions – called 'offensive', 'defensive', 'ministers' aides' and 'contra-mobilisation intelligence' – before returning to

Ulundi where some of them were required to train other Inkatha members.

These details have been denied by the government of kwaZulu and a representative of the SADF said he had no knowledge of the Inkatha training base. However, they have been verified by a former member of the military's Civil Co-Operation Bureau (CCB), a member of the SADF who served in the Caprivi Strip region at the time, and by Inkatha members who were trained at Hippo and have made statements to lawyers about their experiences.

There are also reports that there was, at least until last year, a training camp for Renamo members at Lake Sibaya, near the border between Mozambique and Natal. Prior to that a supply base for Renamo bands operating in southern Mozambique existed at Katwyn village, which is in Ndumu game reserve.

Both of these bases are in kwaZulu and fall under the control of Ulundi. Inkatha officials would have known of these camps. This would have provided extensive opportunity for collusion between members of the Zulu organization and the Mozambican rebels.

A member of the kwaZulu police has made an affidavit stating that one of the camps where Inkatha 'hit-men' are trained is located at Mkuze about 60 kilometres from Ndumu.

The Third Force: Two Hit Squad Men Speak

Eddie Koch and Philippa Garson, *The Weekly Mail*, 24 January 1992

Two 'Black Cats', members of a pro-Inkatha gang that holds the eastern Transvaal township of Wesselton in a grip of fear, have come forward to explain how professional hit-men are able to spread civil strife through a volatile township.

The history of the gang and reign of terror it has imposed on the people of Wesselton since the middle of 1990 provides a vital clue to the way in which mystery 'third force' gunmen have been able to fan the violence that is now endemic in the Transvaal.

The evidence and the two Black Cat members are being placed before Mr Justice R Goldstone, who is heading a special inquiry into Military Intelligence involvement in violence.

Around October 1990, some 'kwaZulu policemen' (known as KZPs) travelled from Ulundi to the township near Ermelo – where tension was running high because of a rent boycott and campaign by the African National Congress-aligned civic organization to depose local councillors – and recruited about 32 young boys and girls from the Black Cats.

These mysterious men from Ulundi were, in fact, part of a 200-strong paramilitary group trained for Inkatha in mid-1986 by the South African Defence Force's Department of Military Intelligence (DMI) at a secret base in the Caprivi Strip in the art of 'offensive warfare'.

The 'KZPs' took the Wesselton youngsters in two mini-buses to Ulundi where they were housed in the old police barracks ... Later the gangsters were transferred to the Mkuze camp and a select group of about 22 were put through an intensive course in how to shoot with AK-47s, 9mm handguns and shotguns. They were also taught how to apprehend people, search and detain them.

The gang then went on the rampage. Backed by a handful of Caprivi graduates who routinely visited Wesselton as members of the KZP, including Mandlanduna (former MK soldier Duloxolo Luthuli), they attacked members of the ANC ...

The manner in which the Black Cats were recruited and trained followed an 'each one teaches 10' principle: small groups of professionals trained by the DMI teach a larger group of gangsters how to use firearms and this group provides a bigger cohort of the gang with the rudimentary skills of killing. In this way Inkatha obtains command over a three-tiered group of trained fighters to use in its contest with the ANC for control over the township, and the level of violence escalates dramatically.

For the First Time: An Insiders' Account of the Third Force

Eddie Koch and Philippa Garson, *The Weekly Mail*, 24 January 1992

A pair of Black Cat vigilantes, members of a notorious gang that operates in the eastern Transvaal township of Wesselton, describe how white police officers used the gang to bomb the office of a human rights lawyer and helped orchestrate a string of murders, assaults and arson attacks.

And the very police officer responsible for some of these attacks, a Warrant Officer Van Zwiel, was appointed to investigate complaints against the Black Cats, say the dissident gangsters.

The gang members decided to speak to the press because they had been threatened by other Black Cat members for voicing criticism of the gang's activities and its close alliance with Inkatha. They are now in hiding in fear of their lives and their names have been changed to protect them. The gang is still operating in the township.

Other evidence supplied by the Black Cats confirms earlier *Weekly Mail* reports, based on testimony from high-ranking Inkatha defector Mbongeni Khumalo, that members of the South African Police in Ermelo released professional hit-men from Ulundi in August 1990 after they had been arrested for shooting up an ANC funeral and killing two of the mourners.

After suffering several defeats at the hands of the 'comrades', 32 Black Cats were taken to Ulundi and then Mkuze camp, where they underwent military training. They returned with instructions to establish themselves as an Inkatha force in the area.

And although the two Black Cats told their stories separately to *The Weekly Mail*, there is a startling consistency to their accounts.

Lucas recounts how white policemen picked three of the strongest Black Cats to petrol bomb the offices of lawyer Stephen Ngwenya as well as the shop, truck and homes of local businessmen in 1990.

... (Lucas tells) how on the night of July 22 and into the

next morning the Black Cats — named after the black whips they brandish — ran amok in the location, breaking doors and windows of civic leaders and known ANC supporters, and attacking several people with pangas, knives and axes. At least eight people were admitted to hospital.

The Weekly Mail is in possession of affidavits made to lawyers by victims and witnesses at the time. Lawyers' attempts to get a restraining order on the activities of the gang proved futile. No arrests were made and the violence escalated.

In his disclosures to *The Weekly Mail*, Khumalo described how a colleague had told him how members of a team of Inkatha hit-men, trained by the Department of Military Intelligence (DMI), had gone to the Wesselton funeral and ambushed the procession, opening fire on mourners and spraying bullets into the coffin.

Lucas, who was with the team of hit-men — the 'eight KZPs' — on that day, tells the inside story ... 'When the funeral procession came past (the KZPs) started shooting. We were watching. The one carrying the flag fell near the coffin. The coffin was dropped. The one who fell, Jabulani Sibanyoni, was not dead. The one KZP (identified as Nhlanhla Khawula) ran forward and shot him in the head. He opened the coffin and shot the dead body many times,' he said.

That evening SADF troops arrested about 30 people, including the eight KZPs, and confiscated their weapons.

'A couple of days later they were all released and came to the (gang leader)'s house,' he said.

Khumalo told *The Weekly Mail* that after the kwaZulu hit-men were released, their confiscated weapons were also returned to Ulundi.

1994, ZIMBABWE

Zimbabwe's land grab

INTRODUCED BY ANTONY SGUAZZIN

In early 1994, less than two months after I had started working as a professional journalist, rumours began to circulate in Zimbabwe's farming community that land bought from white commercial farmers by the government and earmarked for redistribution to subsistence farmers was being handed to cabinet ministers and other prominent officials.

At the *Daily Gazette*, Zimbabwe's first privately owned daily newspaper, that instantly struck a chord as a story that would go to the heart of an issue that divides Zimbabwean society and played a part in causing the country's civil war in the 1970s – who rightfully owns the land?

Brian Latham, the editor of the *Daily Gazette* at the time, assigned Basildon Peta, the newspaper's most prominent reporter at the time, and myself to dig deeper.

First, we drove 70 kilometres east of the capital, Harare, to the fertile farming district of Wedza where we investigated a farm that had been bought by the government under the so-called willing buyer, willing seller programme for the supposed resettlement of 33 families. Instead, it had been leased to Witness Mangwende, the education minister.

The property, Bath Farm, was a sorry sight. While golden tasselled maize stood 2m tall on adjacent farms, Mangwende's crop had been planted late and was ankle height, a rookie mistake by an inexperienced farmer. Workers at the farm, who had been retained by the minister, said that some of their colleagues had been retrenched because the crop would yield little money.

We spoke to farmers in the district and then confirmed the arrangement with a source at the land ministry who said that the farm has been leased to the politician under the so-called Tenant Resettlement Programme, which had not been publicly announced. We published the story on 3 March.

The reaction was instant. Protests were made by farming unions and civil society groups and tips about similar situations flooded in. While the government said very little, some members of Parliament objected, as did former President Canaan Banana.

Over the next few weeks Peta and I traversed Zimbabwe's prime commercial farmlands across the north central area of the country. We drove west to Chegutu, north to Mhangura and Matetepa. We spoke to farmers, snooped around farming districts and spoke to workers and people who lived in the areas, picking up hitchhikers and spending time in rural villages where the new landowners were the main topic of conversation.

When asked difficult questions by security staff, Peta and our driver passed themselves off as civil servants, while I was assumed to be a German aid worker.

To many of those we spoke to, the programme was seen as a betrayal of the ideals for which the liberation war had been fought. Rather than the transfer of land from white colonists to disenfranchised poor black Zimbabweans, farms had ended up in the hands of a politically connected elite.

Public money had been spent on fertile and costly farms that, while originally destined for resettlement, were now controlled by senior civil servants, army and police officers and politicians.

Beneficiaries ranged from Charles Utete, secretary to the president and cabinet and Airforce Chief Perence Shiri and a one-time mayor of Harare, Tizirai Gwata.

Reports surfaced of heavy-handed treatment of small-scale farmers whose livestock strayed onto farms now held by the new owners and excessive hunting of wildlife with automatic weapons.

For the most part, the farms were seen as considerably less productive than they had been under their previous owners. The new owners paid occasional visits and had little farming experience. Crops were planted late and withered.

With our series of stories, dubbed the 'Land Grab Scandal' by our newspaper, it wasn't long before the international media followed and President Robert Mugabe was forced to defend the policy at international forums.

As the protests grew, the pressure on the government increased and eventually Mugabe was forced to declare a commission of inquiry into the programme. That effectively brought it to an end.

In March 1995, Peta and I jointly won the News Reporter of the Year award, a competition backed by Reuters, for this work. It was the first time the award had been given to journalists working for a private news organisation.

While our stories stopped this programme of land seizures by government officials in its tracks, the victory was only temporary. In 2000 the programme of violent land seizures began, leading to the ruin of the Zimbabwean economy. And while much of that land has ended up in the hands of poor black citizens, many properties were soon, once again, occupied by politicians and senior civil servants.

Designated Farm Leased to Mangwende

Anthony Sguazzin and Basildon Peta, *Daily Gazette*, 3 March 1994

WEDZA: A commercial farm here, that was originally acquired for the resettlement of 33 families, has been leased to a cabinet minister for five years.

The property, Bath Farm, that had been planned as a Model A resettlement farm for the families to grow crops and rear cattle, is now under the control of the Minister of Education and Culture, Mr Witness Mangwende.

A senior official in the Ministry of Land, Agriculture and Water Development confirmed the lease of the 1,232-hectare farm on Tuesday. The official said the lease between the State and Mr Mangwende had been reached under the provisions of the 'tenant resettlement' scheme.

The tenant resettlement scheme, the official said, had been devised by the government late last year and entailed the leasing of State farms, acquired for resettlement, to individuals for five-year periods or less.

'There are now two types of resettlements, that is communal resettlement and tenant resettlement. The latter is aimed at promoting indigenous commercial farmers through leasing State farms to individuals,' the official said.

She said it was in this context that Bath Farm had been leased to Mr Mangwende for a five-year period and other individuals who she could not reveal.

'There is nothing sinister about the lease. It was leased under a specific and noble programme by the government to assist genuine black farmers regardless of their type of current employment,' she said.

Mr Peter MacSporran, vice-president of the Commercial Farmers' Union (CFU), said that his organization had never heard of the tenant resettlement scheme. As far as they knew, Bath Farm had been acquired to make available for 33 settlers. He said the CFU would be following up to inquire about this new scheme.

However, sources within the CFU have previously stated that the replacement of one farmer by another on a property was abuse of the resettlement programme which was supposed to broaden the number of landowners and thus alleviate the chronic shortage of land ...

When a *Daily Gazette* team visited the farm, some farm labourers, who had served under the original owner before the acquisition, said Mr Mangwende had been running the farm since last November ... 'We requested him (Mr Mike van Menerty, the previous owner) to help us be part of the families to be resettled so that we could start developing our own villages and fields here,' one labourer said.

'We were assured that this would be possible but the next thing we heard was the farm was no longer for resettlement and someone would come to occupy. Mr Mangwende then came in November and we are very grateful that he retained us' ...

Utete also got Govt farm

Daily Gazette, 23 March 1994

Although the government has declined to name senior government officials who have benefitted from the tenant resettlement programme, the *Daily Gazette* has, through painstaking investigations, uncovered a number of these leases.

Today we confine ourselves to some of the leases in the fertile Doma farming area near Mhangua. However, the *Daily Gazette* will be publishing details of other State-leased farms to senior government officials in a series of articles in due course.

The secretary to the President and Cabinet, Dr Charles Utete, has taken over the 4,000-hectre Rudziwe Farm in Doma, which was allegedly under-utlised by its former owner, a Mr Potgieter, whose family had been on the farm for 19 years. Dr Utete acquired the lease for the farm in 1991, almost three years before the government went public about the 'tenant resettlement programme'.

In the same area, the deputy permanent secretary for Industry and Commerce, Mr James Chinanga, has acquired the 3,000-hectare Wilderness Farm ...

Resettlement farm given to Air Force boss

Daily Gazette, 25 March 1994

The commander of the Air Force of Zimbabwe, Air Marshall Perence Shiri, is now leasing a farm in Matepatepa near Bindura, which was bought by the state in 1989 on a willing-buyer, willing-seller basis for resettlement ...

The 2,832-hectare property, Audrey Farm, known locally as Rufa Falls, was sold to the state by Mr Roger Desa and is considered one of the best farms in the district. The firm has a well-developed irrigation system and potential, with a half share in a dam with 1,400-million-gallon capacity.

A former owner, Mr Pat Johnson, who preceded Mr Desa, was once the biggest individual burley tobacco grower in the world. Since the sale of the farm to the government, a farmer has been leasing it on a yearly basis because it was understood the government was not ready to resettle families on the property ... The farmer was required to leave the farm in the first week of last November ...

Reports of excessive hunting on the farm, which has a high population of kudu, have surfaced since Mr Shiri took over. Relentless efforts to get a comment from Mr Shiri were unsuccessful ...

New twist: Tenants already owners

Daily Gazette, 7 April 1994

In a new twist to the 'tenant resettlement' scandal, the *Daily Gazette* has established that government has leased commercial farms originally acquired for resettlement to prominent people already in possession of other private farms.

Examples of such beneficiaries are former army commander General Tapfumanyeni Mujuru and the first black mayor of Harare and current Zanu (PF) councillor in the capital city, Dr Tizirai Gwata. Dr Gwata, who is a specialist physician, recently acquired a lease on the 4,000-acre Meadows Farm I Concession, about 50 kilometres north of Harare.

The former mayor already owns Pamberi Farm in Ruwa, which he bought. Dr Gwata also owns a private clinic along Fife Avenue in Harare and a number of surgeries in Harare. Dr Gwata is married to Dr Charles Utete's sister. Dr Utete, who is the Secretary to the President and Cabinet, has already benefited through 'tenant resettlement' by acquiring Ruziwe Farm in Doma.

When contacted for comment yesterday, Dr Gwata did not want to commit himself or reveal the details on his new lease ... 'It is wrong to say I benefited from a scheme because this is a simple and straightforward thing that has been occurring for years ...'

When asked to comment on Pamberi Farm in Ruwa, he could only say 'that small plot', but Gwata declined to disclose its hectarage...

1995, ANGOLA

Angola's first muckraker

INTRODUCED BY CLAUDIA GASTROW

Ricardo de Mello, Angola's first investigative journalist, was murdered at the age of 38.

Born in Lisbon on 26 September 1956 to an Angolan mother and Portuguese father, Mello grew up in Luanda where he eventually read for a degree in law at the University of Agostinho Neto. His passion, however, was journalism. He cut his teeth in the 1980s and 1990s reporting on Angola's civil war for Voice of America and the BBC. At the time, private media was illegal in the country, making the official *Jornal de Angola* the only source of locally produced information.

This changed with the abandonment of socialism and superficial adoption of multi-party democracy in 1992. Mello embraced the openings created by the legalisation of independent press. In February 1995, in collaboration with Jaime Gonçalves, an Angolan businessman, Mello launched *Imparcial Fax* (Impartial Fax), an investigative news bulletin, which was published five days a week and faxed directly to subscribers.

Imparcial Fax quickly gained a reputation as one of the few (or arguably the only) source of independent investigative journalism in the country. In its founding statutes, it explicitly aligned itself with a human rights agenda, identifying censorship, corruption and 'political totalitarianism' as its nemeses. In order to preserve its integrity, journalists who worked with *Imparcial Fax* were prohibited from holding positions within the state, political parties or any other kind of employment that could compromise their reporting. This was necessary, as the ruling MPLA (Popular Movement for the Liberation of Angola) had inveigled its way into almost all institutions, providing it with powerful financial and political means to co-opt and silence critics.

War and corruption stood at the centre of *Imparcial Fax*'s reporting. By 1995, Angola's civil war had been dragging on for 20 years, with information on the MPLA and National Union for the Total Independence of Angola (UNITA)'s activities heavily censored. Mello became the first journalist to break through state propaganda, drawing on his links to MPLA elites to gather information about what was really happening. Simultaneously, he began to focus on the extensive corruption that plagued the country. Angola was in the midst of a transition from a socialist planned economy to a free-market orientated one, and the elites were reaping the spoils. Prior to Mello, these actions, although discussed on the street, did not face public scrutiny. *Imparcial Fax* interrupted the feasting by highlighting the collapse of state-owned enterprises, and the corrupt patronage that lay behind accumulation, such as the involvement of First Lady Ana Paula dos Santos in business dealings.

Investigative journalism is risky anywhere, but in Angola, those risks rapidly escalate. Despite only having 300 official subscribers, the information from *Imparcial Fax* reached significantly more people, and also indicated that there were people from within the state willing to leak information. This caused anger among the powerful. Mello and other journalists began to frequently receive threats directed not only at them, but their families. As just one example, Mariano Costa, a journalist working for *Imparcial Fax*, was detained at Luanda's airport and held for 28 hours. In January 1995, just a few months after publishing an exposé about the uses of psychological warfare by the MPLA state, Mello was warned that his life was in danger and he began to receive a deluge of anonymous threats. He was not dissuaded however, and *Imparcial Fax* continued its work.

On 18 January 1995, however, the threats to his life were acted upon. Returning home in the early hours of the morning, he was shot point-blank in his apartment block and then injected with an unknown substance. A neighbour's child found Mello and alerted his wife. His killers have never been brought to justice, nor were they ever formally identified. However, based on information apparently leaked from DNIC (National Directorate for Criminal Investigations), it is widely believed in Angola that his assassination was orchestrated by a man nicknamed 'Carlitos', the nephew of then minister of interior, André Pitra 'Petroff'. The murderers had rented an apartment opposite his the month before, following his daily routines and actions, apparently simply withdrawing into the apartment after murdering him.

Following Mello's murder, *Imparcial Fax* collapsed, the assassination having 'paralyse(d) the entire profession' (IRBC, 1999) of independent journalism in Angola by acting as a warning to both journalists and whistleblowers. On the same day that Mello was killed, two other journalists associated with *Imparcial Fax* were assaulted, and within the week, Mariano Costa was attacked and almost kidnapped by unknown assailants (IRBC, 1999). Many of those linked to the paper sought refuge in other countries.

The opening, which Mello had attempted to grasp, was shut down by the Angolan regime, which, through the 1990s and into the present has continued to harass journalists, with a notable number being threatened, assaulted and interrogated. In Angola, Ricardo de Mello continues to be a symbol of how much can be achieved with little resources and overwhelming political opposition to one's work. While embassies, international organisations and NGOs turned a blind eye to the Angolan regime's impunity, Mello and his team stared these abuses in the face, revealing the potential of independent investigative journalism under even the most adverse conditions.

References

Immigration and Refugee Board of Canada (IRBC). 1999. 'Angola: The Luanda-based newspaper "Jornal Imparcial Fax", in particular whether the paper and its employees were targeted by the dos Santos government and/or police because it published stories critical of the government', (update to AGO21980.E of 14 November 1995). Available at: www.refworld.org/docid/3ae6ad4624.html, accessed on 10 June 2018.

While the Braga is the Treasurer[2]

Ricardo de Mello, *Imparcial Fax*, 18 October 1994
Translated by Claudia Gastrow

The appetites of employees, from the highest in the hierarchy to the lowliest of police, have now turned to privatisations. The transfer of every one of the state's small properties to individuals creates an environment for corruption which is increasingly open, blatant. However, the relevant authorities continue to fail to react due to an alleged 'lack of proof' despite flagrant

---

2   A proverb referencing a context in which there are opportunities for corruption or when money has been embezzled or misappropriated.

examples that have appeared in the public eye. One of them, just one more, is evident in the document published today by IF.

The story is short. In 1975, when the Portuguese colonizers hastily retreated to 'the garden at the edge of the plateau'[3] the legal status of their properties became messy. The old Pensão Lusitana (Hotel Lusitana) on 18 Adolfo Pina Road was left in this situation. In the confusion, the management of the said establishment landed up in the charge of Eugénio Teixeira Furtado, at the time, a businessman. Due to circumstances, in 1978, the former TPR [*Tribunal Popular Revolucionário*] condemned Furtado to two years in prison. Having completed his sentence, he found the hotel operated by the state. He appealed the situation and won. It was decided that the management of Pensão Lusitana should be returned to him, now that he was once again free. However, this never occurred, despite the relevant authorities emitting a dispatch. Eugénio Furtado had to wait for better days, until June 1993, to obtain a new dispatch in his favour, restoring his rights. But, this is where the pig twists its tail again.[4]

After a long process that culminated in an order, signed by both the office holders of the Ministry of Commerce, to return the management [to Furtado], everything remained impeded again. This is because the present director of Pensão Lusitana, currently the Escola de Hotelaria [Hotel School], openly refused to comply with the order of the Minister and Vice-Minister of Commerce. He declared that he would not return the establishment to the previous legitimate manager, paying no attention to the orders of the hierarchy. The Minister and respective Vice-Minister, on their part, proved themselves powerless to make him comply. The current director of the hotel, a state employee, argues that the Pensão Lusitana has to be sold to him and the ministerial order can go to hell! To that effect, he has already submitted his request under the name of a phantom trading company. Since then, not even [Commerce Minister] Celestino Dias could make him stay on the right track

---

3   A phrase from the Salazar years referring to Portugal, which was 'the garden'.
4   A proverb meaning that this was the decisive moment when things started going wrong again.

by following ministerial decisions.

The most mysterious is that, even confronted with these facts (a state employee buying state properties), it continues to be repeated that 'there is no proof' of corruption. Worse still, even when this is provided, as in this situation, the fight against corruption costs money and 'can't burden the OGE [state budget],' as was explained a few days ago by the president of the parliament, França van Dúnen ... Accordingly, everything compounds itself. Will the Pensão Lusitana still be sold to the state employee placed there by the state? Or, will the fact that the fight against corruption is postponed for financial reasons be exploited while 'the Braga is the treasurer'.

The Peace from Afar

Ricardo de Mello, *Imparcial Fax*, 11 October 1994

Definitely, the Lusaka negotiations appear to be experiencing a negotiators' syndrome in which every time it seems that they will be shortly concluded, new questions emerge.

The latest (presented as the only issue still pending), relates to the municipalities. The government delegation travelled to Luanda to hold discussions and returned, having resumed negotiations. The fact that UNITA has claimed the municipalities of Soyo and Lobito has 'muddied' the process and, in Luanda, it is said that the protocol will only be signed after the end of October. Moreover, it is claimed that 'UNITA has to know who is in charge and, because of this, it is only after taking Huambo that it will be possible to proceed with the process'. It is the hardliners that are dictating the rules while the people die in all manners imaginable: hunger, war and a lack of medical assistance.

On the part of the government, the radicals believe that:
- Savimbi is 'off-side' and that with this lack of leadership, UNITA finds itself directionless;
- The divisions among the rebels will not be overcome anytime soon and so now is the moment to apply military pressure;
- Huambo is an easy victory, regardless of the obstacles

presented by the Waku-Kungo/Huambo, Benguela/Huambo, and Kuito/Huambo axes;
- The airpower of the government leaves little room for manoeuvre for Savimbi's men;
- Once militarily defeated, UNITA's officials will not return to guerilla warfare.

On the part of the rebels, the official position is firm:
- If there is any military action against Huambo it will be the end of Lusaka and a return to square one;
- The distribution of posts (power-sharing) should avoid (making it appear) that the peace accord functions as an act of surrender.

There is therefore little room for maneuver, with the two players pushing the limits to the maximum as they attempt to restrict their adversary's wiggle room.

It is a return to the logic of war (if ever it ceased to exist) and the militaries have assumed command of politics, a space that does not belong to them.

1999, MOZAMBIQUE

Who wants to kill Albano Silva and why?

INTRODUCED BY ERIKA RODRIGUES

Carlos Cardoso was a fearless and hardworking investigative journalist who dedicated his life to exposing injustice and corruption in Mozambique and in Africa. Originally a strong supporter of the Marxist-Leninist government that took office in 1975 after Mozambique's independence from Portugal, Cardoso became increasingly disillusioned with the rapacity of officials after the country transitioned to democracy in 1994.

In 2000, Cardoso, 49, was murdered after uncovering a bank fraud involving prominent Mozambican businessmen protected by the police and the judiciary system. He is still remembered as a hero.

Born in 1951 in Beira in the centre of Mozambique, Cardoso began his journalistic career in South Africa. While a student at Wits University in Johannesburg during the 1970s, he wrote extensively against the then-ruling apartheid government, which led to his deportation to Portugal on the eve of Mozambique's independence in 1975.

Cardoso was invited back to Mozambique soon after the Mozambique Liberation Front (FRELIMO) took power. As a reporter at the state-run magazine *Tempo* in 1976, he became known for his meticulous investigative reporting and his emphasis on nation building and social justice. Cardoso 'fought for a journalism of invention, a journalism that was openly political and ideological,' remembered his colleague Paul Fauvet.

Cardoso also continued his campaign against the apartheid governments in Rhodesia and South Africa, which caused tension with South Africa and often made conservative members of FRELIMO uncomfortable. Cardoso's close intellectual relationship with the first Mozambican president, the charismatic

Samora Moisés Machel, allowed him to continue with this work. He eventually became a close adviser of Machel's, even if the two didn't always agree.

When Machel died in 1986 in a bizarre aviation accident, which Carlos Cardoso investigated (See Page XX), socialism in Mozambique died too. Cardoso became deeply disillusioned with the rise of a neoliberal economy run by the International Monetary Fund and the World Bank. Cardoso ended up leaving AIM, the government's information agency, in 1989, which he had led since 1987, and dedicating himself to poetry and painting. After private media were legalised and censorship outlawed in 1991, he joined *Mediacoop*, the country's first independent cooperative of journalists, founded by some of the biggest names in Mozambican journalism.

Mediacoop conducted groundbreaking investigations of corruption and the country's economy. Cardoso focused especially on defending Mozambique's domestic industries against detrimental Bretton Woods policies backed by the new government.

The cooperative also drew attention to the decaying moral fabric of Mozambican society, where theft and bribery had become common practice. Cardoso's articles, published in *Mediafax*, *Mediacoop's* daily news sheet, quickly became famous for their quality and his dogged determination to follow stories wherever they led.

Despite the popularity of *Mediafax*, Cardoso eventually left due to an internal disagreement. He formed a similar daily fax sheet named after Mozambique's currency, *Metical*, dedicated mainly to economic issues. At *Metical*, Cardoso investigated land-grabbing allegations against the then-first lady, wife of former president Joaquim Chissano; the obscure business manoeuvres of the president's son, Nyimpine Chissano; the local treatment of toxic waste; and organised crime activities in Mozambique. He wrote fierce editorials against the 'gangsterisation of the economy' by political and business elites.

Cardoso also began probing the largest bank fraud in Mozambique's history, the theft of US$14 million from the Commercial Bank of Mozambique (BCM). Cardoso had investigated the privatisation of the two public banks, BCM in 1996 and the People's Development Bank (BPD) in 1997. Focusing on BCM, Cardoso revealed that the buying consortium, headed by the Portuguese Mello bank, had been put together by Portuguese businessman António Simões, who owned two companies in Mozambique, Cardoso wrote articles questioning US$17 million in loans, never repaid, that Simões's companies had received from the BCM between 1992 and 1994. Cardoso speculated that Simões had used them to buy his share of the bank.

The BCM scandal had begun before its privatisation. In 1996, private accounts opened by the Satar brothers, notorious loan sharks in Mozambique, were drained of US$14 million. The bank transactions were made possible by a BCM branch manager, Vicente Ramaya. The fraud was detected in 1996, but the investigation was blocked. Cardoso dwelt relentlessly on this case and on 9 May 2000, he dedicated an entire issue of *Metical* to the illicit activities of the Satars. He was becoming a liability for the influential businessmen and state officials involved.

On 22 November 2000, Carlos Cardoso was shot dead on his way home from work. The trial that followed was the first ever conducted in open court and televised live. All six accused – the Satar brothers, Ramaya, and three hit men – received the maximum penalty, but the president's son, Nyimpine Chissano, whose key involvement in the murder was revealed during the trial, escaped punishment. Cardoso was posthumously awarded a number of journalism prizes, including the 2000 Index Courage in Journalism award, sponsored by *The Economist*, in 2001.

Today, Mozambique is enjoying a mining and natural gas boom. Concerns about the misuse of the revenues it is bringing have reached new heights. But, still struggling to fulfil its role as watchdog, the media are starting to show promising glimmers of hope. Thanks to new media technology, bloggers, citizen reporting, and dedicated newspapers like @Verdade and SAVANA, a new generation of investigative reporters is emerging, ready to take up Cardoso's vision. He remains an inspiration to all.

The Tip of the Iceberg: Who Wants to Kill Albano Silva and Why?

Carlos Cardoso, *Metical*, 1999

The assassination attempt on the lawyer Albano Silva on Monday seems to be only the tip of the iceberg, whose explosion will be felt by the judicial, police and financial apparatus in the country. It is about the $14 million theft at BCM that the lawyer was investigating.

It happened around 8:30 p.m. on Monday. Albano Silva was driving on Mao Tse Tung, in the direction of Julius Nyerere.

He was driving at around forty to fifty kilometres per hour with the window on his side open. As he passed the student residence between Amilcar Cabral and the third police station, a small dark car approached from his right. Moments later, the passenger in front brandished a Makarov and fired at close range. Miraculously, the bullet missed the lawyer and smashed the back window on the opposite side.

Albano immediately pulled up by the sidewalk, where a group of students had witnessed the incident. Soon after, officers from the third police station showed up.

Yesterday, one of the students told *Metical*: 'We were watching television when, suddenly, we heard a bang. Initially, it sounded like a tire explosion but when we looked outside the window we saw a man parking his car and he looked very worried. He left the car door open and ran to the residence asking for help. He was very worried and asked us to take him to the police station.'

The same student added: 'Before we went to call the police, Dr. Albano Silva asked us to go to his car and get his briefcase, which was open, and a cellphone. We did that and then called the police. After he went to the station, a team from the criminal investigation police (PIC) came by. We don't know what happened afterward.'

Yesterday morning, a police official from the third police station stated that he was not authorized to talk, but he offered two facts: he confirmed the presence of the lawyer at the station around 8:45 p.m. and declared that the two policemen on duty that night were surprised how quickly two SAVANA reporters had made it to the area. 'They appeared within three or five minutes and wanted to speak to Dr. Albano Silva himself, but he refused. Afterward they tried to photograph the car but we didn't allow it.'

The two SAVANA reports were journalist Paulo Machava and photographer José Mathlombe. The latter told *Metical* yesterday that 'we were alerted by a witness. And what the commander is saying about us trying to take pictures is a lie because there is no way we can take photographs at night when the flash is not connected to the camera. I only showed Paulo Machava the car window of Dr. Albano Silva's car, which was broken by the bullet. This is more or less what happened.'

According to another source, one of the eyewitnesses got into a car and took off in the direction of the SAVANA headquarters. In his opinion, this might explain the swift arrival of reporters at the 3rd police station ...

A little bit of the rest of the iceberg

What could be behind this attempt, which took place barely three months after the lawyer suffered an odd armed robbery in Maputo? Could it be the Kapendra case, as suggested by a couple of his friends? The Mcbride case? A combination of all the difficult cases he has taken on?

The main suspicion falls on the BCM case, the famous $14 million fraud that remains unsolved. Yesterday, Albano Silva indicated to the police that he viewed the Satar brothers – Momade Assif, Ayob, and Asslam Abdul Satar (the latter currently not in the country) – owners of the currency exchange business 'Unicâmbios,' as the main suspects behind the attempt.

Yesterday we heard from Ayob Abdul Satar. He denied any kind of involvement. 'Dr. Albano Silva is the bank's lawyer, as everybody knows. This does not mean he is our enemy. We have nothing against him. We are really sorry for what happened.'

When probed about the lawyer's suspicions, Ayob retorted: 'Dr. Albano Silva needs to substantiate his claims. It is not enough to say that he has suspicions. We deplore what happened. Like him, we want the truth to emerge.' In response to one of our questions, he said that as of yesterday at 12:30 p.m., when the brief contact with *Metical* took place, the police hadn't contacted him.

The BCM case is explosive. In total, the investigation focuses on twenty people: the three Satar brothers, the manager of the BCM Sommerschield branch, Vincente Norotam, various Criminal Investigation Police agents, and five prosecutors (for withholding evidence and bribery), three of them from the Republic's Attorney General. Two of the investigations requested by BCM focus on the former attorney general, Sinai Nhatitima, and on the current one, António Namburete.

Last week, during the national judiciary meeting of the Public Administration, Albano Silva, who was attending as a guest, was able to talk after a brief debate on whether a guest should be able to voice his opinion. He spoke little. They cut him off, arguing that it was not in the tradition of these encounters to discuss specific cases. But he spoke enough to inform all that the prosecutors that there was, in his opinion, enough evidence in the BCM case to incriminate leading figures of the Public Administration.

2000, SOUTH AFRICA

When the lion wakes up

INTRODUCED BY TANYA PAMPALONE

Like 'Mbube', the tune which emerged from Solomon Linda and fell onto a recording track back in 1939 Johannesburg, Rian Malan's *Rolling Stone* story of the man behind the song – or more accurately, the stolen copyright behind the song behind the man – is legendary.

Those around the world who can hum the tune can't always place Linda's name. But they're usually familiar with the epic battle with Disney – which featured it as 'The lion sleeps tonight' in the smash hit movie, *The Lion King* – and how the multinational media conglomerate was eventually forced to admit its part in the scheme and negotiate a settlement that finally gave Linda's family a cut of the song's earnings.

Of course, this was no 'single-fact story', though it might have been if Malan hadn't got his pen around it. But the single fact did boil down to this: a bunch of clever Americans took what they had conveniently dubbed a 'traditional' African song, transferred it through a series of copyrights and ended up all but cutting the original song-maker out of the deal.

It's not likely it would have stayed that way. The song played on South Africa's – and the world's – lyrical landscape without raising any legal flags for years, the song-maker dying in penury in the 1960s, his family living their lives much the same way. But rumours about a copyright violation were floating around the Johannesburg music scene in the late nineties. Something was not right, and those in the know knew as much.

Jay Savage, who was cleaning up discographic information for the Mechanical Copyright Protection Society in London in the late 1990s, says he stumbled across suspicious signatures on documents related to the copyright back then. And by 1999 filmmaker François Verster had been commissioned by SABC3 to do, he says, 'a short piece on the transformation of "Mbube" into (Pete Seeger's) "Wimoweh" and then (Disney's) "The Lion Sleeps Tonight" and in the process discovered there was a far bigger political/investigative story at stake.' He went on to make a documentary, *The Lion's Trail*, which aired on public television back in 2002 and featured Malan, whose story had come out in May 2000. Malan says he first got onto the story at a braai, hearing it from none other than South African musician Johnny Clegg.

The point being, the Solomon Linda story had been out there for someone to grab. Someone, more likely than not, would have, eventually reported on the violation. But on other key points, without Malan on the case, it would have failed.

Would it, for example, have resulted in justice for the family? Malan hooked them up with a lawyer and followed it through until its just ending, all the way to the 2006 Disney settlement which, as he says, put the family members comfortably in the middle classes.

Would it, without Malan, have had the resonance it did?

With his deep, fly-on-the-wall style, imbued with his signature voice, rich characters, vivid scenes and rock 'n roll dialogue, we follow Linda's biblical tale from one Sir Henry Brougham Loch back in the late 1800s through the folk singing days at Seeger in the 1950s and into staid New York conference rooms in the 1990s, all the way back to the Linda family household in post-apartheid Johannesburg.

'He's better than Capote,' says Bongani Madondo, the longform flaneur whose own style is, well, Madondoesque, noting that Malan holds his own among the old 'new journalism' crowd of Didion, Wolfe, Thompson and Talese. Novelist Justin Cartwright, who sat with Malan on a literary stage a few years back, commented in *The Independent* that the prolific journalist told the crowd he didn't have much to say about his own literary success other than: 'Don't ask me, I'm a one-hit wonder.'

But Malan, whose only books since the seminal *My Traitor's Heart* have been collections of his reported pieces, is being dishonest. He's a consummate storyteller who reveals his tales as we sit around the campfire, slack-jawed and begging for more. Some complain that he makes up dialogue he couldn't possibly have heard, that attribution isn't always inserted – it makes pieces stumble, he says. But don't mistake him for someone who hasn't done his homework.

'I learnt my trade working for American monthlies that cut off your head if you made embarrassing errors. Yes, to make those scenes as vivid and "real" as possible, and the reporting had to be accurate; if it wasn't, you got red-lined by the dragons in the fact department, and that was very embarrassing. So, if I said, "It was a dark stormy night as John Doe stepped out into the cold, cradling his night-vision goggles and shotgun", you can bet those details were accurate.'

It was the tail end of the glory days of American magazine journalism, which came along with gun-blazing fact-checkers, generous budgets and editors who believed in the slow simmer of good reporting. Malan spent somewhere between four to six months writing and reporting the 10,000-word piece.

'I flew to New York to interview the Americans but they all stiffed me,' he says of the copyright violators he tried to talk to. 'Didn't return my calls and left me standing in the cold and rain, fruitlessly ringing their doorbells. They were rich and lawyered to the hilt and clearly thought there was no need to take me or any Zulu seriously, coming as we did from an obscure country on the southern tip of Africa. It was like, you can't touch us, so we'll just ignore you. Struck me as profoundly arrogant and insulting. I thought, bugger this, I'm going to score an equaliser.'

As Tom Rosenstiel and Bill Kovach note in *The Elements of Journalism*, it's not just the job of the journalist to seek truth, to verify, to serve as an independent monitor of power and to stay loyal to citizens, journalists also have an 'obligation to personal conscience'. Malan wasn't about to let justice slip on this one. But there's another element that is core to the practice, something often neglected by investigative journalists bent on getting out information in a crush that can leave even the most exciting stories reading like dry intelligence briefings. Journalists have a duty, say Rosenstiel and Kovach, to 'make the significant interesting and relevant'.

Taken together, it's what makes Malan not just a great journalist but one of the best nonfiction narrative writers of his generation.

'People aren't going to read to the end of a long piece unless they're engaged and entertained,' he says. 'You need to plant a hook in their imagination and drag them onward into the narrative. If you engage them on a human level, they're willing to endure screeds of boring reportage between those novelistic scenes.'

It was this sort of storytelling which, among other accolades, landed Malan's 'In the jungle: Inside the long, hidden genealogy of "The lion sleeps tonight"' in the *Best of American Magazine Writing 2001*, alongside David Foster Wallace, Donna Tartt and Malcolm Gladwell, and also ensured that the story is not over. It, like Linda's legacy and Mbube, will live on.

Netflix was recently in town shooting the story for a documentary series, while the Linda family recently re-emerged in the *Sunday Times* in March 2018, irritated that the government of KwaZulu-Natal put out a tender inviting bids to create a life-size statue of Linda – something they forgot to talk to the family about. The songwriter's granddaughter Zee Nzama told the reporter who called to ask the family about their involvement: 'This is the first we have heard about it,' she said. You can bet it won't be the last.

How American music legends made millions off the work of a Zulu tribesman who died a pauper

Rian Malan, *Rolling Stone* (USA), May 2000

Once upon a time, a long time ago, a small miracle took place in the brain of a man named Solomon Linda. It was 1939, and he was standing in front of a microphone in the only recording studio in black Africa when it happened. He hadn't composed the melody or written it down or anything. He just opened his mouth and out it came, a haunting skein of fifteen notes that flowed down the wires and into a trembling stylus that cut tiny grooves into a spinning block of beeswax, which was taken to England and turned into a record that became a very big hit in that part of Africa.

Later, the song took flight and landed in America, where it mutated into a truly immortal pop epiphany that soared to the top of the charts here and then everywhere, again and again, returning every decade or so under different names and guises. Navajo Indians sing it at powwows. Japanese teenagers know it as ライオンは寝ている. The French have a version sung in Congolese. Phish perform it live. It has been recorded by artists as diverse as R.E.M. and Glen Campbell, Brian Eno and Chet Atkins, the Nylons and Muzak schlockmeister Bert Kaempfert. The New Zealand army band turned it into a march. England's 1986 World Cup soccer squad turned it into a joke. Hollywood put it in *Ace Ventura: Pet Detective*. It has logged nearly three decades of continuous radio airplay in the U.S. alone. It is the most famous melody ever to emerge from Africa, a tune that has penetrated so deep into the human consciousness over so many generations that one can truly say, here is a song the whole world knows.

Its epic transcultural saga is also, in a way, the story of popular music, which limped pale-skinned and anemic into the twentieth century but danced out the other side vastly invigorated by transfusions of ragtime and rap, jazz, blues and soul, all of whose bloodlines run back to Africa via slave ships and plantations and ghettos. It was in the nature of this transaction that black men gave more than they got and often ended up with nothing. This one's for Solomon Linda, then, a Zulu who wrote a melody that earned untold millions for white men but died so poor that his widow couldn't afford a stone for his grave. Let's take it from the top, as they say in the trade.

A story about money

The story begins in 1939, when Solomon Linda was visited by angels in Africa's only recording studio. At the time, Johannesburg was a hick mining town where music deals were concluded according to trading principles as old as Moses: record companies bought recordings for whatever they thought the music might be worth in the marketplace; stars generally got several guineas for a session, unknowns got almost nothing. No one got royalties, and copyright was unknown. Solomon Linda didn't even get a contract. He walked out of that session with about ten shillings in his pocket, and the music thereafter belonged to the record company, with no further obligations to anyone. When 'Mbube' became a local hit, the loot went to Eric Gallo, the playboy who owned the company. All Solomon Linda got was a menial job at the boss's packing plant, where he worked for the rest of his days.

When 'Mbube' took flight and turned into the Weavers' hit 'Wimoweh', Gallo could have made a fortune if he had played his cards right. Instead, he struck a handshake deal with Larry Richmond's dad, trading 'Mbube' to TRO in return for the dubious privilege of administering 'Wimoweh' in such bush territories as South Africa and Rhodesia. Control of Solomon

Linda's destiny thus passed into the hands of Howie Richmond and his faithful sidekick, one Albert Brackman.

Howie and Al shared an apartment in the '30s, when they were ambitious young go-getters on Tin Pan Alley. Howie was tall and handsome, Al was short and fat, but otherwise, they were blood brothers, with shared passions for nightlife and big-band jazz. After World War II, Howie worked as a song promoter before deciding to become a publisher in his own right. He says he found a catchy old music-hall number, had a pal write new lyrics and placed the song with Guy Lombardo, who took it to Number Ten as 'Hop Scotch Polka'. Howie was on his way. Al joined up in 1949, and together they put a whole slew of novelty songs on the hit parade. Then they moved into the burgeoning folk-music sector, where big opportunities were opening up for sharp guys with a shrewd understanding of copyright.

After all, what was a folk song? Who owned it? It was just out there, like a wild horse or a tract of virgin land on an unconquered continent. Fortune awaited the man bold enough to name himself as the composer of some ancient tune like, say, 'Greensleeves'. A certain Jessie Cavanaugh did exactly that in the early fifties, only it wasn't really Jessie at all — it was Howie Richmond under an alias. This was a common practice on Tin Pan Alley at the time, and it wasn't illegal or anything. The object was to claim writer royalties on new versions of old songs that belonged to no one. The aliases seem to have been a way to avoid potential embarrassment, just in case word got out that Howard S. Richmond was presenting himself as the author of a madrigal from Shakespeare's day.

Much the same happened with 'Frankie & Johnny,' the hoary old frontier ballad, or 'Rovin' Kind,' a ribald ditty from the clipper-ship era. There's no way Al Brackman could really have written such songs, so when he filed royalty claims with the performing rights society BMI, he attributed the compositions to Albert Stanton, a fictitious tunesmith who often worked closely with the imaginary Mr. Cavanaugh, penning such standards as 'John Henry' and 'Michael Row the Boat Ashore.' Cavanaugh even claimed credit for 'Battle Hymn of the Republic,' a feat eclipsed only by a certain Harold Leventhal, who accidentally copyrighted an obscure whatnot that turned out to be India's national anthem.

Leventhal started out as a gofer for Irving Berlin and wound up promoting concerts for Bob Dylan, but in between, he developed a serious crush on the Weavers. In 1949, he showed up at the Village Vanguard with an old friend in tow — Pete Kameron, a suave charmer who was scouting around an entree into showbiz. Leventhal performed some introductions, and Kameron became the Weavers' manager. Since all these players knew one another, it was natural that they should combine to take charge of the left-wingers' business affairs. Leventhal advised; Kameron handled bookings and tried to fend off the redbaiters. Howie and Al took on the publishing, arranging it so that Kameron owned a fifty-percent stake. The Weavers sang the songs and cut the records, and together they sold around 4 million platters in 18 months or so.

Toward the end of 1951, these men found themselves contemplating the fateful 78 rpm record from Africa and wondering exactly what manner of beast it could be. The label said 'Mbube,' by Solomon Linda and the Evening Birds, but it had never been copyrighted. Anything not copyrighted was a wild horse, strictly speaking, and wild horses in the Weavers' repertoire were usually attributed to one Paul Campbell. The Weavers' version of 'Hush Little Baby' was a Paul Campbell composition, for instance. The same was true of 'Rock Island Line' and 'Kisses Sweeter than Wine,' tunes the folkies had learned off Leadbelly at Village hoots and reworked in their own style.

On the surface of things, Paul Campbell was thus one of the most successful songwriters of the era, but of course the name was just another alias used to claim royalties on songs from the public domain. 'Mbube' wasn't public domain at all, but it was the next best thing — an uncopyrighted song owned by an obscure foreign record label that had shown absolutely no interest in protecting Solomon Linda's rights as a writer. So the Zulu's song was tossed in among the Weavers' wild horses, and released as 'Wimoweh,' by Paul Campbell.

As the song found its fans, money started rolling in. Every record sale triggered a mechanical royalty. Every radio play counted as a performance, which also required payment, and there was always the hope that someone might take out a 'synch license' to use the tune in a movie or TV ad.

Al, Howie and Pete Kameron divided the standard publisher's fifty percent among themselves and distributed the other half to the writers — or in this case, adapters: Pete Seeger and the Weavers. Solomon Linda was entitled to nothing.

2002, Swaziland

Tackling a high-flying king

Introduced by Mbongeni Mbingo

In 2002, the *Times of Swaziland* once again rallied to the cause of enforcing government accountability, this time with an exposé by Vusi Ginindza on the unlawful purchase of a jet for King Mswati III.

On 7 July 2002 the publication dropped a bombshell: the government was secretly engaged in a process of buying the king a Bombadier Global Express Jet.

'In what has been government's most sternly guarded secret for the past two years, it emerges that the state has since made several payments for the purchase of a US$45 million state of the art executive jet for the King …'

The report came as a shock to the Swazi nation and parliament, because it came in the face of serious socio-economic challenges. The nation was E3 billion (US$230 million) in debt; the HIV/AIDS prevalence rate had risen by 40 per cent and the country had just taken over from Botswana the distinction of having the highest infection rate in the world; and the population was being ravaged by famine with approximately 230,000 people going hungry every day.

The revelation had a substantial impact on public opinion and parliament. Parliament was outraged at being bypassed for the purchase of this luxury item. It was particularly vexed because the issue of the feasibility of a private jet had been raised before in parliament in 2000. A committee had been assigned the task to look into the matter but it never came back with a report.

The royalists and traditionalists realised they could no longer get away with undisputed decision-making and a debate (with parliament involved) was opened on the issue. A parliamentary probe was carried out where the ministers involved had to give an account on how the acquisition had gone through. The audacious misuse of public funds was regarded as 'theft' by the members of parliament since the money used for the purchase was meant for development projects. The majority called for the resignation of Prime Minister Sibusiso Barnabas Dlamini. However, not all legislators were against the acquisition of the jet. Some thought it was 'not too bad an idea' as it would cut costs incurred by the 'frequency of the royal travels abroad'.

The public would have none of it. The normally passive citizenry stood up in arms at this extravagant purchase. Protests were scheduled by labour movements and unofficial 'opposition' parties. They wanted to pressure the government to cancel the purchase and put the money where it was most needed: addressing the AIDS and famine calamities. The international community looked on aghast at the audacity of cabinet's actions. Donor agencies threatened to withdraw aid if the purchase went through.

Ultimately the deal was stopped and government was ordered to get a refund. The media had once again played a critical role in the promotion of good governance.

Top of the range jet

Vusi Giningdza, *Times of Swaziland*, 7 July 2002

The government is engaged in a secret mission to purchase a private jet for King Mswati III for an incredible E450 or US$45m.

The aircraft has not simply been identified or merely admired for later consideration but a Sales Agreement plus a down payment of over US$2 million (E20 million) has been made through cryptic transactions, some of which were not entirely authorised by the government.

As it is, government is struggling to raise a monthly instalment of about US$480,000 (E4.8 million).

The 14-seater Global Express Bombardier, one of the new class of ultra long-range corporate jets, competes against the Gallstream V, Boeing 737 BBJ (used by South Africa's president Thabo Mbeki) and Airbus A319C. It is designed to fly long distances at high speed and its range is such that it can fly between any two points on the globe and needs only one refuelling stop, while it can fly non-stop between intercontinental destinations such as Cape Town/London, Sydney/Los Angeles, New York/Tokyo and Tapei/Chicago ...

The process to buy this jet started over a year ago, during which period it was kept as a foremost state secret but accelerated this year as the minister of Works and Transport Titus Mlangeni desperately tried to get rid of two national aircraft in what cabinet sources explained as an 'attempt to raise the deposit for the private jet'.

Minister Mlangeni has since the start of the year taken at least two trips to Canada where the plane is manufactured.

The purchase, according to highly placed sources who declined to be named, was facilitated through the help of two Swazi pilots, one working for South African Airways and another working for Execulet in South Africa. Execulet is a representative of Bombardier Aerospace, the manufacturer in Canada.

At least two Cabinet ministers have been invited for demonstration flights, including Prince Guduza who was then Minister of Works and Transport.

The need for the king's private aircraft was first raised two years ago by Lobamba MP Marwick Khumalo and supported by many of his colleagues who felt that the king was losing a lot of face among his contemporaries by using general passenger planes when other leaders owned private jets for state business. Another concern was the condition of the two national aircraft, now put up for sale, which had mechanical problems, coupled with reports that Swaziland's airspace was highly suspect according to international aviation monitors.

'At the time the economy as not was bad as it is today ...'

What's the fuss about jet?

Alec Lushaba, *Times of Swaziland*, 10 August 2002

His Majesty King Mswati III yesterday said he is aware that government plans to buy him a private jet, which he would use on his many travels abroad.

Speaking at a press conference ... the king told all what he knows about his yet to be delivered jet, an E450 million Bombardier Global Express ... Journalists defied an unwarranted warning from an over-zealous Foreign Affairs Minister Abednego Ntshangase that anything outside the king's smart partnership trip shouldn't be asked. Ntshangase seemingly enjoys dictating to journalists what to or not to ask the king in press conferences.

The king was happy to answer the question on government's plans to buy him a private jet and he conceded that to some people it might appear an extravagant and unnecessary expenditure. He said it is up to the cabinet to explain everything to the people.

What king's jet?

Alec Lushaba, *Times of Swaziland*, 24 July 2002

The Swazi National Council (SNC) has not been briefed on the purchase of the king's private jet worth E450 million, equivalent to about US$45 million.

SNC secretary Sam Mkhombe disclosed in an interview recently that the matter was to be dealt with by cabinet, but it has not yet reached them.

'There is nothing I can say or claim to know about the jet because it has not been brought to the Council's attention. Government can be in a better position to comment on the issue,' Mkhombe said.

It is said that the Government has already paid over E20 million as a ... down payment, some of which has not been entirely approved by government.

It is said that Prime Minister Sibusiso Dlamini's Government is struggling to raise the monthly instalment of about US$480,000 dollars (E4.8 million) ...

Who got the big bucks?

Vusi Ginindza, *Times of Swaziland*, 13 October 2002

Of the numerous controversies that currently beleaguer the Swaziland government, one is a closely guarded secret which, if exposed, could end several careers within the Cabinet. Who received US$1.5 million (about E15 million) as 'commission' for the purchase of the Global Express Bombardier?

This is an executive jet ordered for exclusive use of the King, the Queen Mother and their selected entourage due for delivery before the end of next month.

The *Times* can reveal that it is a standing policy of the manufacturer, Bombardier — as it is with many makers of aeroplanes — to give commissions to buyers once the initial agreement of purchase is concluded.

Experts close to the matter said in the case of this particular deal, a commission of 1.5 percent (of the total purchase price of US$45 million) was paid out to 'a representative' of the buyer, but the ministry of finance has not seen such a deposit into any government account.

Sources in Cabinet said this issue is avoided like a plague every Tuesday when ministers gather for their weekly meetings. 'The Cabinet is decidedly divided on many issues but this one crowns them all,' a minister who asked not to be named revealed. 'Maybe some of us are jealous, you may never know, but the general feeling is that the matter should be discussed openly so that it does not taint all of us. The people who were active in this deal are known' ...

US QUESTIONS PM ON KING'S JET

Musa Magagula, *Times of Swaziland*, 20 October 2002

Prime Minister Sibusiso Dlamini saved the day during his recent trip to the United States when White House officials expressed reluctance to host His Majesty for the Songs for Life launch, because of plans to buy him a jet. The premier is said to have met White House, health and ... service officials whom he convinced the purchase of the king's jet would not get in the way of the objectives of the Royal Initiative to Combat AIDS (RICA) project.

The king is expected to be a guest at the White House where he will attend a reception with President George W Bush ...

2002, SOUTH AFRICA

The tenacious, pugnacious corporate vigilante

INTRODUCED BY REG RUMNEY

The column chosen to illustrate the work of the late Deon Basson will strike those who know his work as remarkably clear, free of numbers and in parts philosophical. Basson, pugnacious and tenacious, did not, according to at least one editor, take kindly to being edited, or as he probably saw it, oversimplified. The writing of the six-time winner of the country's prestigious Sanlam Financial Journalist of the Year Award could be dense and demanding.

This piece of writing by Basson, however, demonstrates what Pulitzer Prize-winning reporter David Cay Johnston says is essential for investigative journalism: 'start with underlying principles and theory' to understand the mechanics (Gutfreund, 2014). Investigative journalism is as much about ideas as ferreting out facts and figures.

The theme of the August 2002 award-winning column was the failure of the supposed regulatory watchdogs to protect investors against the wolves of the financial world. It focused on what seemed to be a quasi unit trust scheme, PSC Guaranteed Growth (PSCGG), an unlisted, and therefore non-transparent, company headed by self-proclaimed share trading expert Jack Milne. As the article notes, Milne flatly refused to disclose the scheme's investment portfolio, and Basson stresses the need for transparency as an essential element of the market system and capitalism itself.

Basson posed a deceptively simple question: Who is supposed to be regulating this scheme and why are they not doing their job? Hovering in the background was the spectacular US accounting scandal and collapse of energy company Enron, which had raised a big question mark over Western corporate culture. Basson had earlier written a column (excerpted here) urging the trade and industry minister to intervene to investigate Tigon, the listed company supposedly underwriting PSCGG and run by Gary Porritt (Wessels, 2003), assisted by his close associate Sue Bennet. Basson noted that it might prove to be South Africa's own mini-Enron (Slabbert, 2016).

Milne's company was raising huge sums from thousands of investors. As it turned out, Basson's hint that investors might once again lose money because of the non-disclosure and fragmented supervision came to pass. Around eight months after Basson wrote the article, Milne confessed to defrauding investors, blaming Porritt (Wessels, 2003) and, after a plea bargain, served 11 months of a five-year jail sentence. He confessed again in 2016 that with Porritt and Bennet he had deliberately defrauded investors by making misrepresentations in a company prospectus (Slabbert, 2016).

Investor money, meant to be put into a diversified portfolio by PSCGG, was diverted solely into shares of Tigon and its subsidiary Shawcell – something which Porritt has disputed in court was even fraudulent (Slabbert, 2018a). PSCGG was liquidated and its investors lost around R160 million.

More than 15 years after being arrested, Porritt and Bennet were still in court in 2018, the PSCGG matter being one among 3000 charges of fraud, racketeering and contraventions of the Income Tax Act, Securities Exchanges Control Act and the Companies Act they faced. Porritt was accused of adopting Stalingrad tactics to delay facing justice by a Supreme Court of Appeals judge (Slabbert, 2018b).

The state also claimed that despite pleading indigence and eschewing legal representation, Porritt had access to R100 million (Slabbert, 2017). Journalism is not renowned for enriching its practitioners, and Basson was unlikely to have had a small fraction of that sum. He struggled with legal costs when he was forced later to defend himself against a defamation suit without the aid of the company, Media24, with whom he had been associated for many years (Cameron, 2008). As resilient as Basson was – he faced severe personal attacks in his investigations, including having his bi-polar medical history revealed – he was not invulnerable. In 2008 at the age of 53, he died of a heart attack attributed to stress at having to fight off lawfare by the property syndication company, Sharemax, on which he focused several chapters of his draft book 'Public Interest Warriors'. Sharemax tried to interdict publication of chapters of the book that dealt with the company, and finally managed to censor it entirely by buying it from his widow (Heystek, 2013).

However, thanks to international publication by Wikileaks, the chapters that Sharemax did not want published are available online. The chapters that do not deal with Sharemax, and discuss PSCGG for instance, are not publicly available.

This is a pity because the book is not simply a history of the Sharemax, Tigon, PSCGG or other corporate debacles, but takes up the deeper ideas presented in Basson's *Finance Week* column, which still resonate a decade later: the failure of the bodies that are supposed to protect investors. In the book he goes beyond regulation, to accuse the media of having its critical facilities blunted by commercial interests, and is scathing of the auditing profession. In the light of the various scandals that have dented the credibility of one of the biggest auditing firms in the world, KPMG, in South Africa (Niselow, 2018), this was prescient. Basson noted that auditing firms have become marketing stalls to sell other lucrative services to clients – calling to mind the so-called discredited South African Revenue Services 'rogue unit' report, for which the firm apologised (Hosken, 2017).

A partial comfort is that one of the moves Basson suggested, a single regulator for the financial services sector, one of the peaks of South Africa's new twin peaks regulation, will become a reality. Basson would be amused that the 'liberalists' are still complaining about new business regulation (Zyl, 2017). However, Basson's history shows that regulators are not all knowing and an independent and well-resourced media must be able to shine a light on what needs to be regulated.

References

Cameron, B. 2008. 'A tribute to Deon Basson, a public interest warrior'. Available at: www.iol.co.za/personal-finance/a-tribute-to-deon-basson-a-public-interest-warrior-997674, accessed on 16 May 2018.

Gutfreund, H. 2014. 'An interview with David Cay Johnston, Pulitzer Prize winner', *The Politic*. Available at: http://thepolitic.org/an-interview-with-david-cay-johnston/, accessed on 16 May 2018.

Heystek, M. 2013. 'Deon Basson was right about Sharemax', *Moneyweb*. Available at: www.moneyweb.co.za/archive/soapbox-tribute-to-deon-basson-and-other-bravehear/, accessed on 16 May 2018.

Hosken, G. 2017. 'KPMG cans SARS "rogue unit" report, apologises to Gordhan'. Available at: www.timeslive.co.za/politics/2017-09-15-kpmg-cans-sars-rogue-unit-report-apologises-to-gordhan/, accessed on 16 May 2018.

Niselow, T. 2018. 'KPMG acknowledges its failings damaged auditing profession', *The M&G Online*. Available at: https://mg.co.za/article/2018-05-07-kpmg-acknowledges-its-failings-damaged-auditing-profession/, accessed on 16 May 2018.

Slabbert, A. 2018a. 'No obligation to diversify PSCGG investments – Porritt', *Moneyweb*. Available at: www.moneyweb.co.za/news/south-africa/no-obligation-to-

diversify-pscgg-investments-porritt/, accessed on 16 May 2018.
Slabbert, A. 2018b. 'Porritt acts just like Zuma, court finds', *Moneyweb*. Available at: www.moneyweb.co.za/news/south-africa/porritt-acts-just-like-zuma-court-finds/, accessed on 16 May 2018.
Slabbert, A. 2017. 'Porritt is a R100-million man, state says', *The Citizen*.
Slabbert, A. 2016. 'Porritt, Bennett and I committed deliberate fraud – Milne', *The Citizen*.
Wessels, V. 2003. 'PSC fugitive Jack Milne breaks his silence'. Available at: www.iol.co.za/news/south-africa/psc-fugitive-jack-milne-breaks-his-silence-105392, accessed on 16 May 2018.
Zyl, G. van. 2017. 'Twin Peaks now law – "sad day" for SA financial services consumers – FMF'. Available at: www.biznews.com/sa-investing/2017/08/23/twin-peaks-now-law-sa-financial-services-consumers-fmf/, accessed on 16 May 2018.

Stand up, real PSCGG regulator

Deon Basson, *Finance Week*, 16 August 2002

The time has come for the PSC Guaranteed Growth (PSCGG) regulator to stand up and be counted so that the SA investing public knows who is supposed to be protecting its interests.

PSCGG is an investment company that markets its unlisted, low voting ordinary shares exceptionally aggressively. In the normal course of events you would, technically speaking, expect the Registrar of Companies to be the 'regulator' of a scheme like PSCGG because of its function of registering the prospectus.

Approval of the prospectus implies only that the Registrar is satisfied that all the requirements of the Companies Act are met. This includes ensuring that the information that must be disclosed in terms of the Companies Act is contained in the prospectus. But it is not the Registrar's job to weigh up the merits of the offer.

PSCGG has been marketing shares without a valid prospectus for more than two years since the validity of the original and prospectus expired on 15 June 2000. Its prominent advertising campaign should have alerted the Registrar that the marketing of new shares continued actively after that date.

It could be argued that PSCGG is not a company in the normal sense and is actually meant to be a unit trust scheme. In this case, why is the Financial Services Board (FSB) not the regulator? But whether it is a company or a unit trust scheme, PSCGG simply refuses to disclose its investment portfolio. Whatever it is, PSCGG is contravening either the Companies Act or the Unit Trusts Act.

But there could be a third possibility. Due to its non-disclosure of its investment portfolio and selling investments without a valid prospectus, it could perhaps be seen as a deposit-taking institution. In this case, the SA Reserve Bank's bank supervision department would be the regulator.

But it is possible that PSCGG is craftily slipping through all three legislative nets — the Companies Act, the Unit Trusts Act and the Banks Act — and making fools of all three regulators.

Looking at the case study of the well-known Ref group and the alleged circumvention of three Acts by PSCGG which are meant to protect investors, a case can even be made for the Business Practices Committee to investigate PSCGG.

The Ref group, under the leadership of David Romero, was investigated by the Business Practices Committee and was severely taken to task in a 77-page report published in the Government Gazette on 30 October 1996. This is a precedent that cannot be ignored.

The power of regulators reminds me of a time 10 years ago when unlisted debentures were all the rage. One of the smaller schemes was OTC Finance International, managed by Freek Viljoen. In one of his marketing documents, he praised capitalism as 'the only moral economic and political system' which existed in history. During an interview, he made emotional use of further slogans by famous economists like Milton Friedman to support his argument.

Liberalists are sometimes the most intolerant people when it comes to expression of alternative views. Similarly, some capitalists are among the most intolerant people when it comes to the disclosure of information.

Let's follow the laissez-faire attitude of Viljoen and his colleagues and scale regulation down to the minimum. Limit regulation to disclosure. Then give investors the freedom and the information to decide for themselves.

The problem is that people like OTC's Viljoen and PSCGG's

Jack Milne want all the freedom of capitalism to collect money from investors. But they conveniently object to disclosure as an essential counterbalance.

Give us a single and modern regulator in SA that strictly enforces simple and meaningful disclosure. I have a feeling that in such circumstances, the market mechanism will function much better than it does now. I am in favour of a market mechanism that provides a level-playing field but certainly not the kind of medieval concoction Milne and others are now trying to dish up.

The Nel Commission, investigating investor protection in SA after the Masterbond debacle, found in 1997: 'The fragmentation of supervision between the Registrar of Banks and the FSB and its predecessor led to inadequate supervision of the Masterbond, Owen Wiggins and Supreme group of companies with resultant losses to investors.

'This can be illustrated by excerpts from an exchange of letters in 1994. There was reason to suspect that certain companies in these groups were carrying on business in contravention of the Banks Act.'

Hopefully PSCGG will not lead to a recurrence of these unfortunate events. Meanwhile, please tell us who PSCGG's regulator is and what will be done about the apparent violations of the Companies Act.

An open letter to [Minister of Trade and Industry] Alec Erwin

Deon Basson, *Finance Week*, 28 June 2002

There is a compelling reason for writing to you. *Finance Week* has been investigating Tigon, a company listed on the JSE Securities Exchange, for a while now.

I believe it's time for you to use your powers in terms of section 258(2) of the Companies Act to appoint an inspector or two to investigate Tigon's affairs.

The media has at its disposal freedom of speech in terms of section 16 of the Constitution. We don't have the power to search, summon or interrogate and it would be inappropriate to have those powers. An inspector would have such powers.

I think it is fair comment to say that for once at least SA's financial media have made a contribution in exposing Tigon's unusual business and accounting practices. On that score, we have done better than our US counterparts with regard to Enron ...

Finance Week will continue to investigate Tigon and publish the results as they become known. But I consider it prudent to warn you that in Tigon, SA may, on a smaller scale, have its own Enron-in-waiting. I do not say that the company acted corruptly or fraudulently. I cannot speak for them, but I would venture to say that if you consult institutions such as the Financial Services Board, the SA Reserve Bank, the SA Revenue Service, the SA Institute of Chartered Accountants and the JSE Securities Exchange, you will probably find that they will largely share my opinion.

Your colleague, Finance Minister Trevor Manuel, highlighted the demise of LeisureNet, Macmed, Regal Treasury Bank and Unifer in his Budget speech earlier this year. In all these instances, investigations followed only after the train smash. As the reports of the Nel Commission show, SA regulatory institutions regularly wait for the accident to happen and do little to avert it.

2006, Tanzania

A local story becomes a national scandal and ousts a prime minister

Introduced by Finnigan wa Simbeye

In 2005, while working at *The Citizen* newspaper, I read in its local Kiswahili sister paper, *Mwanachi*, that parliamentary energy and minerals committee chair, Njeru Kasaka, had ordered the ministry of energy and minerals (MEM) to give a contract to build a 1000-kilometre Dar es Salaam–Mwanza oil pipeline back to a Tanzanian company, Africommerce International Limited.

Africommerce founder and CEO, Elisante Muro, had complained to the parliamentary committee that his company had invested over US$3 milllion in a feasibility study and even marketed the pipeline project to the landlocked neighbouring countries of Burundi, DR Congo, Rwanda and Uganda, when the project was snatched away by MEM and given to a US-based firm, Richmond Development Company LLC (RDC).

After hearing from both sides, including Minister for Energy and Minerals Daniel Yona, Kasaka's committee concluded that the project should be returned to Muro's Company, which should find a strategic partner to implement the multi-million dollar project.

I decided to follow up by getting in touch with Muro, who gave me a briefing of all that transpired and gave me a tip that Richmond was not an established energy company at all, but a briefcase firm controlled by some crooked politicians.

I used my internet searching skills to find out more about RDC, and found the company's website full of false claims. The company, jointly owned by a Tanzanian businessman based in Texas and his Pakistani friend, said that it was constructing the 60,000-seater national stadium in Dar es Salaam and also that it owned the Dar–Mwanza oil pipeline project.

The national stadium was a Chinese-funded project, implemented by a Chinese contractor. The Dar–Mwanza pipeline was also under dispute, so it was inaccurate to claim it belonged to the RDC.

In response to emailed questions, one of the RDC directors, a Pakistani economist named Mohamed Huque, warned me and my newspaper to stop following up the story and threatened that his company would take legal measures against us. I wrote the story and it was published in *The Citizen*.

When President Jakaya Kikwete took over from Benjamin Mkapa after the 2005 general election, Kikwete picked his long-time political ally, Edward Lowassa, as his prime minister despite resistance by some ruling party heavyweights who regarded Lowassa as corrupt. Kikwete's administration was greeted by the worst droughts in the country's history when electricity generated by water plummeted by over 50 per cent and the country started experiencing daily 12-hour power cuts.

With World Bank and other donors, it was agreed that the energy sector, monopolised by the state utility Tanesco, would be partly liberalised with independent power producers allowed to generate electricity and sell it to Tanesco. By January 2006, when Tanesco selected private companies to sell it electricity, RDC got the largest share of 100MW for $US192 million.

When I saw the company included on the list, I sensed foul play and chose to follow up the story by talking to different stakeholders including Yona himself, Africommerce's Muro and his technical director, Dr Athumani Mfutakamba, and then went back to Mohamed Huque, who was now even more threatening. I now worked for *ThisDay* newspaper.

I established that RDC was a shell company with no premises in Texas but run out of a simple internet shop in Dar es Salaam. It had top-level connections to the then ruling party treasurer, Rostam Aziz, whose Caspian Construction Limited shared offices, bank account number and local directors when it registered locally as Richmond Development Tanzania Limited.

When in 2007 RDC failed to import the power-generating turbines as required by the contract and instead sold its contract to Dubai-based Dowans Holdings Limited, it became a national scandal. The parliamentary Speaker, Samuel Sitta, appointed a probe team led by Dr Harrison Mwakyembe to establish who was behind RDC and how, despite violating the 2005 contract, they were allowed to sell it to another company.

When Dr Mwakyembe's probe team submitted its report to Parliament in February 2008, it advised MPs to demand Lowassa's resignation or call a vote of no confidence in him. *The Guardian* reported it this way: 'Courteous norms and sugar-coated language were set aside as fiery MPs spoke with bitterness as they contributed to the debate on the findings of the select committee. Opposition and government CCM MPs spoke with one voice in criticising the contract imposed by top government officials on Tanesco ... It was a "born-again" Parliament, with MPs clearly stating that the time for tolerating vice and the signing of bad contracts by ministers and other public officials while Parliament looked on helplessly were gone for good.'

Lowassa resigned as Prime Minister.

When we were doing the story, there were a lot of monetary offers to abandon it and also not to cooperate with the parliamentary committee. Millions of shillings were promised to us by people allied to Rostam Aziz and Edward Lowassa. Threats were also issued and our publisher, Reginald Mengi, advised us to be careful when going out, avoid being alone and suggested that we should apply for gun registrations to allow us to carry a weapon, if necessary. Some of my fellow journalist got guns, but I declined.

What was important was that the publisher was very supportive and when the story became a national issue, all media outlets took up the matter so it was not easy to target one media house. Likewise, at my newspaper, we were working as a team, so the risk was spread.

Msabaha 'dives' for cover over suspect pipeline deal

Finnigan wa Simbeye, *ThisDay*, January 2006

Rejected only the other day, an American company is back with a lucrative deal, apparently all signed and sealed, to supply power to the national electricity grid, *ThisDay* can reveal.

At first attempt, the Third Phase government rejected a bid by Messrs Richmond Development Company (RDC) to secure a TZS650-billion pipeline project. But the same firm has just scooped the lucrative deal.

ThisDay can now reveal that the RDC failed to win the tender for the oil pipeline project floated by the Third Phase government on grounds that it had submitted 'a poor project implementation proposal'.

But to the surprise of stakeholders in the construction

industry, heightened by a highly suspect move, the same company recently received a bond worth $100 million (about TZS130 billion) from the CRDB Bank, with which it has just secured a contract from TANESCO to supply 100 megawatts of power to the national electricity grid.

'When the Third Phase government was about to end its tenure towards the end of last year, we had rejected Richmond's proposal,' former energy minister, Daniel Yona told *ThisDay*.

He added: 'As to what is happening now, you had better contact the current minister (Dr Msabaha).'

When contacted for comment, Dr Msabaha dithered: 'You better come to my office; I don't give interviews over the phone.' But when *ThisDay* visited the minister's office, his aides demanded a written questionnaire.

The US company, based at Houston, Texas was about to win the lucrative oil pipeline project which was initiated by a local company, Africommerce International Limited (AIL), but it failed in its bid after it allegedly failed to submit a satisfactory proposal on how to implement the project.

The former minister dismissed allegations that the US firm had won the bond through his 'influence-peddling' by virtue of his membership to the CRDB Board.

'Those reports are absolutely untrue, I first knew Richmond during my tenure at the ministry when they approached us with a view to taking over the Dar es Salaam–Mwanza oil pipeline project,' Yona insisted.

The AIL which initiated the project in the 1990s had sunk over TZS3 billion by last year when the former energy and minerals minister decided that the company had failed to deliver over the years.

After a long silence, Richmond resurfaced in the local media last week when press reports revealed that the company had secured a last-minute bond from CRDB after failing to do as a pre-condition to import 20MW General Electric gas turbines to supply power to Tanesco.

The RDC is one of the four private power-generating companies awarded a tender last week to supply Tanesco with energy. But reports said the US firm had failed to import a

20MW gas turbine early this month due to failure to raise a bank guarantee but which the CRDB finally provided.

At a news conference last week, Minister for Energy and Minerals Dr Ibrahim Msabaha – who served as deputy to Mr Yona during the last five years of President Benjamin Mkapa's administration – confirmed that CRDB had 'rescued' the American company in its desperate bid to clinch the Dar es Salaam–Mwanza oil pipeline.

Investigations by *ThisDay* have since established that RDC had earlier failed to secure a bank bond both at home in the US and locally because of stringent US bank demands on credibility and project viability of the loan seeker.

On its website, the RDC which is jointly owned by businessman Mohammed Gire and economist Dr Mohammed Huque, does not give any details of its finances other than giving a general notice on projects covered.

'RDC team has brought to financial close several projects totalling some $500m (approx. TZS650 billion). RDC's current development includes civil constructions, oil pipelines and 200MW Power Plant, and a 200,000 bpd Refinery Project in Brazil,' the company says on its website.

Without naming where the projects are specifically located, the RDC further claims it is undertaking an 'oil pipeline' project and a '60,000-seat national stadium' project; both projects located within East Africa, according to the website.

2006, LESOTHO

On the wrong side of development

INTRODUCED BY JOHN AERNI-FLESSNER

For much of Lesotho's history, there was little to no investigative journalism in the country. There has long been a vibrant local press, writing in both Sesotho and English, dating back to the first publication of *Leselinyana la Lesotho* in 1863 and the publication of the first issues of *Naledi ea Lesotho*, the first independent secular paper in 1904. Much of the journalism through the period of colonial rule and after independence has focused on local politics, religion and the plight of Basotho migrants to South Africa. Despite the arrival of independence in 1966, Lesotho experienced a 23-year period of autocratic rule from 1970 to 1993. During this time, many journalists were not able to operate freely with full legal protections. This is best illustrated by the assassination of *Leselinyana* editor Edgar Mahlomola Motuba in 1981 by individuals upset that the paper was publishing articles critical of the government. Even now, however, journalists can still be at risk, as the shooting of *Lesotho Times* editor Lloyd Mutungamiri and the flight of journalist Keiso Mohloboli into exile in July 2016 demonstrated.

The sometimes-hostile climate toward journalists in Lesotho helps explain the lack of robust investigative reporting, although the 2016 formation of the MNN Centre for Investigative Journalism, an outfit funded in part by the Open Society Initiative for Southern Africa, is heartening.

With a lack of investigative reporting in Lesotho, much of the responsibility for breaking news of public scandals and keeping a watch on policy implementation has fallen on non-governmental organisations (NGOs) based in Lesotho and abroad. The series of excerpts below highlight how the lack of democratic structures, viable avenues for public participation in big projects and local investigative journalism have led to negative outcomes for many individuals and communities impacted by the construction of the mountain dams that supply water to South Africa. In this excerpt, the authors highlight the impact that corruption has played on the Lesotho Highlands Water Project (LHWP), how the compensation scheme for those Basotho displaced by the project has been inadequate, and how viable local partnerships with affected communities can be built. While the published report came too late to mitigate most of the problems with the first phase of the LHWP, it has led to significant changes in later stages of the project. The reporting also highlighted the need for more high-quality investigative work in Lesotho.

The excerpts were written by four individuals. The co-editors of the overall report were Mabusetsa Lenka Thamae, a Mosotho who worked for the Maseru-based Transformation Resource Centre (TRC), and Lori Pottinger, an American working for International Rivers. Both of them authored part of the excerpt as well. Additionally, acclaimed sociologist Thayer Scudder and Korina Horta, an economist working for Environmental Defense, also appear as authors. With most of the authors of the report based outside Lesotho, the report also highlighted the need to include more local voices in reporting projects.

The LHWP was first negotiated in the mid-1980s between the apartheid South African government and a military regime in Lesotho that had been put in power largely through the machinations of the apartheid regime. Thus, the treaty that governs the project was implemented when the rule of law was limited in both countries and the freedom of the press curtailed. This meant that the interests of both governments regarding revenue and the flow of water largely superseded the interests of individuals and communities displaced by the project.

While this report came out too late to change processes involved in the uprooting of communities for the construction of Katse and Mohale Dams in Phases IA and IB, the efforts of the individual authors and of the NGOs involved have kept the interests of communities slated for displacement closer to the centre of Phase II negotiations. The first contracts for the latest dam were awarded in late 2017. The jury is still out, however, on whether communities affected by the new Polihali Dam will receive meaningfully better compensation. The burgeoning investigative press in Lesotho will hopefully pick up the important work that this consortium of NGOs started. To do so, they will have to continue the meaningful collaboration with individuals and communities that the TRC and International Rivers pioneered. They will remain indebted to these NGOs for the publication of reports like this one that have forced the government in Lesotho to be more responsive to the needs of its own citizens and have pushed multi-lateral organisations like the World Bank to be more responsive to problems within projects they are funding.

On the Wrong Side of Development

Transformation Resource Centre, Edited by Mabusetsa Lenka Thamae and Lori Pottinger, 2006

Corruption

By Korina Horta and Lori Pottinger

The Lesotho Courts have shown that the project was marred by corruption from its earliest days. A dozen major multinational firms and consortia on the project were accused of bribing the CEO of LHDA, the agency in charge of the project, after a Swiss bank account in his name was discovered. Starting in 1999, the Lesotho courts have waged an unprecedented fight against corruption, which represents a path-breaking model for the courts in other countries. So far Lesotho has successfully convicted three of the world's leading construction and dam building companies: Acres of Canada, Lahmeyer GmbH of Germany and Spie Batignolles of France. The Canadian and German companies have also lost their appeals in the Lesotho Courts. Other major international companies are still being investigated.

The Lesotho government remains undaunted by the vested interests behind the big companies it has chosen to prosecute. It is essential to show 'zero tolerance' for bribery, says Leaba Thetsane of Public Prosecutions. 'We have demonstrated to the international community that corruption is not just a Third World problem,' he said. But the cost of prosecuting these companies has been high. According to the Lesotho Attorney General, Fine Maema, the court cases have cost the government $4.3 million as of 2004 – 2% of the country's annual budget for public services. Lesotho believed that international donors like the World Bank had promised to provide financial assistance to fund the cases, but no such funding has been given to date, and the World Bank denies that it ever promised financial support.

The Lesotho court case is the only national-level prosecution involving multinational companies building a World Bank-financed project that we know of. So how has the World Bank reacted to the bribery convictions in Lesotho? After initially declaring that there was too little evidence to debar Acres International, the Bank finally debarred the company in July 2004 – barely a week after testimony by the chief prosecutor for the Lesotho courts in front of the United States Senate, and two years after the Lesotho courts had found Acres guilty ... In view of the emphasis of the G8 and northern countries more broadly on 'corruption in Africa' being an obstacle to development, the Lesotho court cases make it very clear that northern companies play a key role in this corruption and may often initiate it in the first place.

The World Bank's Resettlement Policies

By Thayer Scudder

The Bank's resettlement policies, along with the 1986 Treaty's emphasis on 'maintaining' living standards (as opposed to providing new development opportunities to affected individuals and communities), are a major cause for an unsatisfactory resettlement process ... (This approach) has been shown by research not only to not restore incomes but rather to leave the majority worse off, which is why I consider Bank policies as partly responsible for its documented record of failed resettlement. There are several explanations for such a result.

First, the Commission assumed wrongly that a compensation policy, as opposed to a balance between compensation and development initiatives, could restore living standards. The Bank's most recent resettlement policy (2001) also is at fault here, 'compensation' being mentioned 19 times while 'development' is mentioned only four times.

Second, a restoration approach fails to take into consideration the fact that living standards for a majority of resettlers tend to drop during the long planning process (often over ten years) that precedes construction (or first disturbance as mentioned in the

Treaty) and during the initial years immediately after physical removal. One reason is that government services and other external investments, including schools, clinics and economic development programs, are stopped or put on hold while those to be resettled are often told to stop improving housing, upgrading farms and making other investments in what planners assume will be a future reservoir or project area. In addition, the process of physical removal makes heavy demands on resettlers that delay for one or more years their reestablishing themselves in a new area, with a new host population with whom resettlers must compete for land, social services and jobs, and with, more often than not, increased government control of resettler activities.

Third, pre-project surveys carried out to establish a benchmark against which restoration can be measured are known to underestimate income and living standards which have already been lowered due to project-related cessation of investments in the area.

Fourth, the Bank's safeguard policies deal only with direct economic and social impacts. Ignored are a wide range of socio-cultural effects associated with forced removal from a preferred homeland, the psychological stress affecting the elderly and women in particular, and increased rates of illness and death that have been reported in resettlement areas where, more often than not, population densities increase, and water supplies and food (at least during initial years) are apt to be inadequate.

Fifth, resettlement tends to be associated with increased cash expenditures because many resettlers, as with LHWP, are moved to less fertile soils which require costly inputs to provide equivalent yields, have less access to common property resources for grazing, fuel, building materials and for foraging, and become more dependent on credit and the risk of indebtedness.

Public Participation

By Mabusetsa Lenka Thamae

Public participation is a process of engaging communities, informing, involving, and making them aware of their rights in connection to the Project. It means participation of all potential stakeholders who may have an interest in the project, whether directly or indirectly ... We have come to learn that public participation should be facilitated by the presence of a democratic culture. There are now many grievances coming from the communities which ought to have been anticipated and put right, if Lesotho had been a democratic state when the LHWP Treaty was concluded between the governments of Lesotho and the Republic of South Africa. The then-military government in Lesotho and the Apartheid South Africa did not create a conducive atmosphere for soliciting public opinion and meaningful participation in the (Lesotho Highlands Development Authority) (LHDA) compensation policy.

LHDA had what was called a community participation office, which was really doing office work rather than community work in the field. LHDA should have offices in the field, close to the communities. This would have made it easier to respond on the spot to the many grievances and concerns from the communities. The absence of offices has resulted in community members going in their hundreds to LHDA offices; this did not only show the inefficiency of LHDA but it was embarrassing as well to see so many people around the offices. The LHDA participation office set up community committees to make work easier. The community liaison committees (CLAs), as they were called, were supposed to take concerns of the communities to LHDA and to get responses back to the communities. While this was not a totally bad idea, it came as a surprise to TRC field workers that the issues taken up by the community representatives were often at variance with those of the larger community ... The authorities must go to the villages to check if the committees do the work for which they were established. This office should really use participatory methods to capture the concerns. The approach should equally be a respecting one because if communities have a feeling that they are not respected, they will not cooperate as is required. Our experience has also been that it is not enough to just go to the communities once or three times and claim that results have been forthcoming; it must be a patient, deliberate engagement.

Further reading

Devitt, Paul and Robert K. Hitchcock. 2010. 'Who Drives Resettlement? The Case of Lesotho's Mohale Dam,' *African Study Monographs*, 31(2), 57–106.

Hitchcock, Robert K. 2015. 'The Lesotho Highlands Water Project: Dams, Development, and the World Bank,' *Sociology and Anthropology*, 3(10), 526–538.

Mwangi, Oscar. 2007. 'Hydropolitics, Ecocide and Human Security in Lesotho: A Case Study of the Lesotho Highlands Water Project,' *Journal of Southern African Studies*, 33(1), 3–17.

Thabane, Motlatsi. 2000. 'Shifts from Old to New Social and Ecological Environments in the Lesotho Highlands Water Scheme: Relocating Residents of the Mohale Dam Area,' *Journal of Southern African Studies*, 26(4), 633–654.

2007, SOUTH AFRICA

Why Mount Frere's babies die

INTRODUCED BY HARRY DUGMORE

Early in 2007, a whistleblower contacted local journalists with alarming stories of a surge of infant deaths in Frere Hospital, the main public health facility in East London in South Africa. The source said stillbirth rates and deaths of babies under the age of one month had long been high but were getting worse. Newspapers had carried some stories about conditions at the hospital, but local health department officials, and staff working at the hospital, would rarely respond to reporters' questions, or, if they did, would outright deny that there was anything amiss.

A team of journalists from the *Daily Dispatch*, East London's long-established city newspaper, backed by its editor, believing it was unlikely that any officials connected to these deaths would ever talk on the record, decided to go undercover to find out what was really going on at the Frere maternity ward in particular. Justifying their use of hidden cameras and recorders due to the urgent and compelling public interest, a small team – Brett Horner, Chandre Prince and Ntando Makhubu – with the support of editor Phylicia Opphelt and deputy editor Andrew Trench worked on the investigation for three months before they published their first story.

What they discovered horrified them and their readers. Between 1994 and 2007, more than 2000 infants had died in Frere Hospital and it was clear that many of these deaths were preventable.

Given the political sensitivities of what was still regarded as a 'transition' from the apartheid-era health system to a democratic one, including the rapid deracialising of a previously segregated hospital system, the investigative team knew they had to be right on every single fact.

Starting with the initial breaking story, 'Why Frere's babies die' on 12 July 2007, and continuing with a series of investigative pieces over the next few weeks, the reporting revealed how those terrible conditions had been allowed to develop in the Frere Hospital and its smaller feeder hospitals and clinics. A common thread was the failure to control infections through basic hygiene measures in maternity wards and in the hospital more generally, but inadequate staffing levels, incompetence and lack of equipment all played a role too.

Front-line staff were not always directly to blame – there were substantial staff shortages and a large number of unfilled posts, causing a great deal of stress, burnout and low morale among nurses in particular – but it became clear there was also a good deal of negligence.

The journalists were determined to share the broader health context in their stories, acknowledging the social determinants of the situation the hospital found itself in, including the impact of the AIDS epidemic and the high levels of poverty in the area. The stories were carefully researched, well written, poignant and emotionally wrenching. Responses were always sought from those implicated and detailed lists of questions were sent to the health department and hospital managers, but these were rarely answered with more than disavowals.

The story also elicited strong denials from the highest office in in the land. Then president, Thabo Mbeki, castigated the reporting in the strongest terms and went as far as to fire one of his ministers, Nozizwe Madlala-Routledge, then deputy minister of health, who had responded by saying that what was happening at Frere Hospital (and other hospitals in the Eastern Cape) was indeed a 'national emergency'.

The minister of health at the time, the notoriously inept Manto Tshabalala-Msimang, also responded initially with furious denials. Her national health department took out paid ads in newspapers in an attempt to refute the allegations. A long-time AIDS denialist, Minister Tshabalala-Msimang had, with President Mbeki, effectively delayed the provision of live-saving anti-retroviral medication to millions of South Africans.

The story marked something of a turning point in the struggle for a more responsive healthcare system under the ANC government. A year later, President Thabo Mbeki was recalled as president after an internal coup within the ANC. His AIDS denialism might have played a small part in his recall. Minister Tshabalala-Msimang was removed from her post at the same time and replaced by Barbara Hogan, who declared, on her first day of office, that the era of AIDS denialism was over.

Despite the denials that anything was wrong at Frere Hospital, equipment maintenance budgets were soon doubled and then doubled again, and extra nurses and doctors were hired. But the department of health in the province still moved harshly against one of the original whistleblowers: Dr Nokuzola Ntshona was found guilty on charges of 'speaking out' about Frere Hospital maternity deaths and summarily dismissed.

The same pattern – of refusing to allow media to investigate properly nor permitting health officials to talk to the media, and the seeking out and punishing of whistle-blowers – continues to the present day. This has led, in part, to the Life Esidimeni Crisis in Guateng province where 1,700 mental health patients were moved from a long-standing service provider, without proper checks of the new facilities they were being moved to, and 150 of these patients died.

At least, national infant mortality rates have fallen since the Frere story: under-five mortality rate had declined from 77.2 deaths per 1,000 live births in 2002 to 45.1 deaths per 1,000 live births in 2015.

The *Daily Dispatch* team responsible for the series of stories of baby deaths at Frere hospital won the 2007 Taco Kuiper Award for Investigative Journalism. The judges wrote: 'The paper uncovered every aspect of the story, from the highly technical to the human interest; to get to the evidence, they had to use imagination, creativity and some unusual methodology; it had an enormous impact on the country as a whole; and, when facing pressure and criticism, their story held up well, leading to major positive results for the ordinary people they were writing about.'

Noting that the story started from just a single source, the judges in 2007 praised the editors for encouraging reporters to dig deeper: 'Great stories often involve taking a single case and building it into a larger picture which lays out the context, examines the cause and points fingers at the culprits – and therefore has maximum impact. This is what the *Daily Dispatch* did. It is a testament to the power and value of the best kind of journalism …'

Why Frere's babies die

Brett Horner, Chandre Prince & Ntando Makhubu, *Daily Dispatch*, 12 July 2007

Hundreds of newborns are dying every year at Frere Hospital's overburdened maternity section – and the institution's own records reveal the scale of negligence behind many of the deaths.

A *Daily Dispatch* investigation has found that the situation is so bad that a cleaner delivered a baby in front of shocked students.

Exhausted staff are stretched so thin they must abandon the nursery at night to assist doctors in theatre. Mothers are also victims of negligence. A swab was left inside of a patient after a Caesarean-section while another's placenta was removed a full 24 hours after she gave birth.

The *Dispatch* team spent nearly two months walking the maternity wards with hidden cameras, attending the mass burial of dead babies and interviewing medical staff and heartbroken mothers.

Reporters even staffed the Frere mortuary for an afternoon, answering the phone and dispatching porters to collect bodies. Internal documents show that senior management knew the situation was out of control for years, but did little to address the crisis … Two thousand babies were stillborn in the past 14 years at Frere, according to the abortions and stillbirths book in the labour ward.

Last year's figures appear to be the highest on record, when at least 199 babies were stillborn. Frere's official baby mortality rate exceeds provincial and national figures as contained in an unpublished report by a unit of the Medical Research Council. Worse is that hospital staff concede in documents that 'most' maternal deaths and stillbirths 'are avoidable due to care'.

References are also made to the worrying increase in the number of maternal and neo-natal deaths from 2005 to 2006. The pattern of death is illustrated at the Haven Hills Cemetery where batches of up to 45 babies in tiny white coffins are buried in mass pauper funerals every month.

Two weeks ago, 43 babies were buried. The burial included two tots who died in October 2004 and another in December 2005. Their bodies had remained in maternity's cold storage for years …

Renata Coetzee went to Frere in labour, but was turned away by an intern who, she said, confessed he could not read the CTG machine, which monitors the foetal heartbeat and other vital signs. An hour later, Coetzee's baby was stillborn …

Other moms complained of sitting on wooden benches in

prolonged labour, wearing blood-soaked clothes and being left unattended during and after birth. Some mothers blamed insufficient vital equipment for babies dying. A maternity nurse concurred: 'You feel so helpless as deaths could have been avoided if there was enough equipment.'

Again, the hospital's own documents points to crippling shortages of staff and equipment, like CTGs and oxygen points. The situation has become so critical that a long-serving cleaner is known to have delivered babies and dispensed medication.

'I once saw a cleaner doing a delivery ...' said a student nurse, a claim corroborated by a veteran of Frere's maternity wards.

Soon after the *Dispatch* investigation began and emergency inventory was ordered of all equipment and staff needed in the maternity section.

'Frere does not have even half the number of required staff, leaving those available exhausted and burnt out ...' said a former Frere midwife.

Another nurse said staff shortages often forced them to leave the nursery unattended to assist with theatre duties.

A mother's pain

Brett Horner, Chandre Prince and Ntando Makhubu, *Daily Dispatch*, 13 July 2007

Baby Liano King. Born May 22, 2007. Died May 22, 2007. Buried July 3, 2007.

At his graveside in the Haven Hills Cemetery, his mother Murichia King bowed her head and allowed herself to grieve.

Hers was a subdued grief, a silent grief. Her eyes filled with tears, but she had her composure as Pastor Charles Gallagher intoned a blessing that should have been cause for uncontrollable emotion.

'Lord God, ever caring and gentle,' said Pastor Gallagher, 'we commit to your love this little baby who would have brought so much joy to the lives of his parents and many others.'

King was mourning the death of her first child, who was stillborn at Frere Hospital's maternity unit – a death she solely blames on the hospital's 'negligent' staff ...

A week before Baby Liano's funeral, on June 27, 43 other babies were interred in a mass pauper burial at Haven Hills ... Cemetery documentation revealed that 35 of the 43 babies were stillborns from Frere Hospital, while the other eight died between either a day or four days after birth. However, all their death certificates stipulate the cause of death as 'stillborn'.

A stand-out feature of these deaths is that nearly all of them occurred over the course of this year, from January 29 to June 12.

But most shocking of all was the discovery by the *Dispatch* of three babies who had been forgotten in the maternity unit's cold storage for years. Two of the babies were stillborn in October 2004 and the other in December 2005.

The death certificates of two clearly show an attempt to change the date of death to this year. But a copy of a hospital stillborn register in the possession of the *Dispatch* confirms that the babies died years ago.

Also, 18 out of the 43 babies who were buried did not appear in the same register ...

HRC and health council join Frere fray

Brett Horner, Chandre Prince and Ntando Makhubu, *Daily Dispatch*, 14 July 2007

As the public outcry over baby deaths at Frere Hospital continued to grow yesterday, the Health Professions Council of South Africa (HPCSA) and South African Human Rights Commission (SAHRC) vowed to find the culprits and prosecute them.

This follows an in-depth investigation by the *Daily Dispatch* that revealed at least 2000 babies were stillborn at the hospital in 14 years – many of these avoidable and the problem was getting worse.

HPCSA head of legal services advocate Tshepo Boikanyo yesterday said a team would be descending on the hospital without warning to investigate.

'We don't want Frere to know when we're coming ... documents go missing if they know this. In terms of regulations, if we find any cases of misconduct, we go directly and prosecute individuals,' he said.

Internal documents obtained by the *Dispatch* acknowledged that lack of staff, equipment and general negligence were key factors to increased maternal and baby mortality rates.

The HPCSA is the statutory body for investigating malpractice complaints against all health professionals. Boikanyo said their objectives were more about holding health professionals to account than the hospital as an institution. But he warned 'we won't do this thing subtly'.

The SAHRC's chairperson, Jody Kollapen, said he would formally write to the council to offer their services in any investigation.

'This is clearly a matter of human rights because babies are dying. We will either monitor, share, assist or become part of any investigation process,' he pledged.

Kollapen contacted the *Dispatch* after the newspaper's story on the Frere baby deaths was debated on SAFM's After 8 Debate with host Jeremy Maggs yesterday morning ...

Thirza Clarke, a former nurse at Frere, called in to say the crisis warranted the closure of the hospital and immediate evacuation of babies ...

Speaking on behalf of the national Health Department, Professor Ronald Green-Thompson said the hospital had 'ruthlessly and robustly' employed nurses over the past few months.

Maggs quipped: 'You would need a brigade of nurses to address this issue.'

Green-Thompson said that Health Minister Manto Tshabalala-Msimang had spoken to provincial Health MEC Nomsa Jaula on Thursday about the reports. 'The matter will be addressed in whatever way,' he said.

2008, Tanzania

The dark, deadly art of witchcraft and the plight of albinos

Introduced by Bob Wekesa

Tanzanian journalist Vicky Ntetema, 59, is always watching her back after daring to upset a macabre apple cart. She had to flee her country to escape the ire of ritualistic criminals. After 'exile' stints in the United Kingdom and Kenya, she has returned home, but must always be on guard lest those she exposed kill her. Her house is reportedly a fortress.

Investigative journalism has often focused on political and economic issues, with the cultural aspects of society not having gained as much purchase. The case of witchcraft – the superstitious belief in magical powers – is compelling. It is not uncommon for Tanzanian media to report on the vice, including cases of people killing their children and spouses on the advice of witch doctors and in the pursuit of wealth. Because of the underground nature of witchcraft claims and suspicions, law enforcement agencies have often had difficulty arresting and charging alleged perpetrators in modern law courts. Witchcraft is hard to prove, even with evidence such as a witchdoctor's paraphernalia, unless death or other secondary crimes are involved.

In these circumstances, citizens have often opted for 'street justice' in which suspects are summarily killed. Often a claim that someone has bewitched another is enough for a killing to occur. In some cases, the suspicion may be based on as flimsy a ground as someone having red eyes or a strange facial expression.

It is the belief in witchcraft that has brought the targeting for attack of an African minority group, albinos or persons with albinism (PWAs). Sources indicate that attacks on albinos are more pronounced in Africa than elsewhere. Large swathes of eastern and southern Africa report the highest attacks, with

Tanzania said to be in the lead.

Albinos lack pigmentation or melanin in their skin, hair and eyes due to hereditary factors. It is a rare condition, but a highly visible one, and this puts albinos in harm's way (Burke et al, 2014). Besides the stigma, some people also think albinos have special powers, and this is nothing short of deadly. In Tanzania, albinos are referred to as *Zeru Zeru*, meaning 'ghosts'.

The belief is that the blood, body parts (hands, legs, bones) and organs (skin, the heart, liver) of the supposed 'ghosts' have the power to heal diseases, enrich people, help win elections and earn promotions at work. For these reasons, albinos have been targeted by witchdoctors and their clients as key ingredients in sick rituals. This has led to an underground market for albinos as bringers of good luck in agriculture, fishing, mining, education ... just about everything.

Although albinos have been vulnerable to killings for many years, there was a rise in the spate of killings in the mid-2000s. As a journalist working for the BBC, Ntetema, educated in the Soviet Union in the 1980s, noticed the trend (Wray, 2010). The information she received from police was sketchy. She decided to undertake undercover work with a view to understanding the networks that fuelled the killings. She would uncover a link between witchdoctors and their clients as well as unearth the role that corrupt policemen played in the gruesome mix. The investigative work entailed going to 'ground' in the areas where the witchcraft practice was rampant – the Lake Victoria region.

For her work, Ntetema received the 2010 Courage Journalism Award from the International Women's Media Foundation (BBC, 2010). She went on to be honoured with the US Secretary of State's International Women of Courage Award in 2016 (US Dept of State, 2016). This capped a career that started in 1991 as a Swahili translator at the BBC's London hub. In a write-up to celebrate her achievement, the organisation noted her impact as well as the great risk she faced at the height of her investigations into albinism (Wray, 2010). On some occasions, tape recorders concealed on her body fell to the ground as she went about her investigation. A particularly unlucky incident was when she was busted by a police officer who had links with one of the witchdoctors she was investigating. Her investigation was eventually aired by the BBC, on 21 July 2008. Soon after the broadcast, she was forced to flee first to London and eventually to Kenya as the syndicate of witchdoctors and police officers plotted her death.

As a result of her investigative and campaigning work, a number of people were convicted for crimes against albinos. In 2010, she became executive director of Under The Same Sun (UTSS), an NGO advocating and raising awareness about people living with albinism. She left the position in May 2018 after serving for eight years.

References

BBC. 2010. 'Vicky Ntetema wins bravery award for BBC albino report', 11 May. Available at: http://news.bbc.co.uk/2/hi/africa/8674440.stm, accessed on 13 August 2018.
Burke, Jean, Theresa J. Kaijage & Johannes jon-Langba. 2014. 'Media analysis of albino killings in Tanzania: A social work and human rights perspective', *Ethics and Social Welfare*, 8(2): 117–34.
U.S. Department of State. 2016. 'Biographies of 2016 award winners. Available at: https://2009-2017.state.gov/s/gwi/iwoc/2016/bio/index.htm, accessed on 13 August 2018.
Wray, L. 2010. 'Vicky Ntetema: International Women's Media Foundation'. Available at: www.iwmf.org/community/vicky-ntetema/, accessed on 13 August 2018.

In hiding for exposing Tanzania witchdoctors

Vicky Ntetema, BBC News, 24 July 2008

I am living in hiding after I received threats because of my undercover work exposing the threat from witchdoctors to albinos living in Tanzania.

This year, at least 25 people with albinism have been killed, mostly in the Lake Victoria Zone, especially the Mwanza, Shinyanga and Mara areas.

They are being killed because local witchdoctors say their body parts provide the potent ingredient for magic charms, which many local people use to bring success in business and love.

The bodies are left limbless and sometimes with a huge hole in the neck, from where blood would have been drained.

Families not only grieve because of the loss of their loved ones but are also shocked at the state in which the bodies are left by these murderers.

As if that is not enough, they have to bury their dead in the house, guard the graves on their farm and or build them with stones, metal bars and cement to prevent the killers from stealing the body parts.

So I posed as a businesswoman who wanted to get rich and 'consulted' 10 witchdoctors.

The consultations included talking to a hedge and telling my problems to a chicken.

Once, albinos used to seek shelter from the sun. Now they have gone into hiding simply to survive, after a series of killings linked to witchcraft.

These (the albinos) are regarded as intermediaries between the witchdoctor, their ancestors and the spirits, or 'jinns'.

They used old German and English coins with holes in the middle, cowry shells, pebbles, nails, nuts and bolts, screws, crosses with the little figure representing Jesus, and beads which they would shake in a red or white cloth and throw on the ground, while incense burned from all around.

Sticky green stems or old money notes are put between pages from the Koran.

Then the witchdoctors would speak in Arabic and the local Sukuma language and translate or use an interpreter to get the message through to me.

I presented the same case to all of them and got different solutions.

The consultation fee ranged from $20 to $100 per session, with a promise of returning for a further problem-solving process.

All of them gave me different suggestions of who my enemies were – not by name but by description.

None got anything right, most importantly my true mission.

But that did not stop me from praying for my safety, as that was the only defence I had.

Never in my life had it occurred to me that I would one day be sitting in front of a witchdoctor, also known as sangomas or voodoo priests and priestesses.

I met a registered traditional healer who uses African herbs to cure ailments in Magu, the town that shares the name with the district which is known to be the hub of sorcery.

This man condemned the way 'conmen and foreign witchdoctors' lured locals into trusting them, before hiring murderers to organise raids on homes of albinos just after sunset.

Two witchdoctors promised to get me a magic concoction mixed with ground albino organs. The starting price was $2000 for the vital organs.

Another told me that the police were among his customers and that he could make a special potion mixed with ground male and female private parts to enable people to commit armed robbery without being caught.

The encounter with witchdoctor number three was in a village called Gambusi, the most feared area in the region.

The compound had about eight huts around the outside, with a more elaborate structure in the middle.

Here a man in his forties wearing a white T-shirt and khaki trousers with a mobile phone on his belt asked me whether I had brought a chicken.

A gang of men went round the small town where we had stayed, searching all the guest houses.

'What for?' I asked.

He laughed and said that I was forgiven because he realised that I was a novice in the business.

He demanded $2 for a tiny three-week-old chicken and $3 for the fortune-telling.

I was then told to get out of the compound, face south-east where I hail from – Dar es Salaam – spit on the bird's head, back, tail and on my hand, and have a heart-to-heart talk with the chick revealing all my problems.

He asked for $200 for the consultations and said I should spend two nights there before completing the process.

But when I told him that I had only $30 he told me to go away and return when I had the full amount.

When I went back with other BBC colleagues, his nephew was there to receive me.

He said he knew what I wanted and said he would find me albino blood, hair, leg and palms for $2000.

He charged me $55 for the initial consultations and asked me to return with the rest of the money.

I found the last witchdoctor in Lamadi, a tiny rural town which lies at the junction of the roads leading to Kenya and Uganda.

He charged me $100 for the first session and said he would give me the magic potion with albino and other human organs for a price.

While I was there, a man came for a consultation – the witchdoctor said he was a police officer but he was wearing civilian clothes.

However, he was made to wait until my session was over and, I later learned, told the witchdoctor that I was involved in a sting operation.

Shortly afterwards, the threatening phone calls started.

And a gang of men went round the small town of Magu, where we had briefly stayed, searching all the guest houses. Luckily, we had already moved on to the nearest city, Mwanza.

One particularly chilling message came on my mobile phone: 'What have you done now? Watch your back.'

The witchdoctor had boasted of working with a powerful network across East Africa, which included police officers and armed robbers.

I knew they were involved in the murder of albinos, so I was terrified.

At first, I did regret taking on this mission, especially for the sake of my family.

Had I put their lives at risk?

But then I realised that I had done the right thing.

Even if I die today, those involved will have been exposed.

2009, SOUTH AFRICA

The truth about President Jacob Zuma laid bare

Introduced by Nic Dawes

Mandy Rossouw did not go to Nkandla looking for scandal. She travelled there, on a road cratered with potholes, in search of insight.

In November 2009, Jacob Zuma had been president for just six months and the investigative team at the *Mail & Guardian* – where I was editor-in-chief – was quietly building a picture of the sprawling business empire that was springing up around him and his family. That work would begin to emerge piecemeal in 2010 and would culminate seven years later in the multi-billion rand state-capture scandal that led to his ejection from the Presidency.

But Rossouw's story was, in its way, as consequential. The insight she found among the hills of northern KwaZulu-Natal was that Zuma's character is scandal: venal, self-seeking and reckless, secure in the comfort of his absolute entitlement.

'President Jacob Zuma is expanding his remote family homestead at Nkandla in rural KwaZulu-Natal for a whopping price of R65 million – and the taxpayer is footing the largest chunk of the bill,' she wrote.

'The expansion will turn the presidential homestead into a sprawling precinct that will include a police station, helicopter pad, military clinic, visitors' centre, parking lot with parking for at least 40 vehicles and at least three smaller houses that will serve as staff quarters.'

She had established the price tag by assiduously working sources connected with the project, even as official spokespeople denied any work was being done at all.

'It is R65 million, but it will probably be more in the end. You know how it goes with building, the prices always go up and up,' one said.

By the time the public protector, Thuli Madonsela, completed her report on the project three-and-a-half years later, the figure was 'conservatively' R246 million. A staggering amount in South Africa. Eight times what had been spent around Nelson Mandela's rural homestead, 30 times the cost of security arrangements at Mbeki's post-retirement home. Worse, it was clear that every rule of government procurement had been broken to deliver to the President the home of his dreams, with a cattle kraal, an amphitheatre, a deluxe chicken run and a swimming pool styled as a 'fire pool', paid for from the budget for safety measures.

Like many of the best stories, this one began, not with a tip-off, a dossier under the door or a hint from a disgruntled civil servant, but with a hunch that there was something to be found in those hills.

The newspaper's year-end edition is a blockbuster. It is an annual ritual for loyal readers, with longform stories, trend pieces and an uncharacteristic amount of humour, designed to be read over South Africa's lazy year-end vacation. So when we sat around a table in our Rosebank office to plan the 2009 edition, we not only weren't looking for scandal, we were actively uninterested in it. Mandy wanted to go to the President's hometown, as neglected by the national press as it was by the roads department, to have a look, and to better understand someone who clearly set great store by his rural background.

Mandy was not above a bit of breathless enthusiasm when in possession of a new piece of political gossip, but she liked to deliver a real scoop with an air of great calm. And that is what she did when she returned. She had found an earthmover, she explained, and the beginnings of building work. She had talked her way into the construction office, where she saw plans, and got a sense of the scale of the project and, working the phone, she had established what was really going on.

The story of a lavish new home for the President, hitherto kept completely secret, was, of course, a much better return on the trip than an insight piece for year-end. I was probably less good at concealing my enthusiasm than Mandy was. This would not wait for Christmas.

We spent much of the following week in an attempt to elicit comment from the Presidency and the department of public works. They stonewalled us, flatly denying that any work was under way and then, late on Thursday, as the *M&G* was going to press, released a statement to all media, broadly confirming the outlines of Mandy's reporting and insisting there was no impropriety of any kind. It was an obvious attempt to take the sting out of the story, and we released a furious statement of our own, so that our competitors would know the true source of this strange evening windfall.

That minor combat, of course, would soon be forgotten.

The story caused a minor flurry when it came out, but in the months that followed, as costs escalated, and more details of Zuma's personal role in the project began to emerge in the *M&G*, *City Press* and other papers, it built to become the defining scandal of his first term.

Madonsela's 2014 report 'Secure in comfort', calmly outlined the sheer scale of the boondoggle. Zuma, and his administration, she said, should have reacted when the *M&G* first published, to comply with the Executive Code of Ethics and contract regulations. Instead, a builder working for both Zuma and the state had allowed costs to balloon and luxury features to be conflated with security measures.

Madonsela insisted on remedial action, including that Zuma pay back a portion of the costs, and that he reprimand the ministers involved in sanctioning and overseeing the work.

The report, prompted by opposition complaints, was a remarkably brave piece of work, carried out in the face of intense pressure and intimidation and it landed in a climate of economic malaise and escalating concern over corruption at the apex of the government and ANC.

'Pay back the money' quickly became a rallying cry for an invigorated opposition.

Mandy, who would have revelled in reporting these developments, did not live to see them. She had died suddenly at just 33 in March 2013.

But what happened next would, I am quite sure, have elicited one of her warm, broad grins. The parliamentary ANC, in thrall to its whippery and heedless of the consequences, voted to exonerate Zuma, treating Madonsela's orders as mere recommendations. That, in turn, drew a court challenge from the Democratic Alliance and Economic Freedom Fighters. Where one key institution had shirked its duty, the courts, at the last, would not.

In March 2016, Chief Justice, Mogoeng Mogoeng, appointed by Zuma himself, read out the full judgment of the court. It was a primer in the structure of constitutional state, the responsibilities of the legislature and the duties of the President. Both the presidency and parliament had failed in their duties and were to comply with the Public Protector's orders.

It was a stunning rebuke and it ought to have led to Zuma's immediate resignation, or a vote of no-confidence. That it did not was a sign of how deeply the ruling party, ANC, had been captured by the apparatus of corruption he had built.

But his presidency was now holed below the water-line. When the #GuptaLeaks emails were released a year later, and the numbers in play escalated from hundreds of millions to hundreds of billions, what they revealed was what Mandy had already found, at the far end of a shattered road on a warm November day: the truth about Jacob Zuma, in broad daylight, if we would only look at it.

Zuma's R65m Nkandla splurge

Mandy Roussow, *Mail & Guardian*, 4 December 2009
Additional reporting by Niren Tolsi

President Jacob Zuma is expanding his remote family homestead at Nkandla in rural KwaZulu-Natal for a whopping price of R65 million — and the taxpayer is footing the largest chunk of the bill.

The expansion will turn the presidential homestead into a sprawling precinct that will include a police station, helicopter pad, military clinic, visitors' centre, parking lot with parking for at least 40 vehicles and at least three smaller houses that will serve as staff quarters.

Phase one of the project, comprising two houses, one of them a double-storey structure, and a guesthouse, is already under way.

Given that state money is involved, how future presidents will benefit from the development remains unclear.

Government insisted this week that it has no record of such a development and no hand in any of Zuma's personal property endeavours.

Shortly before the *Mail & Guardian*'s deadline the presidency released a statement changing its tune. The statement reads: The Zuma family planned before the elections to extend the Nkandla residence, and this is being done at own cost. No government funding will be utilised for the construction work.

'Outside the perimeter of the Zuma household, a few metres from the house, the State is to undertake construction work in line with the security and medical requirements relating to Heads of State in the Republic. The security services have to construct accommodation facilities for their staff that attend to the President, erect a helipad to ensure safe landing for the Presidential helicopter and a clinic as per medical requirements.'

Public works spokesperson Koketso Sachane said on Wednesday: 'Please note that there is no work or extension project taking place at President Jacob Zuma's homestead at Nkandla.'

The presidency also claimed no knowledge of such a project, saying that Nkandla is Zuma's private home and therefore no business of the state.

It accused the *M&G* of 'setting out to embarrass the president' by publishing a story.

Further attempts to obtain comment from communications head Vusi Mona were futile.

On Thursday December 3 Mona promised to consult Zuma and get back to the *M&G*, but he did not respond to calls later in the day.

However, the *M&G* understands that a meeting to discuss the project was held at Nkandla on August 2, attended by the surgeon general, Vejay Ramlakan, and a representative of the department of public works.

Ramlakan, through his spokesperson, referred all queries to the presidency 'because it is happening at the president's homestead, so it is his matter to comment on'.

When the *M&G* visited Nkandla last weekend, an earth-mover was excavating the ground next to the existing homestead to prepare for the construction of the initial phase of the project.

Two cement mixers and two water tanks were on site as well as construction offices where the architectural plans for the construction are kept.

About 12 construction workers were working overtime to ensure the project gets off the ground.

The site was devoid of company signage.

The contractor told the *M&G* the three new houses would cost R4.1 million and would be funded by Zuma in his personal capacity. However, this was only phase one of the project.

The total cost of the development will run to R65 million, according to sources closely involved with it. 'It is R65 million, but it will probably be more in the end. You know how it goes with building, the prices always go up and up,' one said.

There is no time frame for the completion of the development.

The *M&G* understands part of the reasoning behind the mammoth extension is to enhance the homestead's capacity to host VIP guests and their retinues.

On election day this year, former Nigerian president Olusegun Obasanjo – in the country as an election monitor – popped into Zuma's home after a helicopter flight. More of such visits are expected in the future.

A military source said there was also a need to extend the homestead's capacity to house Zuma's health and security staff, most of whom stay in Eshowe when Zuma is at Nkandla.

A source said: 'This is cumbersome in terms of response time, so the idea was to build a bigger facility to house all the support staff in Nkandla when the president is there.'

The houses are apparently being built to accommodate two wives currently living at Nxamalala, MaNtuli Zuma and MaMbhija Zuma.

The complex already includes a house for his first wife, Sizakhele, built in 2000 shortly after he became deputy president.

Sizakhele uses the main house with various relatives, mostly women and children, who live in rondavel-type structures around her. A silver E-class Mercedes and a white Toyota Prado 4x4 are parked outside and serve as the first lady's transport.

During the corruption trial of Zuma's former financial adviser Schabir Shaik in 2004, the state produced evidence that alleged bribes flowing from French arms firm Thales helped finance the building of the homestead.

Zuma's last visit to Nkandla was in September according to a security guard, but he is expected to spend time there over the Christmas period.

He will then host the annual Christmas party for children and attend to the long queues of local people who line up outside to visit him and discuss issues pertaining to the village.

According to architectural plans shown to the *M&G*, the precinct will include a garden that will house ancestral graves.

The area is due to be cordoned off by a brick wall which will make provision for only one entrance.

The two new main houses are kidney-shaped and contain his-and-hers bathrooms, formal living rooms, walk-in closets and a study.

One house contains four bedrooms, while the smaller has three.

Double-volume ceilings will be fitted to the homes, which will sport thatched roofs, in the same style as the current homestead, which is cordoned off by green palisade fencing.

The plans were drawn up in August by Durban architects, the names of whom the *M&G* was unable to establish. However, no record of the plans could be found at the local deeds office in uThungulu municipality in Richards Bay.

Nkandla houses 13,000 people, many of whom have no access to electricity, and in-house water is a rarity. Work is taking place on the road leading to the presidential homestead to make it more accessible.

2012, South Africa

Killing Rhinos for Profit

Introduced by Ron Nixon

Julian Rademeyer never set out to investigate rhino horn poaching. Rademeyer, a longtime investigative reporter for a number of South African publications who had never really written about the environment or conservation issues, stumbled into the story.

The tipping point was when he came across a story about rifles being smuggled across the border into Zimbabwe to be used to kill rhinos for their horns. The discovery would eventually lead him to quit his job as a reporter and journey through a number of countries tracking the networks behind the global trade in rhino horns. Along the way he would talk to lawmen, mercenaries, corrupt politicians, diplomats, gunrunners and prostitutes. What emerged was the book *Killing for Profit*, an impressive global investigation that takes readers deep inside the illicit trade in rhino horns.

The fact that poachers were decimating rhino populations wasn't new. Nor was it new that the horns can fetch a hefty price in Asian countries – horns are still worth more per kilogram than gold, platinum, cocaine or heroin. In many Asian countries, especially Vietnam and China, rhino horns are believed to cure ailments like headaches and hangovers, and a single rhino horn can fetch up to US$60,000. The horns are also made into libation cups and are considered a symbol of wealth among the emerging middle class in Asian countries. Illegal wildlife trafficking, of which rhino horns are a significant part, is estimated to be roughly US$20 billion a year enterprise globally, ranking fourth just behind drugs, humans and arms, according to the World Economic Forum.

What was new was that Rademeyer approached the story from the standpoint of organised crime, rather than as an environmental or conservation story.

'I looked at this as a chance to look into the criminal syndicates involved,' Rademeyer told me shortly after the book came out in 2015. 'I wanted to know who were the people and organisations that profited off the rhino horn trade.'

The journey to expose the criminal syndicates behind the sale in rhino horns would last two years and take Rademeyer from southern Africa to the United States and those Asian countries at the centre of the illegal rhino trade – Vietnam, Thailand and Laos.

In the book, we come face to face with apartheid-era figures who helped Jonas Savambi, the Angolan rebel leader backed by Pretoria, finance his war against the Angolan government through the illegal sale of wildlife, including rhino horns. It also reveals that the South African Defence Forces engaged in widespread trafficking of wildlife, from rhino horns to ivory. The military covertly involved in the receipt, transportation, sale and export of the items from Angola and Namibia to South Africa.

The investigation sheds light on the shadowy world of hunting for sport and lodges who organise the hunts for rhinos. We meet the diminutive Vietnamese women, posing suggestively in pictures over dead rhino, who purport to be hunters, but are in fact fronts for criminal organisations looking to use the legal permits that allow for the hunting of rhino as trophies to procure the horns.

Rademeyer shows that killing of rhino goes beyond southern African poachers, criminals and Asian buyers. He brings to light the involvement of international criminal enterprises such as the Rathkeale Rovers, a global Irish gang implicated in money laundering and drug dealing. He would find that in the United States, rhino horn trafficking is also prevalent and a number of antique dealers and even a former rodeo cowboy have been prosecuted for selling the horns.

Still, for all the carnage surrounding the killing of rhinos outlined in the book, Rademeyer also manages to tell the story of the brave and dedicated law enforcement officials, prosecutors, environmentalists and game farmers, who with few resources and amid great danger, work to save the animals. Globally, countries in Europe and the United States have pledged resources to help South Africa fight back against the poaching of rhinos. Former US President Barack Obama signed an executive order calling wildlife trafficking a national security issue.

Sadly, nearly six years after the publication of *Killing for Profit*, the slaughter of animals continues. According to the most recent poaching statistics, 1,028 rhinos were illegally killed in 2017 in South Africa, which is home to about 80 per cent of the world's population. That's 26 fewer rhinos killed than in 2016 but still well above the 13 killed in 2007.

Killing for Profit is a meticulously reported and well-written account of the dark underworld of trafficking of rhino horns, its effect on local communities and most of all the creatures who are being killed for the very thing that is supposed to serve as their defence. The book ranks as one of the most important works of investigative reporting to come out of the southern Africa region, exposing the greed, corruption and international demand that has decimated one of the area's most precious resources – its wildlife.

KILLING FOR PROTECT: EXPOSING THE ILLEGAL RHINO HORN TRADE

Julian Rademeyer, Zed Press, 2012

23 April 2008: Tommy Tuan is trapped. Spread out on a bed in Room 122 at the Road Lodge in Kimberley are wads of cash. Thick bundles of hundred-rand bills held together with rubber bands. One million, two hundred and eighty thousand rand, plus change. There's also a duffle bag and ten rhino horns weighing just over twenty kilos.

Hidden under an armchair, where he can't reach it, is a 635mm pistol. Its compact, light and – unless you know what you're doing – more likely to hurt someone or piss them off than kill them. Outside, in the parking lot is a grey Honda Accord with red diplomatic license plates. But between Tommy and the door are three cops ...

Tommy arrives in Kimberley after dark and hours late for the meeting with the seller. He goes straight to the Road Lodge and checks into a room. He isn't alone. He's brought along a friend to look after the money and act as the bagman during the deal. Tommy calls the seller and asks him to come to the hotel.

The man agrees. He asks Tommy if he'll mind if the owner of the horn comes along too. Tommy doesn't. They meet in the parking lot. Tommy tells the men he has brought R1.4 million in cash, but he doesn't have it with him. He insists on doing the transaction at the Road Lodge and not at another hotel, as originally planned. He doesn't know the town well and doesn't want to drive around. He confides that he is scared to go anywhere else, because it could be a 'police trap'.

The men relent. To avoid any misunderstandings about the legality of the deal, they warn Tommy that they don't have permits for the horns. It won't be necessary, he says.

An hour later, they are back. One of the men carries a heavy duffel bag over his shoulder.

Tommy is waiting for them in the lobby and guides them up the stairs to his room on the first floor. They lock the door, shut the windows and close the curtains. There is an electronic scale on a table. Tommy switches it on and begins weighing the horns. On the bed, an ashtray slowly smoulders, filling up with cigarette butts, blackened and burnt to the quick.

Tommy jots down the weights in red ink on a scrap of paper. Some of the horns still have ragged pieces of nasal cartilage attached to the bases. The final tally is 20.559 kilograms. Tommy subtracts 200 grams to factor in the unwanted cartilage. At R63,000 a kilo, it comes to a total of R1,282,617. They round the figure off to R1.280 million.

Tommy places a call on his cellphone. A few minutes later, someone raps on the door. Knock. Pause. Knock-knock. Pause. Knock. Satisfied, Tommy unlocks it. A pair of white takkies flashes into view and disappears.

Tommy reaches into the corridor, picks up a black carry-bag and returns to the room. He locks the door, then heaves the bag onto the bed and begins unpacking the cash. He is so absorbed in his task that he doesn't notice one of the men press the green dial button on his cellphone. Somewhere outside, another cellphone rings briefly and then stops.

There's a hard knock at the door. Tommy goes to see who it is. But the seller is already in front of him, pulling on the handle, and then another man pushes his way into the room. He's saying something. About being a policeman. Tommy freezes. Then the disbelief and shock kick in.

Tommy's wrists are cuffed. The money on the bed is photographed, packed into two large plastic evidence bags, and numbered. Someone finds the pistol, six rounds of 6.35mm ammo and a single 9mm round.

Once the room has been searched, Tommy is taken away. The

bagman has vanished. In the hotel parking lot, police find and impound the Honda. Earlier in the day, everyone involved in the operation had been briefed to keep an eye out for it. Under no circumstances, they were told, should Tommy be allowed to transfer the horns to the car. The vehicle's registration number is D BBB127D: 'D' for 'diplomatic'. The registered owner is Pham Cong Dung, the political counsellor at the Vietnamese embassy. Next to the ambassador, he is the most senior Vietnamese diplomat in South Africa.

For some time now, the embassy in Brooklyn, Pretoria, has been a thorn in the flesh of the cops investigating the illegal rhino horn trade. Two years before Tommy Tuan's arrest, police had uncovered evidence that the embassy's economic attaché, Nguyen Khanh Toan, was using his diplomatic immunity and the diplomatic bag to smuggle rhino horns out of South Africa.

There was little they could do about it other than complain. South Africa's Department of Foreign Affairs wrote a nasty letter to their Vietnamese counterparts and Nguyen was recalled to Vietnam.

That same year, in Hanoi, a corruption scandal involving a senior Vietnamese bureaucrat, Nguyen Van Lam, led to further damaging revelations of high-level involvement in the rhino horn trade. Lam – the deputy head of the Vietnamese 'Government Office' – had reportedly 'admitted shortcomings' in accepting 'cash gifts' from state agencies three years earlier. He was forced to resign.

The bribes had come to light years earlier after Lam forgot a suitcase at Hanoi Airport in 2003. Security staff opened the case and found ten envelopes inside it, stuffed with cash. Lam's explanation was startling. He said most of the cash was from 'friends and colleagues' who wanted him to buy 'rhino horns' for them.

In South Africa, increasing numbers of Vietnamese couriers and middle-men were appearing in court on charges of smuggling rhino horns. Most of them were either unable or unwilling to speak English and, as a result, the courts were heavily reliant on the Vietnamese embassy for referrals to qualified interpreters. Tommy's brother – as it so happened – was one of these 'preferred' translators.

It wasn't long before police investigators found evidence directly impacting some of the interpreters in the illicit trade. In one instance, police at the Kempton Park Organised Crime Unit obtained a photograph of a man posing next to the carcass of a rhino, rifle in hand. A detective instantly recognised him as one of the interpreters in the trial of a courier who had been arrested at OR Tambo International Airport with rhino horn stuffed in his bag.

Two days after Tommy's arrest, police receive a letter from Dung. He wants his car back. He has an explanation. 'On 23rd April 2008, Mr. Nguyen Thien Taun, acquaintance [sic] of my relative Nguyen Anh Bao, dropped in my residence and said his car was out of order, and asked Mr. Bao to borrow the car. Then he took my car and went away until yesterday, 24 April when I was informed that my car was catched [sic] by police in Kemberly [sic]. I assure hereby that I know nothing about Mr. Taun's doing neither the borrowing of the car and would like my car back for use as soon as possible.' The Department of Foreign Affairs leaned on the cops. Four days later, Ngyuen Anh Bao, armed with a letter from Dung, collects the car in Kimberley.

But Dung's ignorance will be challenged seven months later. On 17 November 2008, the environmental television programme 50/50 airs grainy surveillance video of a Vietnamese embassy official receiving a number of rhino horns from a known trafficker. The horns are transferred from the boot of a car that has stopped in the street outside the embassy. Dung's Honda is parked nearby. The recipient of the horns is later identified as Vu Moc Ahn, the embassy first secretary.

2013–17, BOTSWANA

'Never set foot in this place ever again'

INTRODUCED BY JOEL KONOPO

Only those very close to President Ian Khama knew what was happening in Mosu, a tiny and sleepy village some 600 kilometres northeast of the Botswana capital Gaborone, and they kept it a closely guarded secret.

A whistleblower provided the breakthrough in 2013. *Sunday Standard*, a local newspaper, published a sensational story charging President Ian Khama of constructing an airstrip in his private land using resources from the military. The government dismissed this report as nothing but 'lies by the irresponsible media'. A few months later, reporters at the *Botswana Guardian* led by Ntibinyane Ntibinyane (investigations head) and Joel Konopo (editor) published more details of what was happening at Mosu: the Botswana Defence Force was not only constructing an airstrip in Khama's private plot, but was also involved in the construction of his compound.

The government's public relations arm used the state television, radio and newspaper to dismiss these allegations. Government made counter-claims that the airstrip was outside the president's compound and was constructed to facilitate his movements around the country. Further, the government alleged that the country's civil aviation regulator was the custodian of the airstrip.

But the *Botswana Guardian*'s sources within the military gave a conflicting picture. The newspaper insisted that the airstrip was, in fact, inside Khama's plot and the military was heavily involved in the construction. When an opposition MP asked a question in parliament about it, the government made one critical concession. The airstrip was in Khama's private land. The government, however, denied the involvement of the military in the construction of Khama's compound. It was a slight victory for the media, but more questions remained. If the military was involved in the development of both the airstrip and Khama's compound, how much was the taxpayer paying for the development? How big was the airstrip? How big was the compound?

The government was not talking.

After the initial flurry of media interest, the story appeared to die a natural death. In 2017, two years after Ntibinyane and Konopo established the INK Centre for Investigative Journalism, they received more information from well-placed sources in government. In preparation for his retirement, construction at the president's holiday home had intensified and the military had deployed equipment to the area. In March 2017, Ntibinyane, Konopo and another reporter, Kaombona Kanani embarked on a trip to Mosu to verify the claims and get a first-hand view of developments.

Some 5 kilometres before reaching the compound, the three journalists were ambushed by armed presidential guards, detained and interrogated for several hours before being released with a stern warning. 'Don't ever set foot in this place ever again. If you do, we are going to shoot and kill you.' The journalists reported these threats to the police but no action was taken against the over-zealous officers.

A week later, the three journalists devised a plan to obtain an image of the president's compound. They decided to commission a local satellite imaging company to get a real-time image of the area. A week after agreeing to sell the image, the company chose not to proceed with acquiring the image on the basis that what the journalists wanted was 'sensitive material'.

Through the assistance of a Florida-based company Digital Globe, INK Centre for Investigative Journalism was able to obtain an image from a South African-based satellite image reseller. INK paid US$5,000 to obtain the 65.1MB image covering an area of 21-by-19 square kilometres.

The image revealed that the military was constructing a massive airstrip, and was also involved in the construction of Khama's private residence adjacent to the airstrip, all contrary to the government's denials. With the help of a topographer, the centre was able to establish that the compound was not as small as the government initially suggested. The involvement of the military was no longer in doubt.

For the first time, the country was able to have a glimpse of what was happening at the much talked about compound. A former army general with knowledge of the construction for the first time admitted that the budget from the military was used in the construction of the compound and the airstrip.

The story was published with *Sunday Standard* newspaper and later with the *Daily Maverick* in South Africa as well as on the centre's website. In the face of this evidence, government resistance broke down. They issued a two-line statement denying wrongdoing.

The use of a satellite image to hold the powers accountable was a new development in journalism in Botswana. While the president refused to take responsibility for misusing taxpayers' funds, the use of the images caused much shame and embarrassment to his administration.

BDF building airfield on Khama's private land

Ntibinyani Ntibinyani & Joel Konopo, *Sunday Standard*, 22 September 2013

Botswana Defence Force is constructing an airfield in Mosu on a private piece of land owned by President Ian Khama.

Once completed the airfield will form part of the president's elaborate array of holiday resort infrastructure.

Because the airfield is being built by the army, no Environmental Impact Assessment has been conducted, notwithstanding the fact that it is not a military installation. BDF and the Directorate of Intelligence Services are by law exempted from the exigencies of Environmental Impact Assessment.

This however does not take account of the fact that the facility is on a private piece of land situated on the pristine and ecologically sensitive Makgadikgadi Salt Pans.

According to the Presidency, the airfield is expected to facilitate President Ian Khama's air travel.

At the time that *Sunday Standard* was investigating this story, heavy machinery, almost all of it owned by Botswana Defence Force had started a massive de-bushing exercise to clear a chunk of land where the airfield is going to be constructed.

'It is indeed true that the BDF is constructing a landing strip near Mosu for His Excellency the President. The construction of this airstrip is to facilitate the air movements of His Excellency the President,' said the Head of Government Communications, Jeff Ramsay in response to a set of questions that *Sunday Standard* had sent to his office and the Botswana Defence Force ...

Khama's Mosu built with public funds

INK/*Sunday Standard*, 2017

Botswana Defence Force (BDF) funds, equipment and personnel are being diverted towards constructing and developing President Ian Khama's private lodge at Mosu, on the southern shore of Makgadikgadi Salt Pans, a prime tourism destination.

Investigations by INK and *Sunday Standard* have also revealed that Khama, who is one of the biggest tourism investors in Botswana, appropriated a chunk of land to add to the 60ha in Mosu which he has been allocated by the Letlhakane sub-land board for a commercial tourism business.

Satellite images have revealed for the first time how government has for years maintained a veil of secrecy over the huge construction work going on at the president's property in Mosu, consistently downplaying the size, scale and scope of the controversial project. INK and *Sunday Standard* contracted DigitalGlobe, a New York-listed commercial imagery firm, to capture a high-resolution 50cm worldview image over Mosu private property and airstrip. DigitalGlobe sub-contracted Johannesburg-based Swift Geospatial Solutions.

In July 2014, the Office of the President claimed that: 'The President's house is a single bedroom cottage with a kitchen and a sitting room, while his brothers between them have a two-bedroom cottage and a single-room chalet.

'There is also an additional single room chalet at the compound. During all phases of the construction undertaken at the compound, that is on the homes of HE the President, his brothers and the guest chalet, no Government personnel were engaged. Neither was any government money spent on the structures.'

The satellite impressions commissioned by INK and *Sunday Standard* contradict the official narrative that BDF resources have not been deployed in Mosu for the President's personal gain. Imaging satellites operated by Swift Geospatial Solutions exposed the President's property as a huge military installation which is much larger than previously stated by the Office of the

President. One of the plots is 15ha of military equipment: earth moving machinery, water bowsers, large trucks, smaller utility trucks, a solar panel plant, a large generator and and three rectangular structures — which, according to an architect contracted by INK, resemble army barracks.

A fireplace (kgotla) enjoys the pride of place among military hardware at the centre of the compound. Completing the picture of a luxury eco-retreat outback is a 79-square metre helipad and a tower jutting out of a sprawling housing complex of 22 buildings linked to a 45 hectare airstrip with a 1.6 kilometre runway — long enough to accommodate even the Directorate of Intelligence and Security Services (DISS) Pilatus PC-24 twin engine business jet ...

Government statements on the President's residence have tried to divorce his residential plot from the airstrip. The official spin sought to exonerate the President from any private benefit arising from the BDF involvement in Mosu by implying that the airstrip is neither for his personal use nor in his property. The Mosu residence-cum-lodge, which is nestled in the south of Sua Pan, in the eastern half of Makgadikgadi Pan, is a major migratory path for bird life and a gateway to the already rich eco-tourism destination.

While major construction sites are required by law to post signboards cataloguing the civil engineers, construction companies and quality surveys carrying out the works, there is no signage at Mosu to indicate that major construction work is in progress ...

A soldier engaged on the development has revealed that following media revelations of BDF deployment at Mosu in 2013, heavy construction only resumed in earnest last year October (2016) for the final phase of extensions and developments to the property in preparation for Khama's retirement in nine months.

The source told INK that equipment on site includes two BDF-registered earth-movers, a cement-mixer, a grader and 'more than 60 BDF construction workers'.

Another security force source revealed that the use of BDF personnel for Khama's private interests was not a new development. He added that members of the BDF have 'always' been deployed for Khama's personal benefit ...

2015–16, Angola

Diamonds, soldiers, torture and corruption

Introduced by Justin Pearce

In 2002, Angola's MPLA government defeated Unita, which was its adversary in a 27-year war. A year later, the war in Iraq and the energy demands of a rapidly industrialising China combined to send the oil price soaring. It was against this background that Rafael Marques, already a well-established figure in Angolan journalism, founded the investigative website *Maka Angola*, which for more than a decade has documented how former President José Eduardo dos Santos and those around him have pocketed the profits of the post-war boom.

One focus of Marques's work has been on the diamond mining industry in north-eastern Angola. The mine owners investigated by Marques were all high officers in the Angolan Armed Forces, who had been handed diamond concessions as a reward for their loyalty to the government during the war. The concession areas were carved out of what had been communal land where people had made a living from farming or panning through river gravel in search of alluvial diamonds. The generals' positions allowed them to use soldiers and police as private security guards. Travelling to the diamond fields at great personal risk, Marques recorded 500 cases of torture and over 100 killings by security guards. Victims included not only the small-time diamond diggers, but people trying to access their fields or draw water from a river.

Marques made known his research findings in a book, *Diamantes de Sangue: Tortura e Corrupção em Angola* (*Blood Diamonds: Torture and Corruption in Angola*), published in Portugal in September 2011. In November 2012, nine generals attempted to sue Marques in a Lisbon court for libel and defamation. When the Portuguese Attorney General dismissed the case, the generals turned to the Angolan courts to sue Marques for defamation and libel. After a tortuous judicial process, in 2015 Marques received a six-month prison sentence, suspended for two years.

The trial and conviction did not halt Marques's efforts to expose corruption at the highest levels of the Angolan state. In 2013 an investigation co-authored with Kerry Dolan of *Forbes* magazine revealed to readers beyond Angola that Isabel dos Santos, the then-president's daughter, had amassed a fortune of US$3 billion. The title of 'Africa's richest woman' has stuck since then. And it was *Maka Angola* that brought Isabel's brother, José Filomeno ('Zénu') dos Santos into the spotlight. In 2012 Zénu was put in charge of the Angola Sovereign Fund, a US$5-billion nest egg supposedly created to help Angola survive future oil price shocks. Investigations by Marques showed how money from the fund was flowing freely into business ventures controlled by Zénu and his Swiss-Angolan friend Jean-Claude Bastos de Morais. A year later the Panama Papers leak provided further evidence for this.

At the same time as exposing the perpetrators of corruption, Marques has continued to document its consequences. His account of conditions at Luanda's main hospital, during a yellow fever epidemic that could have been prevented through investment in sanitation and public health, bears witness to the lives and deaths of those for whom Angola's economic transformation means little.

References

Marques de Morais, Rafael. 2011. *Blood Diamonds: Corruption and Torture in Angola*. Lisbon: Tinta da China. Available at www.tintadachina.pt/pdfs/626c1154352f7b4f9 6324bf928831b86-insideENG.pdf, accessed on 29 May 2018.

Marques de Morais, Rafael & Dolan, Kerry A. 2013. 'Daddy's girl: How an African "Princess" banked $3 Billion in a Country living on $2 a day', *Forbes*, 2 September. Available at: www.forbes.com/sites/kerryadolan/2013/08/14/how-isabel-dos-santos-took-the-short-route-to-become-africas-richest-woman/#2cd8fb4a45f5, accessed on 29 May 2018.

Angola's Sovereign Fund Pays $100 Million to a Shell Company

Rafael Marques de Morais, *Maka Angola*, 12 April 2015

On 22 January 2015, Angola's Sovereign Wealth Fund (FSDEA) transferred the sum of K9,948,750,000 kwanzas (US$10 million) to the company Kijinga SA. This company is nothing more than a shell company set up as a front for shady transactions by Banco Kwanza Invest (BKI), a bank created by the 36-year-old José Filomeno dos Santos 'Zenú', the current chair of the FSDEA and the son of the President of the Republic.

Kijinga SA shares an office with BKI at 150 Avenida Comandante Jika, next to the Maternity Hospital in Luanda. This address has only one business door, which opens into a small waiting room where there is a reception area and two chairs for visitors. One of these chairs is usually occupied by a security guard, in addition to the guard on duty outside the door. The windows are darkened glass, which does not allow a glimpse inside. From the waiting room all one can see is a door leading to the bank and Kijinga SA.

According to documents in the possession of *Maka Angola*, FSDEA transferred the funds already mentioned from its account at the state-owned Banco de Poupança e Crédito, to account AO06005700000014010400124, which is in the name of Kijinga SA at BKI. The transfer was carried out with the knowledge of the Central Bank of Angola. The transfer is identified only as the payment of a bill dated 13 January 2015.

A document from the General Tax Administration of the finance ministry, in the possession of *Maka Angola* and dated 5 February 2015, shows that Kijinga SA does not have a single employee.

How can a company without a single employee provide services to the Sovereign Wealth Fund valuing nearly US$100 million? That is the question.

Kijinga SA was legally constituted on 4 December 2012. Its formal shareholders are Pascoalina Natacha Daniel Sambo, Sendji Alexandre Vieira Dias, Mário Augusto dos Santos Mangueira, Cira Cláudia Ferreira Custódio Medrôa and Djanir de Nazaré Ferreira da Conceição (now Junqueira).

Maka Angola has conducted a brief investigation into these shareholders. Pascoalina Sambo's CV states that she has served as a sub-director of the BKI legal department since July 2012. Cira Cláudia Ferreira Custódio Medrôa has been on the staff of BKI since October 2012. According to her CV, she started working at the bank as executive secretary and supervisor of the receptionists, and is currently the compliance officer.

Djanir de Nazaré Ferreira da Conceição (now Junqueira) was also working at BKI at the time when the company was set up.

Mário Augusto dos Santos Mangueira has since 2012 been a manager of the Fundo Activo de Capital de Risco (FACRA) a venture capital fund created by President José Eduardo dos Santos, through presidential decree 108/12, using public money, to support micro, small and medium-sized businesses. FACRA's funds are exclusively managed by BKI.

The chief nominal shareholder of BKI, Jean-Claude Bastos de Morais, who holds 85% of the bank's shares, is one of three members of FACRA's highest body, the Supervisory Council. FACRA's investment committee is chaired by Marcel Kruse, BKI's CEO ...

The only individual on the list who does not appear to have any institutional links with BKI or its shareholders or managers is Sendji Alexandre Vieira Dias, who works for the state diamond company, Endiama.

When contacted by *Maka Angola*, Mário Augusto dos Santos Mangueira denied having any relationship with BKI or with Kijinga SA. 'It is very strange that you are phoning me to ask this question,' he stated. He promised to organise a meeting to discuss the matter when his schedule permitted; however, a month later he has not found the time to do so ...

*The full report can be found at www.makaangola.org/2015/04/angolas-sovereign-fund-pays-us-100-million-to-a-shell-company/

The Morgue

Rafael Marques de Morais, *Maka Angola*, 24 March 2016

It's barely 2am at Luanda's Josina Machel Hospital, the largest in Angola, but already vehicles are queuing in a long line at the entrance.

Most carry coffins. Others bear the unboxed bodies. Over

the next five hours they will remove the mortal remains of 235 luckless Angolans for burial. It will be at a rate of a coffin for each 1.2 minutes. This macabre harvest is routine.

The Angolan government can massage the statistics but it only takes one observer to stand and count, as, one by one, grim-faced morticians and weeping relatives carry away the dead.

Angola is in the grip of a yellow fever epidemic that the authorities would prefer to downplay. Malaria too is reaping a rich harvest. This year, these two treatable conditions are the main causes of death in Luanda, an overcrowded metropolis of more than six million souls.

The tiny few who make it to the Josina Machel Hospital give a glimpse of the true situation: 'Not worth it, sir. Too many people dying. I've never seen the like,' says one of the people charged with guarding the removal of the bodies at the morgue. Shaking his head, he takes up position to wait for the next, and the next.

In a small two-door coupe sit three women wearing the false cheer of colourful cotton wraps, each embracing a tiny shrouded body. Waiting to depart.

The clock ticks on: 3.30am and now traffic to and from the morgue entrance is chaotic as the comings and goings multiply in the pre-dawn hours.

Not a minute's rest in the morgue reception area. There should be an orderly line, in order of arrival, but there are space problems given the demand for the release of bodies. On the side, someone has established a 'parallel business': a space up front for a handful of kwanzas.

There is no computer, no typewriter. Release forms are scrawled hurriedly by hand.

I make my way to the refrigerated units in the body holding area. It has to be seen to be believed. I can't ask for names, causes of death. I can only watch, listen, be present, and bear witness to the terrible truth.

In the open space at the back of the morgue are the family members of the recently departed. Each carries their own 20-litre yellow jerry can of water, a plastic tub and soap: the necessities for washing the dead.

I count more than 20 bodies laid out in the open air as

they are washed, dressed and tidied up by their loved ones in preparation for that final goodbye.

The bathwater has nowhere to drain away. It pools on the floor, along with blood, discarded medical gloves, surgical masks, the clothes they were wearing when they died. There is a single drain. It's blocked, putrid.

'What a country this is. What a country this is,' laments one of the relatives.

*The full report can be found at www.makaangola.org/2016/03/the-morgue/

2015, ANGOLA

The massacre of Huambo

INTRODUCED BY JUSTIN PEARCE

Reports of a massacre involving a mysterious religious cult gripped Angola's attention early in 2015. In the province of Huambo in the Central Highlands, a preacher called José Julino Kalupeteka had convinced his followers that the apocalypse was nigh, and led them to set up camp on the Mount Sumi hillside to await the end. When police entered the site in March, a shootout ensued. The state rejected calls for an investigation and sealed off the site. Official accounts declared that sect members had killed nine police and that the police had shot 13 of the faithful. But rumours of deaths numbering in the hundreds continued to circulate, fed by the accounts of believers who had fled the area.

Luísa Rogério and photographer Ampe Rogério were the first journalists to gain admission to the site once the authorities agreed to lift the barricade. They published their impressions on *Rede Angola* (Network Angola), an online magazine whose founding as a space for informed debate and quality long-form journalism was a landmark in the development of a public sphere in Angola. Although some basic facts could not be established – bodies had been removed or buried before the journalists arrived – their reporting marked a moment when Angola was forced to take a look at itself. The government had spent 13 years congratulating itself on ending a civil war and getting fat on the oil boom that followed. That same government's façade of modernity and sophistication was shattered by the revelation that when confronted with the eccentric behaviour of a religious crank, its instinct was to respond by firing on civilians. Luanda's often inward-looking civil society was forced to turn its eyes to the interior provinces where, more than a decade after the war, a heavy state security presence still limits participation in political and civic life.

In 2016 Kalupeteka was sentenced to 28 years' prison over the killing of the police officers. No charges have ever been brought in connection with the deaths of the civilians, who remain uncounted and unnamed.

The Silence of Death

Luísa Rogério, *Rede Angola*, 8 May 2015
Translated by Ana Rocha

Rede Angola went to the site where religious cult Luz do Mundo (Light of the World) set up their camp. Around it, hushed conversations about Kalupeteka!

The glare of shacks on the mountain top was visible from the detour of the tar road into the bush trails. Further ahead, four motor-bikers slowed down to let the police car go past. Children played outside. Pets roamed the streets. There was life in the village of Km25 – named after the distance separating it from the town of Caála in Huambo province. We went up bumpy roads. In the valley, a small lake surrounded by maize and sugar cane plantations. Charming vision of the lush green mountain chain silhouetted by a dying sun, on one side, the camp on the other side. Reports associated with this place are in stark contrast with the landscape – they are appallingly horrific.

On a fact-finding mission to the cult of self-proclaimed prophet Kalupeteka, the reporters from *Rede Angola* visited the place where it all happened, staying around for two hours. Escorted by a vehicle with a police siren, we reached Mount Sumi on a mid-Sunday afternoon. Approximately two weeks after the death of nine policemen, in circumstances still unclear, traces of severe events were still visible on the camp.

Small zinc-roof houses overlapped all the way to the mountaintop. A bigger house, called 'logistic base', shown as pastor Julino Kalupeteka's dwelling, differed from all others. Just before the house, there was a pole next to a lamp post. António Mendes, provincial director of social media in Huambo, who drove the reporting team to the scene of the incidents, was not available for interviews – he just guided and followed. Police officers provided occasional explanations to most recurrent questions.

'Catumbela died here,' an agent said pointing to the pole — a common indicator to the otherwise different versions we were able to gather on the incidents. Another common factor suggested that agents had taken the warrant of arrest while a religious cult was being held. Women and children were chanting religious songs while men were putting into practice those acts which would lead to the death of the police agents. 'The choir sang while officers were being slaughtered with sticks, machetes and stones. The police commander came running because the others were already here,' someone said. After the massacre, there was silence. When backup police officers realized their colleagues were dead, after supposedly being warned by cult members who ordered them to collect the corpses, a shootout against civilians ensued. Sources close to civilian organizations and opposition political parties stated that Angolan Armed Forces and National Police started to shoot indiscriminately and burned everything.

What happened exactly remains a mystery. Reality shows that this camp continues to show evidence of destruction. Burnt out houses and signs of arson in various places clearly stand out. Despite witnesses heard under anonymity referring to the noise of 'bombs as in time of war' and the explosions from heavy artillery used exclusively by the Army, as PKM machine guns and RPG7 grenade launchers, we did not see any bullet signs. The same cannot be said about the gross vandalizing of the place, hardly attributable to cross-fire.

A cult without worshippers

Before that fateful day, access to camp was preceded by three control posts. Now only yellow police tapes were left to demarcate a crime scene. We did not register the presence of soldiers on camp — the same camp where children were not allowed to go to school because Jesus never studied. The high level of destruction mirrored the utmost violence — a burnt-out car and several motorbikes. A bulldozer, used for agriculture, and an industrial generator, both charred, stood out in the idyllic landscape now transformed into a valley of horrors. Despite the gruesome scenery, the well-structured configuration of the camp was still noticeable.

In the different sections of the camp, there was a main outdoor area reserved for cult practices and an open-air auditorium with rocks used as stools. Important religious announcements and notices on community life were divulged here. Warehouses were aligned according to the type of goods they stored. In one, we found salt, maize and beans in the other two. Perishables were kept in deep freezers. We counted two of these and a stove, both destroyed. Only the gas bottle was intact, laying a few metres from Kalupeteka's house.

The last battle. Jesus is coming. Are you ready?

In this landscape, once a paradise on earth, traces of blood were visible in some places. In front of the cult leader's house, there was an esplanade, an all-around observation post. It had electric current from the generator. It had running water. We saw the bathroom, in the rear of the house, and noticed the tiles, although the entrance was barred by corrugated iron sheets darkened by smoke. It was impossible to peep through the windows. Despite the poor housing conditions, the natives of Kalupeteka's mountain did not live quite like in the time of Jesus. The satellite dish, with its missing top, did not take them to a heavenly world but brought the world to camp. Numerous details clearly evidenced a functional community system. Sporadic signs of modernity could be seen: a music mixer, a cell phone data board or a television card.

In a notebook on the floor, we found important observations. No names or telephone numbers — simply bible quotes. 'The last battle. Jesus is coming. Are you ready?' This was the suggestive title on a cassette. Two huge suitcases were left behind. Women and children's clothes were strewn around as well as shirts, jackets and men's trousers, shoes and blue rubber boots! Somewhere else, two blackjacks. A bloody machete lying next to a child's blue outfit precluded any conceived peaceful environment. We asked ourselves whether the Criminal Laboratory team was ever present in this place.

It was late afternoon and the wind carried a strong scent. It was, undoubtedly, something putrid. We dared not imagine what. The smell of roasted corn managed to conceal it. And the number of doves on top of the roof of pastor Kalupeteka's house just kept increasing. And the wind. Again! This time it made a noise similar to a whistling sound. These whistles were a gentle reminder that people lived here, people who left almost no trace of their present location.

Water gushed, non-stop, onto a blue basin. It dripped on the floor. It dispersed into the bush. Hundreds of plates, mugs, forks, knives and kitchen utensils led us to believe they were stored in the same place. Pots with parched food remnants were on the floor. Burners placed on three rocks, typical of rural areas, managed to survive the chaos. We tripped over firewood, jerry cans and perfume bottles. Crocs and children's outfits caught our attention. They were just kids. Wherever they were now, they never had the opportunity to understand what happened.

Camera clicks broke the silence. Shivering fits were unavoidable. Any resemblance to a haunted place was not a mere coincidence. When we left the place, only the doves could be seen perched on top of Kalupeteka's house. Where are the village folk now, where are the worshippers?

2016, BOTSWANA

Shattering the stereotype: Botswana's Military Millionaires

Introduced by Evelyn Groenink

The unearthing of Botswana's decades-long military build-up under President Ian Khama, as Tshireletso Motlogelwa and Matteo Civillini do in 'Military millionaires', challenged superficial and comfortable assumptions about the country and its leadership. Botswana was known as happy. Not too poor, it was given epithets like the 'Switzerland of Africa' and even had a progressive multiracial legend to hold on to: the romance between homegrown prince Seretse Khama and the English woman Ruth Williams, recently made into a Hollywood movie. Tourists, for their part, focused on desert and wildlife, which in many a travel brochure includes the San 'Bushmen' people.

'Military millionaires' shows, among other things, the military build-up, started by President Ian Khama, the son of the first president who was elected in 2008, and the rise of a securocracy – with the diamond-based funding by multinational De Beers – which would protect the wealth of the ruling dynasty, terrorise and jail critical journalists, kill protesting students and be linked to the deaths of several politicians and businessmen standing in its way.

It is by working together across borders that Tshireletso Motlogelwa of Botswana's *Business Weekly and Review* and Matteo Civillini of Italy's investigative reporting project IRPI succeeded in shattering the stereotype and attracted international attention to the rise of this securocracy. By publishing on the African Investigative Publishing Collective's *ZAM* online platform and in Swiss online publication *Sept.info* – Switzerland being a major supplier of Khama's military – as well as in the local newspaper, they sent a signal to Western countries that had been supplying Khama's army and to their own rulers that their behaviour would no longer go unnoticed.

Their collaboration meant that Civillini, who was in the UK at the time, could access UK foreign affairs ministry documents and company registry papers that were inaccessible in Botswana, where the government had ensured that vital arms trade documents could not be traced.

Changes have certainly taken place in Botswana since the story was published in 2016. Elections were won in April 2018 by Mokgweetsi Masisi, who is now the president and is not linked to the security establishment. His election was preceded by extensive debate in the country around the dismantling of the power networks of his predecessor, a debate that is ongoing and, arguably, has already influenced the new president. Masisi has fired Khama's right-hand man, former chief intelligence head Isaac Kgosi, and there are indications that some of Khama's envisaged military acquisition projects will be changed or stopped.

It would be too much to attribute these developments solely to one story. But the *Business Weekly and Review*'s international linkage on this particular one has helped to boost its role as a leading news source in Botswana itself. Its courage and professional investigative journalism has also encouraged other media houses – together with concerned citizens and pressure groups – to stand up to demand a return to democratic rule, less expenditure on arms deals and the security service, and an end to Khama's authoritarian and nepotistic governing style.

Further reading

Motlogelwa, Tshireletso and Civillini, Matteo. 2016. 'Military Millionaires'. *ZAM* magazine. www.zammagazine.com/chronicle/chronicle-20/317-military-millionaires, accessed on 18 August 2018.

Motlogwelwa, Tshireletso. 2015. 'The Diamond Connection'. *ZAM* magazine. Available at: www.zammagazine.com/chronicle/chronicle-13/225-the-diamond-connection, accessed on 18 August 2018.

Military Millionaires

Tshireletso Motlogelwa & Matteo Civillini, *ZAM* magazine, 31 March 2016

In 1981, a British High Commissioner warned in a letter to his superiors in London that the Botswana Defence Force (BDF) had become a 'monster absorbing more of the country's national wealth than can be afforded'. As could be gleaned from the first sentence in the letter – 'I am sure you will think that by now I am paranoid about the BDF' – his superiors didn't take High Commissioner William Turner's concerns very seriously.

The international image of Botswana was then, as it is now, that of a peaceful, friendly country ... Reports that a new 'monstrous' army – gobbling up close to 4% of the country's GDP in 1980 – had been set up because of 'pressure' from President Ian Khama 'through his mother [Ruth, wife of the founding president Sir Seretse Khama],' as the High Commissioner's letter said, did not fit with that narrative and were duly ignored.

There were arguments to support heavy spending on the military in 1981. Up to 1977, Botswana had never had an army, mainly because President Seretse Khama had held a steady focus on development and preferred to spend on health and education. But in the late 1970s ... apartheid South Africa and white Rhodesia had become a threat to the country's borders. However, even though the relatively high budgets allocated to the army during those years can be understood, the need for the specific acquisitions was never explained either to parliament or public. Parliamentarians at the time 'did not even have the required basic knowledge of defence needs to mount any type of criticism against the spending,' confides a former Cabinet Minister. And military expert Dan Henk expressed doubts that there was ever even a point in trying to match powerful South Africa's army. 'Botswana's military improvements could never match its neighbour's might, nor could the BDF [Botswana Defence Force] deter attacks against suspected insurgent targets,' he wrote in *African Security Review* in 2004, illustrating this with the example of the 'brazen, large-scale South African raid in June 1985 against African National Congress (ANC) targets in (Botswana's capital) Gaborone that left six people wounded and twelve dead'.

Botswana kept up the spending even when apartheid was gone. Though military budgets did go down in 1994 with the election of Nelson Mandela as South Africa's first democratic president, they were soon up to close to 4% of GDP again in 1998 for no apparent reason. In 2014 military expenditure fell to 1.9%, but the country was still the 10th highest military spender in Africa, ranking 37 on the global 'big spender' list – on par with Turkey. In late 2015, Botswana taxpayers would fork out over US$75m in a 'stimulus package' for the purchase of six new fighter jets with accompanying systems.

Botswana's numerous military purchases over the past four decades have enriched two parties in particular: the mainly European arms manufacturers that sold the tanks, jets, armoured personnel carriers, guns, ammunition, missiles and sundry spare parts: Alvis Vickers (UK), Swiss Pilatus, French Thales, Israeli Elbit and German Steyr-Daimler and the Khama family, in particular twins Anthony and Tshekedi Khama, brothers of current President Ian Khama.

The lead in this build-up was taken by Ian Khama himself, first as deputy and later as full commander of the Botswana Defence Force. In tandem with their big brother's career, by 1989, Ian's younger brothers, twins Anthony and Tshekedi – the latter is now also Minister for the Environment, Wildlife and Tourism – had established their company Seleka Springs as the dominant agency for military acquisitions for the country.

For decades, the detail of most of the Khama brothers' contracts and suppliers contracting parties remained secret and out of the grasp of the Botswana public. But finally, in March 2015, opposition parliamentarian Pius Mokgware asked Minister of Defence Shaw Kgathi to state the companies which Seleka Springs represented as agents since 1989 for the supply of goods and services to Botswana Defence Force (BDF) and the Botswana Police Services (BPS). Mokgware further wanted to know details of the contracts and amounts awarded to the companies, as well as the amounts of money Seleka Springs had received.

At first Minister Kgathi denied that the Khama brothers at Seleka Springs had ever been awarded tenders from the BDF between 1989 and 1998, the period whilst Ian Khama was in charge of the army. (It was then that, for the first time in Botswana history, a sitting Minister was called a liar by the parliament's deputy speaker, who pointed out that a former minister had already confirmed just that.) Kgathi was made to retract his statement and, a few months later, indeed produced a list of contracts and their value. It was a very short list, though, and the total value of the contracts quoted – around US$10m – was almost laughably small in view of the fact that SIPRI's arms trade register shows several known Seleka Springs deals as amounting to about US$100 million.

The concentration of military power in the presidency, presidential brothers and a few other anointed friends and relatives has accompanied the growth of a Khama-led securocracy in Botswana. In 2008, when Ian Khama was sworn in as President, he immediately promoted his private secretary Isaac Kgosi to head the newly established Directorate for Intelligence and Security (DIS). Khama also gave DIS agents firearms as well as wide-ranging arrest and detention powers. The agency soon became notorious for using these powers to suppress opposition: in 2009, striking students were abducted, threatened and intimidated; twelve 'suspects' were shot in broad daylight.

Subsequent extrajudicial killings were not so much about social protest, but centred more on corruption, scandal and extortion around Ian Khama and his circle of close friends and relatives. Still in 2009, former Khama friend John Kalafatis was shot in public on the streets of Gaborone. It was alleged that he had tried to blackmail 'high profile' individuals with an incriminating videotape. In 2010, state diamond mining company Debswana's managing director Louis Nchindo's body was found, eaten by cheetahs, in the bush: he had allegedly threatened to lift the lid on a diamond-funding scandal from which the ruling party had benefited. On 30 July 2014, opposition leader Gomolemo Motswaledi died when his car rolled over about 90 kilometres south of Gaborone. Botswana police released a statement pronouncing it a traffic accident, but members of the opposition were and are convinced that this was an assassination. And on 6 May 2015 the offices of the *Botswana Gazette* were raided by Botswana government officials with an urgent warrant to search and confiscate any material used for the publication of a recent story about individuals who had used their influence in the ruling party to secure oil contracts. In the same year, President Ian Khama started to visit suppliers for new BDF jets in South Korea and Sweden. His engagement on these last deals is still ongoing.

2016, MOZAMBIQUE

All the generals' licences

INTRODUCED BY EVELYN GROENINK

When reference is made to the 'plunder' of Africa, or, in more technical terms, to 'illicit financial outflows,' the focus is usually on exploitative multinational mining companies, under-declaration of exports and tax evasion by the private sector. The Panama and Paradise papers showed how billions of dollars that rightfully belong in tax coffers have been siphoned off to Swiss bank accounts and tax havens like the Bahamas and Mauritius. In 2018, the West Africa Leaks shed a spotlight on the stark consequences of this phenomenon for poor African countries that, in spite of massive natural wealth, don't provide even proper roads to citizens, let alone healthcare or education. But one important factor in the plunder of Africa's resources often escapes scrutiny: the accountability of Africa's political leaders themselves.

Estacio Valoi is a freelancer who lives and works in Pemba, northern Mozambique, where he says he witnesses cargo ships taking out his country's wealth on a daily basis. He reports on this for the Oxpeckers environmental unit, 100 Reporters and the online magazine *ZAM*, and is a member of the African Investigative Publishing Collective (AIPC). Valoi's reporting on the looting of ruby and other natural resources in his country, Mozambique, provides much-needed scrutiny.

His chapter in the larger transnational investigation into African oligarchs published by AIPC shows how foreign companies are drawn into partnerships with the ruling Frelimo party elite, who hold the licences that provide access to the natural resources. Valoi shows, using the Extractive Industries Transparency Initiative (EITI) and company registry data, that nearly all the licences to exploit natural wealth in northern Mozambique have been allocated to local ruling party-connected individuals first, before the foreign companies came in.

Valoi's identification of Frelimo politicians, lawyers and generals as beneficiaries of these licences also shows that this is not an issue of 'indigenisation' of Mozambique's extractive sector. It is not Mozambique's working business people or artisanal miners who benefit from the foreign investment and expertise. The powerful individuals who end up owning up to half of these joint ventures are conduits: the foreign company does the work, takes out the goods and hands a share of the profit to the local partner.

Where does the tax evasion come in? This part of what Valoi unearthed really shatters the notion that only foreign looters are to blame for this scourge. The main multinational in the area, gemstone giant Gemfields/Pallinghurst, has been faithfully paying the agreed 10 per cent of profits in royalties to the Mozambican state. Montepuez citizens have not benefitted from these moneys at all, in spite of an arrangement with the company that close to a third of the royalties should directly be put to good use in the region. This is not the fault of Gemfields/Pallinghurst, but of Mozambican bureaucrats who have ignored the requirement. In another case unearthed by Valoi, a local-foreign joint venture was able to take out rubies worth over US$110m without the necessary licence. It was thanks to high-level political connections that they bypassed the provincial mining authority with impunity.

Valoi's third achievement in this piece is that he shows how a political 'plunder' elite erodes the state itself. Why have a system of licences and a provincial mining authority if its rules and regulations can be ignored? Why have a tax authority if the moneys it collects do not benefit the citizens? Why even have human rights laws and artisanal mining agreements if – as Valoi also documents – powerful individuals can bypass regular police command and unleash militias and Special Forces on farmers and villagers?

Valoi's relentless reporting, often while risking his life, in the forests, fisheries, export ships and mining sites, has had significant impact in Montepuez. He reports that Gemfields/Pallinghurst works less directly with the generals now, and more with the local state and justice structures. A company with a globally advertised corporate social responsibility and environment-friendly image cannot afford to be called, as one of Valoi's stories was titled, 'Friends with the general'.

Further reading

Valoi, Estacio and Mohammad, Gesbeen. 2016. The Ruby Plunder of Montepuez. *ZAM* magazine. Available at: www.zammagazine.com/chronicle/chronicle-22/318-the-ruby-plunder-wars-of-montepuez, accessed on 18 August 2018.

AIPC. 2017. The Plunder Route to Panama. How Arican oligarchs steal from their countries. *ZAM* magazine. Available at: www.zammagazine.com/images/pdf/documents/African_Oligarchs.pdf, accessed on 18 August 2018.

All the Generals' Licenses

Estacio Valoi, *ZAM* magazine, 12 April 2016

The mining concession map of Montepuez, drawn up by Mozambique's mining and energy department in compliance with international Extractive Industries Transparency Initiative (EITI) requirements, is so completely covered in squares, rectangles and other angularly shaped blocks that it begs the question where the *people* are going to live. The entire region seems to have been allocated to mining, with only space on the side for a nature reserve.

Company papers related to the ruby concessions in the area show that practically all these concession areas are owned by a set of well-networked, ruling party-connected generals and security supremos, politicians and former and present high-ranking ruling party members, as well as the Mayor of Maputo. The biggest concession, of Montepuez Ruby Mining, aka MRM Gemfields – the only one that has already been legally owning, producing and exporting rubies from Mozambique for the past five years – is partly owned by Mozambican General Raimundo Domingos Pachinuapa, a powerful member of Mozambique's ruling party, former liberation movement Frelimo. General Pachinuapa's company Mwiriti holds 25% of MRM, of which the other 75% is owned by UK multinational Gemfields, recently taken over by Pallinghurst. Pachinuapa also holds a quarter each of Gemfields/Pallinghurst's other concessions, Megaruma and Eastern Ruby, as well as 20 other licencses of his own for ruby mining in Montepuez. His son Raime is MRM's manager for corporate affairs.

The General doesn't answer several requests for interviews. The closest I ever come to him is in a bar in Pemba, on an afternoon in 2016, when a lawyer known to be 'well-connected', suddenly sits next to me and tells me how 'generous' the general is known to be to his 'friends'. These friends are most likely not the common inhabitants of Montepuez, though, since no one has been particularly generous to them since mining started. The damage to, in some cases destruction of, villages and farms has not been compensated by an increase in services to the population — electricity, water, schools or shops — as promised by the company and its governing elite partners at the time, in 2014. Mining jobs at MRM — 1,100, says MRM, much less, say locals — have also not compensated for the loss in income experienced by 1,500 artisanal mining families in the region.

In the early days — before the partnership was formed between Mwiriti and Gemfields to create MRM — these artisanal miners had been selling rubies to the Mwiriti operation. But, according to locals, it had been no more than 'two weeks after the arrival of Gemfields' that the artisanal mining associations had been destroyed and the first accounts of violence against artisanal miners by *nacatanas*, militias working for the company, were recorded.

'Formal' mining is still officially supposed to benefit the Montepuez region. According to provincial financial department administrator Fernando Djange, MRM Gemfields has an agreement with the Mozambican state to pay it 10% of the sales value of each ruby auction in royalties. Of this, 2.75%, says Djange, is 'paid to the Montepuez district in royalties at the end of every budget year'. With over nine auctions to date, with according to Gemfields a total revenue of US$288m, royalties would amount to close to US$29m, with 2.75% of that being over US$7m. Seven million American dollars for a sparsely populated district could do a lot of good. Only it never came.

Perusing the budget records at the Cabo Delgado provincial administration, under which Montepuez falls, I only see one input from MRM Gemfields of 6m meticais (US$ one hundred thousand) in 2016. There is no input over the other years. 'We'll check with the finance department,' says Dange. 'It is definitely there.' But neither he nor the finance department come back to clarify the issue. Montepuez district administrator Etelvina Fevereiro, asked if her department ever received the money, explains that 'we only get it two years after the auction. So the money from the auction in 2017, we'll get it in 2019.' But two auctions were held in 2014, totaling over US$76m in revenue. Royalties would amount to close to US$2m, 20 times the amount actually paid in 2016. Fevereiro says she doesn't know about that. 'You should check with the Cabo Delgado provincial financial administration.' Gemfields maintains in an email that all royalties have been paid and notes that 'allocation and distribution' is the responsibility of the Mozambican government.

Whether Gemfields is responsible for the fact that millions of dollars in benefits from its mining are not reaching the villagers, or the Mozambican state, is difficult to answer. Gemfields' operational partners *are* the Mozambican state, after all.

Several others among Mozambique's Who's Who list of ruby concession owners have also found international partners with substantial mining capacity. Felicio Zacarias's company, Regius, features as a partner in UK Redstone mining; Zacarias and prominent Frelimo lawyer Lukman Assade Amane are also partners in Australian Mustang resources. According to *Mining Weekly* of 20 January 2017, 'Mustang Resources announced in late January that it had dispatched its "first commercial parcel of the precious stones of 6,221 carat of rubies from its project in (Mozambique) to the US". Mustang's website estimates the value of one carat of rough Mozambican rubies between US$18,000 and US$42,000, which would place the value of the parcel at at least US$112m.

Informed about this, Montepuez mining director Ramiro Nguiraz says he has 'dispatched an inspection team' to the Mustang concession in Montepuez. 'Mustang only has a prospecting licence. They are not allowed to produce and sell. We think there are few things they did against the law.' Mustang managing director Christiaan Jordaan is adamant, however, that the company's exploration and prospecting licence allows the right to export and sell rubies 'to finance further exploration'. He adds that 'all Mustang's exports have been approved by the Department of Minerals and the Department of Customs' and that 'regarding the export of rubies from Mozambique, including the parcel mentioned by you that was exported at the start of this year ... we have gone through all the official channels with the

Mining Department to secure the necessary export permits and we paid the royalties as calculated by the department.' Jordaan does not respond to an email in which we ask him to provide the text of the licence.

There are more such, let's call it communication gaps, between Montepuez's civil servants trying to do their job and those involved in the mining. Last year, then district administrator Arcanjo Cassia complained that he did not know where to turn to demand delivery on the promised Corporate Social Responsibility Projects (schools, employment projects, water wells among others). In another case, provincial Attorney General Pompilio Uazanguia was demoted from his position after he had attempted to prosecute militia killers of artisanal miners. The demotion took place amid unsubstantiated rumours that Uazanguia was 'involved in timber smuggling,' which were then echoed as fact in a letter sent by Gemfields to a publication that had quoted Uazanguia. (Uazanguia has started a defamation lawsuit against Gemfields/Pallinghurst for airing the accusation.)

2016, Congo

Joseph Kabila's family fortune

Introduced by Franz Wild

As early as 2015, the signs were growing that Democratic Republic of Congo's President Joseph Kabila would try to outstay his two-term limit and jeopardise its carefully crafted peace. If Kabila was to be in power beyond December 2016, he would technically be staying beyond his term limit and Congo would stumble into a constitutional crisis. And it was obvious that elections would be seriously delayed. The question was always why someone who didn't seem to actually want to govern would want to hang on so badly. Many Congolese suspected he was protecting his family's business interests, but no one knew what they were. No one could name a single one.

As three Bloomberg reporters who had each been based in Kinshasa for various periods over the past decade, Michael Kavanagh, Thomas Wilson and I had always wondered the same thing. It so happened that public company records were being digitised and we were able to compile an enormous database of filings. We scoured it for references to Kabila's relatives (often using variations of their real name) and were able to identify dozens of companies they were involved in. With that in hand, we went out to figure out what the story behind each company was. It was all the usual stuff – speaking with old and new sources, getting information from other organisations that had dealt with the companies and finding references in filings in other countries. We went to see the farms in the east, the copper mines in the south and the diamond mines in the west, all remote places controlled by the president's personal guard.

The most breath-taking breakthrough came when a whistleblower emerged towards the end of our reporting process. Jean-Jacques Lumumba had worked for Kabila's brother at a Congolese bank and came forward with credible information on several of the companies and how they operated. He had made it to Europe, but he was literally risking his life.

The story was published days before the official end of Kabila's second term. The mood in Kinshasa was tense. Police were brutally breaking up demonstrations against his rule. When our story came out it immediately became a talking point in the political scene from Congolese opposition politicians to John Kerry, the US Secretary of State, trying to put pressure on Kabila to leave office. Kabila didn't budge and outmanoeuvred his opponents.

After the revelations, a flurry of articles from other major international news organisations and a detailed research report on the Kabila family's assets followed. An area that had seemed totally impenetrable suddenly started producing fascinating details about the first family. Importantly, everyone now has a deeper understanding of who Kabila is and what he's protecting.

We spent about 18 months on this article and crisscrossed sub-Saharan Africa's largest country which would've been an unthinkable investment for a Congolese organisation. Journalism has next to no funding in the Congo. In most instances, newspapers are as much a platform for the rich and powerful to elevate themselves. That said, there are some publications that are working incredibly hard and on very little money to publish independent news.

Snooping around mines with presidential guards patrolling wasn't risk-free for us, but it's a world away from the risks faced by Congolese journalists. They would not be operating on the understanding that a Western government or news organisation could intervene should their rights not be respected. During Kabila's rule, a number of journalists have disappeared or been killed with impunity.

At the time of writing, Kabila's government had just announced that he wouldn't stand in December 2018 elections and that a long-time loyalist would replace him as the ruling coalition's candidate.

* *The original reporting was also supported by the Pulitzer Center on Crisis Reporting and the Congo Research Group at New York University.*

References

Congo Research Group. 2017. 'All the president's wealth: The Kabila family's business'. Available at: http://pulitzercenter.org/sites/default/files/all-the-presidents-wealth-eng.pdf, accessed on 18 August 2018.

With His Family's Fortune at Stake, President Kabila Digs In

Michael Kavanagh, Thomas Wilson and Franz Wild, *Bloomberg News*, 15 December 2016

In his only public speech this year, Joseph Kabila, president of the Democratic Republic of Congo, was defiant about his refusal to hand over power when his final term ends on Dec 19. 'I cannot allow the republic to be taken hostage by a fringe of the political class,' he told parliament last month as members cheered.

His presidency had brought peace and economic growth to Congo, the 45-year-old said, outlining reforms he'd made in telecommunications, mining, energy and banking. What he didn't say is how some of his own family members are among the biggest beneficiaries of those changes — including his sister Jaynet and brother Zoe, who both listened from the front row as elected members of parliament.

Together the Kabilas have built a network of businesses that reaches into every corner of Congo's economy and has brought hundreds of millions of dollars to the family, a *Bloomberg News* investigation has found. The sprawling network may help explain why the president is ignoring pleas by the US, the European Union and a majority of the Congolese people to hand over power next week, though his advisers dispute this.

... Kabila and his siblings have assembled an international business network stretching across at least 70 companies, according to a *Bloomberg News* analysis of thousands of company documents and court filings as well as dozens of interviews with bankers, businessmen, miners, farmers and former government officials.

While Congolese law doesn't prohibit politicians or their families from having business interests, the scope of that empire has only recently become visible, in publicly available corporate and government records that Congolese regulators have computerized and made searchable in just the past few years. *Bloomberg News*, with support from the Pulitzer Center on Crisis Reporting, traced the Kabilas' interests by amassing an archive of hundreds of thousands of pages of corporate documents that shows his wife, two children and eight of his siblings control more than 120 permits to dig gold, diamonds, copper, cobalt and other minerals.

Two of the family's businesses alone own diamond permits that stretch more than 450 miles across Congo's southwestern border with Angola. Family members also have stakes in banks, farms, fuel distributors, airline operators, a road builder, hotels, a pharmaceutical supplier, travel agencies, boutiques and nightclubs. Another venture even tried to launch a rat into space on a rocket.

In Congo's largely informal, cash-based economy where the family stakes are almost all in privately held companies, the exact value of the businesses isn't known. The few figures available in publicly accessible documents show investments worth more than $30 million in just two companies. Estimated revenue for another company exceeds $350 million over four years – in a country where World Bank data show that nearly two-thirds of the 77 million people live on less than $1.90 per day.

While some of the businesses are owned directly, the family also has dozens of joint ventures and shell corporations through which it holds stakes to varying degrees in all manner of industries. That creates a system so pervasive that even seemingly innocuous payments – such as rent paid by the UN for a police station – end up finding their way to the Kabila family, an analysis of the network shows. It can be a ham-handed operation: Perhaps in its eagerness to tap the country's resource wealth, the family has sometimes driven away outside investment that would have made some of its members even more money.

Government spokesman Lambert Mende said he couldn't comment on issues concerning the president's family, which he considered a private matter. When asked how *Bloomberg News* could direct questions to Kabila, he said the president does not talk to Western media. Theodore Mugalu, who handles the family's personal affairs, didn't respond to a series of phone calls and text messages requesting comment ...

Joseph Kabila grew up with his siblings in exile in Tanzania, the children of Laurent-Desire Kabila. Their childhood was modest but full of intrigue, as their heavyset, charismatic, rebel father moved from country to country using fake passports and trying to gin up support for his fight against the US-backed dictator Mobutu Sese Seko ...

After their father became president in 1997 by overthrowing Mobutu with the help of a coalition of African governments, he immediately set about making money for his government — and for family and friends, according to Kennes's biography.

The places he'd fought in the bush as a young rebel became the names of commercial interests. Hewa Bora, the rebel base where his twins Jaynet and Joseph were born, became an airline, a fuel station, a farm and a mining site. Wimbi Dira, another rear base, gave its name to a second airline.

Since then, the Kabila family's businesses have grown with Congo's developing economy. And they now enjoy a perk of presidential power: the protection of the Republican Guard, an elite army unit that is supposed to protect Kabila himself. In July 2015, guard members accompanied his wife, Olive, after she had bought a cattle farm in the grassy hills of North Kivu. According to three laborers who were displaced, she demanded they remove their makeshift homes or watch soldiers destroy them. Olive didn't respond to multiple phone calls and text messages sent to her assistant.

Many of the companies are run by Jaynet, Joseph Kabila's twin sister. After their father's death, documents show, she set up companies across Congo, as well as in the US, Panama, Tanzania and on the South Pacific island of Niue. Company filings show she is or has been a shareholder or director in at least 28 companies. In some, she controlled a majority of shares while in others she held minority stakes, the filings show. It's unclear how many of those companies are still active.

The lack of transparency in some of the family's dealings has hurt Congo's economy. In 2012, the International Monetary Fund cut its half-billion dollar loan program with Congo after the government declined to publish contracts related to a 2011 deal for a copper mine known as Comide. One of the companies involved in the deal, Goma Mining, was at least 10 percent owned by the family and chaired by Kabila's sister, Josephine, according to court records from 2013.

The family's involvement in mining – diamonds, cobalt and copper – comes in part through a company called Acacia, which was majority-owned by Jaynet; younger brother Masengo; Joseph Kabila's 16-year-old daughter, Sifa; and his financial assistant, Emmanuel Adrupiako, based on corporate records from September 2014.

In the remote southern town of Tembo, people haven't heard of Acacia or another family-controlled company called Kwango Mines that together hold 96 mining permits. But they seem to know who controls the diamonds in the river. 'All the documents for this project are now in the hands of Jaynet Kabila, the twin sister,' said diamond trader Jauvin Manzaza, pointing to the wide Kwango River that tracks the border with Angola.

Kabila-controlled companies first arrived here in 1998, Manzaza said, armed with tractors and machinery to dig for diamonds 15 miles south of the town. In 2003, a company controlled by Selemani and Kabila's younger brothers Zoe and Masengo sold more than $12 million of gems, export data show. Diamonds accounted for three-quarters of Congo's export revenue that year, which also marked the end of the country's civil war, attracting international diamond companies.

Once there, those firms found they had no choice but to negotiate with the Kabila clan, said Mike De Wit, head of exploration in Congo from 2003 to 2007 for the world's largest diamond producer, De Beers. In 2006, De Beers signed an agreement to explore with permits belonging to a company controlled by Olive Lembe, a few months before she married the new president, De Wit said. That company is now called Olive Sifa Laurent, or Osifal for short, named after its shareholders: Olive, the couple's daughter, Sifa, and eight-year-old son, Laurent-Desire.

'When Kabila came to power, he looked like an honest guy and business was actually doable, so that's why De Beers went into there,' De Wit said in an interview. 'With time, it became obvious that that wasn't the case' ...

Thirty miles to the south, men in restitched wetsuits dive for diamonds off the edge of a flotilla of 20 multicolored dinghies, scraping gravel from the riverbed. When Republican Guard soldiers come by, the divers hand over buckets of potentially gem-filled gravel as an informal tax.

It's unclear how much revenue diamonds generate for Kabila family businesses today. Congo's diamond production has halved since 2005, overtaken by copper, cobalt and gold.

Acacia turned its attention some 500 miles southeast of Tembo in 2010, when the prices of copper and cobalt, now Congo's biggest exports, surged. The region, known as Katanga, is bursting with copper and other metals. Hundreds of thousands of men, desperate for work, use spades, picks and hammers to scrape ore out of the bottom of tunnels that at times descend more than 130 feet below ground.

Near the town of Luisha, about 4,500 diggers work an area of six mines that officially belong to state-owned miner Gecamines. Teams of four diggers each produce an average of about half a ton of copper and cobalt ore per day, according to a 2014 World Bank-funded report.

Three of the mines are run by Acacia, the 2014 report said, even though Gecamines has never announced any partnership with the company. Soldiers on the sites force diggers to sell their minerals only to Acacia at below-market prices, according to the report, which was written by French consulting firm Sofreco for a World Bank program on improving governance in Congo's mining sector. A Gecamines spokesman declined to comment for this story …

In the Congolese capital of Kinshasa, behind the reflecting windows of the BGFI bank, the Kabila family has built its most sophisticated investment: the country branch of a Gabon-based banking group.

BGFI in Congo is dominated by the presidential family. When the lender set up in the country in 2010, Kabila's sister Gloria Mteyu took a 40 percent stake, then worth $10 million, according to company registration documents from that year. Gabon-based Groupe BGFI Bank SA, which has ventures in 11 countries, holds 60 percent.

In 2014, BGFI in Congo recapitalized, raising its share capital to $38 million, and Gloria maintained her 40 percent shareholding, according to corporate records from that year, the most recent available. Last December, the bank had $374 million in assets, making it Congo's sixth-biggest lender. Gloria also has a stake in a new banking venture via a stake in Kwanza Capital, shareholding records show. BGFI loaned Kwanza $3.45 million in April, according to a term sheet reviewed by Bloomberg.

A 32-year-old fashion designer, Gloria said in a telephone interview that she returned to Congo in 2012 to launch Kinshasa Fashion Week after studying in New York, Milan and Paris.

Asked about her businesses, she said she was a private person and didn't want to talk about ventures that weren't related to fashion. She said she didn't have a stake in BGFI.

At a November press conference in Kinshasa, though, Abdel Kader Diop, deputy managing director of the Congo unit, said Gloria was a shareholder. An outside spokesman for BGFI in Gabon said the chief executive officer of the bank was too busy to comment for this story.

BGFI's Gabonese parent hired PricewaterhouseCoopers to audit BGFI in 2015. The audit found that the Congolese bank had failed to follow internal controls 19 times and paid middlemen for business without knowing who would ultimately receive the funds.

Jean-Jacques Lumumba, head of credit at the bank, found suspicious transactions soon after he started working there in 2014.

Lumumba discovered that the nation's central bank – which isn't allowed to make commercial loans – had lent a food distribution company $43 million and transferred the money to an account at BGFI. The food company's incorporation documents show that it's run by business partners of President Kabila, whose brother Selemani is the bank's CEO.

Lumumba said he confronted Selemani in his boss's office, where he found him sitting in front of a photo of Kabila and another of Selemani with some of the men involved in the transaction.

Selemani stared at him for a moment, then leaned back in his chair, allowing his jacket to fall behind the dark hilt of a pistol protruding from his pants. 'Are you making problems for me?' Lumumba recalled him yelling. 'You know I will deal with you if I have to. Just do as I tell you' …

2016–17, Botswana

Fake degrees and documents

Introduced by Letshwiti Batlhalefi Tutwane

The two investigative stories which we feature in this chapter were published by the *Botswana Gazette* and *Mmegi* newspapers in collaboration with the INK Centre for Investigative Journalism, a new organisation founded by Joel Konopo and Ntibinyane Ntibinyane around 2015.

The first story, 'Botho fires "Dr Fake" as BAC panics', published by the *Botswana Gazette* on 31 August 2016, exposes academic staff at mainly private tertiary institutions in Botswana with fake degrees. The story took at least two months to investigate and covered two local universities, Botho University and Botswana Accountancy College.

The journalists demonstrated that two universities from which the academics in these institutions had received their degrees, New World Mission Dunamis International University (NWMD) in Cape Town and the Northern Ireland Institute of Business Technology (NIIBT) in Belfast, were bogus. They undertook physical checks, travelling to the location of these 'universities' to ascertain how they look and what happens there. They established that the address of NWMD in South Africa is just an office and in London just coffee shops and a parking lot. The website does not state the location of the university, a huge pointer to fraud. As for NIIBT, the journalists revealed that it is not only a shell company but that the provided postcode leads to a property company with no links with education.

The journalists also demonstrated their understanding of academic operational issues. A PhD is an onerous degree which takes at least three years to finish in most universities globally and it would raise eyebrows if anybody claims to have finished two PhDs simultaneously, as a Botho University business sciences lecturer did. Accreditation was another issue. Most universities would seek prestigious accreditation for their programmes and any institution not linked to such accreditation bodies like these two would engender serious suspicion. In addition, a PhD is a demonstration of original research, a major contribution to the field by a graduate. If he or she can't produce their thesis, then that is a strong signal of a dubious doctorate.

The story is significant for two reasons. First it put the national qualifications watchdog, the Botswana Qualifications Authority, on the spot, challenging them to be more circumspect in their work. Secondly, a good investigative story normally has consequences. In this case, the authorities at Botho College dismissed the lecturers.

The INK Centre followed up with another article dated 28 July 2017 titled, 'DIS report on opposition is fake'. What is remarkable about this article is that the report was not equivocal about what was claimed. It boldly stated that a report on alleged state intelligence agency interference in the opposition was fraudulent.

After making the declaration, the INK Centre justified its conclusion. The metadata on the document revealed the authors of the article. It also revealed that the document was created in July 2017 and not 2016 as claimed in it. Significantly, it was created at the time when the two warring factions in the opposition party, the Botswana Movement for Democracy (BMD), were due to hold a congress. It was meant to give an edge to one of the factions in anticipation of the chaos that eventually erupted at the Congress. The Centre was able to tell the dates, times and place the document was created, the kind of computer used and the total time spent creating it.

The document also contained information which was plagiarised from media articles, prompting the Centre to conclude that the work was amateurish. The plagiarism included verbatim quotes from one newspaper article, with no attempt to edit them. The Centre picked out even more basic mistakes like out-dated facts about the place of employment of the wife of one of the opposition leaders who had left her previous job over five years ago. Even the designation of the purported author of the report was not the director at DISS, as claimed. These pointed to serious credibility issues.

The presentation and formatting of the report also gave it away, the Centre observed. Intelligence agents do not normally reveal their identities, often using codes. But in this document, the purported author gave out his identity number.

The Centre would not have managed to do this outstanding investigation without resources. They called on the International Consortium of Investigative Journalists (ICIJ) whose software engineer, Matthew Caruana Galizia, helped them analyse the document, as well as local experts on intelligence and metadata.

Botho fires 'Dr Fake' as BAC panics

Queen Mosare, Lawrence Seretse & Joel Konopo, *Botswana Gazette*, 1 September 2016

Two lecturers have been fired from a Botswana college for obtaining fake degrees from a university apparently based in the wilds of the Northern Cape.

Botho University, a private college in Botswana specialising in business and IT education, has fired two lecturers after discovering that they obtained their doctoral degrees from a 'university' apparently based in the wilds of the Northern Cape.

The institution in question is the New World Mission Dunamis International University (NWMD), which claims on its website to be based in Cape Town but offers no address.

However, a source in the Botswana Qualifications Authority said its application to the authority gave its address as 'Globbershoop' – apparently a misspelling of the remote Northern Cape town of Groblershoop. According to South Africa's most recent census, Groblershoop has a population of about 5000.

In its list of private educational institutions, updated in August 2016, South Africa's department of higher education and training brands the organisation as 'a complete fraud'.

In the United States, the Michigan Civil Service Commission has said that NWMD's degrees do not satisfy the educational requirements indicated for job specifications.

This emerged from an investigation by the *Botswana Gazette* newspaper and the Gaborone-based INK Centre for Investigative Journalism.

Botho pro-vice chancellor Lucky Moahi confirmed that business science lecturers Stanley Thuku Waithaka and Busisiwe Ndlovu were employed on the strength of PhD degrees from NWMD.

He added: 'However, in July 2016, when we were alerted to the fact that the ... institution was not approved by the regulators, we immediately took the necessary action and have since terminated their contracts of employment ...'

The source said Ndlovu received two doctoral degrees in one year, 2012, from the alleged learning institution ...

(NIBBT) offers a 'fast-track programme' that allows students to complete their degrees in a shorter time. Using this programme students can earn a first degree for $300 or R2500.

However, it adds that 'some qualifications may not be recognised by your country of governmental departments' and warns that 'employers and others have got the right to reject your qualifications and that this is not our responsibility'.

A BA programme costs R3000 or R3500, and an MA degree R4000 or R4500.

Ndlovu, whose student number was 29-140-245, enrolled for a PhD at NWMD in 2010 'majoring in leadership, business administration', and graduated in June 2013. He also has an MBA from an institution called the National University of Science and Technology.

Ndlovu did not respond to questions sent to him three weeks ago.

Documents show that Waithaka 'enrolled' for a PhD at about the same time as Ndlovu and graduated with two PhDs, in business studies and business administration, in 2012. It takes an average of between three and five years to complete a PhD at a conventional university.

The fact that Botho employed the two unqualified lecturers for several years has raised questions about its recruitment and verification processes.

The institution's head of 'employability and development', Preya Iyer, said the university relies on Securitas and InfoTrack to screen the qualifications of its academic staff members.

Botho said the two lecturers are still employed by Botho but are serving out notice periods.

Meanwhile, the INK/*Botswana Gazette* investigation also raised questions about the qualifications of Andrew Anyona, a Kenyan-born business lecturer at the Botswana Accountancy College.

Anyona acquired a PhD in 2010 from an outfit calling itself the Northern Ireland Institute of Business and Technology (British) – NIIBT.

On the internet, the NIIBT gives its address as Premier

Business, 20 Adelaide Street, Belfast, Northern Ireland. However, a Google Earth search of this address goes to a lottery centre.

In an online posting, Richard Harriman of Botswana's Consumer Watchdog says the NIIBT does not appear on the company registers of either Britain or the Republic of Ireland.

Its Malaysian addresses, he says, are 'no more than post boxes'.

Harriman comments that the Irish companies register records the existence of the Royal Ireland Institute of Business and Technology, but that this was dissolved in 2012.

The *Botswana Gazette* asked Anyona to supply a copy of his doctoral thesis. He responded that he was not obliged to make the thesis public.

In response to questions about his doctoral degree, he said that the Botswana Qualifications Authority had successfully evaluated his qualifications and that they were recognised in Kenya.

He added that the degree was recognised by the Open University Europa, a member of the International Council for Open and Distance Education.

Asked about Anyona's qualifications, BAC spokesperson Mpho Mokgosi said: 'We are constrained in discussing employee personal information ... and trust that he is best placed to respond to questions of personal nature.'

Mokgosi said the BAC followed a rigorous and transparent recruitment process when it employed the Kenyan in 2012, and that BAC lecturers are accredited by the Botswana Qualifications Authority and 'partner universities' in the UK.

'Our partner universities also subscribe to international higher learning bodies which accredits all lecturer qualifications attained internationally,' he said.

According to the UK's education department, as many as 200 institutions offer bogus degrees in Britain.

The Botswana authority monitors and audits all accredited institutions to ensure 'continued compliance' in accordance with the law, but has never revoked the licence of a major institution on grounds that it employs lecturers with qualifications from 'degree mills'.

DIS report on opposition is fake

INK Centre, *Mmegi*, 28 July 2017

Soon after the opposition Botswana Movement for Democracy (BMD) returned from a violent congress in Bobonong, the media was awash with a document — code named Tholwana Borethe — claiming to reveal a secret plot by the spy agency to disrupt the opposition Umbrella for Democratic Change (UDC) from toppling the ruling Botswana Democratic Party (BDP) in the 2019 general election.

INK Centre analysed the document with the help of International Consortium of Investigative Journalists (ICIJ) software engineer Matthew Caruana Galizia and other local experts on intelligence and metadata, and established that the Tholwana Borethe was done in haste and carried serious and elementary errors.

The metadata inadvertently left on the purported intelligence report lucidly exposed the authors of the documents. The most interesting finding is that the document was created a few days before the last BMD congress in Bobonong, not in 2016 as previously stated. The report was created on two different dates in July. The first document, which was first sent to *Botswana Guardian*, was created on July 10, 2017, at 9:17pm and was last saved on July 12, 2017 at 09:29am.

The document was created from a desktop computer at a Gaborone suburb, which the metadata identified as using Microsoft Word 2001–2004. The total time for editing and writing the document is 139 minutes, according to the document's metadata.

The other report, which was later passed to *Mmegi*, *Sunday Standard*, *Business Weekly* and *Botswana Gazette* was created on July 12, 2017 at 12:46pm using the same computer. The PDF document also offers hints about its authenticity and origins. It was created using MS Word 2001–2004, and later by the latest MS Word 2016, the metadata left on the PDF document show. The document was later converted to PDF using Adobe 1.5 (Acrobat 6.x) version.

Furthermore, what is emerging from the Tholwana Borethe documents are the stark and obvious inconsistencies regarding the fake dates the report was prepared for the DIS Director, Isaac Kgosi. The dates do not correspond with the dates left on the metadata.

The first report passed to the *Botswana Guardian* was allegedly authored by DIS Special Task Team 'director', Tsosoloso Mosinki on February 28, 2016. It is not clear why the report passed on to other publications on the same report claimed that the report was produced on June 28, 2016. A security and intelligence expert engaged by INK Centre concluded that, 'Clearly the report was manufactured by amateurs. They failed the basic test of covering their tracks.' Another commented, 'It is possible to forge the creation date, but I don't think there's a logical reason for them to have done that.'

What is emerging from the analysis of the report is that unlike most intelligence reports, which rely on newly obtained intelligence gathered from sources within political movements, the report was an act of plagiarism that further missed key and basic facts. While the intelligence communities often use open source intelligence (OSINT), the level of plagiarism on the report raises red flags. For example, at least 80% of the contents of the 'intelligence report' are picked from news articles by *Mmegi* newspaper. The report also plagiarised articles by Gabz FM and *European Times* reporters ...

One of the greatest blemishes in the Tholwana Borethe report is that it missed key facts. For example, it missed facts about Saleshando wife Dineo's employment. The report says that Dineo works for Standard Chartered Bank as head of Retail, Credit Policy for Southern Africa. In actual fact Dineo left Standard Chartered Bank more than five years ago, and now works for Barclays Bank ...

The format used by the authors of the document is wanting. Intelligence reports are often laced with secret code names. In the intelligence world, this is policy. At least two sources consulted by INK Centre have confirmed.

The agents who put together intelligence reports often do not identify themselves, but rather use code names, or code numbers in the internal reports. The Tholwana Borethe report identifies the writer and also his national identity number, something which is strange in the intelligence community.

2017, Tanzania

Reporting mystery murders, Gwanda became one

Introduced by Bob Wekesa

From 2015, 'unknown assailants' started a spate of murders in the Pwani coastal region of Tanzania. The epicentre of the shootings was the districts of Kibiti, Rufiji and Mkuranga, and they were brought to light by journalist Azory Gwanda.

Gwanda had moved from his home village of Msimba in the Kigoma region of north-western Tanzania to work as a freelancer in the districts of Kibiti, Rufiji and for *The Citizen* and *Mwananchi* newspapers, imprints of Mwananchi Communications Limited, part of East Africa's Nation Media Group.

Almost every week, Gwanda exhibited great courage as he reported on the grisly murders, over 40 people in a two-year period, the victims including local politicians, government officials, policemen and residents. He became the consistent chronicler of a devastating crime by faceless criminals, but the murders remained unresolved, the culprits not arrested.

The sense of bewilderment at the murders can be seen in Gwanda's reporting. Leaders as high up in the Tanzanian government as President John Pombe Magufuli and Prime Minister Kassim Majaliwa suggested that the government was on the verge of apprehending the perpetrators. Such statements only seemed to fuel the murders. At one point, the police indicated that foreigners were involved in the murders. The objective was to cause civil strife in the region and the country, a senior police officer explained. But no arrests were made.

Nobody was safe from the obscure killers. The murders reported by Gwanda included those of police officers, up to 12 of them, including the local head of criminal investigations. Faced with the perplexing challenge, the police resorted to summary execution of suspects, harassment of residents and imposition of curfews, as reported by Gwanda. At some point, the army was called in.

Then, in November 2017, the 42-year-old Gwanda disappeared.

On the morning of 21 November 2017, he went to a farm near his home where his wife, Anna Pinoni, was working. Reportedly, he was in the company of four unknown people in a white Toyota Land Cruiser. He asked for the keys to his house which his wife handed over. He said he had an emergency, work-related trip and would return the following evening. During this exchange, Gwanda remained in the vehicle and communicated through the car window. The vehicle drove off and that was the last time he was seen.

On returning home, his wife found that the house had been ransacked, with paper scattered all over. She called his mobile phone number only to find that it was switched off. She became even more alarmed when Gwanda failed to return the following evening. She made a formal report at the Kibiti Police Station and case file Kibiti/RB/1496/2017 was opened on 23 November 2018. His employer, Mwananchi Communications Limited, learnt of his disappearance only on 30 November, over a week after his abduction (Kolumbia, 2017).

Searches, investigations and pressure by colleagues, rights campaigners and civic leaders since then have not yielded fruit, giving rise to the grim possibility that he might never be found. A media campaign, under the Twitter hashtags #WhereIsAzory and #BringBackAzory was launched in December 2017. The highly publicised initiative brought together the Tanzanian media fraternity including the Tanzania Editors Forum, Media Council of Tanzania, the Media Institute of Southern Africa – Tanzania chapter and the Union of Tanzania Press Clubs, led by Francis Nanai, chief executive officer of Mwananchi Communications. Local and international rights groups weighed in. But to no avail: the campaign has not helped locate Gwanda. Initial statements from the authorities – including the police, government officials and politicians – promising intensified investigations have fizzled out (Legal and Human Rights Centre/Zanzibar Legal Services Centre, 2017).

Gwanda became a victim of the crimes he courageously reported. Most commentators in Tanzania believe his disappearance is based on his investigative journalism work, specifically the murders in Pwani region.

His disappearance triggered debate on the rising violence in Tanzania, a country hitherto considered one of the most tranquil in Africa. Cameraman Daudi Mwangosi died in 2012 after a tear gas canister was fired at him after a quarrel with police officers (Rhodes 2017). In 2013, journalist Absalom Kibanda was attacked, the top of his right ring-finger chopped off, fingernails removed, left eye gorged out and several teeth knocked out (Rhodes 2013). Spates of disappearances, assaults, killings have been on the rise since the mid-2000s but more so in the past two years. Media reports indicate cases of extra-judicial killings involving the police. These range from cases of the police killing suspects during arrests and in custody to the police abusing their power by killing people who differ with them.

Commentators have cited these events to show that Tanzania has embarked on an authoritarian path under populist President John Pombe Magufuli, marked by inept handling of security situations and a clampdown on all forms of expression (Legal and Human Rights Centre/Zanzibar Legal Services Centre, 2017).

Opposition politicians, journalists and artistes such as musicians have been arrested or otherwise harassed on grounds such as 'insulting' the president. In September 2017 for instance, Tundu Lissu, a critical opposition MP and chairman of the Tanzania Law Society was shot in the capital Dodoma and survived only after being speedily airlifted to Nairobi for emergency treatment. In another case, Godfrey Luena, an opposition politician who campaigned against land grabs, was murdered with machetes outside his home in Morogoro (Kamagi, 2018).

In 2017, a senior regional official stormed a radio station, Cloud FM, demanding that it air a programme critical of his opponent. Arising out of the incident, an information minister, Nape Nnauye was fired for apparently siding with Cloud FM. In September 2017, *Mwahalisi*, an independent newspaper, was forced to stop circulation for two years on the flimsy grounds of publishing seditious and false news. Journalists have been arrested arbitrarily (Legal and Human Rights Centre/Zanzibar Legal Services Centre, 2017).

Repressive laws have been enacted, aimed at curtailing freedom of expression. For instance, the Statistics Act stipulates that statistics can be sourced only from official government agencies. The Electronic and Postal Communications (Online Content) Regulations of 2017 tightly regulated blogging and the management of internet cafés (Legal and Human Rights Centre/Zanzibar Legal Services Centre, 2017).

Gwanda's disappearance became the take-off point for discussions on this rise in violence and repression.

References

Kamagi, Deogratius. 2018. 'More voices urge national dialogue to tackle attack', *The Citizen*, 5 February. Available at: www.thecitizen.co.tz/News/More-voices-urge-national-dialogue-to-tackle-attacks/1840340-4318860-tc0asjz/index.html, accessed on 13 August 2018.

Kolumbia, Louis. 2017. 'Disappearance of Azory: What we know so far', *The Citizen*, 17 December. Available at: www.thecitizen.co.tz/News/Disappearance-of-Azory--what-we-know-so-far/1840340-4231716-r17bs4z/index.html, accessed on 13 August 2018.

Legal and Human Rights Centre and Zanzibar Legal Services Centre. 2017. 'Unknown Assailants': A Threat to Human Rights: Tanzania Human Rights Report – 2017. Available at: http://humanrights.or.tz/assets/attachments/1524659401.pdf, accessed on 13 August 2018.

Rhodes, Tom. 2013. 'The invisible plight of the Tanzanian press'. Available at: https://cpj.org/reports/2013/08/the-invisible-plight-of-the-tanzanian-press.php, accessed on 13 August 2018.

Unexplained murders in the Pwani region of Tanzania

Azory Gwanda, *The Citizen*, 2017

Uncertainty over the motive and individuals behind a spate of cold-blooded killings of local government leaders in parts of the Coast Region has left residents with many unanswered questions and fear over who the next target could be.

The most recent killing of Emmanuel Ndinhu, by unknown gunmen has raised concern not only from residents, but also from the ruling Chama Cha Mapinduzi (CCM), who now want authorities to give a reassurance that they would remain safe. All of the 11 victims of the murders are local government leaders elected on the CCM ticket.

After executing the Monday night killing, the assailants left a written warning which reads: 'Fellow citizen, we announce to you that we are doing this because of injustices committed by the Police Force in collaboration with local government leaders against *wananchi* (citizens). We are not ready to tolerate these evils. We shall make sure that everyone who is involved is treated equally. We thank all the citizens for their good cooperation. A peaceful Tanzania is what we dream of.'

Yesterday, Inspector General of Police (IGP) Ernest Mangu declined to comment on the situation and directed *The Citizen* to contact Coast Regional Police Commander (RPC) Bonaventure Mushongi. But in what appears to be the difficulty authorities are having in putting their finger on the motive of the killings and who the perpetrators are, Mr Mushongi curtly told *The Citizen* when reached on phone: 'Leave me alone with regard to that question.'

The IGP and Home Affairs Minister Mwigulu Nchemba have visited the area and assured *wananchi* that they would end the killings. They had even banned the use of motorcycles, mostly used by the killers, as a way of restoring safety. Again yesterday, Coast Regional Commissioner Evarist Ndikilo re-introduced the ban on motorcycles, which, after all, never helped to eradicate crime in the past.

The ruling CCM expressed concern over the killings and expressed disappointment on the performance of the police, the Tanzania Intelligence and Security Services (TISS) and other security organs with regard to the killings.

2 April 2017
A few days after the Coast Region defence and security committee restricted the use of motorcycles in Rufiji District from 6am to 6pm due to killings of local government leaders, Regional Commissioner Evarist Ndikilo has said it is only a temporary measure. He said this in response to public complaints, noting that the restriction was meant to restore peace and security in the area and urged residents to cooperate with the district government.

In light of this, all shops should also operate from 6am to 6pm. There have been complaints from businesspeople in Ikwiriri that they are being assaulted by the police if their shops are found open after 6pm.

But traders complain that the ban has led to the fall of their sales and that some of their colleagues are forced to close their businesses. (Some traders) said there were some dishonest police officers, who stole their merchandise during patrols.

17 April 2017
Islamic religious leaders from Mkuranga, Kibiti and Rufiji districts in Coast Region ... called upon residents in the districts to cooperate with security and defence organs. The call was made ... at the main mosque in Ikwiriri during special prayers for order, security and tranquillity in the three districts that have been hit by a spate of killings of local government leaders and law keepers.

Earlier, speaking to reporters on Friday in Dar es Salaam, Police Commissioner for Training and Operations Nsato Marijani said the spate of killings in the districts was not associated with terrorism. He said they were the work of a criminal gang comprising a few people, which had been prevented by police from committing crime.

18 April 2017
CCM members in Kibiti and Rufiji districts, Coast Region, [were] apprehensive about collecting forms for leadership positions at the grassroots and branch levels for fear of being killed once in office.

The main reason members were afraid of picking up forms was their fear of being killed in the wake of the killing of the party's branch leaders and members of village governments, hamlets and villages chosen through the party.

23 May 2017
The son of late ruling Chama Cha Mapinduzi (CCM) chairman in Njia Nne ward Mr Iddy Kirungi ... died at Muhimbili National Hospital, where he was admitted after he was shot on the stomach by unknown people, who killed his father in Muyuyu village on Wednesday May 17.

18 May 2017
Unknown people have killed the ruling Chama Cha Mapinduzi (CCM) Muyuyu village chairman Mr Iddy Kirungi in Kibiti District, Coast Region ... the bandits injured his son Nurdin Kirungi, who was shot on stomach.

The medical officer in charge of Ikwiriri Health Centre, Dr

Rashid Omar said Mr Nurdin, who sustained a serious injury in his stomach has been referred to Nchuki hospital.

7 June 2017
Unidentified gunmen shot dead a militiaman in Rufiji District on the eve of a visit by newly appointed Inspector General of Police (IGP) Simon Sirro to launch a new approach to end a spate of mysterious killings, which target local leaders and the police.

The killing of Mr Erick Mwarabu, 37, has brought to a total of 33 people, who have been killed in cold blood since January 2015.

Mr Sirro vowed shortly after he was sworn in at the State House in Dar es Salaam last week to wipe out the killers, who continued the killings in Rufiji, Mkuranga and Kilwa districts, which are said to have prompted President John Magufuli to fire Mr Sirro's predecessor Ernest Mangu.

With the police looking clueless as to who exactly are executing the killings and what the motive is, local government leaders have abandoned offices and their houses and gone into hiding with their families for fear of the assailants. The police have also been blamed for using excessive force and sometimes turning brutal as they hunt for the culprits.

Investigation by *The Citizen* shows that insecurity has paralysed local government and economic activities, bringing to a standstill health services, education, trade and transport services in Coast Region districts.

10 June 2017
Fresh security concerns surfaced in the region this week following the cold-blooded murder of a militiaman, Erick Mwarabu, a resident of Kifuru in the Kazamoyo division.

The 37-year-old was shot dead by unknown assailants who broke into his house at around 3am on Tuesday, ransacked his house before they found him under the bed where he was hiding, and pulled the trigger.

... The situation took a new twist this week. What changed this time round is the timing by the assailants, who normally spread their attacks over up to a month, but in the latest spate carried out their 'mission' in a matter of days.

This week alone, they perpetuated four attacks. The first killing took place just hours before the new Inspector General of Police (IGP) Simon Sirro embarked on his maiden tour of the area, one of the very things he had to do as the country's top cop.

21 June 2017
Two police traffic officers who were shot by unknown assailants have been identified as Sergeant Salum and Constable Masola, according to information from the police.

The two police officers ... were injured after unknown people shot them at Bungu B village in Kibiti. According to eye witnesses, the assailants, who were riding on a motorcycle, opened fire to the police who were on duty along the Dar es Salaam–Mtwara road.

10 July 2017
A 54-year-old man, Hamis Ndikanye a resident of Hanga village in Kibiti, has been shot dead by unknown men on Friday night. Kibiti healthcare centre medical-in-charge Dr Sadock Bandiko confirmed to have received the deceased body. Dr Bandiko said the deceased suffered two bullet wounds on his head and shoulder.

11 July 2017
This time around, (they took) the life of a man in Kibiti District, Coastal Region on Sunday night. The incident occurred at 0500hrs as unidentified men allegedly shot eight bullets that killed Mr Ramadhani Mzuzuri (45) and wounded his wife who was identified by one name, Halima.

[The killers] asked the children to show them where their father was. Then they broke into Mzuzuri's room where he and his wife were sleeping, together with their three-month baby. The relative explains that as the gunmen were breaking the two doors, Mzuzuri tried to climb up the roof to hide. However, when they found Ms Halima, they asked her to show them where her husband was. They then started searching for him, lighting their torch everywhere in the room until they found him.

21 July 2017
Unidentified people have shot dead Mr Rahim Kwangaya, a resident of Mandela, Ikwiriri, in Rufiji District, Coast Region, and then thrown his body into a rubbish dump.

The killers also wounded his wife Tatu Mnete on her left breast. Mr Kwangaya is the 41st victim to have been shot dead in Coast Region so far.

2017, South Africa

#GuptaLeaks: 'We have a game changer'

Introduced by Anton Harber

A panda bear emoji was part of the unravelling of a story that shook the South African state to its core.

Independent investigative unit amaBhungane had been writing about the Gupta brothers and their questionable links to President Jacob Zuma, his family and his political circle since March 2010, when they produced a spread in the *Mail & Guardian* newspaper headlined 'Zuma Inc'. 'People starting tell us of the Guptas giving instructions to cabinet ministers, and strange deals. It was just allegations and rumours at that stage, but it told us this was something to focus on,' says amaBhungane's Stefaans Brümmer. They began to put resources into a comprehensive study of the three Gupta brothers, systematically combing through company, property and other records.

Brümmer recalls his colleague Drew Forrest asking repeatedly at weekly news conferences, 'When are we going to get a story?' Brümmer told him what investigative reporters are always telling their editors: this is the kind of work you do to be ready for when the story comes. This attitude may explain why they chose the name amaBhungane, the isiZulu word for a dung beetle, an insect that painstakingly gathers cow dung in which to lay its eggs. But this slowly, slowly approach was also to cost them when it came to breaking the big story.

The story that brought the Guptas into the national spotlight was in 2013 when *Eyewitness News* reported that a Gupta-chartered plane bringing guests to their daughter's lavish wedding had landed at Waterkloof air force base and guests were given police escorts to Sun City. It was a relatively minor abuse of state resources, but there was an outburst of public outrage.

Other stories followed, such as an amaBhungane story on a state farming venture in Vrede, in the Free State province, where it later emerged that the Guptas had siphoned off huge funds to pay for the wedding; and of other money laundering ventures. AmaBhungane did a number of stories around money laundering and the Gupta's malign influence at major state-owned enterprises (SOEs) like Eskom and Transnet. 'We started proving quite convincingly that their modus operandi was to deploy people to state-owned companies and government positions, and then use their connectivity with the presidency and deployees to control state contracts. So while they did apparently very little business with the state, they were the gatekeepers, the toll-keepers, of SOE contracts and they would extract these tolls outside of their known companies, often off-shore.'

The story became red-hot in 2016/17 with the firing of Finance Minister Nhlanhla Nene, who was replaced by one of the Guptas' close allies, and the statement by Deputy Finance Minister Ncebisi Jonas that the Guptas had offered him a R600 million bribe and the finance minister's job if he worked with them.

Brümmer will not identify the sources that gave them the hard drive of tens of thousands of Gupta emails other than to say it was more than one person who 'accidentally-ish' came into possession of the information and decided it had to come out. A go-between contacted Branko Brkic, who runs the influential news and opinion website, *The Daily Maverick*.

Brkic texted his chief executive, Styli Charamlambous: 'We have a game changer.'

Brkic knew that his small team could not handle this massive dump of information. 'I immediately thought, this is bigger than *Daily Maverick*, this had to be industry-wide.' He called Brümmer, they met over coffee and he told Brümmer about the email tranche that he had not even seen yet. It was midday, but Brümmer ordered a vodka. He is ambivalent about whether the drink was celebratory or needed to calm his nerves, because it was immediately clear to them that this was a risky story. 'We knew we had something that would go to the heart of the Gupta empire. This would end plausible deniability. This was not individual stories, but the whole thing laid out clearly. But we did not know what the reaction would be. We knew that once we started with this story, we were in uncharted territory. We had to be extremely careful, for ourselves and for everyone involved.' They hammered out a cooperation agreement between their two operations.

Brkic was given a USB drive containing a small sample of the emails and dropped it off with Brümmer after midnight in a small town where he was taking a weekend off. Brümmer sat up all night assessing the material and at first light sent Brkic his signal that the emails looked authentic: a smiley face.

While Brümmer and his team started digging deep into the material, Brkic started organising for them and their sources to leave the country with the material. 'We always wanted to do this properly and thoroughly. We had to look after the sources, and we wanted to prepare for a timed release – to drip-feed the stories so that we could prepare them properly and the public could absorb them. We had to be safe and ready, so that they could not stop us once we started.'

They raised money, hired people and bought a new set of laptops that were kept off their books and off the internet for security reasons. When they needed software, they went to internet cafés, opened bogus accounts and downloaded. They did not discuss the matter anywhere near a phone and stuck to face-to-face meetings in safe places.

This is where the panda bear came in. When Brümmer and Brkic needed to speak, they would slip a panda bear emoji into a message and meet a short while later in a park. 'We would leave our phones behind and walk through the woods.'

They chose Ireland as the place to go to because there were no visa requirements for South Africans. Members of the team would travel separately, so as not to draw attention.

Brkic was on his way to Ireland when a *Sunday Times* tweet alerted them that they were running the next day with elements of the story, as were *City Press*. It turned out that a person they had let into their inner circle had secretly copied the material and passed it on to political figures who wanted to get the material out before a critical ANC executive meeting. 'They published it as a blunt political tool. The whistleblowers were still in the country and they rushed it, so they got some things wrong and threw some big stories away,' Brkic says. The betrayal cut them to the quick and they were worried about the safety of the sources. They had to drop their plans for a slow, safe release of the material. 'But at least the material was now so widely available that nobody could stop it coming out,' Brkic said.

AmaBhungane and *Daily Maverick* put their teams together into a war room and they were soon joined by News24, which brought a much bigger audience. Across town, the *Sunday Times* and its sister papers did the same, and the race was on. 'We were forced into the game of scooping each other, which isn't the way we wanted it.'

The Sunday papers had broken the story first, but the *Daily Maverick/*

amaBhungane team was able to weave together information from hundreds of emails and their prior knowledge into a coherent picture showing a level of criminality that went beyond everyone's worst imagining.

The story, it turned out, was a triumph simultaneously for cooperation among large teams and competition between two different teams. For the next few weeks, the public enjoyed a flow of stories from data trawled from and pieced together from the emails.

The mass of emails was too large to read them all, so they used word searches. And they homed in on emails with financial statements, diary entries and other attachments. Then they could trawl backwards to piece together the narratives.

It was the sheer weight and scale of the evidence that gave it authenticity. Nobody could fabricate so much, and the time sequences on the emails would have showed up any attempt to slip fake material among real emails.

One of the most remarkable stories was one in which News24 exposed its own bosses, revealing a shady deal between the national broadcaster SABC, the ANN7 TV channel owned by the Guptas and Naspers, the parent company of News24. It was a notable display of journalistic independence.

President Zuma was forced to call a judicial inquiry into the allegations, parliament began a series of hearings which for the first time subjected ministers and SOE chief executives to intense questioning, and police opened a number of investigations. President Zuma was ousted from office shortly thereafter.

It was also a turning point for amaBhungane and *Daily Maverick*. AmaBhungane raised a previously unimaginable R2.3 million in crowd-funding that year, up from about R800,000 the previous year.

The saga also had its comic moments. When they finally got their hands on the material, they could not access the hard drive. There was panic until they realised that someone had got one letter wrong in the password. And when they put someone on a plane to take a copy of the material overseas for safekeeping, the person left it behind and another trip had to be made.

When the joint team won the Taco Kuiper Award for Investigative Reporting, the judges said: 'There are only a few times in the history of a nation when journalists have played such a clear and crucial role in bringing a country back from the brink.'

On the day that Cyril Ramaphosa was named ANC president, partly on the back of an anti-corruption campaign powered by #GuptaLeaks, Brkic received a message from his chief executive: 'We have a game-changer.'

References

Myburgh, Pieter-Louis. 2017. *The Republic of Gupta*. Johannesburg: Penguin.
Pauw, Jacques. 2017. *The President's Keepers*. Cape Town: Tafelberg.
For full texts of these and other articles, see: www.amabhungane.co.za or www.dailymaverick.co.za or www.news24.com

Zuma Incorporated

amaBhungane, *Mail & Guardian*, 19 March 2010

In the week that the presidency confirmed that Jacob Zuma's women and children are costing the taxpayer more than R15 million a year, an investigation by the *Mail & Guardian* suggests they are also bidding for private benefit from their presidential connections.

Information from Zuma's declaration of interests, finally filed last week, as well as research of company registrations and other public documents, is captured in our graphic (available online).

It gives a disturbing picture of the Zuma family's push into business, especially in the period since Zuma's ascension to the ANC presidency at Polokwane in December 2007.

Of the 16 adults — wives, lovers and children — who can be linked to Zuma, 15 are in business, accounting, with Zuma, for 134 company directorships or memberships of close corporations. Only four of these appear to be Section 21 'not for profit' companies.

At least 83 companies (62%) have been registered in the post-Polokwane period when Zuma's political future was secured. Their interests range across the economic spectrum and include property, resources, trade, mining, telecommunications and information technology.

The *M&G* has not been able to establish what all the companies do — many may be inactive — but reporters asking questions have, with a few exceptions, faced suspicion and hostility.

Information gathered by the *M&G* has already raised some worrying issues:

- Zuma has a history of relying on others to help support his wives and children, notably through his loans of more than R4 million from Schabir Shaik, which led to Shaik's conviction for corruption ...
- The emergence of political entrepreneurs who appear to have used Zuma's children to secure their transition from the Mbeki era to the Zuma camp;
- Business connections and practices in his wider family that are controversial; and Zuma's declaration of interests makes no mention of other properties with which he has been associated, such as the house in Forest Town where he moved shortly after being sacked as deputy president in 2005 and which still seems to be occupied by members of his family. Our investigation suggests public money was used to facilitate the purchase of this home by a Zuma loyalist ...

#GuptaLeaks: Guptas and associates score R5.3bn in locomotives kickbacks

amaBhungane/Scorpio, *Daily Maverick*, 1 June 2017

In our first exposé from the #GuptaLeaks, we show how the president's friends and their associates are diverting billions of rand from Transnet's purchase of locomotives to their offshore accounts.

In a scheme so audacious and lucrative that it puts the notorious arms deal to shame, they:

Entered kickback agreements totalling R5.3 billion with the Chinese manufacturer that became Transnet's favourite locomotive supplier;

Influenced procurement processes through their associates at Transnet;

Are pocketing R10 million from each R50-million locomotive that Transnet is buying.

This story presents the most direct evidence yet of the Guptas and their associates amassing fortunes offshore by tolling contracts at state-owned entities they control ...

#GuptaLeaks: Duduzane Zuma, Kept and Captured

amaBhungane/Scorpio, *Daily Maverick*, 1 June 2017

The 35-year-old son of President Jacob Zuma emerges from the #GuptaLeaks as kept and captured by the Gupta family.

Duduzane Zuma, the 35-year-old son of President Jacob Zuma, emerges from the #GuptaLeaks as kept and captured by the Gupta family, serving as a key channel for influence on official decision-making, including his father's.

The files suggest that the Guptas took care of his every need, from paying for a Mauritian getaway for him and his then girlfriend in 2012, to funding his lavish multimillion-rand marriage to Shanice Stork in April 2015, to setting him up with an R18-million Dubai apartment in the world's tallest skyscraper, the iconic Burj Khalifa.

The Gupta circle was also privy to some of his most sensitive secrets, with Gupta associate Ashu Chawla seemingly enjoying access to Zuma's private gmail account, which shows the same ex-girlfriend sending him suggestive pictures just a day after his new wife told him she was pregnant with their first child.

On the night of February 1, 2014, when Zuma lost control of his Porsche on a rain-soaked Johannesburg highway and slammed into the back of a minibus taxi, killing Phumzile Dube, the first person he telephoned was the youngest Gupta brother, Rajesh 'Tony' Gupta, the e-mails show.

The #GuptaLeaks also show that when the *Sunday Sun* approached the Gupta family in April 2015 saying Duduzane had allegedly made another woman pregnant, the Gupta machine was wheeled into action, providing spin from Oakbay chief executive Nazeem Howa.

Later, company lawyer Gert van der Merwe provided advice on the terms of a R3.5-million maintenance settlement for the child and his mother.

Meanwhile, Duduzane flew backwards and forwards, usually first class; drove fancy cars bought by Gupta group companies; or was chauffeured by limousine and stayed in five-star hotels, among them the Oberoi in Dubai and the Hotel National in Moscow.

Gupta lackeys took care of tiresome details, like sorting out travel arrangements – or mopping up the demands for some R180,000 in arrears on municipal charges that he had built up on his Saxonwold abode, around the corner from the Gupta compound ...

They also paid him extremely well: In March 2015 he drew R300,000 per month in director fees, more than any other director, including the Gupta brothers.

#GuptaLeaks: How Bell Pottinger sought to package SA economic message

Daily Maverick and *News24*, 6 June 2017

In January last year Victoria Geoghegan, British-based PR firm Bell Pottinger's Financial and Corporate partner, met with President Jacob Zuma's son Duduzane to strategise a campaign aimed at marketing a 'narrative that grabs the attention of the grassroots population who must identify with it, connect with it and feel united by it'.

In so doing, the firm directly undermined the ANC's capacity to communicate its own policies and programmes to South Africans and hijacked the ruling party's message, seemingly to benefit the image of the Gupta family.

Victoria Geoghegan later invoiced the Marketing Quotient, a Dubai-based company part-owned by Gupta family lieutenant, Salim Essa, a 'project fee' of £100,000 (about R2.3 million according to exchange rates in January 2016) for a consultation with Duduzane Zuma.

The two met to discuss a brief for a five-month campaign which Duduzane later described in a letter to Geoghegan as 'not primarily one to affect the outcome of the elections (2017) but to turn the tide of our country's trajectory in the long term'.

Earlier Geoghegan wrote to Duduzane that Bell Pottinger was keen to build a long-term partnership with Zuma and that 'we want to stand shoulder-to-shoulder in communicating such a vital message for South Africa. The future of the country in terms of fair economic growth, an inclusive society and political stability, depends on it' ...

'Below is a set of recommendations based upon an initial project, with the opportunity for further projects to evolve:

Create a non-party political narrative around the existence of economic apartheid and the vital need for more economic emancipation. This narrative should appeal to both potential third-party advocates in the business and academic communities and the grass-roots population;

Provide assistance and advice on the setting up of a vehicle (the 'entity') to be the public face of the narrative;

Whilst the narrative/vehicle is intended to be political party-agnostic, it will create opportunities for political commentary and participation;

Bell Pottinger will package the narrative into speeches, press releases, website content, videos/broadcast content, slogans and any other material required;

The initial project would draw on the strengths of both parties:

Bell Pottinger's strategic messaging skills, experience, international reach, and overall brand & credibility; and

This would be complemented by the South African team's access to domestic media outlets, digital capabilities and its in-country network;

Utilise compelling research, case studies and data which illustrate the apartheid that still exists, and the need for truly inclusive growth. Bell Pottinger will analyse the data (for example: power generation, ports) and create fact sheets and easily understood collateral for wider dissemination;

Engage media both domestically in South Africa, and internationally. This will reach both the all-important domestic audience, but also achieve international endorsement which will add credibility to the narrative and feed back into the domestic media also ...'

2017, Lesotho

The Guptas come to Lesotho

Introduced by Lekhetho Ntsukunyane

The Gupta brothers – Ajay, Atul and Rajesh – were already known in South Africa for their audacious attempts to get control of public enterprises and their suspiciously close friendship and influence over President Jacob Zuma and his family. So when in August 2014 Lesotho Prime Minister Tom Thabane appointed Atul Gupta as an 'economic investment envoy' and granted Atul, his associate Salim Essa and a third Gupta associate diplomatic passports, the opposition were enraged and accused Thabane of not following protocol.

When the #GuptaLeaks emails emerged in 2017, there was no way Lesotho could not be implicated.

The MNN Centre for Investigative Journalism (MNNCIJ) is an independent, donor-funded, non-profit company established in March 2016. It is an initiative by four seasoned Basotho journalists, Billy Ntaote, Sechaba Mokhethi, Keiso Mohloboli and myself as editor-in-chief. Combined, we have over 35 years working for various national newspapers including *Public Eye*, *Lesotho Times* and *Sunday Express*.

We forged a formal working relationship with South Africa's amaBhungane Centre for Investigative Journalism. During 2017, MNNCIJ communicated with amaBhungane about #GuptaLeaks, but it was only when Lekhetho and Ntaote visited Botswana's INK Centre for Investigative Journalism in September 2017 and met amaBhungane's Susan Comrie that the material could be checked for Lesotho references. Two areas came up: the Lesotho Highlands Water Project and the country's mining sector.

Lekhetho, who has vast experience writing about mines in Lesotho, returned to Maseru to dig for more information, while Susan continued to scour the emails. They created an online system to share information.

What emerged was how Prime Minister Thomas Thabane's government had signed away a diamond mine to a company linked to the Guptas on the eve of the highly contested February 2015 elections. They summarily withdrew the mineral licence of a Canadian company and illegally offered it to the Tequesta Group, whose address was a small flat on the 15th floor of the Hong Kong's Hillier Commercial Building, surrounded by nail salons and massage parlours. Records from the Hong Kong business registry showed that at the time the sole director was Salim Essa, business partner of the Guptas.

At the time Tequesta was little more than a letterbox company with no presence in Lesotho or track record in mining. The #GuptaLeaks showed that the company's primary business was acting as a conduit for billions of rand in highly questionable sales commissions which flowed from a Chinese rail company to the Gupta family, Essa and the family of President Jacob Zuma.

Our investigation showed how Thabane stood to benefit from the deal. The prime minister's son, Potlako Thabane, told us that Tequesta had approached him to be part of a diamond mining project, although he said he could not remember the name of the mine.

Multiple sources, including the younger Thabane, also confirmed that the Guptas also offered to provide funding to the embattled prime minister's 2014/15 re-election campaign.

That the Guptas were interested in the outcome of the election is evident from the #GuptaLeaks. A week before Khasu's letter arrived, younger brother Tony Gupta commissioned a detailed analysis of each political party's chances in the looming February 2015 election.

The deal appears to have fallen through, but after the story was published the Directorate on Corruption and Economic Offences, the country's anti-corruption body, opened an investigation into Thabane and his son, Potlako.

How family hijacked (and then lost) a Lesotho diamond mine

MNNCIJ, 1 December 2017

On the eve of the highly contested February 2015 elections, Prime Minister Thomas Thabane's government signed away a diamond mine to a company linked to the Guptas.

On 23 October 2014, two identical letters landed on Mining Minister Tlali Khasu's desk. Khasu was then also deputy leader of All Basotho Convention (ABC) – a political party Thabane leads.

Both letters carried the official letterhead of the Ministry of Mining. The letters related to the potentially lucrative but stalled Mothae Diamond Mine. The official who signed both letters on Khasu's behalf assured the readers that 'I remain, Yours Sincerely, Tlali Khasu, honourable minister – mining'.

The difference was that one brought bad news; the other a lucrative opportunity. The two letters appear to have been the first step of an audacious plan orchestrated by the Guptas and their business partner Salim Essa to seize Mothae with the help of Lesotho's political elite.

Khasu's first letter was addressed to the local subsidiary of Lucara Diamonds, a Canadian mining company that held the licence to mine at Mothae, just 5 kilometres away from Lesotho's famous Letšeng mine.

Exploration had confirmed that the mine was 'diamondiferous', but despite Lucara's $38 million (R519 million) investment since 2009, the company had failed to develop a viable commercial plan.

'It has come to my attention that the mine stopped operations in 2012,' the minister's letter stated. 'Subject to the provisions of the Mines and Minerals Act ... I intend to cancel the said mineral concession.'

The second letter, entitled 'Offer of a mining lease at Mothae Mine in Lesotho', was directed to a small flat on the 15th floor of the Hong Kong's Hillier Commercial Building, surrounded by nail salons and massage parlours.

'I am pleased to inform you that the Government of Lesotho is in the process of re-acquiring the mining lease of the above-mentioned mine ... the mine will be on offer to you as soon as the Government re-acquires it,' it stated.

This second letter was addressed to Tequesta Group, whose humble location hid the company's powerful backers – records from the Hong Kong business registry show that at the time the sole director was Salim Essa, the charismatic business partner of the Guptas.

'Looking forward to doing business with you,' the minister

signed off in an altogether friendlier tone.

At the time Tequesta was little more than a letterbox company with no presence in Lesotho or track record in mining. The #GuptaLeaks showed that the company's primary business was acting as a conduit for billions of rands in highly questionable sales commissions which flowed from a Chinese rail company to the Gupta family, Essa and even the family of president Jacob Zuma.

Just two months earlier, in August 2014, Thabane had appointed Atul Gupta as a special advisor and had granted him, Essa and a third Gupta associate diplomatic passports. When confronted he reportedly told journalists that Zuma had recommended the Guptas ...

Thabane was in a precarious political position. In June 2014, he had suspended parliament in order to prevent a vote of no confidence, and in August had been forced to flee the country to avoid an attempted coup.

But by October 2014, Thabane was back, thanks to the intervention of the South African Development Community led by South Africa's deputy president Cyril Ramaphosa, but had been forced to call a snap election.

In such a fraught situation, why would Thabane and his mines' minister – besieged by political rivals – take the risk of offering a lucrative diamond mine to the controversial Guptas?

Investigations by MNN Centre for Investigative Journalism (MNNCIJ) and amaBhungane showed that Thabane stood to benefit from the deal.

The prime minister's son, Potlako Thabane, told us (MNNCIJ) late last year (2017) that Tequesta approached him to be part of a diamond mining project, although he said he could not remember the name of the mine.

'I'm a businessman and a politician as well – people come to me with proposals,' he said. 'If memory serves me right they tried to register a local company but that never really took off ... I think we wanted to be partners, but it never happened.'

Multiple sources, including the younger Thabane, also confirmed that the Guptas also offered to provide funding to the embattled prime minister's re-election campaign.

'We wanted (the Guptas) to, we made arrangements for them to provide funding. But then they suddenly lost interest. They never provided a cent,' Potlako Thabane said.

Two sources told the story slightly differently. One, a well-placed source close to Thabane, said that the Guptas had provided some funding for Thabane's election, but failed to deliver on the full amount promised. Another, a senior government official, said the Guptas provided as much as M10 million (R10 million) to Thabane's election campaign. Questions sent to the prime minister's office had not been answered.

That the Guptas were interested in the outcome of the election is evident from the #GuptaLeaks. A week before Khasu's letter arrived, younger brother Tony Gupta commissioned a detailed analysis of each political party's chances in the looming February 2015 election.

The nine-page report, compiled by a data specialist working for the Guptas, provided a minute breakdown of expected voter turnouts, district-by-district voting patterns, and the probability of Thabane's ABC holding onto power.

Thabane could scrape a narrow victory, according to the analysis, but only if ABC teamed up with its estranged coalition partner, the Lesotho Congress for Democracy (LCD) led by then deputy prime minister Mothetjoa Metsing.

In December 2014, two months after Khasu's letter to Lucara, the Canadian miner announced it would voluntarily relinquish its rights to the Mothae diamond mine.

In terms of section 41 of Lesotho's mining legislation, Lucara would have 12 months to find a buyer for its 70 percent stake in Mothae. If it failed to find a buyer, the rights would revert back to the government.

Leaked documents from the ministry of mining indicate that as soon as the shareholder's agreement was signed, Khasu put his signature on a coveted 10-year mining lease (number 0013/ML/2015), gifting Mothae diamond mine to Tequesta Group Lesotho. The lease would become effective immediately.

'You are asking me about things that happened when I was a minister long time ago ... I can't remember anything,' Khasu told us recently.

There were three problems with what Khasu had just done:

Firstly, the Mothae mining right unquestionably still belonged to Canada's Lucara. Although the company had agreed to relinquish its rights in December 2014, the company still had 11 months to find a buyer before the state could assign the licence to someone else.

Secondly, the job of assessing applications for new mining rights is carried out by Lesotho's mining board. A June 2016 memo from the mining board to the minister makes it clear it was never consulted.

And thirdly, a draft of the licence found in the #GuptaLeaks suggest that the deal Tequesta offered would have left the country with little more than diamond dust: a sales tax of between four and eight percent and rental of $87,000 per year, only payable once the company showed a profit.

It is not clear whether this offer was improved before the deal was signed – sources have only been able to locate the first page of the lease signed by Khasu. The official documents that normally accompany a mining lease, spelling out the terms of the agreement, have not been found.

When we spoke to Potlako Thabane, we asked him why the Guptas had, in his words 'suddenly lost interest' in funding the prime minister's re-election campaign.

His explanation: 'They wanted a mine. The mine they were targeting they couldn't get. I think that's why. After that all communication stopped' ...

Acknowledgements

This book flowed from the work done by Anya Shiffrin in two preceding anthologies, *Global Muckraking* and *African Muckraking*, and she is owed thanks for the support and encouragement she gave to this book.

Nothing would have happened without those who lent their expertise to write the introductions and gave of their time and expertise most generously.

Many people have helped us find material. Special thanks to Ben Carton for his energy and ideas, and his willingness to put at least some limit on the length of his prodigious footnotes, and to Peter Delius, who opened up for me the world of historians, who proved to know the material of journalists better than the journalists themselves.

The hard work of editorial assistant Roxanne Joseph, who pestered librarians, writers and publishers for material and permissions, was invaluable.

There were archivists who gave us their time and energy to locate material, notably the staff of the National Library of South Africa, Cape Town, Phillip Kgaphola and Bheki Nzama of Tiso Blackstar and Colette Stott of Penguin Random House Struik. Long-standing friend and colleague Angella Johnson helped us access the *Daily Mail* archives in London.

Special gratitude goes to Justin Pearce for his persistent work in helping us locate copies of *Impartial Fax*, just when we were giving up hope of finding them. And to Angolan journalist Reginaldo Silva, who had them, and made them available to us.

Tiso Blackstar's Andrew Gill generously waived fees to allow the book to happen, as did the Bailey Archive and others. The Konrad Adenauer Stiftung, a long-standing supporter of investigative journalism in this part of the world, gave their assistance to make this book possible.

Bridget Impey of Jacana Media, editor Lara Jacob and the rest of the team are a pleasure to work with.

And my wife Harriet, and children Jesse and Georgia, for their support and patience.

Permissions

Every attempt has been made to contact copyright holders, where the material was not in the public domain. Any omissions will be corrected in subsequent editions.

Excerpt from 'On the wrong side of development: Lessons learned from the Lesotho Highlands Water Project', edited by Mbusetsa Lenka Thamae and Lori Pottinger, 2006. Reprinted with permission from the Transformation Resource Centre.

Excerpt from 'Lesotho PM faces probe over Gupta mining links,' by Lekhetho Ntsukunyane, 2018. Reprinted with permission from the MNN Centre for Investigative Journalism, amaBhungane and the *Daily Maverick*.

Excerpt from 'Zuma's R65m Nkandla splurge,' by Mandy Rossouw, 2009. Reprinted with permission from the *Mail & Guardian*.

Excerpt from 'The living dead,' by Helen Joseph, 1961. Reprinted with permission from *Africa South* c/o the Segal family.

Excerpt from 'The Sekhukhuneland terror,' by James Fairbairn (Jack Halpern), 1958. Reprinted with permission from *Africa South* c/o the Segal family.

Excerpt from 'Why Frere's babies die,' by Chandré Prince, Brett Horner and Ntando Makhubu, 2007. Reprinted with permission from the *Daily Dispatch* c/o Tiso Blackstar.

Excerpt from 'A mother's pain,' by Chandré Prince, 2007. Reprinted with permission from the *Daily Dispatch* c/o Tiso Blackstar.

Excerpt from 'HRC and health council join Frere fray,' by Chandré Prince, Brett Horner and Ntando Makhubu, 2007. Reprinted with permission from the *Daily Dispatch* c/o Tiso Blackstar.

Excerpt from 'Tell me lies about Matola,' by Paul Fauvet, 1983. Reprinted with permission from the Mozambique News Agency (AIM).

Excerpt from 'Samora Machel's death and South African radar,' by Paul Fauvet, 1986. Reprinted with permission from the Mozambique News Agency (AIM).

Excerpt from 'Inkatha's secret training base,' by Eddie Koch, 1990. Reprinted with permission from the *Mail & Guardian*.

Excerpt from 'How a small group of hitmen held a township to ransom,' by Eddie Koch and Philippa Garson, 1992. Reprinted with permission from the *Mail & Guardian*.

Excerpt from 'Military millionaries,' by Tshireletso Motlogelwa and Matteo Civillini, 2015. Reprinted with permission by *ZAM* magazine and the African Investigative Publishing Collective.

Excerpt from 'The plunder route to Panama: How African oligarchs steal from their countries,' by Estacio Valoi, 2017. Reprinted with permission by *ZAM* magazine and the African Investigative Publishing Collective.

Excerpt from 'The story of Bethal,' by Henry Nxumalo, 1952. Reprinted with permission from Prospero Bailey.

Excerpts from 'Two to tango: The story of Zuma and the Guptas,' 2016, by amaBhungane and Scorpio. Reprinted with permission by amaBhungane, the *Daily Maverick* and *News24*.

Excerpt from 'Top Natal education jobs go to Afrikaners,' by Ivor Wilkins, 1977. Reprinted with permission from the *Sunday Times* c/o Tiso Blackstar.

Excerpt from 'Broeder master plan exposed,' by Ivor Wilkins, 1978. Reprinted with permission from the *Sunday Times* c/o Tiso Blackstar.

Excerpt from 'Broederbond plans for more white babies,' by Ivor Wilkins, 1978. Reprinted with permission from the *Sunday Times* c/o Tiso Blackstar.

Excerpt from 'New leaks show up the Broeder turmoil,' by Hans Strydom, 1978. Reprinted with permission from the *Sunday Times* c/o Tiso Blackstar.

Excerpt from 'Who's who in the Broederbond?' by Ivor Wilkins and Hans Strydom, 1978. Reprinted with permission from the *Sunday Times* c/o Tiso Blackstar.

Excerpt from 'How the Broederbond captures those top jobs,' by Ivor Wilkins and Hans Strydom. Reprinted with permission from the *Sunday Times* c/o Tiso Blackstar.

Excerpt from 'The Bond: Master or servant?' by Patrick Laurence, 1978. Reprinted with permission from the *Rand Daily Mail* c/o Tiso Blackstar.

Excerpt from 'Expected budget concessions,' by George Heard, 1937. Reprinted with permission from the *Sunday Times* c/o Tiso Blackstar.

Excerpt from 'Tried to stop war message by Gen. Smuts,' by George Heard, 1939. Reprinted with permission from the *Sunday Times* c/o Tiso Blackstar.

Excerpt from 'Brandwag is a menace to S.A,' by George Heard, 1940. Reprinted with permission from the *Sunday Times* c/o Tiso Blackstar.

Excerpt from 'Menace of the "fifth column" in South Africa,' by George Heard, 1940. Reprinted with permission from the *Sunday Times* c/o Tiso Blackstar.

Excerpt from 'Storm troops mean new racialism,' by George Heard, 1940. Reprinted with permission from the *Sunday Times* c/o Tiso Blackstar.

Excerpt from '£600,000 wasted on useless defence experiments,' by George Heard, 1940. Reprinted with permission from the *Sunday Times* c/o Tiso Blackstar.

Excerpt from 'Missing millions,' by Mervyn Rees, 1978. Reprinted with permission from the *Rand Daily Mail* c/o Tiso Blackstar.

Excerpt from 'Info's US paper bid,' by Mervyn Rees, 1978. Reprinted with permission from the *Rand Daily Mail* c/o Tiso Blackstar.

Excerpt from 'Mulder hit as Nat paper alters stance,' by Martin Schneider, 1978. Reprinted with permission from the *Rand Daily Mail* c/o Tiso Blackstar.

Excerpt from 'Flop you paid for,' by Mervyn Rees, 1978. Reprinted with permission from the *Rand Daily Mail* c/o Tiso Blackstar.

Excerpt from 'It's all true!' by Mervyn Rees, 1978. Reprinted with permission from the *Rand Daily Mail* c/o Tiso Blackstar.

Excerpt from 'A nation swindled,' by Staff Reporters, 1978. Reprinted with permission from the *Rand Daily Mail* c/o Tiso Blackstar.

Excerpt from 'Dept spent R32m to fund *The Citizen*,' by Staff Reporters, 1978. Reprinted with permission from the *Rand Daily Mail* c/o Tiso Blackstar.

Excerpt from 'Rhoodie's mansion in Miami's millionaire row,' by Mervyn Rees, 1978. Reprinted with permission from the *Rand Daily Mail* c/o Tiso Blackstar.

Excerpt from 'EXCLUSIVE: Khama's Mosu built with public funds,' by INK

Permissions

Reporters, 2013. Reprinted with permission from the INK Centre for Investigative Journalism and the *Daily Maverick*.

Excerpt from 'Botswana: Asylum-seekers accuse prison officials of ill-treatment and sexual assault,' by Joel Konopo and Ntibinyane Ntibinyane, 2018. Reprinted with permission from the INK Centre for Investigative Journalism and the *Daily Maverick*.

Excerpt from 'Parade of death,' by Staff Reporters, 1987. Reprinted with permission from the *Namibian*.

'Peace,' 1902. Reprinted with permission from the *Daily Mail of London*.

Excerpt from 'Top of the range jet,' by Vusie Ginindza, 2002. Reprinted with permission from the *Times of Swaziland*.

Excerpt from 'What's the fuss about jet?' by Alec Lushaba, 2002. Reprinted with permission from the *Times of Swaziland*.

Excerpt from 'What king's jet?' 2002. Reprinted with permission from the *Times of Swaziland*.

Excerpt from 'Who's got the big bucks?' by Vusie Ginindza, 2002. Reprinted with permission from the *Times of Swaziland*.

Excerpt from 'US questions PM on king's jet,' by Musa Magagula, 2002. Reprinted with permission from the *Times of Swaziland*.

Excerpt from 'Mugabe troops leave trail of death,' by Nick Worrall, 1983. Reprinted with permission from the *Guardian*.

Excerpt from 'The fifth column that is shaking Zimbabwe,' by Nick Worrall, 1983. Reprinted with permission from the *Guardian*.

Excerpt from 'Hundreds reported killed in attacks by Zimbabwean troops,' by Jay Ross 1983. Reprinted with permission from the *Washington Post*.

Excerpt from 'Zimbabwe's curfew "cuts off food to drought-hit areas",' by Andrew Meldrum, 1984. Reprinted with permission from the *Guardian*.

Excerpt from 'Zimbabwe massacre bodies found in mine,' by Peter Godwin, 1984. Reprinted with permission from the *Sunday Times*.

Excerpt from 'Stench of death everywhere in Mugabe's siege of Matebeleland,' by Peter Godwin, 1984. Reprinted with permission from the *Sunday Times*.

Excerpt from 'Protected villages on the increase,' by Sister Janice McLaughlin, 1977. Reprinted with permission from the Catholic Institute for International Relations and the Legal Resources Foundation.

Excerpt from 'Rhodesian army pursues policy of systemic torture,' by Sister Janice McLaughlin, 1977. Reprinted with permission from the Catholic Institute for International Relations and the Legal Resources Foundation.

Excerpt from 'Killing for profit,' by Julian Rademyer, 2012. Reprinted with permission from the author and Penguin Random House Struik.

Excerpt from 'Big racket in new cars,' by Geoffrey Nyarota, 1988. Reprinted with permission from the *Chronicle*.

Excerpt from 'In the jungle: How American music legends made millions off the work of a Zulu tribesman who died a pauper,' by Rian Malan, 2000. Reprinted with permission from the author and *Rolling Stone* magazine.

Excerpt from 'Sume, silêncio de morte,' by Luísa Rogério, 2015. Reprinted with permission from the author and *Rede Angola*.

Excerpt from 'Rafael Marques placed under investigation in Angola,' by *Maka Angola*, 2013. Reprinted with permission from the author and *Maka Angola*.

Excerpt from 'Isabel dos Santos: Africa's richest woman and the lie of her assets,' by Rafael Marques de Morais, 2016. Reprinted with permission from the author and *Maka Angola*.

Excerpt from 'Angola's Sovereign Fund pays US$100 million to a shell company,' by Rafael Marques de Morais, 2015. Reprinted with permission from the author and *Maka Angola*.

Excerpt from 'Grim hunt in the bush for their food,' by Benjamin Pogrund, 1962. Reprinted with permission from the *Rand Daily Mail* c/o Tiso Blackstar.

Excerpt from 'Hunger: the facts are in sick beds,' by Benjamin Pogrund, 1962. Reprinted with permission from the *Rand Daily Mail* c/o Tiso Blackstar.

Excerpt from 'The children suffer more than any,' by Benjamin Pogrund, 1962. Reprinted with permission from the *Rand Daily Mail* c/o Tiso Blackstar.

Excerpt from 'Three years "inside",' by Harold Strachan as told to Benjamin Pogrund, 1965. Reprinted with permission from the *Rand Daily Mail* c/o Tiso Blackstar.

Excerpt from 'Ordeal in a prison yard,' by Benjamin Pogrund, 1965. Reprinted with permission from the *Rand Daily Mail* c/o Tiso Blackstar.

Excerpt from 'The Cinderella jail massage,' by Benjamin Pogrund, 1965. Reprinted with permission from the *Rand Daily Mail* c/o Tiso Blackstar.

Excerpt from 'Stand up, real PSCGG regular,' by Deon Basson, 2002. Reprinted with permission by *FinWeek*.

Excerpt from 'Designated farm leased to Mangwende,' by Staff Reporters, 1994. Reprinted with permission from the *Daily Gazette* c/o Brian Latham.

Excerpt from 'The trial of 800,' by Allister Sparks, 1965. Reprinted with permission from the *Rand Daily Mail* c/o Tiso Blackstar.

Excerpt from 'Botho fires "Dr. Fake" as BAC panics,' by Queen Mosarwe, Lawrence Seretse and Joel Konopo. Reprinted with permission from the *Botswana Gazette*.

Excerpt from 'DIS report on opposition is fake,' from the INK Centre for Investigative Journalism, 2017. Reprinted with permission from the *Botswana Gazette*.

Excerpt from 'Msabaha pledges to come "clean" over delayed turbines,' by Finnigan Wa Simbeye, 2006. Reprinted with permission from the author and *ThisDay*.

Excerpt from 'Msabaha "dives" for cover over suspect pipeline deal,' by Finnigan Wa Simbeye, 2006. Reprinted with permission from the author and *ThisDay*.

Excerpt from 'Kibiti DC calls back leaders who fled since peace restored,' by Azory Gwanda, 2017. Reprinted with permission from the *Citizen*.

Excerpt from 'Another person killed by unidentified assailants in Rufiji,' by Azory Gwanda, 2017. Reprinted with permission from the *Citizen*.

Excerpt from 'Relative narrates brutal Kibiti killing,' by Azory Gwanda, 2017. Reprinted with permission from the *Citizen*.

Excerpt from 'Another man feared dead in Kibiti,' by Azory Gwanda, 2017. Reprinted with permission from the *Citizen*.

Excerpt from 'Another man killed in Kibiti,' by Azory Gwanda, 2017. Reprinted with permission from the *Citizen*.

Excerpt from 'Two police shot, injured in Kibiti by unknown people,' by Azory Gwanda, 2017. Reprinted with permission from the *Citizen*.

Excerpt from 'Bizarre Rufiji killings take another turn,' by Azory Gwanda, 2017. Reprinted with permission from the *Citizen*.

Excerpt from 'Another militiaman shot in Ikwiriri,' by Azory Gwanda, 2017. Reprinted with permission from the *Citizen*.

Excerpt from 'Militiaman shot dead on even of IGP visit to Rufiji,' by Azory Gwanda, 2017. Reprinted with permission from the *Citizen*.

Excerpt from 'Wounded son of deceased CCM ward chairman in Kibiti dies,' by Azory Gwanda, 2017. Reprinted with permission from the *Citizen*.

Excerpt from 'Another CCM leader killed in Kibiti,' by Azory Gwanda, 2017. Reprinted with permission from the *Citizen*.

Permissions

Excerpt from 'CCM members fear for their lives ahead of party elections,' by Azory Gwanda, 2017. Reprinted with permission from the *Citizen*.

Excerpt from 'Sheikhs call on wananchi to back police in hunt for killers,' by Azory Gwanda, 2017. Reprinted with permission from the *Citizen*.

Excerpt from 'Restriction on motorcycle use only temporary measures: RC,' by Azory Gwanda, 2017. Reprinted with permission from the *Citizen*.

Excerpt from 'Hard questions in wake of Rufiji leaders killings,' by Azory Gwanda, 2017. Reprinted with permission from the *Citizen*.

Excerpt from 'In hiding for exposing Tanzania witchdoctors,' by Vicky Ntetema, 2008. Reprinted with permission from BBC News.

The Contributors

John Aerni-Flessner is an assistant professor at Michigan State University's Residential College in the Arts and Humanities. He is a historian whose first book, *Dreams for Lesotho: Independence, Foreign Assistance, and Development*, was published in 2018 by the University of Notre Dame Press. His research focuses on Lesotho and he has published articles on the history of development, decolonisation, and the history of the border between Lesotho and South Africa. He became interested in the history of Lesotho while teaching high school for a year in the rural Maseru district.

Jo-Ann Bekker (Thesen) has an honours degree in History from the University of Witwatersrand and a masters in creative writing from Rhodes. Her collection of short fiction is forthcoming from Modjaji Books. She was a journalist for three decades, reporting for South African newspapers, including the *Eastern Province Herald* and *The Weekly Mail*, a Harare-based African news agency, and newspapers in the Netherlands and Florida, USA. She won a Mondi magazine award for reportage (2003) and the 1984 Stellenbosch Farmers Wineries Award for best reporting under pressure for her coverage of community resistance in Cradock, Eastern Cape.

Benedict Carton is the Robert T. Hawkes Professor of History at George Mason University in Fairfax, Virginia, USA. He studies cultural and social change in southern Africa. Carton is the author of *Blood from Your Children: The Colonial Origins of Generational Conflict in South Africa* (2000) and co-editor/co-author of *Zulu Identities: Being Zulu, Past and Present* (2008/2009). His articles have appeared in the *Journal of African History*, *Journal of Southern African Studies*, *Africa*, *Journal of Social History*, among others. His forthcoming book, with Robert Vinson, is titled 'Shaka's progeny: Americans and Zulus in a global world'.

Kevin Davie is business editor at the *Mail & Guardian* and teaches economics and narrative journalism at the University of the Witwatersrand. A journalist for more than 30 years, he was the Nieman Fellow at Harvard in 1995/96 and has held senior positions at titles such as *Business Day, Business Times (Sunday Times)* and *ThisDay*. Davie was a pioneer in cyberspace, establishing news publication WOZA and South Africa's first online stockbroker. An enthusiastic cyclist, he often researches his stories from the saddle of a bicycle. Davie has run the Comrades 11 times, paddled the Dusi 29 times and is the author of *Freedom Rider: 10,000 kms by Mountain Bike Across South Africa*.

Nic Dawes was editor-in-chief of the *Mail & Guardian* when it broke the Nkandla story, after which he was chief editorial and content officer at the *Hindustan Times* (India). He is currently Deputy Executive Director: Media at Human Rights Watch in New York, where he leads a global press, digital publishing, video and campaigns teams.

Indra de Lanerolle is an experienced journalist, television and documentary producer who has worked in Africa, the Americas and Europe, and was a senior producer on the BBC's *Newsnight* and *Panorama*. His work has been recognised with a Peabody Award, an Emmy nomination and the Japan Prize. He teaches courses in television journalism and media innovation and entrepreneurship at the University of the Witwatersrand, Johannesburg, and is the director of the Journalism and Media Lab at Tshimologong Digital Innovation Precinct, Africa's first journalism and media accelerator and innovation lab.

Peter Delius is Professor Emeritus at the University of the Witwatersrand. He has published widely on South African history but his primary research focus has been on rural resistance, migrant labour and struggles over land. His book *A Lion Amongst the Cattle* (1996) includes an in-depth analysis of the Sekhukhuneland Revolt of 1958. In 2014 he co-edited A *Long Way Home, Migrant Worker Worlds 1800–2014*, a collection of essays and images on the experiences, agency and humanity of migrant workers. His most recent book, co-authored with William Beinart and Michelle Hay, is *Rights to Land: A Guide to Tenure Upgrading and Restitution in South Africa*.

Tim du Plessis has been a journalist for 42 years, starting as a news reporter at *Beeld* in 1976. In the span of his career he has been editor of *The Citizen*, *Rapport* and *Beeld*. He is currently the head of news and current affairs at Afrikaans TV channel kykNET. In 1997 Du Plessis led a group of Naspers journalists who, against the wishes of the company, made a statement to the Truth & Reconciliation Commission on the role of their respective papers during apartheid. Du Plessis studied at the universities of Johannesburg and Stellenbosch, and was a Nieman Fellow at Harvard University in 1992/93.

Harry Dugmore teaches at Rhodes University's School of Journalism and Media Studies, where he is an associate professor. He specialises in health journalism, including LGBTIQ+ health and rights, digital journalism studies and media economics. Harry was part of the original script-writing team on the early series of Soul City, and helped coordinate Khomanani, the government's main HIV & AIDS prevention communication programme in the early 2000s. Harry is interested in behaviour change communication and South Africa's AIDS epidemic and, more recently, the role of fast food and sugar-sweetened beverages in driving global obesity levels.

Robert Edgar is Professor of African Studies at Howard University (Washington, DC) and a senior fellow in the history department at Stellenbosch University. He has been a visiting professor at universities in Virginia, Georgetown, Lesotho and South Africa. He specialises in modern religious and political movements in southern Africa. Among his works are *An African American in South Africa: The Travel Notes of Ralph Bunche* (1992), *African Apocalypse: The story of Nontetha Nkwenkwe, a Twentieth-Century South African Prophet* (2000) (co-authored with Hilary Sapire) and *The Finger of God: Enoch Mgijima, the Israelites and the Bulhoek Massacre* (2018).

Paul Fauvet is a British journalist who has lived and worked in Mozambique since 1981. His involvement in southern Africa dates back to the 1960s and his membership of the Committee for Freedom in Mozambique, Angola and Guinea-Bissau, which organised solidarity in the UK for the liberation movements of the Portuguese colonies. Paul worked for the Mozambique, Angola and Guinea Information Centre in London until 1980, when he received an invitation to work on the English desk of the Mozambique News Agency (AIM). He is currently editor of the AIM English service and co-authored the biography, *Carlos Cardoso: Telling the Truth in Mozambique*.

Philippa Garson is a journalist and writer living in New York. She began her career as a trainee reporter at *The Weekly Mail* (now the *Mail & Guardian*) in 1989, and went on to cover township violence, politics, education and many other beats. She then worked as editor of the newspaper's sister publication, *The Teacher*. Today Garson writes about global development, global health, reproductive health and humanitarian issues for a range of publications and clients. Garson has won two media awards and was selected to participate in four UN Foundation Press Fellowships.

Claudia Gastrow is a lecturer in anthropology at the University of Johannesburg. Her research investigates politics and urbanism in Angola, with special focuses on questions of citizenship, governance, housing and land.

Evelyn Groenink is an investigative journalist based in Johannesburg since the mid-1990s, often working with colleagues in other African countries, inter alia, on international arms deals. She co-founded the Forum for African Investigative Reporters in 2003 and now works as investigative editor for the African Investigative Publishing Collective and *ZAM*. She wrote three books on South Africa which were published in the Netherlands, and one that was recently published in South Africa: *Incorruptible*, on the assassinations of southern African freedom fighters Dulcie September, Anton Lubowski and Chris Hani.

Anton Harber holds the Caxton Chair of Journalism at the University of the Witwatersrand. He was founder-editor of *The Weekly Mail* (now the *Mail & Guardian*), editor-in-chief of South Africa's leading television news channel, eNCA, and chief executive of Kagiso Broadcasting. He is a board member of the Global Investigative Journalism Network and former chair of the SA Conference of Editors and the National Association of Broadcasters. Harber wrote *Diepsloot* (2011), *The Gorilla in the Room* (2013) and co-edited the first two editions of *The A–Z of South African Politics, What is Left Unsaid: Reporting the South African HIV Epidemic*, and *Troublemakers: The Best of SA's Investigative Journalism*.

Catherine Higgs is professor of history and head of the history and sociology department in the Irving K. Barber School of Arts and Sciences at the University of British Columbia, Okanagan.

Raymond Joseph began his career as a cadet reporter for the *Rand Daily Mail* in 1974 and has worked for mainstream, community and tabloid newspapers and magazines in senior editorial positions. He is a former ICFJ/Knight International Journalism Fellow, and an ex-editor and board member of *The Big Issue South Africa*, which he helped launch in 1996. After heading up Code for South Africa's media programme and launching its Data Journalism Academy in 2015, he now works as a freelance journalist and trainer, specialising in fact-checking, the verification of online and social media content, and the use of social media as journalism tools.

Joel Konopo is an investigative journalist and managing partner of INK Centre for Investigative Journalism, a non-profit newsroom that produces stories in the public interest for organisations that have significant budgetary constraints in Gaborone, Botswana. Previously, he was editor of the *Botswana Guardian*. He was part of the team of journalists who worked on the Panama Papers that implicated prominent business people in Botswana. Konopo holds a bachelor's degree in political science from the University of Botswana. He is currently a JSK Fellow at Stanford University.

Peter Limb is Emeritus Professor, Michigan State University and research fellow, Gender and Africa Studies Centre, University of the Free State. He has published widely on South African history, journalism and anti-apartheid movements. His books include *The People's Paper: A Centenary History & Anthology of Abantu-Batho* (2012), *Autobiography & Selected Works of AB Xuma* (2012) and *The ANC's Early Years* (2010). His current research includes books on African cartooning (2018) and Free State political history. He co-hosts the popular scholarly podcast series Africa Past & Present (afripod.aodl.org) with leading Africanists across disciplines and continents.

Gwen Lister is a journalist, columnist and press freedom activist. She founded *The Namibian* in 1985 at the height of colonial rule, making her the first woman newspaper editor in southern Africa. The newspaper was constantly the target of right-wingers because it exposed apartheid atrocities and supported the struggle for independence. Lister was jailed twice and won several international awards for her work. She is a founder member of the International Consortium of International Journalists (ICIJ) and currently heads the Namibia Media Trust, which is active in promoting media freedom, freedom of expression and journalism training in Namibia and further afield.

Irwin Manoim was joint founder and editor of *The Weekly Mail* (1985–94) along with Anton Harber, and of the online *Mail & Guardian* (1994–2000), the first digital news operation in Africa. He has researched and taught media theory and history in the Journalism Studies programme at the University of the Witwatersrand.

Mbongeni Mbingo has been the managing editor of the Swazi Observer Group since 2012. He began his career 20 years ago at the *Times of Swaziland*. He has received multiple awards and in 2017 was recognised by the Swaziland Media Institute of Southern Africa with the Media Freedom Award. He is deputy chairman of the Southern African Editors' Forum and chairman of the Swaziland Editors' Forum. Mbingo holds a master's degree in journalism from the University of the Witwatersrand. He has been a guest lecturer at several eSwatini universities, on media ethics, the public sphere and the media in eSwatini.

Andrew Meldrum is an American journalist who worked in Zimbabwe from 1980 until 2003, primarily writing for *The Guardian* and *The Economist*. After a Nieman Fellowship at Harvard University, he was deputy managing editor at *Global Post*. He is currently based in Johannesburg where he is acting Africa editor for *The Associated Press*.

Hlonipha Mokoena received her PhD from the University of Cape Town in 2005. She is currently an associate professor and researcher at WiSER (Wits Institute for Social and Economic Research) at the University of the Witwatersrand. Her articles have been published in *Journal of Natal and Zulu History*, *Journal of Religion in Africa*, *Journal of Southern African Studies*, *Ufahamu: A Journal of African Studies*, *Interventions: International Journal of Postcolonial Studies*, *Image & Text* and *Critical Arts*.

Ron Nixon is *The New York Times*'s homeland security correspondent. He is based in the Washington bureau, where he covers border and aviation security, immigration, counterterrorism, cybercrime and cyber security, transnational crime and violent extremism. He has reported from Rwanda, Uganda, Belgium, Canada, Mexico, South Africa, Nigeria, Senegal, Democratic Republic of Congo, Costa Rica, Kenya and Burundi. Nixon is also the author of *Selling Apartheid: Apartheid South Africa's Global Propaganda War*.

Lekhetho Ntsukunyane is the founding editor of the MNN Centre for Investigative Journalism in Lesotho. He was the winner of the 2016 MISA – Lesotho/US Embassy Maseru Investigative Journalism Award. Lekhetho is a passionate investigative journalist who has published a number of hard-hitting exposés on governance, extractive industries, courts of law, corruption and related crimes since the start of his professional career in 2009. He has published in *Public Eye*, *Lesotho Times* and *Sunday Express*, as well as internationally.

Geoffrey Nyarota was the editor of *The Chronicle* in Bulawayo until 1988, when the Willowgate Scandal caused the abrupt termination of his contract. Graduating with a bachelor's degree from the University of Rhodesia, Nyarota became a cadet journalist at *The Herald* in Harare. He founded *The Daily News* in 1999, which became Zimbabwe's largest selling newspaper. His first book, *Against the Grain*, was published in 2006 and his second, titled 'The Graceless Fall of Robert Mugabe', will be published in August 2018. A fellow of the Nieman Foundation for Journalism at Harvard University, he has won nine international awards for excellence in journalism.

Tanya Pampalone is the managing editor of the Global Investigative Journalism Network, a non-profit based in Washington, DC, and has been moonlighting as a non-fiction editor for Pan Macmillan South Africa since 2013. A former executive editor of *Mail & Guardian*, she won the Standard Bank Sikuvile Award in 2012 for creative writing, and was the 2013 Menell Media Fellow at Duke University's Sanford School of Public Policy. She was the co-editor of two non-fiction narrative collections, *Writing Invisibility: Conversations on the Inner City* (2013) and *I Want To Go Home Forever: Stories of Becoming and Belonging in South Africa's Great Metropolis* (2018).

Justin Pearce lectures in African politics at the University of Cambridge. He began his journalistic career in South Africa and has been writing about Angola since 2001, as a journalist, human rights researcher and academic. After two years in Luanda as the BBC World Service correspondent, he later returned to Angola to research his doctorate on political mobilisation during the Angolan war. He is the author of two books on Angola: *An Outbreak of Peace* (2005) and *Political Identity and Conflict in Central Angola* (2015).

The Contributors

Benjamin Pogrund established mainstream reporting on black politics and life under apartheid, and covered southern African countries, during his 26 years with the *Rand Daily Mail*. He also represented the *Sunday Times* (London) and the *Boston Globe*. He was deputy editor when the *Mail* closed in 1985. He emigrated to Britain, was diplomatic editor of *Today* and then chief foreign sub-editor of *The Independent*. He then moved to Israel to found a dialogue centre and lives in Jerusalem. He has written books about Robert Sobukwe, Nelson Mandela, the press under apartheid, Israel and apartheid, and has co-edited publications about the Israeli-Palestinian dialogue.

Erika Rodrigues is a Columbia University graduate working at UX Information Technologies in Mozambique. She co-wrote a paper on media and the extractive sector in 2013 and has contributed chapters to *Global Muckraking: 100 Years of Investigative Journalism from Around the World* (2014) and *Participatory Democracy and Citizen Journalism in a Networked Africa: A Connected Continent* (2015).

Reg Rumney has extensive experience in South Africa's business news media, having worked for the *Rand Daily Mail* as property editor and *Business Day* as production editor before becoming business editor of *Finance Week* and the *Mail & Guardian*, and then moving into broadcasting as economics editor of SABC News. He was also in charge of research as director of socio-economic thinktank BusinessMap, an organisation that specialised in black empowerment and investment research. Most recently he was director of the SA Reserve Bank Centre for Economics Journalism at Rhodes University, where he researched and taught financial, business and economics journalism at postgraduate level.

Anthony Sguazzin started his career as a business reporter on Zimbabwe's *Daily Gazette*, the country's first privately owned daily, in 1994 and also worked on investigations and features. He later worked for the *Financial Gazette* in Zimbabwe and *Metal Bulletin* and *Dow Jones* in London before joining *Bloomberg News* in Johannesburg in 1998. Today he is the managing editor of Bloomberg's news operations in sub-Saharan Africa. He has an honours degree in African literature from the University of Zimbabwe and a journalism diploma from Rhodes University.

Letshwiti Tutwane is a lecturer in media law and journalism in the department of media studies at the University of Botswana, where he teaches an undergraduate course in investigative journalism. He recently returned from the United States where he was a Fulbright scholar-in-residence at Illinois Central College. Previously he worked as a journalist in Botswana, mainly at *Mmegi* newspaper, where he was a features editor.

Finnigan wa Simbeye has been an investigative journalist for the past 15 years, trained in Tanzania and France. He has worked for several European publications, including the *Indian Ocean Newsletter* of France. He is currently chief reporter of *The Guardian*, a member of the Forum for African Investigative Reporters and a correspondent for the London-based Africa Investigates television agency.

Bob Wekesa has been a postdoctoral fellow in the Department of Journalism and Media Studies, at the University of the Witwatersrand since 2015. He holds a BEd degree in linguistics and literature from the University of Nairobi, a masters in international communication and a PhD which focused on media and public diplomacy, from the Communication University of China. His academic and journalistic interests are in media and geopolitics. He is a research associate with the Wits Africa–China Reporting Project and the Wits African Centre for the Study of the US.

Franz Wild is an investigative reporter with Bloomberg in London with a decade of experience reporting from several sub-Saharan African countries.

Index

#GuptaLeaks exposé (2017) xxi–xxii, 263, 329, 332, 335–6, 338–9

Abantu-Batho (*People*) 42–3, 48–9
Acacia 307
Acres 242
Adrupiako, Emmanuel 306
Africa South 77, 86
African Investigative Publishing Collective (AIPC) xvii, 295
    ZAM xvii, 289, 295, 297
African Methodist Episcopal (AME) Church 26, 35
    revivalism of 27
African National Congress (ANC) 43, 48–9, 64, 69, 71, 82, 118–23, 146–7, 152, 163–4, 182–3, 185–91, 262, 328–9, 333
    banning of (1958) 76, 85, 109, 118, 182
    formerly South African Native National Congress 15
    Polokwane Conference (2007) 330
    Umkhonto weSizwe (MK) 61, 77, 123, 146, 186–7, 190
    unbanning of (1990) 103
African Political Organisation APO 43
African Security Review 291
Africommerce 236
Afrikaans (language) 147, 180
Afrikaner Broederbond 100–6, 108
Agence France-Presse 155
Alcock, Neil 94–5
All Basotho Convention 337
Alvis Vickers 292

amaBhungane 326–33, 335, 338
Amanzimtoti Theological 25
American Board of Commissioners for Foreign Missions (ABCFM) 24–5, 29
    Missionary Herald 25
Amnesty International 78
Anglican Church 78
    Diocese of Namibia 171
Anglo-Boer War (1899–1902) 20
    Vereeniging Peace Treaty (1902) 37, 41
Angola xv–xvi, xxii, 151, 169, 189, 203, 268, 278–9, 284, 304
    Civil War (1975–2002) 203–4
    General Tax Administration 280
    Huambo 284–5
    Luanda 203, 207, 279, 281–2
    Sovereign Wealth Fund (FSDEA) 279–80
apartheid x, 43, 61, 92, 101, 180–1, 183–4
Associated Negro Press (ANP) 49
Association of Black Journalists 174
Australia
    infant mortality rate of 98
    Sydney 224
Aziz, Rostam 236–7

Baartman, Ben 91
Bailey, Jim 69
Banana, Canaan 198
Banco Kwanza Invest (BKI) 280–1
Banda, Hastings 163
Bantu Authorities Act (1951) 79
Bantu Education Act 79
Baobab Books 127
Bapedi Authority 82

disestablishment of 80–1
Baker, Ray Stannard xi
Bandiko, Sadock 324
Bank of Credit and Commerce 177
Barclays Bank 315
Barnett, Claude 49
Barrie, Gerald 135
Basotho (ethnic group) 240
Basson, Deon 228–9
    writings of 230–1
Baumann, Antonie 43
Baumann, Marie 43
Bell Pottinger 333–4
Bennet, Sue 229
Bensonvale Institution 14, 16
Bernstein, Carl 133
BGFI 307–8
Bhambatha Rebellion
    suppression of 36
Black Cats Scandal (1990–1) 190, 193–6
black journalism 71
Black Sash xx
Bloomberg 301
    Bloomberg News 303
Bloomberg, Charles 101–2
BMI 220
Boers 20, 23
Bogaert, Abraham
    Historical Journey (1711) 2
Boikanyo, Tshepo 252–3
Bombardier Aerospace 225, 227
Bombardier Global Express 225–6
Borethe, Tholwana 315–16
Bosman, Kobus 147
Botha, P.W. 107
Botho University 309–11
Botswana xvi–xvii, 141, 275, 289, 311
    Gaborone 273, 291, 293
    Mosu 275–6
Botswana Accountancy College (BAC) 309, 313
Botswana Defence Force (BDF) 273, 275–6, 291–2, 294
Botswana Democratic Party (BDP) 314
Botswana Gazette 293, 309, 312–14
Botswana Guardian 273
Botswana Movement for Democracy (BMD) 310, 314
    Bobonog Congress 314

Botswana Police Services (BPS) 292
Botswana Qualifications Authority 310–11, 313
Brackman, Albert 220
Bredenhann, Wally 170
Bretton Woods 210
British Broadcasting Corporation (BBC) 150, 203, 255, 258
Brkic, Branko 327–9
broadcasting journalism xxiii
Brümmer, Stefaans 326, 328
Bush, George W. 227
Business Days 165
Bureau for State Security (BOSS) 54, 133–4, 138
Burnside, Janet 36
Burundi 235
Business Day xxi
Business Weekly and Review 289–90, 314
Business Practices Committee 232
Buthelezi 190

Cachalia, Amina 86
Campbell, Paul 221
Canada 225, 242, 340
Cape Archives 2–3
Cape Colony 27, 36, 40
    Herschel 14, 16–18
Cape Times 20, 55, 134
Caprivi Trainee Sandal (1990) 189, 191
Cardoso, Carlos xiii–xv, 164, 209–11
    murder of (2000) 209
    writings of 211–12
Cartwright, Justin 216
Caspian Construction Limited 236
Cassia, Arcanjo 300
Catholic Commission for Justice and Peace 157
Catholic Institute for International Relations 126
Catholicism xi, 126, 155
    Maryknoll order 126–7
Cavanaugh, Jessie 220
Central Bank of Angola 280
Cetshwayo (Ketshwayo) 8–10
Chama Cha Mapinduzi (CCM) 320, 322
Chamber of Mines 55, 68
Charamlambous, Styli 327
Charlieman, Tommy 122

Index

Chawla, Ashu 332
Chezi, Barnett 122–3
Chihambakwe, Simplisius 157
Chikurubi Prison 127
China, People's Republic of 267, 278
    Hong Kong 336–7
Chinanga, James 201
Chissano, Joaquim 210
Chissano, Nyimpine 210
Chiweshe Residents Association 130
Christian Institute
    banning of (1977) 101–2
Christianity 4, 24, 26, 286–7
    Bible 25
    conversion to 8
    missionaries 11, 14, 16
Chronicle, The (Bulawayo) 154, 172, 174, 176
Cillie, Piet 112
Cinderella Prison 116–17
Citizen, The 135–7, 235, 321, 323
    Project Annemarie 139
City Press 262, 328
Civillini, Matteo 289–90
    writings of 290–1
Clarke, Thirza 253
Clegg, Johnny 216
Cloud FM 319
Cocksey, Brian xviii
Coetzee, Dirk 181–2, 184–5
Coetzee, Renata 250
Coka, Jameson Gilbert 49–50
    background of 48
    writings of 51–2
Colenso, John W. 8
Commercial Bank of Mozambique (BCM) 210, 214
    privatisation of (1996) 210–11
    Sommerschield branch 213
    theft scandal 210–11, 213
Commercial Farmers' Union (CFU) 200
Committee of Education Heads 105
Companies Act 229, 232–4
Constitution of South Africa
    Section 16 233–4
Cooper, Dr E.D. 99
Corporate Social Responsibility Projects 300
da Costa, Monica 3, 204
Criminal Investigation Police (PIC) 211–13

Cuba 27

Daily Dispatch, The 38–40, 134, 247, 249, 253
Daily Gazette x, 197, 200–2
Daily Mail 19–22
Daily Maverick xxi, 274, 327–9, 332
Daily News xv, xvii
Dar es Salaam-Mwanza Oil Pipeline Project 235–6, 239
da Silva, Antonio Ferreira 148
Day, Chris
    Muldergate (1980) 132–3
da Conceição, Djanir de Nazaré Ferreira 280–1
De Beers 289, 306
De Klerk, F.W. 183, 189–90
De Kock, Eugene 183–4
de Mello, Ricardo xv, 203
    Impartial Fax xxiii
    murder of (1995) 204–5
    writings of 205–8
De Wet van Wyk, C. 83
De Wit, Mike 306
Defence and Aid Fund 118–20
Defence Special Fund 140
Defence White Paper (1979) 167
Democratic Alliance 262
Democratic Republic of Congo (DRC) 104, 235, 301, 303–4
    Hewa Bora 305
    Kinshasa 302
    Luisha 307
    North Kivu 305
    Republican Guard 306–7
    Tembo 306
de Morais, Jean-Claude Bastos 279, 281
Department of Bantu Affairs 85
Department of Information 138–9
Detainees Parents Support Committee xx
development journalism
    concept of xvii
Dhlamini, James 142–3
    writings of 144
Dias, Celestino 206
Dias, Sendji Alexandre Vieira 280–1
Digital Globe 274, 276
Diop, Abdel Kader 308
Directorate of Intelligence and Security (DIS) 293

Directorate of Intelligence Services (DISS) 275, 277
Directorate of Special Tasks
  Operation Marion 191
Directorate on Corruption and Economic Offences 336
Djange, Fernando 298
Dlamini, Sibusiso Barnabas 224, 226–8
Dolan, Kerry 279
Doran, Stuart
  Kingdom, Power, Glory: Mugabe, ZANU and the Quest for Supremacy 1960–1987 157
dos Santos, Ana Paula 204
dos Santos, Isabel 279
dos Santos, José Eduardo 278, 281
dos Santos, José Filomento (Zénu) 279–80
dos Santos Mangueira, Mário Augusto 280–1
Dowans Holdings Limited 236
Drum (1951) xx, 71
  founding of (1951) 69–70
Dube, John Langalibalele xiv, 24–5, 29, 86
  background of 25
  Impi yamakhanda 24
  visits to USA 25, 27
  writings of 33–5
Dube, Nokutela 28
Dube, Phumzile 332
Dunn, Ernst 30
du Preez, Max 180–2
Du Rand, Kierie 169
Dutch East India Company (VoC) 1–2
  Heeren XVII 1–4
Dutch Reformed Church 101

Eagle Printing Press Company 36
Economic Freedom Fighters 262
Economist, The 211
Eduardo, Jose 164
Eduado Mondlane University 64
Egypt
  infant mortality rate of 98
Elbit 292
Electronic and Postal Communications (Online Content) Regulations (2017) 319
Emergency Relief Committee of Christian Care 130

Enron 234
EP Herald 134
Erasmus Commission of Inquiry 133, 139
Eskom 327
Essa, Salim 333, 335–7
Ethiopia 26
European Union (EU) 303
Execulet 225
Executive Code of Ethics 262
Extractive Industries Transparency Initiative (EITI) 295, 297
Eyewitness News 326

fascism 55
Fauvet, Paul
  writings of 146–51, 164–8
Federation of South African Women 85
Fevereiro, Etelvina 298
Finance Week 230–1
Fighting Talk 61
Finance Week 233
Financial Services Board 234
First, Ruth xiv–xv, xx, 64–8, 86
  background of 61–2
  banned from practising journalism (1960) 63
  Barrel of a Gun: Political Power in Africa and the Coup d'État 63
  Black Gold: The Mozambican Miner, Proletarian and Peasant (1983) 61–4
  murder of (1982) 146, 187
First World War (1914–18) 50
Flemington, Archie 186
Forbes 279
Forrest, Drew 326
Fouché, Leo 2
  Diary of Adam Tas (1914) 1, 3
France 133, 242
  Paris 152, 308
Frederikse, Julie
  None but Ourselves 126
Free State Congress 43
Freeman Cohen, Harry 21
Frere Hospital
  infant mortality rate in 247–53
Fundo Activo de Capital de Risco (FACRA) 281
Fürst, Julius 62

Index

Furtado, Eugénio 206
Fuze 8–9
   'A Visit to King Ketshwayo' 9–13

Gabon 307
Galizia, Matthew Caruana 310, 314
Gallo, Eric 219
Gandar, Laurence 92, 112–13
   trial of 112
Gandhi, Mahatma
   founder of *Indian Opinion* 42
Gaozi 11
Garlake, Peter 125
Garson, Philippa 195
Garvey, Marcus
   ideology of 49
Gemfields/Pallinghurst 296, 300
Geohegan, Victoria 333
Germany 133, 242
   Berlin 77
Geyser, Albert 101
Ghana
   infant mortality rate of 98
Gibson, Dave 179
Ginindza, Vusi 223
   writings of 224–7
Global Investigative Journalism Conference 87
Gobizembe 30, 33
Godwin, Peter 156
   writings of 162–3
Golden City Post 109
Goldstone, R. 194
Goldstone Commission of Inquiry (1991) 190–1
Goma Mining 305–6
Gonçalves, Jaime 203
Good Morning, South Africa 165
Gosani, Bob 69–70
Government Gazette 232
Green-Thompson, Ronald 253
Group of Eight (G8) 243
Groupe BGFI Bank SA 307
Guardian, The xx, 61–2, 154, 236–7
Guduza, Prince 225
Gukurahundi Massacre (1983–7) x, 153–4, 156, 172
Gupta, Ajay 334
Gupta, Atul 334, 338
Gupta, Rajesh 'Tony' 326–7, 332, 334, 336, 339
Gupta Brothers 326–7, 333–4, 336–8
GuptaLeaks exposé (2017) xxi–xxii, 263, 329, 332, 335–6, 338–9
Gwanda, Azory xv, 317–18
   writings of 320–3
Gwata, Dr Tizirai 202

Hadebe, Mark 28
Halpern, Jack (James Fairbairn)
   background of 77–8
   death of 78
   South Africa's Hostages: Basutoland, Bechuanaland & Swaziland (1965) 78
Hampton Institute 26
Handhawersbond 59
Hani, Chris 187
Harriman, Richard 313
Havenga, N.C.
   Minister of Finance 57
Health Professions Council of South Africa (HPCSA) 252–3
Heard, George xv, 54
   background of 55
   death of 55–6
   writings of 57–8
Heko xviii
Henson, Geoffrey
   Provincial Commissioner for Internal Affairs 128
Hertzog, General 88
Hitler, Adolf 54–5, 59
HIV/AIDS 223–4, 248
Hoffman, Dustin xii
Hogan, Barbara 248
Holt, Samuel 26
Horner, Brett 247
   writings of 249–52
Howa, Nazeem 332
Human Rights Welfare Committee 85
Huque, Mohamed 236
Husing, Henning 2

Ikwezi le Afrika 48–9
Ilanga laseNatal (*The Natal Sun*) 24, 29
Imparcial Fax (Impartial Fax) 203–5
imperialism
   American 27

British 10
Imvo Zabantsundu (Black Opinion) 14–15, 36
Income Tax Act 229
Independent, The 216
India 221
   infant mortality rate of 98
Indian Opinion 42
Industrial and Commercial Workers' Union (ICU) 48
   Workers' Herald, The 48
Information Scandal xiii, 132–3
INK Centre for Investigative Journalism xvii, xix, 274, 276–7, 309–10, 312, 314–15, 335
Inkatha Freedom Party (IFP) 183, 188–9, 191–2
Inkathagate (1991) 190
Institute of Race Relations 120
Intermark 149
International Consortium of Investigative Journalists (ICIJ) 310
International Council for Open and Distance Education 313
International Monetary Fund (IMF) 305
International Rivers 241
International Women's Media Foundation 255
investigative journalism xvii, xxi, xxiii, 14, 16, 86, 101–5, 180, 203
isiXhosa (language) 14, 28, 36
isiZulu (language) 25, 326
Islam 322
Israel 133
Italy 289
   Milan 308
Iyer, Preya 312
Izwi la Bantu (*Voice of the People*)
   establishment of (1897) 36

Jabavu, John Tengo xiv
   background of 14
   writings of 14–16
Jane Furse Mission School 79
Japan 133
   Tokyo 224
Jaula, Nomsa 253
Johannesburg Star 152, 166

Johnson, Pat 201
Johnston, David Cay 228
Jonas, Ncebisi 327
Jordaan, Christiaan 299
Jornal de Angola 203
Joseph, Helen
   background of 85
   death of 86
   Tomorrow's Sun 86
JSE Securities Exchange 233–4
Judaism 62

Kabila, Jaynet 305
Kabila, Joseph 301–6
Kabila, Josephine 305–8
Kabila, Lauren-Desire 304–5
Kabila, Masengo 306
Kafka, Franz
   Trial, The 112
Kaiyamo, Nico 169
Kalafatis, John 293
Kalupeteka, José Julino 284–5, 287–8
kaMancinza, Bhambatha 29
Kamba, Walter 174
Kameron, Pete 219–21
Kanani, Kaombona 274
Karlen, Henry
   Bishop of Bulawayo 155
Kasaka, Njeru 235
Katabaro, Stan xvii–xviii
Katzin, Kitt 133–4
Kauluma, Bishop James 171
Kaunda, Kenneth 164
Kavanagh, Michael
   writings of 303
Kenya 151, 255, 259
   Mau Mau Uprising (1952–64) 76
Kerry, John 302
Keyter, Carl 94–5
Kgosi, Isaac 315
Khama, Anthony 292
Khama, Ian 273–6, 289, 291, 294
Khama, Seretse 289, 291
Khama, Tshekedi 292
   Minister for Environment, Wildlife and Tourism 292
Khasu, Tlali 339–40
   Mining Minister 336–7

Khawula, Nhlanhla 196
Khumalo, Marwick 225
Khumalo, Mbongeni 190
Kibanda, Absalom 319
Kijinga SA 280–2
Kikwete, Jakaya 236
Kinshasa Fashion Week 308
Kipling, Rudyard 20
Kirungi, Iddy 322
Kiswahili (language) ix, xvii
    newspapers 235
Kitchener, Lord Herbert 20, 22
Koch, Eddie 189, 192, 195
Kona, William 154
Konopo, Joel 273, 275–6
Kovach, Bill
    Elements of Journalism, The 217
Ku Klux Klan (KKK) 27
Kupe, Tawana xiii–xiv
Kupugani (Nutrition Corporation) 92–4
Kwangaya, Rahim 325
Kwango, River 306
Kwango Mines 306
Kwanza Capital 308

Lahmeyer GmbH 242
Lancaster House Agreement (1975) 145, 148
Land Act (1913) xiv, 43
Land Grab Scandal 198
Laos 268
Latham, Brian x
Latvia 62
Legal Resources Foundation 157
LeisureNet 234
Leselinyana la Lesotho 240
Lesotho xix, 141, 151, 240–3, 245, 334–5, 337–8
    Letseng Mine 337
Lesotho Highlands Water Project (LHWP) 241, 245, 335
    Katse and Mohale Dams 241
    Polihali Dam 241
Lesotho Times xix, 240, 335
Letanka, Daniel 42–3
Leuchers, George 30, 33
Leventhal, Harold 220–1
Levitan, Tilly 62

Levy, Langley 55
LHDA 242
Liberia 27
Liebbrandt, H.C.T. 2–3
Linda, Solomon 215, 218–20
Lissu, Tundu 319
Lister, Gwen ix–x
Lithuania 62
Location Vigilance Committee 45
Loch, Sir Henry Brougham 216
Lombardo, Guy 220
Louw, Raymond 113
Lowassa, Edward ix, 237
Lubowski, Anton
    assassination of (1989) 182
Lucara 340
Lugalambi, George xii
Lumumba, Jean-Jacques 301, 308
Lushaba, Alec
    writings of 225–6
Luthuli, Daluxolo 190, 194
Lutuli, Ngazana 28
Luz do Mundo 285

Mabandla, Prince 142, 144
Mabhida, Moses 164
Machava, Paulo 212
Machel, Samora 145, 210
    death of (1986) 163–4, 168, 210
MacLean, Alistair
    Golden Rendezvous 138
Macmed 234
MacSporran, Peter 200
Madlala-Routledge, Nozizwe 248
Madondo, Bongani 216
Madonsela, Thula 261
    'Secure in Comfort' (2014) 262
Magufuli, John Pombe 317, 319, 323
Mail & Guardian (M&G) ix, 260–2, 264–6, 326, 330–2
Majaliwa, Kassim 317
Maka Angola 278–83
Makau, Patrick 187
Makhosetive, Prince 143
Malan, D.F. xiv, 107
Malan, Magnus 163
Malan, Rian 215–16
    My Traitor's Heart 216

writings of 216, 218–19
malaria 282
Malawi 163
Mamatola (tribe) 88
Mandela, Nelson 24, 64, 69, 101, 189, 261
    election of (1994) 291–2
Mandela, Winnie 86
Mangu, Ernest 321, 323
Mangwende, Witness 197, 199–200
    Minister of Education and Culture 199
Manuel, Trevor
    Finance Minister 234
Manzaza, Jauvin 306
Marijani, Nsato 322
Marketing Quotient 333
Marques de Morais, Rafael
    Diamantes de Sangue Tortura e Corrupção em Angola (*Blood Diamonds: Torture and Corruption in Angola*) (2011) 278–9
    writings of 279–82
Maruziva, Davison 173
Maserumule, Frank 83
Masisi, Mokgweetsi 290
Masterbond Debacle 233
Mathlombe, José 212
Matisonn, John
    God, Spies and Lies 102, 135
Matlala Reserve 88–9
Matshana 10–11
Mauritius 295
Mbeki, Thabo 224, 248, 261
McGoff, Daniel J. 140
McGoff, John 137, 140
McLaughlin, Sister Janice xx, 126–7
    writings of 128–31
Mechanical Copyright Protection Society 215
Media Council of Tanzania 318
Media Institute of Southern Africa (MISA) xviii–xix, 318
    So This is Democracy 2017 xvi
Mediacoop 210
Mediafax 210
Medical Research Council 250
Medrôa, Cira Cláudia Ferreira Custódio 280

Melchmar International xviii
Meldrum, Andrew x
    writings of 161–2
Mellet, Patric Tariq 3–4
Memorial, The 4–5
    significance of 1–3
Mende, Lambert 304
Mervis, Joel 56, 101
    Fourth Estate, The 102
Metical 211
Meyer, P.J. 104
Mfunzi 12
Mfutakamba, Dr Athumani 236
Michigan Civil Service Commission 311
Milne, Jack 228, 232–3
Mines and Minerals Act 337
mining 67, 305–7
    cobalt 307
    copper 307
    diamond 307, 336, 339
    gold 67
    labour 67–8
Mining Weekly 299
Mkapa, Benjamin 236
Mkhombe, Sam 226
Mlangeni, Titus
    Minister of Works and Transport 225
Mmegi 309, 314–15
Mnangagwa, Emmerson 157
    Zimbabwean Security Minister 156
Mnete, Tatu 325
MNN Centre for Investigative Journalism (MNNCIJ) xix, 240, 335–9
Mnyamana, Chief Induna 11
Moahi, Lucky 311
Mochochoko, Edward Sauer 43
Modderbee (prison)
    deaths of prisoners at 109
Mogoeng, Mogoeng 262
Mohloboli, Keiso xix, 335
Mohloboli, Ntsukunya xix
Mokgosi, Mpho 313
Mokgware, Pius 292
Mokhethi, Sechaba xix, 335
Montepuez Ruby Mining (MRM Gemfields) 297–8
Mopedi, Chief 89
Morgadinho, Francisco 146, 149
Moroamoche 80–1

Morolong, Joe 86
Morris, Rev. Charles 27
Mosinki, Tsosoloso 315
Mothae Diamond Mine 337, 339
Motlogelwa, Tshireletso
    writings of 290–1
Moto 126
Motsitsi, Casey 69
Motuba, Edgar Mahlomola 240
Moyo, Sikwali 161
Mozambican Liberation Front
    (FRELIMO) 67, 209–10, 295–6, 299
Mozambique xiii, xv–xvi, 64, 67, 125–6,
    151, 163, 165–6, 193, 209, 211, 295
    Beira 145, 209
    Department of Customs 299
    Department of Minerals 299
    Maputo 61, 145, 149, 164, 168, 186,
        213
    Matola 146–8, 151
    Matola River 151
    Ministry of Defence 151
    Montepuez 297–8, 300
    Xai-Xai 149
Mozambique Airlines (LAM) 148, 152
Mozambique National Resistance
    (RENAMO) 145, 163, 189, 192
Mozambique New Agency (AIM) 146,
    164, 210
Mpande 8
Mpendu, Zebia
    trial of (1965) 119
Mpofu, Alford 173, 176
Mpofu, Obert 173, 176
Msabaha, Dr Ibrahim
Minister for Energy and Minerals 239
Msimang, Richard xiv
Mswati III, King 223, 225–6
Mteyu, Gloria 307–8
Mubako, Simbi
    Zimbabwean Minister of Home
        Affairs 161–2
muckraking 24
Mugabe, Robert x, 125, 153, 155, 157, 159,
    172, 198
Mugalu, Theodore 304
Mujuru, Tapfumanyeni 202
Mulder, Connie
    Minister of Information 133, 137

Muro, Elisante 235–6
Mushongi, Bonaventure 321
Mussett, Jack 128
Mustang Resources 299
Mutungamiri, Lloyd 240
    attempted assassination of xix
Mwakyembe, Dr Harrison 236
Mwangosi, Daudi 318–19
Mwarabu, Erick 323
Mwiriti 297
Mxenge, Griffiths 185
Myburgh, Tertius 101, 103
Mzuzuri, Ramadhani 324

Nakasa, Nat 69
Naledi ea Lesotho 240
Namburete, António 213
Namibia xvi, 170, 189, 268
    Caprivi Strip 189, 192
    Hippo 192
    Ongdangu 171
    Ongwediwa 171
    Oshakati 171
    Windhoek 182
Namibian, The 170–1
    founding of (1985) 169
Nanai, Francis 318
Natal (Colony) 8
Natal Mercury 134
Nation Media Group
    Mwananchi Communications
        Limited 317
National Convention 38
National Directorate for Criminal
    Investigation (DNIC) 204
National Nutrition Research Institute
    97–9
National Party 63, 79, 93, 100–2, 108, 139,
    180, 189
National Union for the Total Independence
    of Angola (UNITA) 164, 204, 207–8
nationalism 181
    African 126
    Afrikaner 107
    English 136
    Zulu 24, 188
Nationalist Party 135
Native Administration Bill 88
Native Affairs Department (NAD) 79–80,

82–3
Natives' Land Act (1913) 15
Naude, Beyers 101–2
Nchindo, Louis 293
Ndabezita 12
Ndebele (ethnic group) 153, 160–1, 172
Ndikilo, Evarist 321
Ndinhu, Emmanuel 320
Ndlovu, Busisiwe 311–12
Ndlovu, Callistus Dingiswayo 176
    Zimbabwean Minister of Industry and Technology 178
Ndlovu, Don 177–8
Nederduits Gereformeerde Kerk 104
Nel Commission 233
Nene, Nhlanhla
    Finance Minister 327
Netherlands 133
    Amsterdam 1–2
New Nation 188
New Statesman 77
New World Mission Dunamis International University (NWMD) 309, 311–12
New Zealand 101
News24 xxi
Ngoyi, Lillian 85
Nguiraz, Ramiro 299
Ngulungwa, Brian 185
Ngwenya, Austin 157
Nhatitima, Sinai 213
Nieuwoudt, Adriaan 180
Nilsson, Anders 146
Nixon, Richard
    Watergate Scandal (1972–4) xii, 133
Nkadimeng, Phasoane 82
Nkala, Enos
    Zimbabwean Minister of Defence 173
Nkisimane 12
Nkomati Non-Aggression Pact (1984) 163
Nkomo, Joshua 154, 160–1, 172
Nkosi, Lewis 69
NMM Centre xix
Nofemela, Almond 182, 185
non-governmental organizations (NGOs) xviii, xx, 205, 240–1, 256
Norris, Frank xi
North Korea 153, 158
Northern Ireland Institute of Business Technology (NIIBT) 309, 312–13
Norway 133
Ntaote, Billy xix, 335
Ntetema, Vicky 254–6
    writings of 256–7
Ntibinyane, Ntibinyane 273–6
Ntshangase, Abednego 226
Ntshona, Dr Nokuzola 249
Ntsukunyane, Lekhetho xix
    arrest of xix
Nxumalo, Henry xx, 69–70
    writings of 70–3
Nyagumbo, Maurice 174
Nyarota, Geoffrey
    writings of 175–6
Nyere, Julius 86
Nzama, Zee 218

Obama, Barack 268
Obasanjo, Olusegun 265
Oberlin College 25–6
Ohlange 25
Olive Sifa Laurent (Osifal) 306
Ombe, Ilidio 152
Open Society Institute of Southern Africa (OSISA) xix, 240
Open University Europa 313
Operation Green Leader (1979) 148
Operation Peace and Quiet 121–2
Orange Free State 14, 16
Ossewabrandwag (OB) 54, 56, 58–60
OTC Finance International 232–3
Ovamboland 169

Pachinuapa, Raimundo Domingos 297
Pan-Africanist Congress (PAC)
    banning of (1958) 109, 118
Panama 305
Panama Papers xxi, 279, 295
Panax Corporation 140
Paradise Papers xxi, 295
Pauw, Jacques x, 180, 183
    Tell Me No Lies 183
    writings of 184–5
Payne, Cecil 112
People's Development Bank (BPD)
    privatisation of (1997) 210
Peoples' Liberation Army of Namibia (PLAN) 169

People's United Democratic Movement (PUDEMO) 143
Peres, Dr Jaime 149
persons with albinism (PWAs) 254–8
Peta, Basildon x, 197–9
    writings of 199–200
Philadelphia Inquirer 155
Pietrse, Andre 138
Pilatus 292
Pilgrim's Papers 25
Pinoni, Anna 318
Pitra 'Petroff', André 204
Plaatje, Sol xiv, 43
    founder of *Tsala ea Batho* (*People's Friend*) 42
Pogrund, Benjamin 94–9
Popular Movement for the Liberation of Angola (MPLA) 203, 278
Porritt, Gary 229
Portugal 145–6, 209
Pottinger, Lori 241–2
Pretoria Local Prison 110, 114–16
Pretorius, Estienne 170
PricewaterhouseCoopers (PwC) 308
Prince, Chandre 247
Prinsloo, C.W. 80, 83
Prisons Act (1959) 109
    Section 44(f) 109–10
Progressive Party 101, 181
PSC Guaranteed Growth (PSCGG) 228–33
Public Eye 335
Pulitzer Center on Crisis Reporting 303–4
Pwani Shootings (2015) 317–25

Quass, Dr F.W. 97–9

Rademeyer, Julian 267–8
    Killing for Profit 267–9
    writings of 269–70
Ramaphosa, Cyril 329, 338
Ramare. Frans 89
Ramaya, Vicente 211
Ramlakan, Vejay 264
Ramsay, Jeff 275
Rand Club 55
Rand Daily Mail, The 22, 54, 56, 76, 92, 109–11, 113, 118, 134–8, 147, 149–50
    Pretoria Bureau 92

Rand Revolt (1922) 55–6
Rapport 136, 180, 183
Rathkeale Rovers 268
Red Shirts 27
Rede Angola (Network Angola) 284
Redford, Robert xii
Rees, Mervyn
    Muldergate (1980) 132–3
Regal Treasury Bank 234
Reuters 20
Review of African Political Economy 64
Reynolds News 77
Rhodes, Cecil 15, 25, 36
Rhodesia xx, 62, 65, 90, 125, 128, 219
Rhodesia Herald 125
Rhodesian Bush War (1964–79) 125–9
Rhodesian Central Intelligence Organisation 192
Rhodesian Front 125–6
Rhoodie, Eschel 132, 137, 140
Richmond, Howie 220, 222
Richmond Development Company LLC (RDC) 235–9
Richmond Development Tanzania Limited 236
Richmond, Larry 219–20
Riis, Jacob xii
Rivonia Trial 123
Robben Island 110, 121
Rogério, Ampe 284
Rogério, Luísa 284
    writings of 285–8
Rolling Stone 215
Roosevelt, Theodore xi
Rosenstiel, Tom
    Elements of Journalism, The 217
Ross, Jay
    writings of 160–1
Rossouw, Mandy ix, 260
    writings of 263–4
Royal Initiative to Combat AIDS (RICA) Project 227
Royal Ireland Institute of Business and Technology 313
Rubusana, Walter 36
Russian Empire 15
Russian Federation
    Moscow 333
Rwanda 235

SA Institute of Chartered Accountants 234
SA Reserve Bank 234
SA Revenue Service 234
Sambo, Pascoalina Natacha Daniel 280
Sampson, Anthony 69
Sandura, Wilson 174
Satar Brothers 211, 213
Savage, Jay 215
Savambi, Jonas 268
Schoon, Marius 185
   murder of 187
Scudder, Thayer
   writings of 243–4
Second World War (1939–45) 54, 220
Securities Exchanges Control Act 229
Security Branch 121
Sekhukhune, Godfrey Mogaramedi 78
Sekhukhuneland Revolt (1958) 76–8
Seme, Pixley ka Isaka 48–9
   founder of *Abantu-Batho* (*People*) 42
Sept.info 289
Serfontein, Hennie 101
   Brotherhood of Power 101
Sese Seko, Mobuto 164, 305
Sesotho (language) 91, 240
Sguazzin, Anthony
   writings of 199–200
Shaik, Schabir 265, 331
Shaka 9
Sharemax 229–30
Sharpeville Massacre (1959) 71, 152
Shiffrin, Anya xii
Shiri, Perence 198, 201
Shona (ethnic group) 125–6
Shona (language) 126, 153, 160
Sibanyoni, Jabulani 196
Silva, Albano 211–12, 214
Simelane, James 144
Simões, António 210
Sinclair, Upton xi
Sirro, Simon 323–4
Sisulu, Walter 69, 86
Sitta, Samuel 236
Slovo, Joe 61, 64, 164
Slovo, Shawn
   A World Apart (1988) 62
Smith, Ian 125, 145–6, 148
Smuts, Jan 54, 57–8

Sobantu 12
Sobhuza II, King 141–2
   Decree (1973) 141, 143
Soga, Alan Kirkland 36, 38–9
Soga, Rev. Tiyo 36
Sophiatown Removals (1948) 69
Soros, George xix
South Africa xiii, xvi, 1, 19, 54, 165–6, 186, 230, 245, 271, 334
   Addo 124
   Bethal 62–3, 72
   Bloemfontein 40, 44, 46–7
   Cape Town xix, 1–2, 9–10, 40, 98, 134, 224, 309
   Ciskei 68
   Cradok 124
   Durban 48, 96–8, 103, 110, 134, 149, 185
   East London 36, 40, 247
   Eastern Cape 15, 36, 118, 121, 123
   Edenburg 47
   Free State (Province) 327
   Frenchdale 90
   Graaff-Reinet 124
   Grahamstown 122
   Groblersdaal 89–90
   Gauteng (Province) 249
   Humansdorp 124
   Johannesburg x, xix, 22, 40, 49, 62, 70, 77, 87, 109–11, 118, 149, 188, 209, 215–16, 276, 332
   Kimberley 40, 97, 269
   King Williams Town 36
   Komatipoort 185–6
   Kruger National Park 165
   KwaZulu-Natal ix, 48, 188, 191, 193, 260, 263
   Lamadi 259
   Ministry of Land, Agriculture and Water Development 199
   Ministry of Mining 337
   Natal xiv, 27, 105
   Natal (Province) 37, 191
   Nkandla 260
   Nyasaland 65, 74
   Orange River (Province) 37
   Port Alfred 124
   Port Elizabeth 118–20, 124, 134
   Pretoria 20, 40, 134, 138, 145, 150,

164, 170, 181, 185
Sebokeng 188
Sekhukhuneland 76–9, 81, 84, 91, 95–6
Somerset East 124
Sun City 326
Transkei 68, 82, 90
Transvaal (Province) 37, 79, 91, 94, 96–7, 188, 193
Ulundi 195
Vereeniging 20
Winburg 43–4
Witzieshoek 89
Zeerust 91
South African Air Force 147
South African Airways (SAA) 149, 225
South African Associated Newspapers (SAAN) 112
South African Broadcasting Corporation (SABC) 54, 57–8, 329
SABC3 215
South African Commercial Advertiser 77
South African Communist Party (SACP) 49, 63, 77–8, 122, 146, 163–4
South Africa Worker 49
South African Conspiracy Act 39
South African Defence Force (SADF) 169, 171, 191, 193
  Civil Co-operation Bureau 189
  Department of Military Intelligence (DMI) 194, 196
South African Development Community 338
South African Human Rights Commission (SAHRC) 252
South African Institute of Race Relations (IRR) 77–8
South African Military Intelligence 145
South African Native National Congress 24, 36–7
  as ANC 15
South African Police (SAP) 181–2, 185–6, 195
  Unit C1 181
  Unit C2 183
  Vlakplaas 183–5
South Korea 294
South West African People's Organisation (SWAPO) x, 182

South West African Territorial Force (SWATF) 171
Soviet Union (USSR) 54, 255
Sowetan xxi
Sparks, Allister 119, 134
  Sword and the Pen: Six Decades on the Political Frontier, The 118
Spie Batignolles 242
Squazzin, Antony x
Standard and Diggers News 22
Standard Chartered Bank 315
Star, The 134
State of Emergency (1958) 109
Statistics Act 319
Steffens, Lincoln xi
Steyn, Marais
South African Ambassador to UK 150–1
Steyn, Pierre
Steyn Report (2007) 191
Steyr-Daimler 292
Stork, Shanice 332
Strachan, Harold 110
  imprisonment of 112
  writings of 113–17
Stiglitz, Joseph 87
Strijdom, J.G. 107
Strydom, Hans 107
Super Afrikaners, The (1978) 100–2
Sunday Express xix, 133–6, 138, 335
Sunday News xvii
Sunday Standard 273, 276, 314
Sunday Star 165
Sunday Sun 332
Sunday Times 49, 55–6, 100–2, 104–6, 110, 156, 328
Swahili (language) 255
Swazi National Council (SNC) 226
Swaziland (eSwatini) xiv–xv, 90, 185, 187, 226–7
Sweden 294
Swift Geospatial Solutions 276

Taiwan
  Taipei 224
Tanda Tribal Trust Land 130
Tanesco xviii, 236, 238–9
Tanzania xv, xviii, 255, 304–5, 321
  Coast Region 321–5
  Dar es Salaam 235–6, 239, 258, 322

Dodoma 319
Loliondo xvii–xviii
Ministry of Energy and Mineral 235
Msimba 317
Mwanza 235, 239
Pwani 317–18
Tanzania Editors Forum 318
Tanzania Intelligence and Security Services (TISS) 321
Tanzania Law Society 319
Tarbell, Ida xi
Tas, Adam 1, 3
   background of 1–2
Tekere, Edgar 174
Tempo 209
Tenant Resettlement Programme 197–8
Tequesta Group 336, 338
terrorism 82
Thabane, Potlako 336, 340
Thabane, Tom 335–9
Thailand 268
Thales 292
Thamae, Mabusetsa Lenka 241–2
   writings of 245–6
Theal, George McCall 2
Themba, Can 69, 85
Thetsane, Leaba 242
Third Force 191
Third Reich (1933–45) 54, 57, 59, 77–8
ThisDay 237–8
Times of Swaziland 142, 223
TimesLive xxi
Toan, Nguyen Khanh 271
Traber, Father Michael 126
Transformation Resource Centre (TRC) 241
Transnet 327, 331
Transparency International xviii
Treason Trial (1956–61) 85–6
Trench, Andrew 247
Tribunal Popular Revolucionário (TRP) 206
Tribune 26
Truth and Reconciliation Commission (TRC) 191
   establishment of (1994) 184
Tsala ea Batho (*People's Friend*) 42
Tshabalala-Msimang, Manto 251, 253
Tshikalange, David 185

Tuan, Tommy 269–72
Tugela River 29
Turner, Henry McNeal 27
   Bishop of AME Church 26, 35
Turner, Rick 102–3
Turner, William
   British High Commissioner 291
Tuskegee Institute 25
Tutwana, Dr Lethwiti xvii
Twitter
   hashtag system of 318
Tyson, Harvey
   Editors Under Fire 134

Uazanguia, Pompilio 300
Uganda 235, 259
Uhuru xvii
Uitenhage (ethnic group) 122
Umbrella for Democratic Change (UDC) 314
Under the Same Sun (UTSS) 256
Unifer 234
Union Missionary Training Institute 26
Union of Tanzania Press Clubs 318
Unit Trusts Act 232
United Arab Emirates (UAE)
   Dubai 236, 333
United Democratic Front 188
United Kingdom (UK) 78, 133, 290
   Belfast 309, 312–13
   government of 41
   infant mortality rate of 98
   London 19, 21–2, 36, 40, 46, 61, 86, 110, 126, 150, 215, 224, 255, 291, 309
   Parliament 38
United Nations (UN) 145
United States of America (USA) xii, 26, 36, 126, 133, 137, 164, 174, 227–8, 234, 243, 268, 303, 305
   Chicago, IL 49
   civil rights movement in 86
   infant mortality rate of 98
   Jim Crow Laws 50
   Los Angeles, CA 224
   New York 26, 217, 224, 308
   segregation in 50
United Workers Union of South Africa 190

Unity Accord (1987) 157, 172
University of the Witwatersrand xx, 62
University of Zimbabwe 174
Utete, Charles 198, 201

Vaal River 20
Valoi, Estacio 295–6
    writings of 297–300
Van Brakel, Elizabeth 2
Van Breda, Felix 56
Van den Bergh, Hendrik 54, 133, 138
Van Dúnen, França 207
Van der Merwe, Louis 117
Van der Stel, Willem Adriaan 1, 5–7
    Kortie Deductie 2–3
Van Dyk, Paul 185–6
Van Rooyen, Jan Hendrick 82
Van Schalkwyk, Gysbert 117
Vermeulen, Koos 185
Verster, François 215
Verwoerd, Hendrik xiv, 79–81, 107
Victoria, Queen 8, 10, 16–17
Vieira, Sergio
    Mozambican Agriculture Minister 150–1
Vietnam 267–8
    Hanoi 271
Viljoen, Freek 232
Vlok, Adriaan
    Minister of Law and Order 189
Voice for America 203
Vorster, B.J. 'John' 54, 133
    Minister of Plural Relations 138
Vrye Weekblad x, 180–3, 188–9
    founding of 180

Waaihoek Location 46
Waithaka, Stanley Thuku 311
Wallace, Edgar 19, 22
    background of 19–22
    writings of 23–4
Washington, Booker T. 25, 27, 36–7, 48
Washington Office on Africa 127
Washington Post 155
Washington Star 137, 140
wa Simbeye, Finnigan ix, xvii
    writings of 237–8
Wayburne, Dr Sam 93
Webster, David

    assassination of (1989) 182
Weekly Guardian, The 86
Weekly Mail, The 182, 188, 190–1, 195–6
Wesleyan Society 16
West Africa Leaks 295
Western Native Township 49
White Free State 43
Wilcox, Rev. William 25
Wild, Franz
    writings of 303
Wilde, Dudley 176
Wilkins, Ivor 106–7
    Super Afrikaners, The (1978) 100–2
Williams, Ruth 289
Willowgate Scandal (1988) 172, 174
Willowvale Mazda Motor Industries (WMMI) 173, 175–6, 178
Wilson, Thomas
    writings of 303
Winter, Gordon
    Inside BOSS (1981) 132
Wits University 209
Woodward, Bob 133
World Bank 236, 241–2, 304, 307
World Economic Forum 267
Worrall, Nick
    writings of 154, 157–60

Xhosa (language)
    journalism 14

Yona, Daniel
    Minister for Energy and Minerals 235
Young Communist League 62

Zacarias, Felicio 299
Zaire 164
Zambia xviii–xix, 148, 168
    Lusaka 148, 207–8
    Mbala 164
Zimbabwe x, xv, xxii, 62, 125, 127, 151, 153, 165, 173, 189, 197–9, 267
    Bindura 201
    Bulawayo 154–5, 157–9, 161–2
    Chiweshe TTL 128–9
    Fingo 158
    Harare (Salisbury) 126–8, 154, 173, 202

Independence of (1980) 127, 145, 172
Mashinaland 158
Matabeleland x, 153–6, 159, 162
Matepatepa 198, 201
Mhangura 198
Ministry of Trade and Commerce 177
Zimbabwe African National Union –
  Patriotic Front (ZANU-PF) 153, 156,
  159, 172, 174, 202
Zimbabwe African People's Union
  (ZAPU) 154, 158–9, 161, 172
Zimbabwe Grain Bag Company 173, 176
Zimbabwe National Army
  Fifth Brigade 153–7, 172
Zimbabwe Newspapers 174
Zulu (ethnic group) 8–9, 11–12, 27–8,
  188, 217
Zulu (language)
  newspapers 24
Zululand 8, 10–11, 89
Zuma, Duduzane 332–3
Zuma, Jacob ix, 260, 262–4, 326, 329–33,
  335, 338
Zuma, MaMbhija 265
Zuma, MaNtuli 265